Explorations in the New Economic History

ESSAYS IN HONOR OF DOUGLASS C. NORTH
PRESENTED BY HIS STUDENTS

Terry L. Anderson
Bennett Baack
Philip R. P. Coelho
Lance E. Davis
Gerald A. Gunderson
Jonathan R. T. Hughes
Lloyd J. Mercer
Ramon H. Myers
Roger L. Ransom
Gaston V. Rimlinger
James F. Shepherd
Richard Sutch
Gary M. Walton

On the occasion of his sixtieth birthday, November 5, 1980

Explorations in the New Economic History

ESSAYS IN HONOR OF DOUGLASS C. NORTH

EDITED BY

Roger L. Ransom
Department of Economics
University of California, Riverside
Riverside, California

Richard Sutch
Department of Economics
University of California, Berkeley
Berkeley, California

Gary M. Walton
Graduate School of Administration
University of California, Davis
Davis, California

1982

ACADEMIC PRESS
A Subsidiary of Harcourt Brace Jovanovich, Publishers
New York London
Paris San Diego San Francisco São Paulo
Sydney Tokyo Toronto

ACADEMIC PRESS, INC.
111 Fifth Avenue, New York, New York 10003

United Kingdom Edition published by
ACADEMIC PRESS, INC. (LONDON) LTD.
24/28 Oval Road, London NW1 7DX

Library of Congress Cataloging in Publication Data
Main entry under title:

Explorations in the new economic history.

Includes bibliographical references.
1. Economic history--Addresses, essays, lectures.
2. North, Douglass Cecil--Addresses, essays, lectures.
I. North, Douglass Cecil. II. Ransom, Roger L., Date. III. Sutch, Richard. IV. Walton, Gary M.
HC26.E95 330.9 81-17645
ISBN 0-12-580080-0 AACR2

PRINTED IN THE UNITED STATES OF AMERICA

82 83 84 85 9 8 7 6 5 4 3 2 1

Contents

II
Growth and Welfare

List of Contributors

Numbers in parentheses indicate the pages on which the authors' contributions begin.

Terry L. Anderson (193), Department of Economics, Montana State University, Bozeman, Montana 59715

Bennett Baack (257), Department of Economics, Ohio State University, Columbus, Ohio 43210

Philip R. P. Coelho (213), Department of Economics, George Mason University, Fairfax, Virginia 22030

Lance E. Davis (41), Department of Economics, California Institute of Technology, Pasadena, California 91009

Donald F. Gordon (171), Department of Economics and Finance, Bernard Baruch College, The City University of New York, New York, New York 10010

Gerald A. Gunderson (235), Department of Economics, Trinity College, Hartford,Connecticut 06106

P. J. Hill (193), Department of Economics, Montana State University, Bozeman, Montana 59715

Jonathan R. T. Hughes (3), Department of Economics, Northwestern University, Evanston, Illinois 60201

Robert A. Huttenback (41), Department of Economics, University of California, Santa Barbara, Santa Barbara, California 93106

David R. Knowles (213), Department of Economics, Seattle University, Seattle, Washington 98122

Lloyd J. Mercer (71), Department of Economics, University of California, Santa Barbara, Santa Barbara, California 93106

Ramon H. Myers (273), Hoover Institution on War, Revolution and Peace, Stanford, California 94305

Roger L. Ransom (125), Department of Economics, University of California, Riverside, Riverside, California 92502

Gaston V. Rimlinger (149), Department of Economics, Rice University, Houston, Texas 77005

James F. Shepherd (97), Department of Economics, Whitman College, Walla Walla, Washington 99362

Richard Sutch (13), Department of Economics, University of California, Berkeley, Berkeley, California 94720

Gary M. Walton (171), Graduate School of Administration, University of California, Davis, Davis, California 95616

Preface

Twenty-three years ago, a small but determined band of economic historians—most of them trained in the principles of economics—set out to change the way people studied the economic history of the United States. They sought to bring explicit scientific theory (mostly economic theory of the neoclassical variety) to the study of history, and to employ the rigorous standards of the statistics profession in the manipulation of data and the formal testing of hypotheses. They claimed at the time that their effort would produce a "new" economic history. And they made good on their claim; today the New Economic History is neither new nor the practice of a minor cult; economic history in the English-speaking world is today dominated by those who identify themselves with this philosophy and methodology.

The New Economic History not only brought economic theory and statistical methods to the study of the past, it produced new results as well. Within these past 23 years, there has been in economic history no topic that has not to some extent been revised, reinterpreted, or revolutionized by the new history. And this work of revision is still proceeding. As the title of our volume suggests, the essays presented here explore some of the far reaches of the continually expanding universe of the New Economic History. In terms of geography, the places dealt with are as diverse as the United States, China, Great Britain, India, and Western Europe. In terms of historical time, the topics range from classical antiquity to the present. The diversity of issues notwithstanding, the essays have a very important bond that ties them together: Each has been contributed by a former student of Douglass C. North.

North was among the founding group that launched the New Economic History at a joint conference of the Economic History Association and the National Bureau of Economic Research in September, 1957. There can be no doubt that the power of the philosophy espoused by the New Economic Historians explains the movement's eventual triumph, yet it is also certain that the cause was assisted in no small way by North's persistent enthusiasm, critical attention, and bold leadership. This Berkeley-trained scholar, working at the University of Washington, has contributed more than his share of research and prose to the corpus of the New Economic History. And he has from the beginning been the principal spokesman and theoretician for the movement. He also sought out, inspired, and trained students who themselves carried on research in the field.

In September of 1977 several of his former students gathered together in New Orleans to discuss the possibility of assembling a collection of papers to celebrate Douglass North's sixtieth birthday. Immediately we knew that the project was feasible. North is the mentor of many economic historians, and his students are unusually prolific contributors to the scholarly journals. We quickly settled upon a rule defining potential contributors: Each of the contributing authors was to have been, at one time or another, a participant in North's Seminar in Economic History at the University of Washington. The editors were chosen and everyone present agreed to assist with the project.

There was only one point that troubled us—the lack of a theme to propose to the potential contributors. North's own research interests have ranged from rather specific projects (such as measuring the productivity of ocean shipping or drawing up balance of payments accounts) to broad, sweeping generalizations about whole societies and historical epochs (such as the "rise" of the Western world). He has made major contributions to both American and European economic history. His journal articles include methodological discussions as well as research on historical topics. At various times North has drawn theoretical inspiration from economists as varied as Smith, Marx, Schumpeter, Polanyi, M. M. Knight, Baumol, Arrow, and Buchanan. Not surprisingly, we were unable to find any "school" of economic history associated with North. Although none of us is as far ranging as North himself, taken together, North's students represent as broad and eclectic a group of economic historians as it would be possible to find. No single theme seemed to allow sufficient scope to incorporate the diversity of interests reflected by either North himself or his students. At the time, we decided to let the theme take care of itself.

As soon as the papers began to come in, however, the editors discovered what had eluded them in New Orleans: North's philosophy of history could serve as a theme since it was evident in each of the papers. North has consistently maintained both in his teaching and in his writing that good research in economic history has to satisfy three criteria:

1. The topic chosen for investigation must be relevant to history. North has no tolerance for those who fit regression equations to historical data if the results shed no light on a historical question. Theoretical fantasies divorced from the real world do not interest him. The economic problems people faced in the past and the solutions they found are important to North because they were important to real people living in exciting times.
2. A research effort is successful if it helps us understand the past. This means that the theory that guides the work must be sound and explicit. The simplifying assumptions must be defensible. Douglass North is, above all, an economist and he insists that good economic history must first and always be good economics. He is ruthless when he discovers sloppy thinking or bad theory in the work of others.
3. North also insists that truly good work must be imaginative and original. He demands of himself as well as of his students a continual effort of experimentation and exploration. What excites him are new ideas, fresh applications, and imaginative approaches.

These lessons have not been lost on North's students. The essays they have contributed are truly *Explorations in the New Economic History*. What ties together the thirteen essays offered in this volume is the common influence of these standards of research. Each contribution is an application of economic theory to some identifiable problem in economic history.

Great teachers are indeed rare, but North is certainly one of them. He has been extraordinarily successful in recruiting a steady stream of young scholars to his seminars at the University of Washington, in fostering their interest in problems of economic history, and in inspiring them to try their own hand at the game. North's own breadth of interest and his genuine excitement over any new idea are one of his great strengths as a teacher, but there is more to his success than that. We asked John Hughes to attempt to capture what it is like to be a student in North's graduate seminar and to try to put his finger on North's elusive ability to inspire others.

North's influence on the profession goes far beyond his role as teacher. His own contributions to the field, his leadership of the New Economic History movement, and, most importantly, the audacity and originality of his ideas have in some way attracted the attention of every economic historian. This is a remarkable accomplishment. Richard Sutch has attempted to explore this facet of our story in his assessment of North's contributions to scholarship. His essay is an excellent companion to Hughes's appreciation of North as a teacher. One must read both essays to understand what Douglass North is about. We have placed them—appropriately—at the beginning of the volume in Part I.

Other, more subtle themes also emerged from our collected papers. These themes are reflected in the grouping of papers into Parts II and III.

North has always maintained that economic history deals with two grand topics: *growth and welfare*; hence the title for Part II in which the authors concern themselves with these issues in a variety of settings. In separate essays, Lloyd Mercer and Jim Shepherd deal with explanations of economic growth very near to North's own—the model of export-led economic growth (Chapters 4 and 5). Donald Gordon and Gary Walton examine a rather different situation—the phenomenon of "regenerative" growth following wartime devastation—and turn to modern West Germany for data to test their hypothesis (Chapter 8). An early preoccupation of the New Economic History was measuring the "burden" of the Navigation Acts on the thirteen American colonies. Lance Davis and Robert Huttenback view the other side of this question in their essay on the "costs" of empire—and find that the British had their own imperial problems (Chapter 3). Not all the effects of economic growth and industrial expansion are positive. Both Roger Ransom and Gaston Rimlinger concern themselves with the problems of welfare in industrial societies and with ways in which economic security can be enhanced (Chapters 6 and 7).

Another set of problems that has fascinated Douglass North are those concerning *property rights and institutional change*. These are the problems addressed by several of his students in Part III. Two of the papers in Part III deal with situations where people sought to change their economic environment. Ben Baack examines the impact of changing property rights in Britain during the early years of industrialization (Chapter 12). Terry Anderson and P. J. Hill look at a more subtle type of institutional change—the use of the judiciary as an agency to support efforts to effect transfers from one group to another (Chapter 9). Philip Coelho and David Knowles seek the reasons for government regulation of business in their case study of the tung oil industry and its relations with the government (Chapter 10). The other two papers in Part III deal with societies that are sometimes viewed as being outside the scope of economic analysis because of their reliance on nonmarket forms of economic organization. Both Gerald Gunderson's study of economic behavior in the ancient world (Chapter 11) and Ramon Myers's examination of customary law and property rights in China (Chapter 13) show that important insights can be gained by extending economic analysis to such societies.

North has always been eager to work with others on research topics. His collaboration with Lance Davis on institutional change and with Robert Thomas on Western Europe are two of the more significant examples. Here again, his students have followed his lead. In their own work they have collaborated with one another (Shepherd and Walton on the colonial economy; Ransom and Sutch on the postbellum South; Shepherd and Coelho on price and wage statistics) as well as with scholars outside the fold. In four of the essays for this volume North's students are joined by "outside" collaborators. Robert Huttenback, Donald Gordon, P. J. Hill, and David Knowles were not "students" of North in the same sense as their respective coauthors. But every economic historian who cares equally about history, sound theory, and new ideas has learned something from North. They are students merely one step removed. We are most grateful to these four scholars for their willingness to include their work in this volume.

All of the papers in this volume have been reviewed, refereed, and edited. To assist in this process the editors have asked the help of many people. Each of the contributing authors served as a member of an informal "Board of Editors," reading and commenting on the first drafts of the contributions submitted. In many cases editorial advice was sought from outside of the group. Among those who provided help of one sort or another to the editors are Gunter Conradus, Paul David, Trevor Dick, Dudley Johnson, Victor Lippitt, Donald McCloskey, Carl Mosk, Richard Roehl, and Robert Thomas. The editors wish to thank each one of these colleagues for his help.

After the inevitable process of perfecting and finalizing the drafts, Marian Impolla imposed a stylistic and editorial consistency on the authors' disparate efforts. Each of us is grateful to her for the attention and care she lavished on our prose. Once the volume was complete, Poinka Patuska and Kaylyn Gary typed the manuscript under considerable time pressure. Without their aid we would not have been able to meet the deadline set by North's sixtieth birthday.

Over the past three years, a minor miracle occurred. The organizational meeting in New Orleans, the commitment to this project, and the preparation of this volume have all been kept secret from North. All of those mentioned here must be thanked for this as well as for their assistance in assembling the manuscript. At a surprise party on November 10, 1980, the manuscript of this book was presented to North as a birthday present.

It is with a great deal of pride and appreciation that we dedicate the contributions here to Douglass C. North.

Explorations in the New Economic History

Part I

Douglass North and the New Economic History

A revolution is taking place in economic history in the United States. It is being initiated by a new generation of economic historians who are both skeptical of traditional interpretations of U.S. economic history and convinced that a new economic history must be firmly grounded in sound statistical data.

Douglass C. North

The American Economic Review
March 1963

Chapter 1

Douglass North as a Teacher

Jonathan R.T. Hughes

We thought, naturally, that the University of Washington had just been lucky in the early 1950s to have us, such a talented clutch of graduate students. The University of Washington was not known as a producer of economic historians then, but it soon would be. You went into a seminar room in 1950 and shared space with Lance Davis, Gaston Rimlinger, August Bolino, Herbert Kisch, Irwin Unger, all of whom would someday do major work in economic history. There was already a tradition of good graduate students at the University of Washington. But they tended to get an M.A. and then go elsewhere for their Ph.D.s. Our group mostly went away to finish up too, escaping the old "infinite Ph.D. program" at the University of Washington which had been invented apparently for people with lots of time and money for graduate studies. Later on this tradition changed. The program was reduced to manageable proportions and good students stayed on in Seattle in greater numbers to complete their work. In the 1960s, for example, Roger Ransom, Gary Walton, Jim Shepherd, Lloyd Mercer, Ben Baack, Terry Anderson, and others could be found arguing various issues in Economics 563: "American Economic History." And these students (with the execption of an occasional precocious undergraduate like Richard Sutch) stayed on at the University of Washington to finish their graduate work with Douglass North. So the theories of "luck" and "bunching of talent" to explain North's long string of successful students were wrong. The flow has now continued for nearly three decades.

ISBN 0-12-580080-0

The correct explanation is that North managed to channel more than his share of the University of Washington's students under his own fescue. This is perhaps surprising. Economic history in 1958 was not a field populated heavily by economists, and North had plenty of competition in his quest for students. The young faculty was brilliant and congenial. They made themselves available to the graduate students, and in fact most of them did so more than North. He was hardly ever around at night, and he never went casually off to the Red Robin in the evenings for a beer with the graduate students. Your contact with North was most likely in his office, in the classroom, or at lunch.

At first North was an enigma to us. He was an easterner, and had apparently spent nonmilitary time in Europe—an oddity. He *spoke* French, and he talked about wines as though they were books. He had a slightly reserved, diffident manner about him. He did not ever assert any presumed superiority though; he probably just assumed you would know. You wondered what he would say before he said it. He had been in the merchant marine, and that gave him some status as an "ordinary guy," but he also claimed to be a Marxist, and we thought that hilariously funny. He also was a hunting and fishing enthusiast, and since many of us were from the Northwest, that was old hat to us, of little particular merit. But when it turned out that he could fly an airplane, ears pricked up; when it came out later that he owned his own plane there was real heartfelt admiration. To us, North was obviously, or soon would be, a great man. The Marxism was merely a peculiarity. But it was also a risky thing to call youself in 1950, in the age of Senate investigating committees and Washington State's own Canwell Committee, which had just produced some firings of reputed "communists" on the Washington faculty. So we admired North for his political nerve. But most of us already knew about "the working classes," having just emerged from them. We were trying to escape from them—upward.

Kisch enjoyed references to "temporary acting instructor North," for it was at that modest rank that Doug entered our lives in 1950. He was just finishing his dissertation at Berkeley, and was parked in Seattle in Berkeley's "Ph.D. holding pattern." Kisch had just come to Seattle from the London School of Economics and was perplexed by "that little man" who held the great figures of the profession, past and present, in little or no regard. Kisch respected the great men and works of economics. North had unreserved respect for no one. No work was above criticism. Even though North was claiming to be a Marxist, his criticism of Marx and Marxism was biting and continous. Kisch was offended by the irreverence. The rest of us were merely amused, with a few exceptions, being so ignorant we hardly knew what North was talking about, or why Kisch thought it scandalous.

Doug's long-term love affair with price theory was evident even in his youthful Marxist phase. He constantly criticized the theory we were studying (from others) as frivolous and irrelevant, yet he was already hanging his own research ideas on simple theoretical concepts. Once he started working with a theoretical tool he wielded it like an axe, giving it all the punishment it could take, and sometimes striking stones and other hard objects with it. We were expected to do the same. In his seminar you had to have a point in you paper. You could get such a point, he argued, if you reduced the historical problems to the core of material that theory suggested was relevant. The other parts could be dispensed with. Some found this shocking (I did, and still do), but it was his attitude then and the habit stuck for a long time. His technique in the seminar was to hand out topics for papers, suggest background readings, and then, when the papers were presented, blast away at us, our sources (most of which he had supplied), and our ideas.

The seminar was a place of excitement. North was able to create this atmosphere, and his former students have often compared notes about it, finding it not so easy to do in their own seminars as it appeared to be in Savery Hall during their days of servitude there. You knew you would have to contend with Doug, but it was not certain *ex ante* how, or on what points. We students would tend to support each other in alliance against him. The seminar was shock because North expected and demanded new ideas from us. How could we do that? We knew little or nothing about economic history, and yet North was pressuring us to be critical and original about materials we had scarcely learned. The seminar was a forcing bed for originality, however feeble.

There was a reading list, produced in 1951, which I still have, and it is solid for the time, but no gold mine of exciting new ideas, even by the standards of those days. It also is not of prodigious length. We were expected to know what was in it, although there was no examination about it. The materials in it were thrown into the discussion by North, very skillfully, and so you had to do some reading if you wanted at least to jog along. He called it a "selective bibliography." Oddly enough, one would still be able to conduct a seminar of fundamental depth with the thing, as most of the "cliometric revolution" developed on topics already in those readings. What cliometrics added was the perspective of quantitative analyses. In the seminar in those days North would force life and relevance from the materials by question and argument.

We considered Charles Beard's thesis, but of course from a Marxist position; not only was Beard correct, but so were the "reactionaries" who framed the Constitution. Their attempt to stop "progress" was historically necessary. The reaction was then followed by a great expansion of primitive, preindustrial capitalism. Again, the readings could support such a thesis: Norman Buck on the British finance of the antebellum South, McGrane's count of foreign investment and state repudiation (primitive accumulation without force), Hidy on the comingling of trade and finance—mercantile capitalism.

The reading list continues for a total of 12 pages, but there are fewer than 200 items on it. The list is sound. We read Gray on southern agriculture, laughed at U. B. Phillips on slavery, read Jenks and George Rogers Taylor on the importance of railroads. We studied Victor Clark's account of the rise of manufacturing industry and the later tie with finance capitalism, Moody's *The Masters of Capital,* the Pecora Committee, then Berle and Means, Riply on *Trusts, Pools and Corporations,* the TNEC monographs on corporate control and organization.

Since this was B.E. (before econometrics), the reading list began with an obligatory section on "methodology." There was no teaching even of mathematical statistics in the economics department then. Economic theory was "little games" of logic which, it was asserted, somehow "explained" reality. It was an act of faith to believe that, as there was no technical link available to us between theory and the quantitative evidence of reality. The methodology section had the simplest possible point, therefore: What were we doing studying economic history? The answer was that we were studying something that actually had happened. Economic history could hope to explain at least some real events in the economic world, the past, and, for good Marxists and other true believers, the future as well, if the signs and portents were read correctly. So when we argued about Collingwood's *The Idea of History,* Schumpeter's "Creative Response in Economic History," or the discussion of theory and history in the famous old Social Science Research Council Bulletin 54, we thought we were grappling with important tools of historical understanding. Thus armed, we then would ask with new interest why the American Revolution occurred. And Lawrence Harper was on the reading list to deepen the mystery, along with Andrews, Beer, Nettels, and Richard Morris. There were two interesting ideas about the early Federal period implied in the section headings "Revolution and Counter Revolution" and "The Character of Mercantilist America: Capital Accumulation and Investment." Solid categories—the way one was taught to think about the historic past in the days before econometrics. The whole reading list ended with big issues again, "The Development of American Capitalism: Theories and Evidence." Here were Arthur Cole, Maurice Dobb, N. S. B. Gras, Louis Hacker, Walt Rostow, Schumpeter's *Business Cycles,* and Sweezy's *Theory of Capitalist Development.*

As North matured as a scholar, the seminar's focus shifted subtly away from these classics and increasingly emphasized North's own work and the key documents of the nascent New Economic History. Students of the 1960s recall careful dissection of Conrad and Meyer on slavery, the all important NBER volume (bible?) on *Trends in the American Economy,* North's own book on the economic growth of the United States, and a mimeographed "preliminary report" by Robert Fogel on the economic impact of the railroads. The references to Schumpeter, Marx, George Rogers Taylor *et al.* still peppered North's own comments, but clearly it was the newer ideas that now excited Doug. And it was his excitement about the New Economic History that lit the spark in so many of his students.

North has always been a very effective seminar leader. He pounds away at students about perspective, getting a "feel for history." How does theory "explain" what happened? Where are the gaps? Simplify, abstract, *argue,* present a thesis. Do not just restate what your sources say; be critical, show their errors, produce new arguments.

In the seminar room the student is up close with North, and his low-key style adds to the student's own nervous condition. North makes even the strongest criticism in a low voice. He does not interrupt the speaker; you are always allowed to give your paper as best you can without interruption before there is any action. The tension builds up. North seldom begins the discussion himself, preferring to come into it via someone else's question. He does not hesitate to criticize the speaker's thesis, yet he is willing to defend it when the graduate students attack it. So the discussion is nearly always triangular. North also is careful to say something nice about the speaker's effort no matter how bad it was, and no matter how savagely it has been mauled. He always allows the student to escape, self-respect intact. Discussion can become quite heated, even though North himself hardly ever raises his voice.

But at times in the early days it became hard to maintain order and North would "get tough." One of my vivid memories of a particularly hot session in the seminar was North pounding his fist on the table when two students were talking loudly at once, saying to a future Pulitzer Prize winner, "———, for Christ's sake, shut up." You could get angry, even though he never did. It was not the topics we discussed, it was the nature of the argument, his unwillingness to be convinced, and your gnawing fear that somehow North would turn out to be right after all. I was once involved in a long fracas with him about the

Populists, grain prices, railroad rates, and monopoly power of the railway grain buyers. Such a subject sounds prosaic enough, but North would not buy the argument. I well remember the furious 22-year-old Hughes working into the night in the library gathering regional grain price data to support an argument that would "show him." Another student from those days recalls being asked to read Jefferson to see if he had become a conservative in his old age. Was he ever *really* a revolutionary? Was Hamilton in fact the real revolutionary? North in the end attacked both Jefferson and Hamilton for their inconsistencies, *and* criticized the student for excessive deference to their opinions.

How much of the impact of his seminars is intellectual and how much is the interaction of personalities really is difficult to sort out. North will argue about any thesis, and his personality can disturb the composure of almost anyone. His opinion matters to his students; he somehow makes it matter. He believes economic history to be a deeply important subject, and he conveys to the student a sense of drama and excitement about it. He has a talent for finding and pursuing the parts of topics that have development possibilities.

I never got the impression that his interests were in any sense "art for its own sake." My cohorts mainly went elsewhere to finish up. But when people began staying on in Seattle to write dissertations, there was a tendency for North's students to write on topics upon which he himself was working. Students of those days say North was not at all reticent about recruiting; if he thought you had possibilities he went after you to work with him. He could sense what parts of economic history were "int'resting," and that is where he and his students plunged in: colonial America, the balance of payments, slavery, internal improvements, Ricardian-Malthusian models of long-period change, property rights, institutional change, and the role of government. He wrote on other subjects too, but these central interests of his became also the veins of pay dirt from which his students extracted their theses.

Though North could be brilliant in his graduate seminars, it was a different matter when he taught Economics 160, the big undergraduate course in economic history. Everything was in low gear. A charismatic lecturer he was not. Twenty-five years later an eye witness at one of North's lectures to a large class gave this description:

> He is not terribly well organized in his presentation, in fact, sometimes he is very confusing. But he tosses out a wealth of ideas and suggestions, which often baffle the students. But he gets them to think. He also comes up with a constant stream of opinions and judgments on people and issues. None of his opinions are modest, and some are downright outrageous, but he does not mind being challenged. He very

> much encourages it. One minute he sounds arrogant and the next minute he pokes fun at himself.

The style has been familiar in his big lectures for all these years. It was so when I was his teaching assistant.

In his own work, and that of his students, there has been a precocious (and, it has been charged, sometimes forced) originality, sometimes verging on wildness. He has a knack for forcing out creativity. When he, very quickly, gave up on Marxism and devoted his efforts to imaginative applications of price theory, he dragged the students along with him. He was always willing to change abruptly. I recall his coming out one day, in disgust at our best efforts, with what seemed to be a flat rejection of the whole subject as it then stood. "What we need is a *new* economic history," he said. Price theory applied to problems of historical development was to be the vehicle. His paper on "Location Theory and Regional Economic Growth" was one of his first efforts in this enterprise. But he never gave up yearning for larger systems as explanations of history; later books in collaboration with Lance Davis and Bob Thomas illustrate this continuing interest.

The drive for originality, ever present in the seminar, came through in his students' Ph.D. dissertations. The work had to be clearly focused, have a shape, a point, an argument. As one of his students put it:

> New ideas excite him. Work in an established mold, no matter how scholarly, rates very little with him. He is always chasing some new idea. The mistakes he makes are mainly those of a man working in poorly charted areas. He probably figures that it is better to plunge ahead and make mistakes than to move very slowly and avoid them. So long as you move in the right direction, you can leave it to others to straighten out the path and clear up the debris.

This element in North's attitude toward work was there when he first came to Seattle. It could be a dangerous attitude, but it well fitted the temper of the seminar, and does certainly describe much of North's own work and that of his students. Not that their work is strewn with error. But the errors they have made were usually in opening up new subjects in new ways. North's attitude was partly the product of strong self-confidence (some said in the early days before he became so eminent that it was an extraordinarily inflated ego), together with a shrewd estimate of the talent structure and sociology of the profession. I well recall the thrust of his words to us about these matters, and I have often quoted them to my students regarding taking risks. What he said was something like this:

> Some scholars are original, and some are not. Most people in our profession are not. If you are one of those who can be original, then it is your duty to the profession to write and publish. Do your work and *never look back*. Don't listen to critics until you've finished. Everyone can criticize; very few can produce new ideas. We must have new ideas; without them the field will die.

Now this is reckless and dangerous doctrine, and must produce some work that would be better left alone. But it gave young scholars self-confidence to try; more than that, it gave young scholars *North's* self-confidence, and that was a terribly valuable item to have. We did not know where "historical truth" came from. Obviously certain things had happened in the past, and other things had not happened. The Germans did not win World War I, and Herbert Hoover was not elected to a second term in 1932. But more subtle historical truth, the idea that history came from questions and argument about piles of mute evidence which could be motivated into life and speech by inquiry and argument—this was difficult for the student to comprehend. Were historians mere tellers of stories, fiction writers who made up believable scenarios about the past? Was an hypothesis the truth just because it seemed like the best explanation one could imagine? Were you wrong if everyone disagreed with you? Were you wrong *because* everyone disagreed with you? Could you win the argument and still be wrong? Could you withhold your own belief in the "truth" of a superior argument even if you could not refute it?

It was with such questions that North's own self-confidence gave the student the strength to persist. In North's seminar, majority rule was not the truth. You became fad-proof. In later years he once told me, somewhat plaintively, that he had never received a favorable review of any of his books. Did he mind? Yes. Had he considered trying to write a book that might get favorable reviews? Why bother, he said. By his own example, and the doctrine of his own seminar, you followed your own nose. The result with his students has been that their work has so many times appeared to be an attempt to start an intellectual brawl. There is no "North school" of economic history. There is an attitude, and a style.

It is said that North has a fine taste for talent, and over the years was able to pick out and attract the best of the available talent. But again, the University of Washington was not an international focal point for graduate study in economic history like, say, Oxford or Harvard. The raw material for future economic historians cannot have been so extraordinarily rich. It is only the University of Washington's output of productive economic historians that has been so far above the average. The Devil has to be given his due. To have been in his seminar was a once-and-for-all experience, but also the beginning of a life long dialogue that disturbed the slower ones as well as the gifted. Even the least distinguished of his students can talk for hours, will if given the chance, about the seminar and how it influenced them. It was not a slick, well-planned "course of study." North's interests changed, the subject matter changed, the arguments changed. The students who faced North-the-Marxist and those who confronted North-the-reactionary worked with different intellectual materials. But the critical attitude was a constant, like the drive for focus and creativity.

So what makes a great teacher? Surely not merely charisma as a lecturer. The charisma emanating from North's lectern was slight indeed. A parade of erudition? Not Douglass North. A warm and lovable manner? Not Doug. He went his way, did his thing, followed his instincts. If you were along on part of the journey he would tell you what he was doing, how and why, and what was good or bad about your own work. No words were shaded. He was always perfectly straight in his professional judgment. So when he was wrong everyone knew it, and when he was right, which was often enough, many hated to admit it. He also handed his students a sense of fun and life. The last they do not forget. He always believed he was good, his ideas important, economic history an essential discipline. You were his student, so you were worth something in the world by right. The nice thing about his criticism of you was that he also was always willing to think his adverse judgment might be wrong. Try it out, he dared you. So we did.

ACKNOWLEDGMENTS

The author thanks the editors, and several former students, who will remain anonymous, for additional information supplied on later years in North's teaching career.

Jonathan R. T. Hughes was raised in Idaho and might have escaped an academic career altogether if it had not been for the University of Washington and Douglass North. After receiving a Bachelor's degree at Utah State in 1950, he went to Seattle but was soon redirected toward a British education at Oxford where he received his D.Phil. in 1955. Hughes later became one of the group at Purdue University that was influential in establishing the New Economic History as a recognized approach to the field. Hughes has been a prolific writer, publishing numerous articles and several books on both British and American topics. His major works include **Fluctuations in Trade, Industry, and Finance** (1960); **The Vital Few: American Economic Progress and its Protagonists** (1966); **Social Control in the Colonial Economy** (1976); and **The Government Habit: Economic Controls from Colonial Times to the Present** (1977). Recently he has completed a textbook in American Economic History.

Chapter 2

Douglass North and the New Economic History

Richard Sutch

Some scholars are original, and some are not. . . . Everyone can criticize; very few can produce new ideas. We must have new ideas; without them the field will die

—Douglass North[1]

I can recall North's unhappiness with my first attempt in his seminar to report on a reading assignment. This was in 1963. He found my restatements of the author's arguments redundant: "We've all read the paper!" And when I finished my criticism he said, "It's clear you don't like this paper. Well then, isn't it incumbent upon you to come up with something better?" When I protested that such a feat might be beyond me (I was an undergraduate at the time), North countered with "Well, if you don't, who will?"

There is no doubt that such audacity (which we students could take as North's expression of confidence in our abilities) inspired many of us. But it is an entirely separate issue whether North's doctrine constitutes wise advice for an aspiring scholar. Hughes, at least, has his doubts. North's prescription, he fears, "must produce some work that would be better left alone." Judging North's own scholarly output by the academic reviews it has prompted, Hughes's fear might seem justified. Rarely has

1. John Hughes is quoting Douglass North from recollection of a seminar meeting in the early 1950s. See the preceding essay in this volume (p. 10).

ISBN 0-12-580080-0

North's work received uncritical review, never has it received unqualified praise.

But is has always been noticed. Indeed I would argue, the critical notice North's work has received has been largely the direct consequence of its originality and boldness. New ideas deserve to be taken seriously, and the scholarly profession has always thought it essential to scrutinize closely such arguments and the evidence used to support them. Criticism in such cases should not be taken as an indictment of scholarship.

Quite to the contrary, the profession has honored Douglass North with more than the usual number of offices. He has been an editor of the *Journal of Economic History,* trustee and later president of the Economic History Association, president of the Western Economic Association, member of the board of directors of the National Bureau of Economic Research, associate editor of *Explorations in Economic History,* chair of the Department of Economics at the University of Washington, and so on. Such honors might be expected to soften criticisms of one's work. But not so in North's case. As North himself notes, "everyone can criticize," and we might add that nearly everyone does. North on the other hand has always claimed that the true test of a scholar's contribution is not the popularity but the power of his ideas: their power to excite others, their power to stimulate new research, their power to enliven the field, and their power to survive. Judged on these critieria, North's own work takes on a unique luster.

What are these original ideas? What contributions has North made? What debates has he launched?

I am afraid that originality, like beauty, is in the eye of the beholder. My own answer to these questions might not be the next person's answer, let alone Douglass North's answer. But let us not hesitate to state our opinions for fear of contradiction. North himself has always counseled: "Rush ahead, fear of trespass befits only angles." Rushing ahead then, I shall state my view that North has to date made at least three major contributions to the field of economic history.

1. North conceived the tripartite-economy model of American economic growth, first put forth in *The Economic Growth of the United States, 1790 to 1860* (published in 1961). This view is now the standard framework used in most textbook discussions of the period.
2. In the 1960s, North was a major force behind the movement to establish the New Economic History. His book *Growth and Welfare in the American Past: A New Economic History* (published in 1966) also made him a leading practitioner of the new methodology.

3. Beginning with *Institutional Change and American Economic Growth* (coauthored with Lance Davis, published in 1971) and quickly followed by *The Rise of the Western World* (coauthored with Robert Thomas, published in 1973), North has attempted to explain the historical transformation of property rights, legal systems, and other institutional arrangements by devising an explicit economic model of institutional change.

THE TRIPARTITE ECONOMY

North's idea was essentially a very simple one—most good ideas are.[2] The fledgling American economy in 1815 was not one but three separate economies initially isolated from one another by distance and poor communications:

1. The "North," comprising New England and the seaboard portions of the Middle Atlantic States down through Pennsylvania and northern Delaware.
2. The "South," comprising the bulk of the slave states.
3. The transappalachian "West."

Then the transportation advances of the early nineteenth century gradually began to link the three regions together: water transportation on the western rivers, and in particular the steamboat, would connect the West with the South; an elaborate system of canals would link the West to the North; and increasingly efficient ocean transportation would improve the communication between the North and South, as well as foster increased trade and improved communications between the new world and the old.

In North's view, however, rather than uniting the three parts into an increasingly homogeneous whole, the new transportation networks instead permitted each region to develop its own economic speciality, each pursuing, as it were, its unique comparative advantage. The South, with agricultural labor supplied by a rapidly growing slave population, expanded its production of staple exports—not only sugar, rice, and tobacco, but also, and increasingly, the short-staple cotton whose cultivation was made feasible by Eli Whitney's recently introduced (1793) cotton gin. The North became the financial and commercial center of the nation and then, with labor supplied by both immigration from Europe and surplus labor from the region's agricultural sector (including many

2. North, *The Economic Growth of the United States, 1790 to 1860* (Englewood Cliffs, N. J.: Prentice-Hall, 1961; New York: W. W. Norton, 1966, paperback edition).

young women), developed a substantial manufacturing industry which was particularly successful in adapting the English factory system to the production of low grade cotton cloth, shoes and boots, iron, and iron products such as nails and wrought iron. The West, with its rapidly advancing frontier, specialized in agricultural products—particularly those with high value per unit of weight such as barreled pork, whiskey, animal skins, and flour.

These distinct regional specialties were made possible—indeed, their development was stimulated—because they complemented each other. The northern textile industry required southern cotton which it used to produce the cheap cloth provided to clothe the slaves. New England's shoe factories mass-produced shoes and boots for southern slaves and western farmers out of leathers from western cattle. At the same time, the northern factory workers were able to purchase cheap food (and therefore they were willing to work for less) because of the steady flow of agricultural products from the West. Both the West and the South could economically procure manufactured products from the North, thus reducing the nation's dependence upon European imports. Both the North and the South could fill their agricultural deficits by relying on the abundance of western agriculture.

Thus Douglass North's model of the developing American economy was like a three-legged stool: Each region was dependent upon the other two, and all three were required to support the national economy.

What made North's 1961 conception of the tripartite economy so important was that it pulled together many of the previously disconnected strands of research in economic history, unifying them into a coherent whole. *The Economic Growth of the United States* drew heavily upon, but at the same time gave new importance to, the work by George Rogers Taylor and Louis Schmidt on transportation improvements, the studies by V. S. Clark, Arthur Cole, and others on manufacturing development, Lewis Cecil Gray's monumental *History of Agriculture in the Southern United States,* and Thomas Berry's study of the Cincinnati market in western agricultural development.[3]

3. George Rogers Taylor, *The Transportation Revolution, 1815–1860* (New York: Holt Rinehart, 1951); Louis B. Schmidt, "Internal Commerce and the Development of a National Economy before 1860," *Journal of Political Economy* 47 (December 1939). Also see Guy S. Callender, *Selections from the Economic History of the United States, 1765–1860* (Boston: Ginn and Company, 1909); V. S. Clark, *History of Manufactures in the United States,* 3 vols. (New York: McGraw-Hill, 1929); Arthur H. Cole, *The American Wool Manufacture,* 2 vols. (Cambridge, Mass.: Harvard University Press, 1926); Lance E. Davis, "Sources of Industrial Finance: The American Textile Industry, A Case "Study," *Explorations in Entrepreneurial History* 9 (April 1957); Blanche Hazard, *The Organization of the Boot and Shoe Industry in*

Another factor that helps explain the importance historians have attached to North's tripartite thesis is that his economic model stresses the divergence between the three regional economies as much as their mutual dependence. Thus it provides a convenient framework for an economic interpretation of the growing sectional conflict that ultimately erupted into Civil War. Although North himself did not dwell on this point, there can be little doubt that economic issues—slavery, differential economic development, and the insecurity engendered by the interregional dependencies—fed the interregional animosities which smoldered and flaired until they culminated in Southern secession and war.

Of greatest significance to the discipline, however, was that within North's framework it was possible, really for the first time, to offer a satisfying explanation for American economic growth. The logic of North's explanation of growth is familiar classical economics: Each of the three regions pursued its comparative advantage, specialized in what it could best produce, and traded with the other regions to the advantage of all sections. The source of growth was the progressively improving efficiency with which goods were produced. The increasing efficiency was, in turn, made possible by the expansion of the market and the increasingly fine division of labor.[4] Although firmly rooted in the static principle of comparative advantage, North's model also supplied an essential dynamic mechanism that, he argued, propelled the three-part economy toward the classical result and then helped to sustain economic growth once it had begun.

Massachusetts before 1875 (Cambridge, Mass.: Harvard University Press, 1921); Edgar M. Hoover, Jr., *Location Theory and the Shoe and Leather Industries* (Cambridge, Mass.: Harvard University Press, 1937); Lewis Cecil Gray, *History of Agriculture in the Southern United States to 1860* (Washington, D. C.: Carnegie Institution, 1933). Thomas S. Berry, *Western Prices before 1861: A Study of the Cincinnati Market* (Cambridge, Mass.: Harvard University Press, 1943).

4. The first sentence in *The Economic Growth of the United States* reads "The analytical framework of this study is a composite of several propositions, the most important of which was a cornerstone of *The Wealth of Nations* [p. 1]." On page 10, North cites George J. Stigler, "The Division of Labor is Limited by the Extent of the Market," *Journal of Political Economy* 59 (June 1951), as one inspiration for his emphasis on regional specialization and comparative advantage. Also relevant is North's earlier paper "Location Theory and Regional Economic Growth," *Journal of Political Economy* 63 (June 1955). For a more extensive discussion of the relationship between regional specialization and economic growth, see the introduction (by North and Thomas) to Douglass C. North and Robert Paul Thomas, eds., *The Growth of the American Economy to 1860* in the *Documentary History of the United States,* edited by Richard B. Morris (Columbia, N. C.: University of South Carolina Press, 1968), pp. 1–4.

That driving force was the rapidly growing foreign demand for American exports, primarily cotton. In *The Economic Growth of the United States,* North stated:

> The expanding international economy of the past two centuries has provided the avenue by which one economy after another has accelerated its rate of growth. There are few exceptions to the essential initiating role of a successful export sector in the early stages of accelerated growth of market economies.[5]

The economic theory behind this idea was not, of course, new. The export-led growth model had been earlier introduced by Harold Innis to explain Canadian development.[6] But this demand-oriented growth theory seemed to fit North's purposes exactly. The United States in 1815 was still a small economy dependent in many ways on its trading relationships with Europe (and the West Indies). Also relevant to the theory's applicability was the existence of a good deal of empty land beyond the frontier which could be settled and developed as soon as demand warranted. Moreover, North's earlier work on the United States' balance of payments before 1860 provided the factual underpinnings for an emphasis on the importance of exports in early American history.[7]

The mechanism of export-led growth worked in North's tripartite American economy something like this:[8]

5. North and Thomas, *Growth of the American Economy,* pp. 1–2.

6. Harrold Innis, *The Fur Trade in Canada: An Introduction to Canadian Economic History* (Toronto: University of Toronto Press, 1930); idem, *The Cod Fisheries: The History of an International Economy* (Toronto: University of Toronto Press, 1940). In references to Innis's work the term "staple model" is more common than "export-led growth model," but the two terms are essentially synonymous. Incidentally, North does not cite Innis in *The Economic Growth of the United States.* He does, however, refer (on p. 4) to R. E. Baldwin's important discussion of the impact of staple production, "Patterns of Development in Newly Settled Regions," *Manchester School of Economics and Social Studies* 24 (May 1956). Guy S. Callendar also anticipated North's argument when he emphasized the importance of the American export trade in staples in *Selections from the Economic History of the United States.* North cites Callendar frequently in *The Economic Growth of the United States* and quotes a lengthy passage from the book (on pp. 101–102) on the importance of *interregional* trade, but does not cite Callendar on the importance of *international* trade.

7. Douglass C. North, "The United States Balance of Payments, 1790-1860," *Trends in the American Economy in the Nineteenth Century,* National Bureau of Economic Research, Studies in Income and Wealth, Vol. 24 (Princeton: Princeton University Press, 1960). North makes extensive use of the data developed in this NBER study in his book. In particular, see Chapter 8, "International Economic Flows."

8. This characterization of North's model represents my own interpretation. It is, however, faithful to North's own presentations of the mechanism of growth. In particular see Chapter 6 of North, *Growth and Welfare in the American Past: A New Economic History,* 2nd ed. (Englewood Cliffs, N. J.: Prentice-Hall, 1974).

The industrial revolution in Britain roared ahead unchecked after the end of the Napoleanic wars in Europe. Of primary importance in this development was the rapid expansion of textile manufacturing. As a consequence there was a growing demand for cotton on the part of English manufacturers which soon pushed against the available world wide capacity. Initially cotton prices began to rise and this inspired American planters to put more of their acreage into cotton. Because of the availability of cheap, but fertile, land and the rapidly growing slave population, the southern states were able to expand cotton production rapidly enough to keep pace with the growth in demand. Permissive government land policies explain why this increase in output was primarily accomplished by a rapid westward expansion of cotton culture and an accompanying forced migration of a substantial fraction of the American slave population.

Although the cotton plantations grew much of their own food they nevertheless had food deficits that were filled by purchase from western farmers located north of the Ohio River. Meanwhile, southerners turned to the North to provide banking, insurance, and other commercial services, and, more and more as time went on, for manufactured products as well. In this way the expanding economy of the South created, in turn, growing demands for the products of the North and West. Furthermore, as the North developed its manufacturing industry, it too increasingly turned to the West to feed its growing urban population. Southern growth was translated through the linkages of interregional dependency into northern and western growth as well.

The prosperity in the West brought about by high prices, falling transportation costs, and expanding demand attracted new settlers to the frontier of that region. Thus the westward movement of population proceeded north of the Ohio only slightly more slowly than in the South. Meanwhile, with the advantage of location, northern manufacturing interests were able to penetrate American markets previously dominated by European imports, including the market for cotton textiles. Even more significantly, factory-made goods began to replace home manufactures, enhancing productivity in the rural areas as well as within the more narrow confines of the industrial sector.

According to North, it was during the period 1815-1860 and by the means just sketched that the per capita income of Americans began the acceleration which W. W. Rostow has labeled the "take-off into sustained economic growth." No matter where one turned, the demand for cotton was acting as a force to increase productivity, inspire capital formation, and bring more and more acreage into production. Thus propelled, the American economy not only outpaced the high natural rates of population increase, but also was able to absorb the waves of European immigrants that were attracted to the "new land."

It is an attractive thesis. It is as grand and sweeping as it is elegant and original.

There were also other grand theories of American economic growth offered in the early 1960s. One immediately thinks of W. W. Rostow's historical stages theory of growth which appeared in 1960.[9] However the

9. *The Stages of Economic Growth: A Non-Communist Manifesto* (Cambridge: Cambridge University Press, 1960).

other theories did not survive critical attention, and North's has. The reason, I think is that unlike Rostow's hypothesis, North's model fits the facts.[10] The historical statistics that can be compiled are indeed impressive. This is not the place to recite them; fortunately, however, the interested reader can find a useful compendium of relevant quantitative data in a book edited by Stuart Bruchey.[11]

North's thesis was not, of course, without critics. Albert Fishlow disputed the proposition that southern food imports played a leading role in western development by arguing that the magnitude of the trade flows in the years after 1839 was too small for interregional trade to have had the impact North suggested.[12] North was defended in this case by Robert Fogel.[13] Although later work established that Fishlow's estimates of the trade flows were approximately correct and that North exaggerated the extent of southern dependency upon food imports,[14] these findings did not really strike to the heart of the argument.

In the first place, North had argued that the West-South trade in foodstuffs was a significant factor in the total demand for western agricultural output. Fishlow and others are probably correct to suggest that interregional trade filled only a comparatively tiny fraction of the total demand for food and animal feed in the South, but these trade flows

10. Simon Kuznets, for example, has stated "I can only conclude the available evidence lends no support to Professor Rostow's suggestion." "Notes on the Take-Off," in W. W. Rostow, ed., *The Economics of Take-Off into Sustained Growth* (New York: St. Martin Press, 1964). Also see Chapter 4 of Robert W. Fogel, *Railroads and American Economic Growth: Essays in Econometric History* (Baltimore: Johns Hopkins University Press, 1964), for a detailed criticism of Rostow's thesis.

11. *Cotton and the Growth of the American Economy; 1790-1860: Sources and Readings* (New York: Harcourt, Brace and World, 1967). Bruchey's compilation also includes reprints of numerous historical documents relevant to North's hypothesis.

12. "Antebellum Interregional Trade Reconsidered," *American Economic Review* 54 (May 1964). Also see Fishlow, *American Railroads and the Transformation of the Ante-Bellum Economy* (Cambridge, Mass.: Harvard University Press, 1965), Chapter 7.

13. "A Provisional View of the 'New Economic History,'" *American Economic Review* (May 1964). Also see Fogel, "American Interregional Trade in the Nineteenth Century," in Ralph Andreano, ed., *New Views on American Economic Development: A Selective Anthology of Recent Work* (Cambridge, Mass.: Schenkman Publishing, 1965). The Andreano volume also reprints the previously cited articles by Fishlow and Fogel.

14. Diane Lindstrom, "Southern Dependence upon Interregional Grain Supplies: A Review of the Trade Flows, 1840-1860," *Agricultural History* 44 (January 1970); Robert E. Gallman, "Self-Sufficiency in the Cotton Economy of the Antebellum South," *Agricultural History* 44 (January 1970); and Stanley L. Engerman, "The Antebellum South: What Probably Was and What Should Have Been," *Agricultural History* 44 (January 1970). These three articles have been reprinted in William N. Parker, ed., *The Structure of the Cotton Economy of the Antebellum South* (Berkeley and Los Angeles: University of California Press, 1970).

were nevertheless large enough to account for a significant fraction of western exports.[15]

Second, Fishlow's trade flow figures are for the period after 1839, and reliable southern self-sufficiency estimates have been constructed only for the years 1849 and 1859. However, as Lloyd Mercer points out in his contribution to this volume, North's original argument referred primarily to the period before 1840.[16] Thus much of this criticism has missed its intended target. North's conception of the tripartite economy has stood the test of time remarkably well.[17]

THE NEW ECONOMIC HISTORY

The Economic Growth of the United States is often cited as the pioneering work of the New Economic History, although the book itself barely mentions methodological issues explicitly and never uses the term "the New Economic History." This phrase apparently first appeared in print in the textbook by Lance Davis, John Hughes, and Duncan McDougall which was published in 1961—the same year as North's book.[18] Some years later, Lance Davis credited his coauthor, John Hughes, with coining the phrase.[19] But now we learn from Hughes, in his essay preceding

15. According to Fishlow's own estimates for 1839, the West shipped $14.9 million of merchandise to the South and by contrast only $11.8 million worth to the North. Fishlow, "Antebellum Interregional Trade," Table 3.

16. Lloyd J. Mercer, "The Antebellum Interregional Trade Hypothesis: A Reexamination of Theory and Evidence," Chapter 4. Unfortunately, the available quantitative data—as Mercer points out—cannot be used to estimate directly the extent to which Southern demands had an impact on the transappalachian West in the relevant period from 1815 to 1840.

17. This is not to say that the issue is closed for all time. The skeptic might begin with Lawrence Herbst, "Interregional Commodity Trade from the North to the South and American Economic Development in the Antebellum Period," *Journal of Economic History* 35 (March 1975); and Diane Lindstrom, "Demand, Market, and Eastern Economic Development: Philadelphia 1815-1840," *Journal of Economic History* 35 (March 1975).

18. *American Economic History: The Development of a National Economy* (Richard D. Irwin, 1961), p. vii. (A second edition appeared in 1965, a third in 1969.) My authority for awarding the precedence of usage to Davis *et al.* is George G. S. Murphy, "The 'New' History," *Explorations in Entrepreneurial History, Second Series* 2 (Winter 1965). Davis and Hughes, of course, were students of Douglass North.

19. Lance Davis, "'And It Will Never be Literature;' The New Economic History: A Critique," *Explorations in Entrepreneurial History, Second Series* 6 (Fall 1968), p. 75. Incidentially, this article by Davis, the article by Murphy cited in the preceding footnote, and a number of other commentaries on the methodology of the New Economic History (including one by Hughes) are conveniently reprinted in Ralph L. Andreano, ed., *The New Economic History: Recent Papers on Methodology* (New York: John Wiley and Sons, 1970).

my own in this volume, that it was Douglass North himself who first used the term. Since North was the spokesman and chief theoretician of the movement, it is fitting that he provided its name.[20]

New Economic History is an explicit attempt to subsume the history of the economy into the framework of applied social science. The early advocates of the approach—North among them—rejected mere historical description for description's sake. They proposed that economic historians use the techniques and insights of modern economic theory to frame the questions asked of history, to influence the hypotheses advanced about the past, and to suggest the nature and type of data to be collected from the archives. The New Economic Historians went further; they also advocated that any hypothesis proposed should be rigorously tested against the alternatives, particularly those to be found in the "old" history. This would have to be done by collecting relevant quantitive data and then analyzing them using the tools of statistics and econometrics.[21]

There is no better place to turn for a brief on behalf of this philosophy of economic history than Douglass North's 1965 article in the *American Economic Review.* It is worth quoting at length:

> A moment's reflection on the part of any economist should convince [him or her] that to the extent that economic history moves beyond the simple cataloguing of facts, it must meet of necessity the same set of standards that we attempt to impose by the use of scientific methods in economics. . . . I am well aware that we frequently do not have either adequate theory or the statistical data to develop and test hypotheses in any definitive fashion. My point is that economic historians do not make use of the theory we do have. While it is true that we have no overall theory of economic growth worth the name and that therefore the grand theme of the economic rise and

20. By emulation of both method and nomenclature we now have a New Social History, a New Political History, and a New Demographic History. See Robert E. Gallman, "Some Notes on the New Social History," *Journal of Economic History* 37 (March 1977); Lance E. Davis, "It's a Long, Long Road to Tipperary, or Reflections on Organized Violence, Protection Rates, and Related Topics: The New Political History," *Journal of Economic History* 40 (March 1980); and Maris A. Vinovskis, ed., *Studies in American Historical Demography* (New York:Academic Press, 1979)—a collection of papers on the New Demographic History.

21. The use of quantitative methods in economic history is often called "econometric history." In 1964 this term was employed in the titles of two books: Fogel's *Railroads and American Economic Growth: Essays in Econometric History* and Alfred H. Conrad and John R. Meyer's *The Economics of Slavery and Other Studies in Econometric History* (Chicago: Aldine Publishing). More recently the term "cliometrics" has come into vogue, sometimes to refer only to the use of statistical method in history and at other times more broadly to refer to the application of any social science theory or method to history. See Richard Sutch, "Frontiers of Quantitative Economic History, circa 1975," in Michael D. Intriligator, ed., *Frontiers of Quantitative Economics,* Vol. 3.B (Amsterdam: North Holland, 1977), p. 414.

> fall of nations cannot be treated in a formal fashion, we still know a good deal about productivity change and its sources; but little of the literature in economic history reflects any awareness of this fact. And for the rest of economic history, much of it deals with problems in which various fields of economic theory are directly relevant.[22]

The joint conference held in Williamstown, Massachusetts, by the Economic History Association and the National Bureau of Economic Research in September of 1957 is customarily used to mark the birth of the New Economic History.[23] Alfred H. Conrad and John R. Meyer read two famous papers at those meetings: one on method and one on the economics of slavery.[24] At the same meetings were scholars like William Parker, Robert Gallman, Richard Easterlin, and Stanley Lebergott. Their contributions (Parker and Whartenby on output trends before 1840, Gallman on commodity output, Easterlin on regional income, and Lebergott on employment) were to serve as statistical foundations for much of the subsequent New Economic History written on nineteenth-century America. Douglass North was also in Williamstown.[25] It was there that he presented the paper on "The United States Balance

22. "The State of Economic History," *American Economic Review* 55 (May 1965), pp. 86–87. For other early statements in support of the New Economic History, see Alfred H. Conrad and John R. Meyer, "Economic Theory, Statisitical Inference, and Economic History," *Journal of Economic History* 17 (December 1957); Lance E. Davis, Jonathan R. T. Hughes, and Stanley Reiter, "Aspects of Quantitative Research in Economic History," *Journal of Economic History* 20 (December 1960), reprinted in *Purdue Faculty Papers in Economic History, 1956–1966* (Homewood, Ill.: Richard D. Irwin, 1967); Douglass C. North, "Quantitative Research in American Economic History," *American Economic Review* 53 (March 1963); and the series of contributions by Robert W. Fogel: "A Provisional View of the 'New Economic History,'" *American Economic Review* 54 (May 1964); "Measurement and Theory in the Study of Economic History," in *Railroads and American Economic Growth*, pp. 237–249; "The Reunification of Economic History with Economic Theory," *American Economic Review* 55 (May 1965); and "The New Economic History: Its Findings and Methods," *Economic History Review, Second Series* 26 (December 1966; reprinted in Fogel and Stanley L. Engerman, eds., *The Reinterpretation of American Economic History* [New York: Harper and Row, 1971]).

23. North himself dates the origin of the New Economic History to these 1957 meetings. Douglass C. North, "The New Economic History After Twenty Years," *American Behavioral Scientist* 21 (December 1977), p. 187.

24. Conrad and Meyer, "Economic Theory, Statistical Inference, and Economic History," and "The Economics of Slavery in the Antebellum South," *Journal of Political Economy* 66 (April 1958). Both papers are reprinted in Conrad and Meyer, *Economics of Slavery and Other Studies.*

25. The essays by Parker and Whartenby, Towne and Rasmussen (on agricultural output), Gallman, Easterlin, Lebergott, and North were printed in William Parker, ed., *Trends in the American Economy in the Nineteenth Century,* National Bureau of Economic Research, Studies in Income and Wealth, Vol. 24 (Princeton: Princeton University Press, 1960).

of Payments, 1790–1860" which was later to provide the statistical base for *The Economic Growth of the United States.* North's book appeared in 1861; it was the first book-length monograph to be considered New Economic History.

But it is not North's participation at the beginning of the movement—however noteworthy—that I believe is the most important link between the man and the method. North's key role in the story of the New Economic History was as an articulator, a missionary, and a militant partisan for the new methodology. Between 1960 and 1968 (roughly dated) North championed the New Economic History. As coeditor of the *Journal of Economic History* with William Parker from 1960 through 1966 he was able to ensure that the field's most prestigious journal was hospitable to articles and reviews that made self-conscious use of neoclassical economic theory and/or econometric methodology.[26]

During this period North published a series of three papers (1963, 1965, and 1968) which praised and evaluated the new work,[27] and in a short book, *Growth and Welfare in the American Past* (1966), he demonstrated how powerful and provocative the New Economic History could be.[28] Subtitled *A New Economic History,* the book is really a collection of essays on several key topics in American economic history. In each essay North used simple economic theory and the tabular presentation of

26. During the years North was coeditor of the *Journal of Economic History* there appeared such classics of the New Economic History as Lance E. Davis, "The New England Textile Mills and the Capital Markets: A Study of Industrial Borrowing 1840–1860" (March 1960); Robert W. Fogel, "A Quantitative Approach to the Study of Railroads in American Economic Growth" (June 1962); Albert Fishlow, "Review of *Trends in the American Economy in the Nineteenth Century*" (June 1962); Allan G. Bogue, "Farming in the Prairie Peninsula, 1830-1890" (March 1963); Harry N. Scheiber, "State Policy and the Public Domain: The Ohio Canal Lands" (March 1965); Lance E. Davis, "The Investment Market, 1870–1914: The Evolution of a National Market" (September 1965); Robert P. Swierenga, "Land Speculator 'Profits' Reconsidered: Central Iowa as a Test Case" (March 1966); Peter Temin, "Labor Scarcity and the Problem of American Industrial Efficiency in the 1850's" (September 1966); and Martin L. Primack, "Farm Capital Formation as a Use of Farm Labor in the United States, 1850–1910" (September 1966). In preparing this list, I have excluded papers that appeared in the December issues of the *Journal.* In those years the December issue printed the papers presented at the annual meetings of the Economic History Association and thus were not under the direct control of the *Journal's* editors.

27. "Quantitative Research in American Economic History," *American Economic Review* 53 (March 1963); "The State of Economic History," *American Economic Review* 55 (May 1965); and "Economic History," in David L. Sills, ed., *International Encyclopedia of the Social Sciences,* Vol. 6 (New York: Macmillan, 1968).

28. The first edition was published by Prentice-Hall in 1966. A revised second edition appeared in 1974, and there are now plans for a third edition to be coauthored by North and one of his former students, Terry Anderson.

quantitative data to challange views that were widely held at the time.[29] The book was of major importance at the time for several reasons. It was the first, and for many years the only, textbook of the New Economic History suitable for use in the undergraduate class.[30] As such it was widely used, generally as a supplement to a more substantial text, throughout the country. Not only students, but many teachers as well, were first introduced to the New Economic History through North's essays. And within those essays—where North offered his own reappraisal of American economic history—the significance of the New Economic History to both economics and history was made evident.

On topic after topic North demonstrated how the most elementary economic theory could be used to cast doubt upon venerable interpretations of the past. The book was packed with original and startling ideas, and most of them were completely undeveloped. What a gold mine of new ideas for future research it turned out to be! In Chapter 3, North questioned Lawrence Harper's analysis of the burden of the British Navigation Acts on the colonial American economy.[31] And within a few years a major debate had grown up over the magnitude and proper interpretation of the quantitative estimates of these burdens.[32] In Chap-

29. North once told me that he had orginally intended merely to edit a book that reprinted important articles by other economic historians. But, he related, as he began to draft the critical introductions to the selections he had chosen, he discovered that he had more to say on each topic than the format would allow. Accordingly he scrapped the selected readings and reworked the introductory essays into self-contained expositions of his own views.

30. The textbook by Davis, Hughes, and McDougall was designed to teach basic economic theory along with economic history and was organized around a topical outline.

31. "The Effect of the Navigation Acts on the Thirteen Colonies," in Richard B. Morris, ed., *The Era of the American Revolution* (New York: Columbia University Press, 1939).

32. The debate was started by North's colleague, Robert P. Thomas, "A Quantitative Approach to the Study of the Effects of British Imperial Policy upon Colonial Welfare: Some Preliminary Findings," *Journal of Economic History* 25 (December 1965). Incidentially, in the 1966 edition of *Growth and Welfare,* North acknowledges "numerous lengthy discussions" with Thomas (p. 43) and even cites Thomas's 1965 article (p. 194). However, the text shows evidence that North's own critique of Harper preceded Thomas's. For some of the flavor of the discussion that arose over this issue see Roger L. Ransom, "British Policy and Colonial Growth: Some Implications of the Burden from the Navigation Acts," *Journal of Economic History* 28 (September 1968); Robert P. Thomas, "British Imperial Policy and the Economic Interpretation of the American Revolution," *Journal of Economic History* 28 (September 1968); Peter D. McClelland, "The Cost to America of British Imperial Policy," *American Economic Review* 59 (May 1969); Joseph D. Reid, Jr., "On Navigating the Navigation Acts with Peter D. McClelland: Comment," *American Economic Review* 60 (December 1970); and Gary Walton, "The New Economic History and the Navigation Acts," *Economic*

ter 5, North argued that the period 1793-1807 was unusually prosperous "as a result of peculiar events that lasted for a very short time [p. 74]." This view was later challenged by Paul David on both theoretical and empirical grounds.[33] And soon another debate within the New Economic History was off and running.[34]

In Chapter 7, North cited Richard Easterlin's estimates of personal income per capita by region and suggested that the South "—far from being stagnant—was growing during this period [1840-1860] at a rate approximately equal to the national average [p. 91]."[35] Soon Stanley Engerman developed this idea in a provocative series of papers that culminated in one of the major themes of Fogel and Engerman's *Time on the Cross.* The result was yet another debate between New Economic Historians.[36] A brief comment, also in Chapter 6, on the "viability and profitability of slavery" likewise foreshadowed the extensive debate on this issue.[37]

History Review, Second Series 24 (October 1971). A review of this debate can be found in Chapter 2 of Susan Previant Lee and Peter Passell, *A New Economic View of American History* (New York: W. W. Norton, 1979).

33. "The Growth of Real Product in the U. S. before 1840: New Evidence, Controlled Conjectures," *Journal of Economic History* 27 (June 1967).

34. See Chapter 3 of Lee and Passell's *New Economic View of American History* for a discussion of this debate. A recent contribution stimulated by North's original argument is Claudia D. Goldin and Frank D. Lewis, "The Role of Exports in American Economic Growth during the Napoleonic Wars, 1793 to 1807," *Explorations in Economic History* 17 (January 1980).

35. Richard A. Easterlin, "Regional Income Trends, 1840–1950," in Seymour E. Harris, ed., *American Economic History* (New York: McGraw-Hill, 1961).

36. Stanley L. Engerman, "The Effects of Slavery upon the Southern Economy: A Review of the Recent Debate," *Explorations in Entrepreneurial History, Second Series* 4 (Winter 1967); "Some Economic Factors in Southern Backwardness in the Nineteenth Century," in John F. Kain and John R. Meyer, eds., *Essays in Regional Economics* (Cambridge, Mass.: Harvard University Press, 1971); and Robert W. Fogel and Stanley L. Engerman, *Time on the Cross,* 2 vols. (Boston: Little, Brown & Co., 1974), 1: 247–257. The North-Engerman-Fogel thesis that antebellum growth in the South was comparable to the North's has been criticized by Roger L. Ransom and Richard Sutch, in *One Kind of Freedom: The Economic Consequences of Emancipation* (Cambridge: Cambridge University Press, 1977), pp. 264-269; and in "Growth and Welfare in the American South of the Nineteenth Century," *Explorations in Economic History* 16 (April 1979; reprinted in Gary M. Walton and James F. Shepherd, eds., *Market Institutions and Economic Progress in the New South, 1965–1900* [New York: Academic Press, 1981]).

37. North's comment was apparently inspired by Yasukichi Yasuba, "The Profitability and Viability of Plantation Slavery in the United States," *Economic Studies Quarterly* 12 (September 1961); and by Richard Sutch, "The Profitability of Antebellum Slavery—Revisited," *Southern Economic Journal* 31 (April 1965). For reviews of this debate see Stanley Engerman, "The Effects of Slavery," and Lee and Passell, *New Economic View of American*

In Chapter 10, North "suggest[ed] some hypotheses that must be tested" concerning the effect of public land policies (pp. 131-136). When the second edition of *Growth and Welfare* appeared in 1974, North was able to cite his own student, Lloyd Mercer, on "Land Grants to American Railroads, Social Cost or Social Benefit."[38] In Chapter 11, North argued that the agrarian discontent of the late nineteenth century could not easily be explained by a decline in farm incomes (pp. 145-148). He provided a scattering of evidence that suggested incomes were rising. Soon a number of New Economic Historians were busying themselves in an attempt to solve the puzzle of farm discontent.[39]

Growth and Welfare set more than a few hares off and running. Armed with techniques which gave their owners a feeling of methodological superiority (I can speak from personal experience), a host of newly converted New Economic Historians enthusiastically gave chase. The revolution, thus ignited, was enormously successful. Robert Fogel, installed at the University of Chicago, soon joined with North as a major advocate for the cause. A tireless and effective spokesman, Fogel won attention and support for the movement from many economists outside of the field. As a consequence, the demand for economic historians trained in the new approach soared.

Students from North's seminar at the University of Washington helped fill part of the demand. In the 1960s, Gary Walton, James Shepherd, Roger Ransom, Lloyd Mercer, and Gerald Gunderson received their doctorates from the University of Washington. And by the mid-1960s the economics department at Harvard University was also turning out New Historians at an impressive rate. Albert Fishlow, Paul David, Peter Temin, Peter McClelland, Donald McCloskey, Richard Sylla, Barbara Solow, Stefano Fenoaltea, and Lars Sandberg (to name a

History, Chapter 8. The articles by Yasuba, Sutch, and Engerman are reprinted along with other contributions to the debate in Hugh G. J. Aitken, ed., *Did Slavery Pay? Readings in the Economics of Black Slavery in the United States* (Boston: Houghton Mifflin, 1971).

38. *Business History Review* 43 (Summer 1969). Also see Mercer, "Rate of Return for Land Grant Railroads: The Central Pacific System," *Journal of Economic History* 30 (September 1970). Another important paper on this topic is Robert W. Fogel and Jack L. Rutner, "Efficiency Effects of Federal Land Policy, 1850–1900," in William O. Aydelotte, Allan G. Bogue, and Robert W. Fogel, eds., *The Dimensions of Quantitative Research in History* (Princeton: Princeton University Press, 1972).

39. See Lee and Passell, *New Economic View of American History,* pp. 292–301, for a review. Among those who joined this debate are Robert Higgs, "Railroad Rates and the Populist Uprising," *Agricultural History* 44 (July 1970); Ann Mayhew, "A Reappraisal of the Causes of Farm Protest in the United States, 1870–1900," *Journal of Economic History* 32 (June 1972); and John Bowman and Richard Keehn, "Agricultural Terms of Trade in Four Midwestern States, 1870–1900," *Journal of Economic History* 34 (September 1974).

few) taught each other the new techniques in the seminar convened by Alexander Gerschenkron.[40] Gerschenkron never did New Economic History himself, but he supported its values and shared its goals.[41] Given the excitement then raging in the field, that was all that was required.

The success of the New Economic History was a truly remarkable achievement. Within surprisingly few years New Economic Historians dominated the profession, and it is North and Gerschenkron who share the credit for training and inspiring the bulk of the second generation of New Economic Historians who took up the new positions in departments of economics around the country.

There was criticism of the new approach from those trained in the older methods, of course.[42] But such comments produced only enough hesitation on the part of the committed to produce a round of vigorous rebuttal.[43] The important criticisms—the ones that ultimately changed the way the New Economic History was practiced—came from within the movement. Almost from the outset the "Harvard wing" began to question the followers of Fogel and North about their "excessive" devotion to partial-equilibrium neoclassical economic theory.[44]

The power of neoclassical theory derives from the strong assumptions it makes about the presence of competition, the absence of transactions

40. I was a Ph.D. student at the Massachusetts Institute of Technology from 1965 to 1967 and was privileged to attend Gerschenkron's seminar in those years.

41. For example, see his foreword to Fishlow, *Railroads and the Ante-Bellum Economy*, pp. vii–viii.

42. The best known of these critiques are Fritz Redlich, "'New' and Traditional Approaches to Economic History and Their Interdependence," *Journal of Economic History* 25 (December 1965); Louis M. Hacker, "The New Revolution in Economic History: A Review Article Based on *Railroads and Economic Growth: Essays in Econometric History* by Robert William Fogel," *Explorations in Entrepreneurial History, Second Series* 3 (Spring 1966); Meghnad Desai, "Some Issues in Economic History," *Economic History Review, Second Series* 21 (April 1968); and Fritz Redlich, "Potentialities and Pitfalls in Economic History," *Explorations in Entrepreneurial History, Second Series* 6 (Fall 1968).

43. For example: Robert W. Fogel, "The Specification Problem in Economic History," *Journal of Economic History* 27 (September 1967); Alfred H. Conrad, "Econometrics and Southern History," *Explorations in Entrepreneurial History, Second Series* 6 (Fall 1968); and Peter D. McClelland, *Causal Explanation and Model Building in History, Economics, and the New Economic History* (Ithaca, N. Y.: Cornell University Press, 1975).

44. The expression "Harvard wing" was used by North to characterize the source of this criticism ("The New Economic History after Twenty Years," p. 199). Although graduates of the Harvard seminar played an important role in articulating the critique of neoclassical methodology in economic history, there were other—non-Harvard—members of this group as well. William Parker at Yale and his student, Gavin Wright, should be mentioned prominently.

cost and uncertainty, and the stability of the underlying economic institutions. Many of the most interesting historical problems in economics, however, revolve around the absence or imperfections of competition, the consequences of substantial transactions cost and uncertainty, and changes in the economic institutions of society. The critics from within worried about the limitations of the neoclassical framework when applied to such problems.[45]

At first Fogel and North defended the applicability of neoclassical theory, although North was from the begining willing to express his own reservations concerning what he considered to be sloppy thinking on the part of many New Economic Historians. As early as 1965 he wrote

> There has been some valuable work [in the New Economic History]—particularly in the gathering of statistics—to provide us with some solid footing for analysis, and there have been a few first-rate articles and books, yet the results have been generally disappointing. Too much of it has been dull and unimaginative, and there seems to be a widespread conviction that econometric techniques, the computer, and running a few regressions can substitute for theory and imagination. Some of the new economic history written by economists is of distressingly poor quality. Some of it is so imprecise and fuzzy as to make it difficult, if not impossible, to make any model at all. A good deal of it includes partial-equilibrium analysis of problems with broad general-equilibrium or disequilibrium implications. Too much of it shows that the writer clearly has no fundamental understanding of the way by which an economy operates. In particular, a lot of it shows that the role of prices in resource allocations and the implications of price behavior have completely eluded the writer.[46]

45. In the late 1960s and early 1970s these worries were frequently discussed at the National Science Foundation sponsored Cliometrics Conference held during that time in Madison, Wisconsin. The criticism from the Harvard wing first began to find its way into print in the discussion revolving around Fogel's book, *Railroads and American Economic Growth*. For a few examples, see Peter McClelland, "Railroads, American Growth and the New Economic History," *Journal of Economic History* 28 (March 1968); and Paul A. David, "Transportation Innovations and Economic Growth: Professor Fogel On and Off the Rails," *Economic History Review, Second Series* 22 (December 1969; reprinted as Chapter 6 of David, *Technical Choice, Innovation, and Economic Growth: Essays on American and British Experience in the Nineteenth Century* [Cambridge: Cambridge University Press, 1975]). Explicit methodological discussions can be found in Gavin Wright, "Econometric Studies of History," in Michael D. Intriligator, ed., *Frontiers of Quantitative Economics* (Amsterdam: North Holland, 1971), together with "Comments" by Paul David in the same volume; William Parker, "From New to Old in Economic History," *Journal of Economic History* 31 (March 1971); Paul A. David, "Introduction: Technology, History and Growth," in David, *Technical Choice;* and Richard Sutch, "Frontiers of Quantitative Economic History, circa 1975."

46. "The State of Economic History," p. 90. North went on in this article to castigate Conrad and Meyer's classic paper on the "Economics of Slavery." For another criticism of the use of partial-equilibrium models to analyze general-equilibrium problems in history, see Peter Temin, "General-Equilibrium Models in Economic History," *Journal of Economic History* 31 (March 1971).

North's criticisms, however, soon turned to the inherent deficiencies of the neoclassical framework. In 1971 he wrote

> The tools that the new economic historian inherited from the economist were not intended to deal with long-run economic change as twenty-five years of groping by the economist concerned with development should attest. The economist not only accepted tastes, technology, and population as given, but also he accepted equally the current basic ground rules within which both market and non-market decisions were made. For that matter, the theory did not recognize the possibility of making economic decisions via the political process. Information was assumed to be perfect and costless. That is an awesome collection of deficiencies.[47]

North titled his 1973 presidential address before the Economic History Association "Beyond the New Economic History." Within the course of his remarks he catalogued the limitations of the New Economic History and then went on to add

> The limitations are those of theory. Neo-classical economic theory has two major shortcomings for the economic historian. One, it was not designed to explain long-run economic change; and two, even within the context of the question it was designed to answer, it provides quite limited answers since it is immediately relevant to a world of perfect markets—that is, perfect in the sense of zero transactions costs: the costs of specifying the enforcing property rights. Yet we have come to realize that devising and enforcing a set of rules of the game is hardly ever costless and the nature of these costs is at the very root of all economic system's problems.[48]

The Harvard wing was a minority no longer.[49]

47. "Institutional Change and Economic Growth," *Journal of Economic History* 31 (March 1971), p. 118. I have taken the liberty of correcting an obvious typographical error in the original.

48. *Journal of Economic History* 34 (March 1974), p. 2. Also see "The New Economic History after Twenty Years."

49. With these methodological papers North broke away from Fogel and the neoclassical wing. About this time the rivalry between the two camps became more agitated. Discussions at academic conferences were intense and the criticisms voiced were more pointed. Finally these tensions erupted at a conference in Rochester, New York, in 1974. The conference had been called to assess Fogel and Engerman's controversial work on American slavery, *Time on the Cross.* In their book Fogel and Engerman made sweeping claims for the superiority of the New Economic History and in particular its neoclassical version (see, for example, Volume 1, Chapter 1; Volume 2, Appendix A). For an introduction to the voluminous literature on the *Time on the Cross* controversy see Paul A. David, Herbert G. Gutman, Richard Sutch, Peter Temin, and Gavin Wright, *Reckoning with Slavery: A Critical Study in the Quantitative History of American Negro Slavery* (Oxford: Oxford University Press, 1976). Particularly relevant to the methodological dispute are "The Authors' Preface" and Chapter 8, "*Time on the Cross* and the Burden of Quantitative History." Although the disagreement over the limitations of the neoclassical approach is definitely

The criticism, moreover, was beginning to have a positive effect. Much of the new work that appeared after 1973 attempts (some of it more successfully than other) to address these deficiencies. In the best of this work, models are no longer being borrowed blindly from the neoclassical kit bag, but are instead constructed to fit the special circumstances of the period and topic under study. The New Economic History has been steered in a new direction.[50] This is a development that promises to contribute to economic theory almost as much as it should enrich economic history.

A GENERAL THEORY OF INSTITUTIONAL CHANGE, PROPERTY RIGHTS, AND THE STATE

Douglass North was not content with merely delineating the limitations of received neoclassical theory for the study of history. Indeed, he had scorn for those who made "elaborate disclaimers of the limitations of this approach before proceeding on their merry way of applying the theory to historical problems."[51] In an impressive series of articles and books, North has attempted to set forth a new theoretical paradigm that would explain institutional change, deal with the assignment and enforcement of property rights, and incorporate a theory of the state. As he sees it, "if economics is a theory of choice subject to specified con-

---

an important part of this debate, it would be a mistake to conclude that this was the primary issue. Fogel and Engerman were also sharply criticized for presenting results that could not be replicated by other scholars and for drastically overstating their case. For more detail, see the essays by David and Temin, Gutman and Sutch, and Sutch in *Reckoning with Slavery*.

50. The contributions in Part III of this volume are all examples of this new direction in research. Several other good examples are Gavin Wright, "The Political Economy of New Deal Spending: An Econometric Analysis," *Review of Economics and Statistics* 56 (February 1974); Donald McCloskey, "English Open Fields as Behavior Toward Risk," *Research in Economic History* 1 (1976); J. J. Pincus, *Pressure Groups and Politics in Antebellum Tariffs* (New York: Columbia University Press, 1977); and Gavin Wright, *The Political Economy of the Cotton South: Households, Markets, and Wealth in the Nineteenth Century* (New York: W. W. Norton, 1978). In my own collaborative work with Roger Ransom (*One Kind of Freedom: The Economic Consequences of Emancipation*), we stressed the roles of institutional change, high transactions costs, uncertainty, and racism in explaining the relatively impoverished economic position of the blacks and the lack of economic growth in the postemancipation South. For a view of the type of controversy that can arise over attempts to go outside the rigid neoclassical framework, see the contributions in Walton and Shepherd, *Market Institutions and Economic Progress in the New South*.

51. "The New Economic History After Twenty Years," p. 199.

straints, a task of economic history [is] to theorize about those evolving constraints."[52]

North—it should be understood—is not rejecting neoclassical economics in his recent works. He is critical of its narrow focus and its limited usefulness for historical analysis. One can see in this progression of books and articles that his ultimate goal is the construction of a "general theory" of economic change with a much broader applicability than the neoclassical model but within which the neoclassical model would still reside undisturbed as a special case.[53]

The first step in North's search for a broader theory was taken in a research report that appeared in 1968 on "Sources of Productivity Change in Ocean Shipping, 1600-1850." The conclusion North reached with this research (itself a classic example of the earlier type of New Economic History) was that most of the increase in productivity (output per unit of input) in ocean transportation was attributable, not to technological change, but to improvements in economic organization.[54] Institutions did matter after all!

The heart of the problem, as North came to see it after this discovery, is that the economic historian who seeks to explain economic growth is thus called upon to explain, among other things, the evolution of the particular set of economic institutions, behaviorial constraints, legal rights, and rules that define at any point in history what is commonly called the "economic system." Somewhat later North had taken this point a step further when he wrote (with Robert Thomas), "The factors we have listed (innovation, economies of scale, education, capital accumulation, etc.) are not causes of growth; they *are* growth. . . . Growth will simply not occur unless the existing economic organization is efficient."[55] Simply put, the focus of attention had to be shifted away from the neoclassical causes of growth to the problem of institutional change.

52. North, "Structure and Performance: The Task of Economic History," *Journal of Economic Literature* 16 (September 1978), p. 963. In the passage quoted, North is referring to the views of Schumpeter, Marx, and Smith, but from the context it is clear that he shares their conception of the task of the economic historian.

53. At times North talks about extending the neoclassical framework to enable it to deal with the problems of institutional change. But whether the theoretical innovations are thought to be extensions of the existing neoclassical method or to lie outside of that framework is merely a semantic issue.

54. North, "Sources of Productivity Change in Ocean Shipping, 1600–1850," *Journal of Political Economy* 76 (September 1968), p. 953.

55. Douglass North and Robert Paul Thomas, *The Rise of the Western World: A New Economic History* (Cambridge: Cambridge University Press. 1973; paperback ed., 1976), p. 2.

The neoclassical tradition is of little help in analyzing institutional change since it takes the existing economic organization as given and attempts to explain how humans would behave within such a system. When successful, neoclassical theory can shed light on how the system "works." It is powerless, however, when it comes to explaining where the system "comes from" or how it evolves. This is a major disadvantage to the historian interested in economic growth since no economic system is static. Economic institutions are constantly changing, and the forces that direct and propel that change are themselves endogenous to the economy.

What North sought was a theoretical framework for tackling the problem of institutional change. Since the early 1970s economic historians have ventured in a number of different directions in their attempt to come up with satisfying ways to handle this problem. One of the possibilities that has stimulated a great deal of discussion is North's proposal to use a "choice-theoretic" model to explain how societies choose their institutions from a larger (possibly infinite) set of possible institutions.[56]

"Sources of Productivity Change" was followed 2 years later by "Institutional Change and American Economic Growth: A First Step towards a Theory of Institutional Innovation".[57] In this article with Lance Davis, North argues that institutional change will occur when an action group (either an individual or an organized group) perceives that a modification of the existing institutional rules will yield benefits greater than the costs of innovation. The action group then undertakes the job of bringing about the change. It secures the acquiescence of those who might be opposed by sharing with them the proceeds attributable to the innovation. If the group is successful and if their expectations about costs and benefits prove correct, then the rearrangement of institutions will actually increase the productivity of the economy. In this way institutions will slowly evolve to ever more efficient forms. This, Davis and North suggest, is the fundamental explanation of economic growth.

The argument was quickly elaborated in a book coauthored with Davis, which attempted to put the new theory to work on several topics

56. North drew his inspiration for this approach from W. F. Baumol, *Welfare Economics and the Theory of the State* (London: Longmans, 1952); Anthony Downs, *An Economic Theory of Democracy* (New York: Harper and Row, 1957); James Buchanan and Gordon Tullock, *The Calculus of Consent* (Ann Arbor: University of Michigan Press, 1962); Harold Demsetz, "Towards a Theory of Property Rights," *American Economic Review* 57 (May 1967); and Kenneth Arrow, "Political and Economic Evaluation of Social Effects and Externalities," National Bureau of Economic Research (unpublished).

57. Davis and North, in *Journal of Economic History* 30 (March 1970).

in American economic history.[58] There are chapters on "Land Policy and American Agriculture," "Savings and Investment in the American Economy," "Transportation and Economic Growth," "The Growth of Manufacturing in the United States," "The Service Industries," and "The Labor Force: Organization and Education." It was immediately evident, however, that there are theoretical difficulties with the original Davis-North argument. First, there is the problem of the decision-making process. Who is it that evaluates the costs and benefits of change? And what happens if there is a divergence between the private and social evaluations of these magnitudes? Individual pursuit of self-interest and the freedom to form voluntary action groups are not in themselves sufficient to make North's model determinant.

North recognized this problem from the beginning. Because some individuals outside of the action group may be hurt by the changes proposed, they would have an incentive to organize and oppose the change. If the losers are—say, for ideological reasons—unwilling to be bribed, there is no a priori way to predict the outcome of such conflicts. Thus Davis and North admit they have difficulty explaining the timing of institutional changes.[59] Those who benefit may also be left outside of the action group and thus avoid their appropriate share of the costs involved. Indeed, there is a distinct incentive for individuals in such a situation to become "free riders."[60] Moreover, if too many individuals attempt to be free riders, they will leave behind an insufficient number of members within the "action group" to bear the costs of organization and negotiation. When this happens, the group will collapse (or never form) and institutional progress fails to occur.

In an attempt to deal with these and similar problems, North and Robert Thomas suggested in a 1970 article that a set of "fundamental institutional arrangements" could somehow prevent the polarization of conflicting interest groups and solve the free rider problem.[61] These fundamental institutions are distinct from the "secondary institutional arrangements" analyzed by Davis and North. According to North and Thomas, the fundamental institutions may be specified in a constitution or may simply be a set of customary "ground rules" for economic and political behavior. But in any case, early in the process of growth North's

58. Davis and North, *Institutional Change and American Economic Growth* (Cambridge: Cambridge University Press, 1971); also see North, "Institutional Change and Economic Growth," *Journal of Economic History* 31 (March 1971).

59. Davis and North, *Institutional Change*, p. 263.

60. North and Thomas, *The Rise of the Western World*, pp. 4–5.

61. North and Thomas, "An Economic Theory of the Growth of the Western World," *Economic History Review, Second Series* 23 (April 1970), p. 10.

model requires something like a government to prevent conflicts and to apportion the costs of beneficial change to the would-be free riders. This concept of fundamental and secondary institutions was applied by North and Thomas to explain "The Rise and Fall of the Manorial System" in a second article that appeared in 1971.[62] The ideas in these articles were further developed in a book, *The Rise of the Western World*, which appeared in 1973. Within 159 pages, North and Thomas placed under scrutiny the whole of Europe from A.D. 900 to 1700.[63]

These works have received their share of criticism, much of it focusing on matters of detail. Stefano Fenoaltea, for example, has criticized the North–Thomas model of the manorial system for alleged misinterpretations of the historical record.[64] And misinterpretations there undoubtedly were. But such criticisms do not really negate the basic contribution of these works. Fenoaltea admits as much in his conclusion:

> But one must also recall [North and Thomas's] ambitious attempt to encompass centuries of change in a unified explanation, the pioneering application of transaction-cost analysis to economic history, and the proper formulation of the problem of efficiency with respect to labor obligations. All these remain, and will continue to claim both our gratitude and our admiration.

The real difficulties with the choice-theoretic approach at this point were still theoretical—not the possible failures of application. The distinction between fundamental and secondary institutions seems arbitrary, and North and Thomas's appeal to the different roles played by the rulers of various European states in *The Rise of the Western World* struck many readers as ad hoc. Fenoaltea, for example, complains that the historical explanation offered by North and Thomas "appeals to institutional constraints to an extent that is both empirically unjustified and analytically alarming."[66]

A related theoretical problem arises at this juncture. As long as the historian can take the initial institutional setting at the outset of the time period under study as given (as Davis and North say they do),[67] we can think of new institutional innovations as being brought about within the

62. North and Thomas, "The Rise and Fall of the Manorial System: A Theoretical Model," *Journal of Economic History* 31 (December 1971).

63. North and Thomas, *Rise of the Western World.*

64. Stefano Fenoaltea, "The Rise and Fall of a Theoretical Model: The Manorial System," *Journal of Economic History* 35 (June 1975).

65. Ibid., p. 409.

66. Ibid., pp. 408–409.

67. Davis and North, *Institutional Change,* p. 263.

existing rules of the game—provided those rules of the game are "appropriate" to the Davis–North mechanism; provided, in North's words, that the original "fundamental" institutional organization was "efficient." The rules of the game, of course, may slowly change over time, but by a potentially understandable process. Yet, as soon as the possibility is raised that not all sets of initial institutional rules are necessarily "appropriate" or efficient, a problem arises. What if at some point in history a set of inappropriate institutions exists which pits interest group against interest group and which allows the free rider problem to sap the strength of voluntary organizations? Then there will be no mechanism to change such bad rules to more appropriate ones. It is no good to argue that a set of "metarules" might exist through which such bad fundamental institutions will inevitably be overthrown. What if the metarules are wrong too? Those following this line of argument would be forced into an infinite regression.

These are not mere "what if" questions. Back before growth began, institutions must have been inefficient and inappropriate for growth-inducing institutional change. If they were not, why did not modern economic growth begin earlier? But if the initial institutions were inefficient, the North–Davis–Thomas model cannot explain their transformation and thus cannot explain the onset of economic growth. Since the role of the economic historian is to explain, not just the ongoing process of economic growth, but also the causes and timing of the initiation of growth, the North model is still incomplete.

This conundrum has been used by Alexander Field in a thoughtful critique of the North–Thomas model of the Western world.[68] Field argues that North and Thomas are ultimately trapped by this problem. If one desires to eliminate all references to exogenously given rules in a formal theory of growth, some other mechanism than the choice-theoretic one will have to be found.

> Some basic set of rules needs to be treated as parametric to . . . any model of an economic system that treats individuals as self interested. The proposition that these rules can be understood as resulting from the interaction of agents in an economic model which makes no appeal to some set of rules specified exogenously needs to be rejected, along with the widespread misperception that it is the ultimate task of microeconomic theory to create such models.[69]

68. Alexander James Field, "What's Wrong with NeoClassical Institutional Economics: A Critique with Special Reference to the North/Thomas Model of Pre-1500 Europe," *Explorations in Economic History* 18 (April 1981). I wish to thank Professor Field for allowing me to examine and cite this article in advance of publication.

69. Field, p. 31 in manuscript (October 1980).

North himself seems to recognize the logical problem that Field has pointed out so forcefully. But he would not agree that it is inherently insoluble—at least not if the economic historian is prepared to look beyond "microeconomic theory" for the answers. In a 1978 paper on the "Task of Economic History," North retraces the route he has taken and then makes the following assertions:

> An explanation of this fundamental [institutional] transformation in the structure of the economy is not to be found in the work of new economic historians. Looking elsewhere, we find that Joseph Schumpeter alone amongst the major economists of the twentieth century analyzed this transformation. . . .
>
> It is more than just constitutional rules—it is also the ideological context that determines the acceptable range of choices. In short, tastes have been changing as well. . . .
>
> Strong convictions about injustice do appear to have overcome the free rider problem. . . .
>
> The past century bore witness to a fundamental change in ideological perspective, which Schumpeter described very effectively. I see no way to account for this transformation without the systematic study of the sociology of knowledge. . . .
>
> Ideology can be studied as a positive science and empirically testable propositions can be derived. . . .
>
> Economists and economic historians are not going to make further headway in theorizing about nonmarket decision making until they come to grips with these issues.[70]

The problem of ideology is not the only one North is prepared to come to grips with. Apparently he would agree with Fenoaltea that his references to the role of the state in North and Thomas were ad hoc and theoretically unsatisfactory. In a paper he submitted to a festschrift in honor of his own mentor, M. M. Knight, he offers a "Framework for Analyzing the State in Economic History." It begins as follows: "The creation of a state is an essential precondition for economic growth. . . . Models of the state should be an explicit part of any analysis of secular changes."[71]

Whether or not North succeeds in developing acceptable theories of ideology and the state, the profession can certainly respect and, indeed, applaud his desire to try. That the problems he wishes to solve are difficult, that the theory to deal with them is still grossly inadequate, and

70. North, "Structure and Performance: The Task of Economic History," pp. 965–966, 964–965, 976, 974, 975, 976.

71. North, "A Framework for Analyzing the State in Economic History," *Explorations in Economic History* 16 (October 1979), p. 249.

that a decade of his work (the 1970s) is thought by some to have been misdirected, is not likely to deter Douglass North. He already has a new book underway, entitled *Structure and Change in Economic History*. It will contain another theory of institutional change, but one that attempts to theorize about the evolving role of ideology and the state in the historical process.[72] I do not know what he will say, but I am certain that the book will be full of new ideas. And, as Douglass North himself stated it, "We must have new ideas, without them the field will die."

ACKNOWLEDGMENTS

I wish to acknowledge the extended discussions I have had with Roger Ransom on the two subjects of this review. I have also received helpful advice on an earlier draft from Roger Ransom and Gary Walton.

Richard Sutch was an undergraduate at the University of Washington when he took North's graduate seminar in American Economic History in 1964. His seminar paper "The Profitability of Slavery—Revisited," was subsequently published in the **Southern Economic Journal** in 1965. Although he pursued monetary theory and macroeconomics at the Massachusetts Institute of Technology (where he received a Ph.D. in 1968), the interest in economic history which had been excited by his work with North remained strong.

Sutch joined Roger Ransom as a cofounder of the University of California's Southern Economic History Project in 1968. Ransom and Sutch are co-authors of several articles on the post-Civil War period in southern history and a book, **One Kind of Freedom: The Economic Consequences of Emancipation**, which was published in 1977. Sutch has been a leading figure in one of the major battlefields of the New Economic History—the continuing debates centering on the economics of slavery in the United States. Among his many contributions on this subject are those in **Reckoning with Slavery: A Critical Study in the Quantitive History of American Negro Slavery** with Paul David and others (1976).

Sutch is Professor of Economics at the University of California at Berkeley. He was awarded Berkeley's Distinguished Teaching Award in 1980.

72. North, *Structure and Change in Economic History* (New York: W. W. Norton, 1981).

Part II

Growth and Welfare

Economic history attempts to explain two major issues: (1) the causes of economic growth, decline or stagnation in a society over time and (2) the well-being of different groups in the society over time; that is, it attempts to explain the distribution of income and changes in the distribution of income. Of necessity, such explanations entail analysis of the structure of economic organization and the interrelationship between structure and performance.

Douglass C. North

The American Behavioral Scientist
December 1977

Chapter 3

The Cost of Empire

Lance E. Davis and Robert A. Huttenback

Whether there are lessons to be learned from the study of history is not clear. What is clear is that society seldom learns from history. In 1852 Disraeli wrote, "These wretched colonies . . . are a millstone around our necks."[1] Fifty years later Lord Haldane noted that the power of manipulating people was no doubt of high value but that it was not obvious to him "that we do not in this country pay too high a price for it."[2] Fifty years after Haldane two economists, Mancur Olson and Richard Zeckhauser, provided a general proof as to why at least "western" empires become millstones and cost more than they are worth.[3] Still such "western" empires grow, and if they do not flourish neither do they wither. This paper explores some aspects of three sets of "imperial" relations.

THOSE COSTLY COLONIALS

There are those who argue that Britain never had an imperial policy, while others contend that the empire was conceived in a fit of ab-

1. James Howard Harris, 3rd Earl of Malmesbury, Malmesbury, *Memoirs of an Ex-Minister,* quoted in Joseph Schumpeter, *Imperialist Social Classes: Two Essays by Joseph Schumpeter* (New York: Meridian Bros., 1955), p. 10.

2. Quoted in A. P. Thornton, *Imperialism in the Twentieth Century* (Minneapolis: University of Minnesota Press, 1977), p. 102.

3. Mancur Olson, Jr. and Richard Zeckhauser, "An Economic Theory of Alliances," in Francis A. Beer, ed., *Alliances: Latent War Communities in the Contemporary World* (New York: Holt, Rinehart and Winston 1970; reprinted from *Review of Economics and Statistics* 48 [1966]).

ISBN 0-12-580080-0

sentmindedness. It appears that in the eighteenth century Britain did have at least an enunciated policy of imperial defense, although it may have been honored most often in the breach. It seems that the British were

> willing to spend large sums of money on the defense of the outlying frontiers of the empire and... likewise willing when necessary to establish garrisons in the most exposed colonies.... On the other hand, it was a fundamental principle of British colonial administration that during peace in Europe the defense of each colony against the local enemy would devolve primarily on the colony itself, and that assistance would be given by the mother country only if the situation were so serious as to endanger the empire as a whole.[4]

In the seventeenth and early eighteenth centuries this policy led to the brunt of the Indian wars falling on the American colonists; however, the line between local and empire defense was never clear, and British administrators appear frequently to have drawn it in favor of the colonists. Even when both parties agreed that the incident was purely of local character, Great Britain often sent arms and ammunition, much to the disgust of the Ordinance Board, "which objected to these extraordinary outlays for which parliament had made no provision."[5]

Because of this policy, as well as other defense commitments, the level of per capita defense expenditures in Britain was very high, and—as an empirical, if not theoretical, corollary—so were the levels of taxes. As Table 3.1 indicates, the British were spending only slightly less than 10s. per capita on defense in "peacetime" and something more than twice that amount in time of "war." If the debt deadweight is added to those figures (much of the underlying debt having been incurred in previous wars), the total level varies between £1.9 and roughly twice that amount. To support those levels of expenditure, British taxes yielded about £1 per capita over the entire period of 1740 to 1775. That figure, amounting to about 6% of net national product, was probably the highest in the world. British taxpayers were quite aware of both the tax burden and the distribution of the defense burden between the American colonists and themselves. The year 1767 had seen strong popular opposition to a proposed increase in taxes; and William Samuel Johnson, a Connecticut lawyer, reported from London:

> Great pains have been taken to irritate the people of England against America, especially the freeholders, and to persuade them that they are to pay infinite taxes,

4. George Louis Beer, *British Colonial Policy: 1754–1765* (New York: Peter Smith 1922), pp. 123, 10.
5. Ibid., p. 10.

TABLE 3.1
Great Britain: Expenditures and Taxes (1770 £s)

	(1) Total taxes	(2) Military expenditures	(3) Debt expenditures
1740–1748	.928	.868	.332
1749–1755	.991	.487	.410
1756–1763	1.081	1.414	.438
1764–1775	1.117	.436	.505

Sources: B. R. Mitchell, *Abstract of British Historical Statistics* (Cambridge: Cambridge University Press, 1962) Public Finance I, pp. 386–388, Public Finance II, pp. 389–391; Population and Vital Statistics I, p. 5 (figures used were Richman (1) plus a correction for Scotland); Prices I (consumer goods) p. 468–469.

> and we [the colonists] none; they are to be burdened that we may be eased; and in a word, that the interests of Britain are to be sacrificed to those in America.[6]

Nor were the British perceptions far from reality, as shown by the data on American tax levels in the years before the Revolution, presented in Table 3.2. Since Americans paid no direct taxes and few customs duties to Great Britain, the figures refer to internal taxes within each colony. They largely exclude abnormal military expenditures, which typically were financed by issues of colonial paper money. Although both individual figures and the coverage may be suspect, all appear to tell the same story. In the words of the historian Robert Palmer, "The British Americans enjoyed a lighter tax burden than any [other] people in the western world except Poland—and one knows what happened to Poland."[7] Despite colonial protestations, even Americans were aware of the relative magnitudes of American and British defense burdens. In 1778, the Continental Congress wrote to Benjamin Franklin, then in Paris, that "since the Americans had never been much taxed before the revolution, it would be madness to tax them now"; thus, "the war with Britain made it urgent for them [the Congress] to obtain a loan."[8] Not that the Americans missed a try at obscuring the fact. In 1774, Silas Deane, a member of the Continental Congress, attempted to document "the immense sums that must have been expended" fighting the Seven Years' War; at the end of his labors, however, he was able only to

6. Quoted in Lawrence Henry Gipson, *The Coming of the Revolution: 1763–1775* (New York: Harper, 1954), p. 172.
7. Robert R. Palmer, *The Age of the Democratic Revolution: A Political History of Europe and America, 1760–1800* (Princeton: Princeton University Press, 1959), p. 156.
8. Ibid., p. 57.

TABLE 3.2
Per Capita Taxes (Current £s)

	1740–1748	1749–1754	1765	c. 1775	1785	1785 (1770 £s)
Massachusetts	.023	.059	.050	.071	.900	
New Hampshire				.047		
Rhode Island				.063		
Connecticut			.029	.020		
New York			.033	.024		
Pennsylvania			.050	.016		
New Jersey				.009		
Maryland			.050			
Virginia			.021	.016		
South Carolina				.053		
Great Britain	.868	.915	1.300		1.700	1.42
Ireland					.500	
France					1.050	.42
High—Paris					2.800	2.33
Rouen					1.550	1.29
Lyon					1.250	1.04
Low—Strasbourg					.600	.50
Besincon					.600	.50
Perpegnon					.600	.50
Rennes					.500	.42
Austria						
Austria					.600	.50
Bohemia-Moravia					1.050	.88
Hungary					.700	.58
Transylvania					.350	.29
Lombardy					.250	.80
Austrian Netherlands					.175	.15
Spain					.500	.42
Sweden					.488	.41
Russia					.300	.25
Prussia					.300	.25
Poland					.054	.05

Sources: Massachusetts 1740–1748 and 1749–1754 from J. Gwyn, "War and Economic Change, Louisburg and the New England Economy in the 1740s," in *Melanges d'histoire de Canada Francais* (Ottawa: University of Ottawa Press, 1978), p. 24; Britain from B. R. Mitchell, *Abstract of British Historical Statistics,* pp. 386–389; columns for 1765 and 1785 from Robert R. Palmer, *The Age of the Democratic Revolution: A Political History of Europe and America, 1760–1800* (Princeton, New Jersey: Princeton University Press, 1959); c1775 from Adam Smith, *Wealth of Nations* (New York: E. P. Dutton, 1937; reprinted from the 1910 edition, pp. 540–541).

lament, that "he could find no authentick record of it. . . . Our enemies boldly assert that we have expended nothing but what we have been largely paid for, and we have no record to contradict them."[9]

When confronted, however, the Americans were always ready to argue either that defense expenditures were a matter of imperial concern or that the colonial relationship was so important to the British that Britain should pay for colonial defense. In 1703, for example, the Pennsylvania assembly refused to take action against privateers then interdicting the colony's trade with the West Indies and attacking settlements on Delaware Bay, on the grounds that "it was incumbent upon the British government to afford protection by sea."[10] The same body reaffirmed the position 37 years later with the words "shipping was protected by the British navy without expense to the colonies."[11] Legislative behavior was mirrored in the rhetoric of American politicians. In 1760, when the question of financing the defense of Pennsylvania was pressing, Benjamin Franklin wrote

> Our North American colonies are to be considered the frontier of the British empire on that side. The frontier of any dominion being attached, it becomes not only the cause of the people affected but properly the cause of the whole body.[12]

And 5 years later, when concern had shifted to possible British defense imposts on the colonies, he added

> I know the last war is commonly spoke of here as entered into for the defense, or for the sake of, the people of America. I think it is quite misunderstood. . . . As to the Ohio, the contest there began about your trading rights with the Indians, which the French infringed. . . . They took a fort, which a company of your merchants and their factors and correspondents had erected there to secure that trade. Braddock was sent with an army to retake the fort . . . and to protect your trade. It was not until after your defeat that the colonies were attacked.[13]

It might be difficult to guess that the location of that fort is now a Pittsburgh suburb and that the area under attack was western Pennsylvania.

If the British failed to subsidize American defense on the basis of duty

9. Quoted in Robert Arthur Becker, "The Politics of Taxation in America, 1763–1783" (unpublished doctoral dissertation, University of Wisconsin, 1971).

10. Quoted in Winifred Trexler Root, *The Relations of Pennsylvania with the British Government, 1690–1765* (Philadelphia: Benjamin Franklin, 1912), pp. 270–271.

11. Ibid., pp. 280–283.

12. Ibid., p. 256.

13. Gipson, *Coming of the Revolution*, p. 111.

or guilt, then, it was argued, the colonies should yet be defended for the sake of the British themselves. For example, Ebenezer Devotion wrote in 1766 "why, in the name of wonder, could not Great Britain protect us, . . . for the sake of their trade, which you say the British merchants are very fond of and which raised Great Britain to a pitch of glory beyond every other nation."[14] In a similar vein (a vein that was to be mined by Canadians and Australians in the nineteenth century and by Europeans and Japanese in the twentieth), Richard Bland wrote

> I would prove that the revenues arising from the trade of the colonies and the advantages of their exports to Great Britain in the balance of her trade with the foreign nations, could exceed infinitely all the expenses she has been at, all the expenses she can be at, in their protection.[15]

The tax rates reported in Table 3.1 are not strictly related to defense expenditures, but the American record seems to justify British concern over the relative weights of the defense burden. For example, it is estimated that during the Seven Years' War the colonies contributed a total of £2.5 million but, of this sum, at least £1 million was repaid to them from the British exchequer. Ignoring any adjustment for forgone interest, the colonists were left paying, on average, £.13 per capita per year,[16] about one-tenth the rate prevailing in Great Britain (£1.39) at that time and less than one-fifth the level of support contributed by the British over the entire period 1740–1775.

Although even as small a sum as £.13 may be a weighty burden if income is sufficiently low, it does not appear to have rested heavily on the colonies. For example, New Hampshire, by investing its parliamentary reimbursements, was able to pay all its wartime issues of bills of credit as they came due.[17] From the British viewpoint, Connecticut was probably the most responsive of the colonies; yet 6 years after the end of the war, back taxes on the assessor's book (half again as large as the unpaid war debt) remained uncollected because, it was felt, "the money was simply not needed."[18] Again, in the case of Pennsylvania,

14. "The Examiner Examined: A Letter from a Gentleman in Connecticut to his Friend in London, In Answer to a Letter from a Gentleman in London to his Friend in America" (New London, Connecticut, 1766), Evans collection #10280.

15. *An Inquiry into the Rights of the British Colonies* (Williamsburg, Virginia, 1766), Evans collection #10244.

16. If we assume a 10% rate of interest and a 3-year lag in British payment, the figure rises only to £.16. Using a more reasonable 5% interest and a 2-year lag, the adjustment is only £.01 (a total of £.14).

17. Gipson, *Coming of the Revolution*, p. 121.

18. Ibid., pp. 128–129.

reimbursements were so adequate that no taxes were needed during the war years 1760–1763 and, except for some revenue raised by a liquor tax, that situation continued until the Revolution.[19]

By 1763 the British were aware of the weight of the American defense commitment and also of incipient trouble over western lands acquired from the French. The magnitude of both problems was brought sharply into focus by Pontiac's rebellion. Despite their losses in both lives and property, the colonial governments did nothing to put down the uprising. That task was left to imperial troops.[20] Thus on May 5, 1763, Grenville, through his secretary of state, instructed the Board of Trade to report "in what mode least burdensome and most palatable to the colonists can they contribute towards the support and additional expense that must attend their civil and military establishments in consequence of the newly acquired territories and forts therein."[21]

This policy was, of course, to lead by way of the Stamp, Sugar, Townshend, and Navigation Acts to the American Revolution. Table 3.3 provides an estimate of the possible impact, on both Britain and the colonies, of four alternative policies (two hypothetical and two real) that the British might have adopted, had these policies been in effect since 1740. Case 1 assumes that the British required the Americans to pay the actual amounts spent in their defense;[22] Case 2, that tax burdens were equalized between Britain and the colonies; Cases 3 and 4, respectively, that the British raised £145,000 or £105,000 per year from the colonies. These were the amounts that the British expected to receive from the post-1763 tax legislation. Although total equalization would indeed have imposed a heavy burden on the colonial taxpayer, there is little evidence to suggest that equalization was either the short- or the long-term goal of British imperial policy.[23] In fact, Britain does not seem to have pressed even for payment of actual charges (Case 1) although such a policy would have involved additional tax levels of less than 6% of net national

19. Ibid., p. 136.

20. Palmer, *Age of Democratic Revolution*, p. 158.

21. Quoted in George Louis Beer, *The Commercial Policy of England towards the American Colonies*, Columbia University Studies in Economics, History and Public Law, vol. 3, no. 2, 1893.

22. The data on actual British expenditures in the colonies are from Julien Gwyn, "British Government Spending and the American Balance of Payments" (manuscript, Ottawa, Canada, 1979). Expenditures have been allocated between Canada and the "American Colonies" on the basis of relative populations.

23. The equalization counterfactual is the basis of Professor Joe Reid's belief that the Revolutionary War was justified from the point of view of the Americans. See Reid, "Economic Burden: Spark to the American Revolution," *Journal of Economic History* 38 (1978), pp. 81–100.

TABLE 3.3
Great Britain: Hypothetical Per Capita Burden Transfers of Military Expenditure (Constant 1770 £s)

	G.B. per capita	U.S. expenses	G.B. savings per capita	New G.B.	U.S. burden per capita
		Case 1 (if actual U.S. expenses transferred)			
1740–1748	.868	131	.018	.850	.129
1749–1755	.487	210	.027	.460	.167
1756–1763	1.414	912	.114	1.300	.572
1764–1775	.436	365	.041	.395	.170
		Case 2 (if per capita equalized)			
1740–1748	.868	772	.105	.763	.763
1749–1755	.487	526	.068	.419	.419
1756–1763	1.414	1879	.235	1.179	1.179
1764–1775	.436	713	.104	.332	.332
		Case 3 (if £ 145,000/yr transferred)			
1740–1748	.868	145	.020	.848	.143
1749–1755	.487	145	.019	.468	.116
1756–1763	1.414	145	.018	1.396	.090
1764–1775	.436	145	.016	.368	.068
		Case 4 (if £ 105,000/yr transferred)			
1740–1748	.868	105	.014	.854	.104
1749–1755	.487	105	.014	.473	.084
1756–1763	1.414	105	.013	1.401	.066
1764–1775	.436	105	.012	.387	.049

product even at the height of the Seven Years' War. More reasonable, however, are Cases 3 and 4: Although Britain never managed to raise even the lesser sum, these cases do reflect official policy.

Combining the evidence in Tables 3.2 and 3.3, we find that if the British had managed to raise the full £145 thousand between 1764 and 1775, the American colonies (with a total tax burden of £.11) would have edged past Poland in terms of total tax burden. Nevertheless, they would still have paid per capita rates only two-thirds those of the next region enumerated (the Austrian Netherlands), less than one-tenth those of Great Britain, one-eighth those prevailing in France, and about one-quarter those imposed on the Irish.

The rest of the story is well known. Colonial reaction to the passage of the Stamp Act was so intense and bitter that Parliament was forced to repeal it—although the members continued their attempts to raise tax revenues in America. The succeeding revenue legislation (the Sugar, Townshend, and Navigation Acts) imposed on the colonists a burden of about £.016 per capita per year, or about one-tenth of 1% of gross national product, and this was viewed as so onerous that the colonists would rather "fight than switch." In the words of one nineteenth-century historian: "The Americans would not pay any tax levied on them by a parliament in which they were not represented and they would not pay any which were levied on them by 'a creature of their own making'; that is, they would not pay any at all."[24]

The war was fought and imperial bonds dissolved. Two facts appear worth noting. First, when Parliament repealed the Stamp Act, it did so at least in part in response to pressure brought by British mercantile and manufacturing intereses. These businessmen, already under heavy pressure from the effects of the Nonintercourse Acts, felt that "if civil war did ensue . . . they would be placed in an even more desperate plight."[25] Perhaps Ebenezer Devotion and Richard Bland understood something of the nature of international business; certainly the argument has been often repeated over the past two centuries.

Second, Table 3.4 raises some question about who actually won the revolutionary war. Rhetoric aside, most American politicians felt, even before 1774, that the colonists should pay more taxes—and that group included even Tom Paine.[26] It should not, therefore, be a surprise to any except, perhaps, the colonists themselves, that federal per capita tax rates over the years 1792–1811 soared to more than 10 times those levied by the British between 1765 and 1775, and that federal defense expenditures, although less per capita than the amounts that had been spent by the British in the colonies between 1765 and 1775, were substantially greater than the amount that the British had been attempting to charge the Americans for those services.

WELFARE PAYMENTS AND THE SECOND EMPIRE

Almost any historian is pleased when he can show that some person, group, or nation has benefited "from the lessons of history." By the late nineteenth century it was clear that the British government had learned something (although one may question whether the lesson was the correct one) from the eighteenth century American experience. By 1880,

24. Henry Phillips Jr., written in 1866 and quoted in William Graham Sumner, *The Financier and the Finances of the American Revolution*, 2 vols. (New York: A. M. Kelley, 1968; reprinted from an 1891 edition), 1: 24–25.

25. Gipson, *Coming of the Revolution*, pp. 114–115.

26. Palmer, *Age of Democratic Revolution*, p. 157.

TABLE 3.4
Per Capita Taxes and Expenditure
(Constant 1770 £s)

	U.S. federal military expenditure	U.S. federal tax receipts	U.S. taxes paid to Great Britain (Sugar, Stamp, Townshend, and Navigation Acts)
1765–1774			.016
1792–1801	.075		
1803–1811	.062	.240	
1812–1816	.272	.177	

Source: U.S. Bureau of the Census, *Historical Statistics of the United States, Colonial Times to 1970, Bicentennial Edition, Part 2* (Washington, D.C.: GPO, 1975).

British policy had come to reflect the view that if you want an empire you must be willing to pay for it and under no circumstances should you attempt to assess the subsidiary parts of that empire for their full share of the defense burden. In the nineteenth century, not only did Britain excuse the empire from sharing in the costs of her defense, but, in fact, the transfers were large and in the other direction. Expenditure patterns within and without the empire suggest that in the late nineteenth and early twentieth centuries the United Kingdom had one of the world's highest—if not the highest—level of military expenditure and, concomitantly, of taxes. At the same time, the non-British components of the empire were underwriting so little military support that it became possible for them either to levy few taxes or else to support much higher levels of investment in "productive" sectors at levels of aggregate taxation no higher than those prevailing elsewhere in the world. As Table 3.5 suggests, over the period from 1860 to 1912, Britain was spending annually £1.32 (in constant pounds per capita) as against £.36 for foreign developed countries and £.20 for undeveloped countries. Meantime, India was paying out only £.08 and the self-governing colonies only slight more (£.11). Even more surprisingly, the "true" colonies, Types 2 and 3, spent only £.03 and .05 respectively. With the exception of India, the same story emerges for the fraction of government expenditures directed toward defense (a partial measure of "effort").[27]

27. Type 1 comprises colonies with responsible government (elected parliamentary and executive bodies); Type 2, those with partly responsible government (appointed executive, some elected legislature or consultative body); Type 3, those without responsible government (India excluded).

TABLE 3.5

Hypothetical United Kingdom Defense Expenditures Assuming That Colonies Spent Amounts Equal to Those Spent by Similar Nonempire Political Units

Period	(1) Type 1 as a foreign undeveloped	(2) Type 2 as a foreign undeveloped	(3) Type 3 as a foreign undeveloped	(4) India as a foreign undeveloped	(5) (1) + (2) + (3)	(6) (1) + (2) + (3) + (4)	(7) Foreign developed	(8) Actual U.K.
				Panel A Reductions in U.K. annual average per capita expenditures (constant £s)				
1860–1869	− .05	− .01	− .02	− .48	− .08	− .56		
1870–1879	− .04	− .01	− .01	− .63	− .06	− .73		
1880–1889	− .08	− .01	− .02	− .77	− .11	− .88		
1890–1899	− .09	− .01	− .05	−1.68	− .15	−1.83		
1900–1912	− .09	− .01	− .12	−1.01	− .22	−1.23		
				Panel B New levels of U.K. annual average per capital expenditures (constant £s)				
1860–1869	.89	.93	.92	.46	.86	.39	.27	.94
1870–1879	.76	.79	.79	.17	.74	.11	.24	.80
1880–1889	.90	.97	.96	.22	.87	.10	.41	.98
1890–1899	1.19	1.27	1.23	− .40	1.13	− .55	.40	1.28
1900–1912	2.22	2.30	2.19	1.30	2.09	.79	.43	2.31

Nor are these numbers the statistical artifacts produced by the onset of World War I or even of the South African adventure. The data show a similar story whether the focus is placed on the years 1860–1900 or 1906–1912. It is clear that Britain provided the defense umbrella while the empire stayed out of the rain. Even India, long singled out as the most "exploited" of the colonies, seems to have fared relatively well as compared, not with the rest of the empire, but with the rest of the world. India did supply troops for imperial adventures in Ethiopia, the Sudan, and West Africa (the Ashanti war), but the average per capita level of expenditure, while high by colonial experience, was still low relative to the defense spending of politically independent undeveloped countries.

An analysis of the U.K. Home-1 and -2 estimates confirms this point in a different way. These figures allocate British military and naval expenditures between home and imperial defense.[28] The "home" estimates indicate levels of expenditure slightly higher than the average of all developed countries, but about equal to those of France and Germany. England, therefore, appears to be maintaining two defense establishments: one for the British Isles and a second for the empire.

Table 3.6 tells the same story from the point of view of the British taxpayer. Shifting the defense burden only to the non-Indian empire would have eased the tax load of the average Briton to some extent; but a policy that produced Indian expenditures equivalent to those of the underdeveloped countries included in the survey would have made that taxpayer notably "better off" than his peers in the rest of the developed world. Nor did "learning by doing" appear to make the British more efficient at the operation of empire. The data indicate that the "subsidy" to the non-Indian empire was increasing over time. In the last decade of the period, per capita British support to the colonies with responsible self-government was £.09 and to those with no self-government at all, £.12.

The important question remains: Why did the British allow themselves to be exploited in this fashion? Quantitative evidence provides few clues, but qualitative evidence suggests that even the Victorians fretted over the question. The Treasury in particular expressed continual concern. As early as 1860 Sir Charles Adderley asked in Parliament, "Why should Great Britain contribute £4,000,000 to the cost of security

28. Allocations are made on the basis of the location of manpower. The two estimates differ because of the allocation of the Mediterranean fleet. In 1 it is included in the empire, in 2, in home defense. The naval allocation for the period 1893–1921 is made on the basis of the distribution in 1893. More recently, the data have been rerun with better naval distribution for the post-1893 period, and no substantive changes resulted.

TABLE 3.6

Imperial Defense Expenditures, Per Capita and as a Percentage of the Government Budget, for United Kingdom, Colonies, and Selected Foreign Countries, 1860–1912

Period	U.K. total	U.K.[a] Home 1	U.K.[b] Home 2	France and Germany	Foreign developed	Colonies Type 1[c]	U.K.[a] Imperial 1	U.K.[b] Imperial 2	Foreign undeveloped	India	Colonies Type 2[d]	Colonies Type 3[e]	Colonies Type 2 (including police)	Colonies Type 3
							Panel A Average per capita expenditure on defense (constant £s)							
1860–1869	.94	.38	.45	.39	.27	.05	.56	.49	.17	.09	.01	.04	.12	.10
1870–1879	.80	.39	.44	.52	.24	.07	.41	.36	.18	.08	.04	.04	.16	.11
1880–1889	.98	.46	.53	.58	.41	.11	.52	.45	.18	.08	.06	.04	.18	.12
1890–1899	1.28	.56	.70	.80	.40	.13	.72	.58	.27	.07	.03	.06	.24	.13
1900–1912	2.31	.97	1.20	.77	.43	.19	1.33	1.11	.20	.07	.01	.05	.20	.09
1900–1905	2.96	1.20	1.42	.79	.49	.17	1.74	1.52	.18	.07	.01	.07	.21	.11
1906–1912	1.75	.78	1.00	.76	.39	.20	.97	.76	.22	.07	.01	.04	.20	.08
1860–1912	1.32	.58	.69	.62	.36	.11	.74	.63	.20	.08	.03	.05	.18	.11
							Panel B Average proportion of government budget spent on defense (as percentages)							
1860–1869	38.2	15.3	18.5	16.8	31.4	2.7	22.8	20.3	28.0	33.9	1.4	6.9	12.9	16.0
1870–1879	34.9	17.0	19.1	29.5	25.3	3.3	18.0	15.9	20.9	21.4	4.3	6.3	16.8	16.6
1880–1889	34.9	16.3	18.9	23.1	24.2	1.8	18.6	16.1	15.3	24.2	4.0	4.3	12.8	14.4
1890–1899	38.2	16.7	20.9	27.4	22.2	2.2	21.5	17.4	16.8	27.7	1.2	7.4	12.4	15.6
1900–1912	47.2	20.2	24.9	24.0	21.9	3.1	27.0	22.3	14.4	22.3	.6	10.0	12.4	17.2
1900–1905	55.2	22.7	27.0	24.1	23.7	2.5	32.6	28.2	14.0	21.6	.6	11.5	12.4	18.1
1906–1912	40.3	18.0	23.0	24.0	20.2	3.6	22.2	17.3	14.9	22.8	.7	8.7	12.4	16.4
1860–1912	39.1	17.3	20.7	24.2	24.9	2.7	21.9	18.6	18.8	26.1	2.2	7.1	13.3	16.1

[a] Mediterranean fleet included in imperial expenditures.
[b] Mediterranean fleet included in home expenditures.
[c] Colonies with responsible government (elected parliamentary and executive bodies).
[d] Colonies with partial responsible government (appointed executive, some elected legislative or consultative body).
[e] Colonies without responsible government (India excluded).

while the colonies paid less than £40,000? [Why] should the colonies be exempted from paying for their own defense?" He argued that "it was absolutely unparalleled in the history of the world that any portion of an empire—colonial, provincial or otherwise—should be exempted in purse and person from the costs of its own defenses as was a British colony."[29]

In the case of the self-governing colonies, one part of the answer was relatively simple—they refused to pay, and the British could do very little about it. With the advent of responsible government, the British subsidies were withdrawn, but constitutional autonomy then allowed those colonies to refuse aid on matters of general imperial concern. The British must have remembered 1775, when an attempt to collect some fraction of defense costs led to a costly war and the loss of a large and uniquely British part of the empire. This position was well articulated in a letter from Anderson to Gladstone about the New Zealand situation in 1865:

> It is idle to say (I speak of those colonies only which have responsible government) that there may be cases where the money is absolutely required and cannot be had from any other source. Were we to legislate against the colonies, as in former times, they would soon show us that the money could be otherwise than out of our pockets to defend them against us; and so it can defend them against their own people in rebellion against the law.[30]

In the case of Canada, as another example, the British tried for years without success to collect some payment for the funds spent to put down Louis Real's rebellion on the Red River—a matter of almost purely Canadian concern. Nearly every attempt to increase the Canadian contribution to imperial defense was met with arguments like "the best defense for Canada is no defense at all"—and that statement was made in 1863, when armies of the United States were posing a serious threat to Canadian security.[31] Nor did those attitudes change. When in the early twentieth century the British called on the empire to contribute to the general war then on the horizon, the Canadians responded that "as a maritime nation [Canada] produced a steady stream of seaman and . . . that contribution to the merchant marine was sufficient."[32]

Again New Zealand happily accepted British aid in the Maori war

29. *Hansard*, May 31, 1860.

30. Gladstone Papers, British Museum Additional Ms. 44535, #124: Anderson to Gladstone, September 14, 1865.

31. Newcastle Papers British Museum, Newcastle to Sir Charles Monk, June 20, 1863.

32. Minutes of the Imperial Conference, 1911, Parliamentary Papers cd 574s p. 265.

until the British withdrew support, at which point the New Zealanders refused to carry the war further. Nor did the British withdraw in good humor. Their position was summarized in the Anderson letter to Gladstone:

> The state of things exhibited by the army accounts for New Zealand exhibits a state of their [Prime Minister's] regard to the command of Colonial ministers or other local authorities over the money of the English which, I will venture to say, for injustice and absurdity has no parallel on earth.[33]

Other colonies with self-government repeated the story. In the case of Natal, Garnet Wolsely wrote to Hicks Beach in 1880:

> With all deference to those at home who wish to squeeze £1,000,000 out of the colony, I feel bound even at the risk of giving offense, to say that to ask a colony of 22,500 white souls to subserve such an amount would be neither just nor wise, and I would need scarcely add would only court defeat in the wretched little council.[34]

The reports from Cape Colony suggest even more intransigence. There the local colonial government in 1880 refused to make more than a token contribution to the Ninth Kaffir War and in 1881 announced its intention of halting its £10,000 annual contribution to the cost of the imperial garrison in the colony. On the former issue the imperial government attempted to negotiate, but on the latter it could only lament, while reserving the right to reopen the subject. "My lords cannot, however, leave unnoticed the implication that a colony should not be called upon to contribute towards the cost of a force maintained as an imperial garrison within its territory, with this opinion Milords cannot agree."[35] But agree or not, they were unable to do anything about it.

A 1901 letter from Walter Hely-Hutchinson, the Governor of Cape Colony, to Milner is particularly suggestive of the dilemma faced by the British government:

> With regard to the payment of troops, a very anomalous state of affairs exists. At the commencement of the War in October 1899 a Bond Ministry was in Office. I need not dwell to you upon the many embarrassments caused by this circumstance. One of the points to which the ministry clung most tenaciously was the exclusion of the colonial forces from any part of the struggle. They were willing, not gladly, to allow the Imperial forces to make use of the colony as a base of operations, but they wished

33. Gladstone Papers, 44535, #124: Anderson to Gladstone, September 14, 1865.

34. St. Aldwyn (Hicks Beach) Papers, NRA 3526, Gloucester RO D2455, PPC/6, #19: Garnet Wolsely to Hicks Beach, February 2, 1880.

35. C.O. Domestic Minute Paper, Cape 1247: Treasury to Colonial Office (CO48); January 22, 1881.

> these operations to be conducted exclusively by Imperial troops, without any assistance from the colonials. The invasion of the colony, which followed almost immediately upon declaration of war, enabled me to push them out of this position. Face to face with an invasion of the colony, it was no longer possible to refuse to call out the colonial force for its defense, but in order to get this done instantly—and there was no time to be lost—I had to agree to a single compromise, which was that the Imperial government should pay the difference between the cost of the war to the colonial establishment of the colonial corps and of the peace establishment. That is to say we pay virtually the whole cost of the colonial volunteers as a fighting force. . . . In principle, I have always thought this arrangement monstrous; as a matter of fact, it was the only one possible. . . .[36]

The self-governing colonies not only refused to pay for their own defense but also pushed the imperial government to undertake military operations where the only gains would accrue to the colonists. In the 1880s, for example, the Australians were interested in increasing their sphere of influence, thus in 1883 Derby wrote to Gladstone:

> I have likened one of their [the Australians'] claims to the Monroe Doctrine: but there is one essential difference. The Americans are prepared to fight for their pretensions. The colonists expect us to do their fighting for them. . . . After this preface you will not suspect me of undue tenderness for colonial feelings or fancies and you will believe that it is not very willingly that I come to the conclusions that as regards New Guinea we cannot hold out against the demand for a protectorate. . . .[37]

The overall impact of the self-governing colonies on imperial defense is well summarized in a 1902 breakdown of per capita contributions to the empire's naval commitment: Canada, zero; New South Wales, eight and a half pence; Victoria, one shilling; Queensland, one shilling; Cape Colony, three and a quarter pence; Natal, five and three quarters of a penny, and the United Kingdom, fifteen shillings.[38] The money saved, of course, was often funneled into investment in social overhead capital, and it is hardly surprising that Australian per capita expenditures on roads, fences, lighthouses, education, and research were the highest in the world. As Derby wrote to Gladstone, "It is the same old story; colonies are always willing to help us and stand by us provided we will find all the money and take all the risks."[39]

Over the dependent empire the British should have had more control, and the figures suggest they were actually somewhat more successful.

36. Milner Papers, NRA 14300, Bodleian Library: Hutchinson to Milner, February 28, 1901.

37. Gladstone Papers, 44142: Derby to Gladstone, December 7, 1883.

38. *Hansard*, December 16, 1902.

39. Gladstone Papers, 44141, #124: Derby to Gladstone, July 7, 1883.

Regardless of their state of constitutional development, all colonies were in an advantageous position vis-à-vis the British government when it came to paying for the cost of actual hostilities. Wars were not infrequent along the imperial borders, and the initial expenses were almost always paid by the governor from the treasury chest, a fund of £1 million spread throughout the empire to cover emergencies. Once the imperial monies had been expended and the hostilities concluded, the British Treasury usually recouped few of its monetary advances. Thus, for example, the British taxpayer bore the entire £900,000 cost of the Ashanti war of 1873–1874 and almost all the cost of the Zulu war.

The American experience hung like a cloud even over areas with only minimal white settlement. In 1880 Wolsely wrote to Hicks Beach, the governor of Natal:

> In 1875 I increased the native hut tax from 7/ to 14/ percent remitting some marriage fees at the same time. It was a dangerous experiment but the natives accepted the arrangement on the understanding that the settlement that effected was to continue for many years. . . . If such an attempt [to raise taxes to pay for a war] did not lead to rebellion, it would at least cause the natives to swarm out of a province where they were very oppressed by taxation and whose rulers had broken faith with them.[40]

Even a colony as insignificant as Bermuda succeeded in refusing a Treasury request for a military contribution. And when, as in the case of Mauritius, the government achieved a temporary success, some compromise settlement usually reduced the repayment.

India, however, was the Treasury's ideal, conducting its affairs as a British dependency should. Having self-government, it was subject to whatever plans its governors and the authorities in Whitehall might devise. The expenses of the Indian army and of the British regiments stationed in India were paid from Indian revenues. India provided and almost exclusively funded a military reserve for the whole British empire. Yet examination of the budget suggests that Indian payments were almost certainly less than they would have been had the country not been under British rule—the umbrella worked even there. The levies would have been higher had the Treasury (or even the India Office) had its way, but the Treasury met continual opposition from British governors (who were almost always sympathetic either to the plight of the poor Indians and their need for famine prevention or to the British residents in India who, like other colonists in the empire, had no desire to pay taxes). Lord Ripon, when viceroy, disputed the idea that England should use India as a "reserve to drain" in case of need: "It is dangerous

40. St. Aldwyn Papers, Wolsey to Hicks Beach, February 2, 1880.

to India because our present garrison is less numerous than is required for the maintenance of public tranquility, it is mischievous to England because it helps to foster the jingo spirit and to encourage an aggressive policy.[41]

As Table 3.6 indicates, if the colonies (and particularly India) had assumed levels of defense expenditure about the same as those borne by countries at similar states of development, the tax load on the British taxpayer could have been reduced or government resources could have been freed for more productive purposes with no reduction in consumption income. It may be only a coincidence that during this very period British industry was falling behind that of Germany and the United States. As for the colonies, they certainly received substantial benefits; but those benefits were not evenly distributed. The colonies of white settlement did very well. Others in the empire received a subsidized market basket of government services, but given free choice they might well have chosen not to have bought those benefits even at those sale prices. In Britain, investors in colonial enterprise received some of the fruits of British largess since rates of return on empire investment would have been about 1% less had those investors been forced to shoulder the burden of local defense.

Still some lessons were learned. By the beginning of the twentieth century, Liberal social reformers like Campbell-Bannerman and Lloyd George had learned that an empire was a costly proposition—and that frequently the opportunity cost was social legislation. No one—except perhaps the residents of the colonists in the white settlements—had yet realized the costs in terms of investment in both human and capital resources and in technical change.

AMERICA THE BEAUTIFUL OR AT LEAST BOUNTIFUL

Following the end of World War II, a wide spectrum of America embraced the idea of collective security. Under threat of Russian aggression, many came to believe that the European economic miracle based, they thought, on Marshall Plan aid, had a military corollary in the form of a shared burden for defense. Despite the objections of a few Senators like Robert A. Taft ("let Europe work out its own solutions"),[42] the North Atlantic Pact was signed in 1949. At that time the official policy was one of an equal sharing of costs between the United States and its allies. That, however, was not the European view, even in those heady days. In April, 1950, the *New York Times* reported that "representatives

41. Northbrook Papers, NRA 11218, C144/3: Ripon to Northbrook January 22, 1884.
42. Robert Taft in a television speech reported in the *New York Times*, May 29, 1950, p. 6.

of the smaller countries are frank in declaring that the plan's fulfillment depends on the continuation and perhaps increase of the United States contribution to money and arms."[43]

It was not only the smaller countries that foresaw the potentially high levels of continuing American military support. For example, in public, French officials justified similar expectations with arguments like: Western Europe must fight on two fronts—

> the economic front where the aim is to prevent slumps that would help international communist strategy and the defense front where the aim is to deter aggression. . . . Western Europe could obviously not finance both fights even if it eventually managed to finance the first, which it had been unable to do thus far.[44]

Those words seemed to hold some promise for increased European sharing, at least in the very long run, but beneath them were quite different thoughts. The same article in which these words were quoted reports:

> There is in some quarters an impulse to conclude that since armament is hopelessly costly, Western Europe would do better to give it up and try to be neutral . . . but neutrality would involve forgoing the hope of further United States aid, although Europe would have to do some arming, even in neutral, hence it should explain the economic and financial limits to the armament it can do and call on the United States to bear the rest of the burden.[45]

By 1951 the official position had changed, and "Mr. Acheson accepted for the first time publicly the argument of the Finance Ministers of most North Atlantic Treaty countries that they could not meet the rearmament objectives . . . unless the United States paid the difference between the cost of the program and what they were able to finance themselves."[46]

The reversal of policy had been anticipated by those parts of American society devoted to the idea of collective defense. C. L. Sulzberger concluded that "for an indefinite period the United States will have to assume incomparably the greatest financial share of the costs for building up this western defensive army." However he also held out a ray of hope: "Nevertheless, the European allies are for the most part gradually assuming more important fiscal and economic obligations."[47] The extent of that increasing acceptance of fiscal obligation is apparent in Table 3.7. In 1950 our industrialized European allies were spending at a rate

43. The *New York Times*, April 1, 1950, p. 2.
44. A French official quoted in ibid., by Harold Callender, April 9, 1950, pp. 1–2.
45. Ibid., p. 2.
46. Ibid., September 20, 1951, p. 16.
47. Ibid., February 12, 1951, p. 1.

TABLE 3.7
Per Capita Defense Expenditure
(Constant Dollars 1970 = 100)

	U.S.A.	Belgium	Denmark	France	Federal Republic of Germany	Italy	Nether-lands	Norway
1950	154.7		27.4	62.7	30.9	28.6	52.0	37.3
1951	323.7		32.6	83.0	57.7	31.0	54.3	50.9
1952	445.9	68.0	44.3	94.4	63.1	30.8	63.0	65.9
1953	450.4	67.2	57.9	117.1	49.9	37.7	66.2	83.0
1954	383.6	68.6	56.6	98.2	50.2	30.1	74.3	84.1
1955	355.6	56.7	55.0	90.7	56.7	29.7	76.9	69.4
1956	354.2	54.8	52.6	117.3	53.1	30.0	82.0	66.7
1957	354.9	56.8	55.1	120.5	63.5	31.3	75.7	70.2
1958	349.6	55.8	53.4	110.2	46.7	31.8	65.7	64.8
1959	344.2	56.0	51.9	110.6	73.7	32.7	57.6	67.9
1960	329.6	56.7	57.6	112.9	78.9	33.8	62.7	64.2
1961	337.4	57.2	58.4	115.2	82.0	34.7	72.1	69.3
1962	360.2	60.5	70.5	117.3	102.8	37.9	75.6	75.8
1963	349.9	56.8	70.9	113.3	114.2	41.9	75.6	78.5
1964	333.7	69.5	72.5	115.3	108.2	42.5	81.1	79.1
1965	327.6	67.2	76.3	116.0	105.6	43.7	78.0	90.9
1966	386.2	67.9	74.8	118.4	102.3	46.9	75.0	89.6
1967	441.5	70.8	74.0	123.8	106.1	45.3	82.1	91.6
1968	448.9	73.7	78.4	122.8	93.7	45.9	80.4	96.1
1969	425.6	73.5	76.7	120.1	101.0	44.7	83.1	100.8
1970	380.0	78.2	74.6	118.5	101.9	46.7	84.7	100.3
1971	346.6	79.1	81.3	117.3	108.3	52.5	87.5	102.1
1972	345.2	82.8	80.4	115.1	114.8	57.5	89.4	101.3
1973	326.0	86.2	75.9	120.0	117.6	56.7	93.4	101.3
1974	319.2	89.4	82.6	122.2	123.9	57.3	93.5	103.3
1975	307.3	96.1	89.5	127.7	123.7	45.3	93.0	111.7
1976	314.4	99.5	93.1	133.5	122.6	50.6	90.5	110.4
Averages								
1950–1959	351.7	60.5	48.7	100.5	54.6	30.4	66.8	66.0
1960–1969	374.1	66.3	71.0	117.5	99.5	41.7	76.6	83.6
1970–1976	334.1	87.3	82.5	122.0	116.1	52.4	90.3	104.3
1950–1976	355.4	70.3	65.7	112.4	87.2	40.3	76.5	82.5

Sources: Defense Expenditures from 1952–1976: *SIPRI Yearbook: World Armaments and Disarmament, 1974–1977* (Cambridge, Mass.: MIT Press, 1978); 1950–1951 from Alan Newcombe and James Wert, *An Inter-nation Tensionmeter for the Prediction of War* (Canadian Peace Research Institute: Oakville,

U.K.	Sweden	Australia	Canada	New Zealand	Japan	Singapore	Czechoslovakia	German Democratic People's Republic	USSR
89.9	71.9	46.5	57.9	26.2			63.5		78.3
110.8	79.2	65.7	127.0	36.9			74.6		96.6
137.9	90.6	74.7	183.9	49.5	9.2		75.1		130.2
143.5	101.0	72.1	190.0	53.7	10.0		75.6		138.0
131.8	105.1	64.2	164.0	45.5	9.6		71.6		129.2
125.2	107.6	65.0	164.0	41.6	8.9		97.6		142.6
121.4	107.4	61.8	164.6	40.8	8.7		86.1		127.0
113.9	109.1	55.4	149.3	38.6	8.6		89.1		123.8
110.8	109.7	53.3	135.3	37.3	8.6		84.5	27.4	117.6
110.1	113.7	53.4	122.9	37.8	8.7		85.7		126.5
112.6	111.4	51.9	119.7	38.0	8.5		86.0	17.3	123.3
111.3	116.4	51.4	120.5	34.7	8.8		93.3	17.4	152.9
112.4	124.3	52.5	123.3	33.1	9.5		104.6	46.5	163.0
112.8	131.8	54.4	112.7	33.2	10.0		102.6	48.2	174.5
116.0	137.6	60.0	115.3	38.6	10.9		96.4	50.3	164.2
114.9	144.6	70.0	101.0	41.8	11.2		92.4	53.7	157.7
113.3	144.4	84.9	101.5	43.7	11.8		97.3	55.3	163.3
116.7	139.5	104.9	107.1	40.4	12.4	13.1	109.5	62.2	174.6
113.7	139.1	105.1	99.4	42.2	13.1	16.4	115.0	100.2	199.5
106.1	145.4	98.9	92.4	43.3	14.1	47.5	118.4	108.8	209.7
105.6	148.0	92.9	95.7	47.0	15.3	50.2	122.5	117.6	210.6
110.1	144.9	90.9	95.0	43.2	16.1	67.3	130.4	124.5	208.7
119.7	144.6	90.8	94.0	41.4	18.4	92.6	136.7	132.9	207.0
116.4	143.7	87.4	92.2	38.6	18.8	60.3	142.2	147.7	205.1
119.9	153.9	90.0	98.0	41.5	19.2	56.8	144.7	159.9	199.7
119.8	153.6	88.0	95.8	40.4	19.1	63.6	151.9	172.6	195.5
124.6	148.5	84.8	100.3	33.8	19.3	75.0	157.7	185.4	193.8
119.5	99.6	61.3	145.9	40.8	9.0	—	80.3	27.4	121.0
113.0	133.4	73.4	109.3	38.9	11.0	25.7	101.6	56.0	168.3
116.6	148.2	89.4	95.9	40.8	18.1	66.5	140.9	148.7	202.9
116.3	124.7	73.1	119.4	40.1	12.4	54.3	103.9	77.5	159.7

Ontario, 1972); and Populations from United Nations, *Demographic Yearbook* 1958, 1965, 1976 (New York: United Nations, 1958, 1969, 1977).

slightly less than one-third of ours; by 1955, although the average was up, the relative figure had fallen to about 20%. Over the same period their per capita expenditures fell from 60 to 50% those of Russia.

Responding to American criticism of its lagging defense effort, Belgium stated that "in any case expenditure figures should not be the sole criteria. We know that with a given expenditure, we achieve more than other countries because we manage things much more economically."[48]

American policymakers may have been happy with the prospects that NATO would exist, in the short run at least, on subsidies from the United States; but even in 1951, that feeling was not shared by all on this side of the Atlantic. Besides, Congress was becoming restive.

Ten years later, in 1960, the United States still carried the bulk of the burden and found itself facing a nagging balance of payments problem. As Table 3.7 indicates, a decade of record economic growth in Western Europe had brought no substantial change in the "temporary" allocation of defense burdens. In both relative and real terms, European per capita defense expenditures remained about where they had been in 1955, although they had dropped slightly relative to those of the Soviet Union. From the American point of view, the major problem facing the NATO foreign ministers was to achieve a "reallocation of the military and financial burdens among the western allies, which in effect means an assumption of a larger share of these burdens by our now prosperous European allies."[49] The Europeans, however, were no more interested in shouldering a larger fraction of defense expenditures than they had been a decade earlier.

It was symptomatic of the general attitude that when Secretary of the Treasury Robert Anderson journeyed to West Germany to negotiate a greater permanent German defense effort, the Bonn government, concerned with saving "enough money to have an elective gift for the West German voters next year," pleaded poverty.[50] In words reminiscent of the Pennsylvania legislature's eighteenth-century response to Britain's call for help against the French:

> the total budget burden and hence the tax burden is at least as high in relation to the national income of West Germany as in the United States. Although welfare expenditures of various kinds made up a greater proportion of the German budget than they do the American budget . . . such expenditures are necessary. Because of the

48. An official spokesman of the Belgian Defense Ministry, quoted in ibid., October 25, 1951, p. 7.

49. "New Horizons for NATO," an editorial in ibid., November 15, 1960, p. 42.

50. From the *Frankfurter Rundeschau*, quoted in ibid., November 26, 1960, p. 15.

> country's position next to the iron curtain . . . welfare payments demonstrate that a capitalistic system can prevent poverty.[51]

Another 10 years later, in 1970, there had been a second economic miracle—Japan. Europe's prosperity continued, and the United States balance of payments had worsened. On his way to a meeting of NATO's defense and finance chiefs, Secretary of the Treasury David Kennedy remarked, "What we hope for is to obtain a greater part of support from the European allies. A more fair burden-sharing will be discussed."[52] At that time (see Table 3.7) the European level of per capita defense expenditures was about 23% that of Americans and only 42% that of the Russians—a showing probably as bad as any in the two-decade history of the alliance. On that evidence, one might have doubted that income levels in Europe had achieved near parity with those in the United States.

In Washington, Mike Mansfield, the Senate Majority leader, frustrated by the position of America's European allies, proposed a unilateral withdrawal of American troops from Europe. In the words of James Reston,

> Mike is fed up with the war, with the cost of the military, with the failure of most of the Europeans to hold up their end of the commond defense burden, with the inability of the government to resolve most of these problems. . . . It was the aim of American policy over the last generation—and of Senator Mansfield—to encourage the formation of a strong and unified Europe which could act as equal partners with the United States in a shared defense of a common civilization. Instead the Europeans have preferred to enjoy their prosperity and national independence rather than pay the price of political union, and have counted on the United States for their security rather than one another. This has caused increasing irritation here, particularly when the cost of U.S. arms has contributed to monetary crises abroad and social and economic difficulties at home.[53]

The response of the policymakers and of our allies was rapid and—if one remembered the debate over the original NATO Treaty—predictable. The Administration took exception to the plan:

> The president's advisors . . . argued that United States' influence in Europe—as well as the confidence of its European allies—would be profoundly shaken if the Senate were to order a reduction of American forces. . . . The President himself said, "At this point in time it would be an error of historic proportions for any of the North Atlantic

51. The *New York Times*, November 22, 1960, p. 5.
52. Ibid., December 1, 1970, p. 9.
53. Ibid., May 14, 1971, p. 3.

> Treaty allies to reduce unilaterally the military forces maintained in Europe for the common defense. As the most powerful member of the alliance, the United States bears a responsibility for leadership."[54]

Undersecretary of State Elliot Richardson picked up a train of argument that had been familiar in the colonies before the Revolution. As a political or psychological matter, Mr. Richardson contended,

> Any sudden or major withdrawal of American forces would have a significantly destabilizing effect on the European scene. There would be a deterioration not unlike that which can send prices on the stock market plummeting. . . . Withdrawal of our forces from Europe would be likely to invoke countervailing effects, notably in reduced sale of military equipment to our allies and in general exports to those countries.[55]

Perhaps more relevantly, he also added that "the bulk of any substantial reduction in United States forces would have to be made up by West Germany. But the German people do not relish any enlargement of their country's military establishments."[56]

In Europe too, the voices of 1950 were repeated. "President Pompidou today forcefully conveyed France's desire to strengthen her ties with the United States despite various policy divergences and to see the American military and economic presence maintained in Western Europe."[57] Manlio Brosio, Secretary General of NATO, warned that "a unilateral reduction in United States forces would 'undermine' the Atlantic Alliance."[58] Conrad Ahlers, West German government spokesman, said that "in the present situation in East–West relations, any substantial unilateral reduction of United States fighting strength in Europe would have consequences of the utmost seriousness for European stability, for the prospects for relaxation and for the security of all partners in the alliance including the United States."[59] State Secretary Egon Bahr, of West Germany, told the administration that "members of the North Atlantic Treaty Organization remain eager for the United States to maintain troop levels indefinitely in Western Europe."[60]

Given the share of defense costs that the Europeans had been paying, it is not surprising that they were eager to keep the American military

54. Ibid., May 16, 1971, pp. 2, 22.
55. Reported by Peter Grose, ibid., January 21, 1970, pp. 1, 5.
56. Ibid.
57. *New York Times*, February 25, 1970.
58. John Finney in ibid., May 18, 1971, p. 6.
59. Lawrence Fellows in ibid., June 15, 1971, p. 9.
60. Ibid., August 9, 1970, p. 3.

presence in Europe; and, on May 21, 1970, "the West German government—expressed satisfaction at the United States Senate's rejection of Senator Mike Mansfield's proposal.[61] Table 3.7 suggests that the American pressure at this point may again have had some slight positive effect. A comparison of the first 6 years of the 1970s with the decade of the sixties indicates that, in real terms, European expenditures were up almost $13 a head. Relative to the United States, their contributions had risen almost to the level in 1950 and, although still reflecting efforts less than half those of the USSR, the relative level had risen from 42 to 48%.

It was, however, not Europe alone that posed a problem—the American defense shield covered the western Pacific as well. In the Mutual Security Treaty the United States had guaranteed Japan military protection, and the Japanese proved themselves master of the game of musical burdens. As Table 3.7 indicates, at no time have Japanese expenditures exceeded $20 per head, and never has Japan spent at a rate more than 6% of the American level. At the end of World War II, both parties may have benefited from such a defense pact, but as Japan prospered, it became increasingly clear that the costs were largely on one side and the benefits on the other. In the words of a Japanese government spokesman, "The Japanese do not want to become a military superpower... they *can not afford it* and they *would indeed rather rely on* the *American military umbrella.*"[62]

It is clear that the United States has been almost as successful in preserving its "empire" as were the British a century before. And equally clearly, the opportunity costs in both cases have been high. Table 3.8 provides some estimate of the magnitude of those forgone opportunities. The left-hand panel presents "equal total effort" savings to the United States as calculated under a number of hypothetical redistributions of the defense burden. In Column (1) the calculations assume that the redistribution is made among the industrialized European allies only;[63] Column (2) adds Australia, Canada, and New Zealand to that total; Column (3) adds Japan, as does Column (4). In the latter case, however, the Japanese counterfactual is not the Case 1, 2, or 3 hypotheticals but Singapore. Counterfactual calculations assume for Case 1 that our allies had spent at the same per capita rate as Sweden, Case 2 as Czechoslovakia, and Case 3 as the USSR.

The right-hand panel is an attempt to put into perspective the per

61. Ibid., May 21, 1970, p. 3.

62. Quoted in ibid., October 20, 1970, p. 17.

63. That group includes Belgium, Denmark, France, Federal Republic of Germany, Italy, Netherlands, Norway, and the United Kingdom.

TABLE 3.8
Impact upon the American Economy of Several Hypothetical Savings in Defense Expenditures: Developed Countries Only[a]

	Constant (1970) dollar per capita				Percentages					
	(1)	(2)	(3)	(4)	(5)	(6)	(7)	(8)	(9)	(10)
	U.S. savings I: Europe only[b]	U.S. Savings II: Europe + British Empire[c]	U.S. savings IIIa: Europe + British Empire + Japan (1)[d]	U.S. savings IIIb: Europe + British Empire + Japan (2)[e]	(1) per capita personal disposable income	(2) per capita personal disposable income	(3) per capita personal disposable income	(4) per capita personal disposable income	(1) per capita net personal savings	(2) per capita net personal savings
1950–1959										
Case 1	34.3	32.9	81.6	41.8	1.6	1.5	3.7	1.9	12.8	12.3
Case 2	8.3	3.7	42.0	12.6	.4	.2	1.9	.6	3.1	1.4
Case 3	62.9	64.8	125.0	73.7	2.9	3.0	5.7	3.4	23.4	24.2
1960–1969										
Case 1	53.7	60.9	122.5	68.2	2.1	2.3	4.7	2.6	18.1	20.5
Case 2	13.6	15.3	60.9	22.6	.5	.6	2.3	.9	4.6	5.2
Case 3	97.5	110.7	189.9	118.0	3.7	4.2	7.2	4.5	32.9	37.3
1970–1976										
Case 1	58.4	69.1	136.3	92.5	1.6	1.9	3.7	2.6	21.1	25.0
Case 2	49.4	58.7	122.1	82.1	1.4	1.6	3.4	2.3	17.9	21.3
Case 3	125.3	145.9	241.4	169.3	3.5	4.1	6.7	4.7	45.4	52.9
1950–1976										
Case 1	47.4	52.0	108.9	72.9	1.8	1.9	4.0	2.7	16.9	18.5
Case 2	21.1	22.2	68.5	43.1	.8	.8	2.5	1.6	7.5	7.9
Case 3	91.6	102.2	176.8	123.1	3.4	3.8	6.5	4.6	32.6	36.4

Source: Table 3.7 and U.S. Bureau of the Census, *Historical Statistics of the United States, Colonial Times to 1970, Bicentennial Edition, Part 1* (Washington, D.C.: GPO, 1975), F26, F552, F557, Y533, W109; and U.S. Bureau of the Census, *Statistical Abstract of the United States* (Washington, D.C.: GPO, 1971–1978), F26, F552, F557, Y533, W109.

[a] Case 1: comparison is with Sweden; Case 2: comparison is with Czechoslovakia; Case 3: comparison is with USSR.

capita savings associated with the redistribution. For the sake of illustration, let us take the case most favorable to the American taxpayer (including all allies and with the USSR as the appropriate counterfactual). For the entire post-1950 period, that redistribution would have increased U.S. disposable income by 7%. Although that number may not appear overwhelmingly large, the remainder of the table suggests it represents substantial forgone opportunities. If the funds had been saved, personal savings would have risen by 63%, and the stream of new capital could have risen to reflect the new savings levels. Alternatively, if these funds had been made available to support education, total public support for

Percentages

(11)	(12)	(13)	(14)	(15)	(16)	(17)	(28)	(19)	(20)
(3) per capita net personal savings	(4) per capita net personal savings	(1) per capita public expendi- ture on educa- tion	(2) per capita public expendi- ture on educa- tion	(3) per capita public expendi- ture on educa- tion	(4) per capita public expdendi- ture on educa- tion	(1) per capita expendi- ture on research and develop- ment	(2) per capita expendi- ture on research and develop- ment	(3) per capita expendi- ture on research and develop- ment	(4) per capita expendi- ture on research and develop- ment
30.4	15.6	31.0	29.8	73.8	37.8	49.4	47.3	117.4	60.1
15.7	4.7	7.5	3.3	38.0	11.4	11.9	5.3	60.4	18.1
46.6	27.4	56.9	58.6	113.1	66.7	90.5	93.2	179.9	106.0
41.3	23.0	27.8	31.5	63.4	35.3	43.6	49.4	99.4	55.3
20.5	7.6	7.0	7.9	31.5	11.7	11.0	12.4	49.4	18.3
64.0	39.8	50.5	57.3	98.3	61.1	79.1	89.8	154.0	95.7
49.4	33.5	20.1	23.8	46.9	31.8	47.6	56.3	111.1	75.4
44.2	29.7	17.0	20.2	42.0	28.2	40.3	47.8	99.5	66.9
87.5	61.3	43.1	50.2	83.0	58.2	102.1	118.9	196.7	138.0
38.8	26.0	25.2	27.7	58.0	38.8	44.1	48.4	101.3	67.9
24.4	15.3	11.2	11.8	36.5	22.9	19.6	20.7	63.8	40.1
63.0	43.8	48.7	54.4	94.1	65.5	85.3	95.2	164.6	114.6

[b] Belgium, Denmark, France, FRG, Italy, The Netherlands, Norway, and United Kingdom.
[c] All those above plus Australia, Canada, and New Zealand.
[d] All those above plus Japan.
[e] All those above plus Japan and counterfactual Singapore.

all levels of education would have risen by 94%. If the savings had instead been channeled into research and development, our total expenditures on technical and scientific development would have risen by 165%. Even if we had chosen the worst case—European allies only and with Czechoslovakia as the counterfactual—those latter three percentages would respectively be 8, 11, and 20—hardly insignificant. Given the sluggish rate of productivity growth in the United States since World War II (and particularly over the past decade), the opportunity costs appear highest when measured against the level either of investment or of expenditures on research and development.

Nor are things getting any better. In January of this year, in words reminiscent of the theme song heard so often since 1949, a *Los Angeles Times* editorial writer wrote

> And while they enjoy carping about Carter's shortcomings as a leader, neither Schmidt not France's Valery Giscard d'Estaing nor any other European statesman has the courage to go to his own people and demand the sacrifices that would be required to deal with the big bad world if U.S. power and influence ceased to be effective.[64]

BIG ATLANTIS AND LITTLE ATLANTIS

What, then, is the moral to be drawn from these three historical episodes? First, it costs a lot of money to maintain an empire. Second, some nations seem to learn about the costs of empire more quickly than others. It took Britain the better part of 200 years; and although American economists appear to have discovered it in about the same length of time, the knowledge has still not filtered through to any large body of our policymakers, either elected or appointed. On the European continent, in the empire of white settlement, and in Japan, however, the learning curve has had a much steeper slope. Finally, it appears that although the "empire" business may be a consumer good, it is not an activity to be entered unless one is willing to accept not only short- but long-run losses as well. Perhaps in all those years since the American Revolution the question has been phrased incorrectly. What any profit-maximizing nation should be seeking is the efficient way to get absorbed into somebody else's empire.

In conclusion, it is interesting to note the identity of the American political leader who, in commenting on the sharing of the defense burden among our NATO allies, said

> We were told by the civilian and military leaders of our government that we stand in the greatest of perils. We have inaugurated an immense military program. The consequences of this program to our economic life are already evident. Under it, taxes will take a greater portion of our national income than that taken by most noncommunist countries in Europe. Already we are in the midst of a disastrous wave of inflation from its pressures. We must defer many needed improvements. We can stand this for possibly two or three years pending a genuine rally by the noncommunist world to their full part in defense. But we must in time have relief from a large part of that burden.[65]

64. Ernest Conine in the *Los Angeles Times,* January 29, 1979, p. 5.

65. Herbert Hoover in a radio address, "Where We Are Now," reported in the *New York Times,* October 20, 1950, p. 12.

It was not Mike Mansfield in 1970, nor Teddy Kennedy in 1979, but Herbert Hoover in 1950. Sometimes you don't know who your friends are.

More than any other contributor to this volume **Lance Davis** is associated with Douglass North in professional circles. He was one of the first students at the University of Washington to work with North in the early 1950s. Later he and North collaborated on a series of articles on government and institutional change which culminated in the publication of their book, **Institutional Change and American Economic Growth**, in 1971.

Davis received his Bachelor's degree from the University of Washington in 1950 and worked with North for an additional year before moving to Johns Hopkins where he received his Ph.D. in 1956. He was one of several economic historians who joined together on the faculty at Purdue in the early 1960s and propelled that institution into the forefront of the new economic history movement. Together with Jonathan Hughes, Duncan McDougall, Nathen Rosenberg, Stanley Reiter, and Robert Bassman, Davis organized the now famous Cliometric Meetings which first met at Purdue in December of 1960 and annually thereafter until the group moved to Wisconsin in 1967. Long before the New Economic History came to dominate the teaching of the subject, Lance Davis, John Hughes, and Duncan McDougall wrote **American Economic History** (1961), the first textbook to champion the new methodology. Davis has remained simultaneously one of the most influential proponents as well as one of the most incisive critics of the use of rigourous economic theory and statistical techniques in the study of history.

Davis is widely known for his papers on the development of capital markets. More recently his research interests have turned to the role of empire in the economic history of Britain. The contribution to this volume is an outgrowth of that work.

Davis is joined by coauthor, **Robert A. Huttenback**, currently Professor of History of the University of California, Santa Barbara.

Chapter **4**

The Antebellum Interregional Trade Hypothesis: A Reexamination of Theory and Evidence

Lloyd J. Mercer

The hypothesis that regional interdependence and economic growth in the antebellum United States were built on a network of interregional trade, with emphasis on West-South trade, has been around for at least seven decades. The names of three scholars—Guy S. Callender, Louis B. Schmidt, and Douglass C. North—are most closely associated with the concept. The Callender and Schmidt statements are essentially identical. North builds on their work but goes beyond them in the sophistication of his model of regional interdependence. Thus, although the alternate versions of antebellum interregional trade hypothesis are similar, there are some important differences.[1]

North can be viewed as having made two statements of the trade hypothesis. In his earlier version (1961), relative prices are implicit as a

1. For three simple general equilibrium models of the trade hypothesis, see Appendix Table 4 A.1. What is here labeled the Callender-Schmidt model comes from Guy S. Callender, *Selections from the Economic History of the United States* (Boston: Ginn & Company, 1909), Chapter 7, and from Louis B. Schmidt, "The Internal Grain Trade of the United States, 1850–1860," *Iowa Journal of History and Politics* 18 (1920), pp. 94–124, and idem, "Internal Commerce and the Development of the National Economy before 1860," *Journal of Political Economy* 47 (1939), pp. 798–822. Schmidt's discussion of the interregional trade hypothesis is derived directly from Callender's earlier discussion. See Schmidt, "Internal Grain Trade," pp. 94–96. The North models, referred to as (1961) and (1974), are from, respectively, *The Economic Growth of the United States, 1790-1860* (Englewood Cliffs, N. J.: Prentice-Hall, 1961), especially Chapters 9, 10, and 11, and *Growth and Welfare in the American Past*, 2d ed. (Englewood Cliffs, N. J.: Prentice-Hall, 1974), especially Chapters 6 and 7.

EXPLORATIONS IN THE NEW ECONOMIC HISTORY

ISBN 0-12-580080-0

determinant of trade, but their importance becomes explicit when he later (1974) writes:[2] "Whether or not there was more regional specialization in years of high cotton prices (and therefore more dependence on Western foodstuffs) is still an unresolved question."

North's most significant divergence from the other authors is in respect to this very matter: his view of prices. Callender and Schmidt have virtually nothing to say on that subject. North, on the other hand, gives prices an important role in his early (1961) discussion of the hypothesis and later (1974) emphasizes them still further. The crucial difference among the alternative statements appears most clearly in the posited determinants of southern demand for western foodstuffs. In Callender-Schmidt, that demand depends simply on the extent of cotton (southern) output. In North (1961) it also depends on the price of western grain (foodstuffs); in North (1974) it depends on the relative price of cotton (southern goods) and foodstuffs in lieu of the extent of cotton (southern) output. The differences in these relationships are instructive both for evaluating criticisms of the antebellum interregional trade hypothesis and for reappraising the hypothesis and the evidence.

A review may help to place the hypothesis and the major criticisms of it in perspective. Guy S. Callender was the first scholar to provide a systematic statement of the hypothesis. In his view, internal commerce "was the means by which the economic advantage arising from an increased foreign demand for our extractive products was diffused over the entire country and made to stimulate nearly all its industries."[3]

According to Callender, the crucial factor increasing the size of the market economy and participation in the market economy in the West was the introduction of cotton culture into the South and its extension after 1815 into the Southwest. Callender believed that the profitability of cotton and sugar led to monoculture of these crops in South Carolina and the Gulf States and to the neglect of other agriculture. This is reflected in his statement,

> The gradual absorption of these industries [cotton and sugar] by planters with slave labor increased this tendency [to monoculture] as the one advantage of that labor, viz., its capacity for being organized, could only be utilized in them. Mixed farming could not be profitably carried on by slaves in the South; hence the planters were glad to purchase their agricultural supplies, so far as possible, from other producers.[4]

In Callender's story, this set of circumstances provided the first important market for western farmers and served as a stimulus to growth in

2. *Growth and Welfare,* p. 76.
3. *Selections,* p. 271.
4. Ibid., pp. 272-273.

the western economy as cotton did for the Southwest. This argument, and the similar ones by Schmidt detailed in what follows, determine the southern demand for western foodstuffs in the Callender-Schmidt version of the trade hypothesis. The final link in Callender's version is an increased demand for manufactured products from the Northeast resulting from rising income in the South and West. (This relationship also appears in the Douglass North models.) Callender views the West's major market as shifting to the Northeast in the early 1840s, with the completion of the West-Northeast transportation links. The older slave states are not left out of Callender's story. They share in supplying the Northeast with agricultural produce and find a market for their surplus slaves with the extension of cotton culture into the Southwest.

Louis B. Schmidt, the next major scholar to focus on the hypothesis of antebellum interregional trade and interdependence, set forth his thesis that "the rapid extension of internal commerce after 1815 gave rise to regional specialization."[5] Schmidt saw two early obstacles to western development: (*a*) the difficulty of attracting immigrants to the region, and (*b*) the absence of markets for western products. Schmidt believed that these obstacles were overcome after 1815 by the introduction of the steamboat on western rivers and the extension of cotton culture into the Southwest. According to him, "the Middle West therefore, found its first important market in the South."[6] Like Callender, Schmidt believed that the South Atlantic and Gulf states concentrated on the production of cotton, sugar, and tobacco and neglected other branches of agriculture for which the Middle West possessed natural advantages, with the result that the South became the first important market for the grain and grain derivative products of the Middle West and ended up "depending on the West for a large part of its food supply."[7] Schmidt saw an important export trade developing for the West as a consequence of the reopening of West Indies trade in 1830 and the 1846 repeal of the English Corn Laws. Thus export demand enters the Callender-Schmidt version of the trade hypothesis. Schmidt also emphasized that it was the rise of manufacturing and the growth of industrial population in the East that ultimately provided the principal market for western agricultural products.

Providing the most recent restatement and elaboration of the antebellum interregional trade hypothesis, Douglass North starts with the Callender and Schmidt expositions of the hypothesis, but he extends the sophistication of economic analysis by having prices play an important

5. "Internal Commerce," p. 798.
6. Ibid., p. 801.
7. Ibid., p. 820.

and specific role in the various interregional relationships. Moreover, he sees transport cost as a key determinant of the delivered price of western goods.

North's discussion (especially his 1974 version) can be viewed within the framework of the comparative static analysis of the usual interregional trade model. For this purpose consider two regions: the South and the West. Trade in goods is permitted between regions but, because of specialization, factors are assumed to be relatively immobile. The South's economy can be described by the neoclassical production possibility curve in Figure 4.1. For simplicity, the South is assumed to produce cotton (C) and grain (G). In the following discussion, grain refers to all foodstuffs (i.e., grain, grain derivatives, etc.), and cotton refers more generally to staple production. Efficiency requires that production be divided between C and G so that the marginal rate of substitution between C and G is equal to the ratio of their output prices, P_c/P_g.

Demand for southern cotton was exogenously determined, primarily by demand in Great Britain.[8] Thus, given an existing capacity to produce cotton in the South, the price of cotton (P_c) depended on the exogenously determined level of demand. The price of grain (P_g) was primarily the result of domestic market forces and exogenous factors affecting agricultural production.

Starting from an initial equilibrium (G, C) an exogenous rise in the demand for cotton results in a rise in the price of cotton and an increase of the (absolute) slope of the budget line. To attain a new equilibrium, resources are transferred from grain to cotton production (G', C') with the appropriate lag.[9] Given the existing price of grain and the level of

8. It is a common assumption that the demand for cotton in the South was determined largely outside the United States, primarily from Great Britain (cf. Peter Temin, "The Causes of Cotton Price Fluctuation in the 1820's," *The Review of Economics and Statistics* 53 [1971], p. 463). Gavin Wright, "An Econometric Study of Cotton Production and Trade," *Review of Economics and Statistics* 53 (1971), p. 119, supports this view when he writes "It now appears that the rise in world income (or the steady shift of the world population from subsistence agriculture into the market economy) must have provided the continually expanding market for British cloth." The demand for cotton was, of course, derived from the demand for cloth, and the British textile industry purchased the bulk of the American crop.

9. The only assumption here is that the production frontier is concave, consistent with neoclassical production theory. Presumably, a further response to the rising cotton price would have been an acceleration in the outward shift of the South's production frontier. The evidence on increased land sales in the South supports this expectation (see North, *Economic Growth*, pp. 123-125). This is also supported by Wright's results with respect to his basic supply function for cotton:

$$Y_0 = a_1 + a_2 P_{\text{no},-1} + a_3 L_{-2}$$

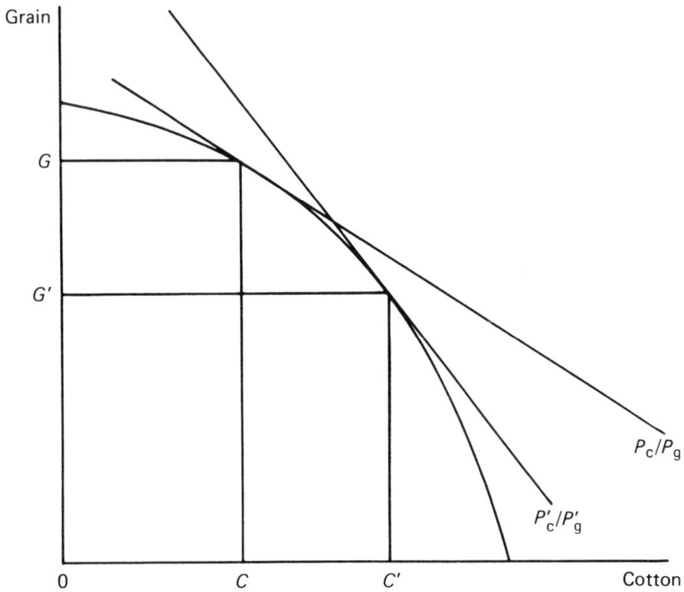

FIGURE 4.1. Relative price and output mix change.

grain demand in the South, an amount equal to $G'G$ will be demanded by southerners but not currently supplied by southerners. A basic premise of the regional interdependence hypothesis is that at least a portion of $G'G$ will be met by increased importation of grain from the West.[10] This relationship is reflected in North's (1974) version of southern demand for western foodstuffs. Under the conditions described, this analysis suggests that the typical trade pattern during periods of substantial expansion of southern cotton production would have been the export of grain from the West to the South.

According to North's later (1974) version of the hypothesis, expansion of the South's export sector (cotton) provided the impetus to western expansion in the following comparative static manner. An increase in

where Y_0 is annual cotton production, $P_{no,-1}$ is the New Orleans cotton price lagged 1 year, and L_{-2} equals cumulative land sales lagged 2 years (see Wright, "Econometric Study," p. 111). As Wright notes, this function implies that planters could be expected to adjust their cotton acreage (out of a given total acreage) on the basis of the existing cotton price. He refers, of course, to the relative price.

10. An eventual result of the outward shift of the production frontier (associated with expansion in the South) would have been an increase in grain supply in the South.

foreign exogenous demand for cotton produced an increase in the price of cotton, raising the ratio of cotton price to grain price, P_c/P_g. As factors shifted from G to C, cotton production increased and the supply of grain was reduced in the South (G', C') in response to the relative output-price change. The reduction in southern grain supply led to a rise in grain prices in the South, producing windfall gains to western grain producers and providing incentive for increases in output of grain in the West and in western grain exports. The response to the higher price of western grain was a movement of capital and labor toward the West, a further opening up of western lands, and (through a multiplier-accelerator process) a speedup in western development. The result of movement of capital and labor toward the West can be represented in comparative static terms by a rightward shift in the supply curve of western grain. This response in the West was reflected in increased land sales, because of the increase in demand for land, and population movements to the West. Of course, after the appropriate lag, the price of grain fell. Depending on the magnitude of the supply response, the final P_g observed may in reality be higher or lower than the initial equilibrium.

North argues that beginning in the 1830s, the West's pattern of trade gradually changed as completion of the Ohio canals was followed by a redirection of western produce to the Northeast and this was in turn accelerated by completion of the East-West railroads. According to him, although western trade with the South increased in absolute terms in the 1850s, it declined in relative terms.

North views growth of income in the West and the West's integration into the national economy as having resulted from the export of grain and grain derivatives. With respect to interregional trade, North cites the most important changes in the western regional economy during the antebellum period as having been (*a*) the surges of westward expansion, (*b*) redirection of western trade from the South to the Northeast and Europe, and (*c*) the accelerated shift of western population from self-sufficiency to the market economy during periods of expansion. He asserts that the waves of western expansion (1816–1818, 1832–1836, 1846–1847, and 1850–1856) reflected the increased profitability of western staples.

North's position regarding West–South trade is summed up by the following statement:

> From 1815 to the mid-forties, the primary market for Western foodstuffs was the South, supplemented by reshipments out of New Orleans to the East, West Indies, and South America; the rapid extension of cotton culture in the Southwest was the major determinant of expanding demand for corn, hogs, bacon, pork, wheat, flour,

and so on. The South remained a market for the West throughout the period, but was displaced by the East in relative terms during the last surge of expansion from 1843–1861.[11]

CRITICISMS OF THE ANTEBELLUM INTERREGIONAL TRADE HYPOTHESIS

Since publication of *The Economic Growth of the United States, 1790-1860,* the antebellum interregional trade hypothesis, and particularly its West-South trade component, has come under frequent and vigorous attack. Examination of the Callender-Schmidt version of the hypothesis reveals a major reason for this assault: According to this version of the hypothesis, southern demand for western exports depended only on the level of cotton (southern staple) production. The South is viewed as engaging in monoculture of staples and "depending on the West for a large part of its food supply."[12] Common sense, a minor stint of economic reasoning, and a casual perusal of data in the U.S. Census for the antebellum years (1840-1860) all suggest that the hypothesis formulated in this manner is surely wrong. Criticisms of the trade hypothesis have for the most part dealt with this exaggeration in the Callender-Schmidt model without coming to grips with the more sophisticated hypothesis in the North model(s).

Perhaps the most blatant error in interpretation of North's statement of the hypothesis involves the point in time to which it applies.[13] Specifically, when was the South-West trade link of particular importance to western development? North indicates it was during the period of 1815-1845 that the South's demand for western exports would have provided the impetus for economic growth in the West. He explicitly recognizes that a redirection of western trade from the South to the Northeast began with the opening of the Erie Canal in 1825. However, he carefully points out that almost two decades passed before this canal significantly affected the movement of western bulk goods to the eastern market.[14] In the final analysis, substantial trade between the West and the Northeast awaited the later construction of canals connecting the

11. *Economic Growth,* p. 141.

12. "Internal Commerce," p. 820.

13. Disregarding the adequacy of the tests themselves, they have simply not been applied to the appropriate points in time so that, even if the tests had been designed correctly, the hypothesis is not tested.

14. *Economic Growth,* p. 142. North argues that the redirection of trade accelerated rapidly after the middle 1840s. It now appears that this acceleration occurred even earlier, in the 1830s.

Great Lakes to the Mississippi River system.[15] Tonnage shipped from the western states to tidewater over the Erie Canal increased rapidly only from the middle 1830s, with tonnage from the western states not exceeding that from western New York State until 1847.[16] Thus, general trade patterns, as indicated by the volume of tonnage, suggest that the period during which exports to the South were potentially crucial to development of the West includes only the decades between 1810 and 1840—that is, the period before transportation developments accelerated the redirection of trade toward the Northeast and provide the West with a significant and expanding alternative domestic market for bulk goods.[17]

A major set of general objections to the interregional trade hypothesis rests on the notion of southern self-sufficiency in grain production and dates at least from Richard A. Easterlin's review of *The Economic Growth of the United States.*[18] As Stanley Engerman has pointed out, there are two possible approaches to a study of the southern imports of foodstuffs.[19] The first involves direct analysis of the available trade flow data; the second, a determination of the probable requirement for grains and meats in the South and a comparison of these requirements with the southern production available to meet them.

Easterlin implicitly relies on the latter method by comparing the three major regions as defined by North with respect to per capita production (or inventory) in 1840 for major agricultural items exported by the West. The data presented are the regional per capita production (or inventory) as a percentage of the national per capita figure for each good. On the assumption that per capita consumption levels were reasonably similar in the three regions, Easterlin concludes that the major food deficit area was the Northeast rather than the South. As further evidence against the trade hypothesis, he offers some preliminary results of research by

15. Ibid., p. 105.

16. As Robert W. Fogel, "Discussion: Reappraisals in American History," *American Economic Review* 54 (1964), p. 382, has pointed out, a significant portion of West–South trade moved eastward to tidewater and then south by the 1850s. The growth of this trade is undoubtedly included in the rise of western tonnage moving to tidewater on the Erie Canal.

17. North, *Economic Growth*, pp. 141–142.

18. "Review: The Economic Growth of the United States, 1790–1860," *Journal of Economic History* 23 (1962), pp. 123–126.

19. Stanley L. Engerman, "The Antebellum South: What Probably Was and What Should Have Been," *Agricultural History* 44 (1970), pp. 122–126. To test the North version of the trade hypothesis one would also want to correctly resolve the colligation problem, that is, pick the right time period for the test.

William N. Parker indicating that southern plantations were probably self-sufficient, farm by farm, in pork and corn in 1850 and 1860.[20]

Robert E. Gallman, in a careful and detailed study based on a sample of farms from the 1860 manuscript census, examines the possibility of self-sufficiency in the production of foodstuffs within the South and the volume of West-South trade required to supplement southern production.[21] Gallman's thesis with respect to the South is that

> the region was normally self-sufficient in food. In good years—and perhaps even average years—there were surpluses for sale to the nonfarm population within the region and outside it. Productive capacity was impressive, but food production remained a secondary activity conducted in considerable measure beyond the discipline of the market. . . . planters as a group . . . did not provide a large and regular market for the output of small farmers.[22]

Examining the question of southern self-sufficiency by studying trade flows to New Orleans for the period 1839–1860, Albert Fishlow concluded that trade between the West and South was always of limited importance to both regions, with the South being neither a major market for western produce nor in dire need of important foodstuffs.[23] Raymond C. Battalio and John Kagel, in a study of South Carolina agriculture in 1860, present results indicating that the farms of the Old South produced a surplus of food above their own needs, and on this basis they concur with the Fishlow finding that the magnitude of West–South trade in general foodstuffs was relatively small.[24] Robert Fogel criticizes Fishlow for ignoring some potential trade routes for foodstuff shipments between West and South, but he also focuses on the 1840–1860 period.[25]

A further study of grain flows in those same two decades has been

20. William N. Parker, "The Slave Plantation in American Agriuclture," in *Contributions,* Première Conférence Internationale d'Histoire Économique, Stockholm, 1960, pp. 321–331, especially p. 326.

21. Robert E. Gallman, "Self-Sufficiency in the Cotton Economy of the Antebellum South," *Agricultural History* 44 (1970), pp. 5–23.

22. Ibid., p. 6.

23. "Antebellum Interregional Trade Reconsidered" and "Postscript" in Ralph Andreano, ed., *New Views on American Economic Development* (Cambridge, Mass.: Schenkman Publishing Company, 1965).

24. "The Structure of Antebellum Southern Agriculture: South Carolina, A Case Study," *Agricultural History* 44 (1970), pp. 25–37.

25. Fogel, "Discussion," p. 389.

conducted by Diane Lindstrom,[26] who concludes that the trade flow data cast doubt on the position that the South relied on western grain supplies. In general, her study supports the findings of Fishlow and Gallman that the South was largely self-sufficient with respect to wheat and corn.[27]

It should be evident that these various critiques are focusing on a period inappropriate for a test of the North hypothesis. For that objective, the appropriate period is from 1815 to about 1840. Tests based on 1850 and 1860 data are particularly inadequate to evaluate North's version of the trade hypothesis.

Moreover, the sort of results obtained by Easterlin should not be too surprising to economists. His conclusion that the Northeast was the major food-deficit area in 1840 would probably be equally true at whatever date one chooses between 1815 and 1860 (or 1981). The point is that a relatively greater food deficit in the Northeast than in the South at any date in the antebellum period would be neither very surprising on an a priori basis nor a test of the trade hypothesis. The Easterlin results are inconclusive. A yet stronger criticism can be leveled against the self-sufficiency and trade flow tests. The evaluations of southern self-sufficiency, even if aimed at the relevant time periods, totally fail to indicate the *importance* of southern imports from the West. There is surely some error of estimate, greater than zero, involved in examination of southern self-sufficiency. As an example, suppose the South was 95% self-sufficient in foodstuffs and that only the remaining 5% was imported. If brought in from the West, this could constitute a substantial part of western exports and production, expecially in the teens and twenties.[28] A similar criticism can be leveled at the evidence from trade flow data. These studies focus only on the direction of flow without considering the importance of this trade *relative* to western output. Thus, the crucial statistic would be to discover what proportion of western output or market sales was represented by western exports to the South. For North's version of the trade hypothesis to hold, southern imports have to be (at the margin) a significant share of the western surplus of export commodities.[29] Given the considerations discussed

26. "Southern Dependence on Interregional Grain Supplies: A Review of the Trade Flows, 1840-1860," *Agricultural History* 44 (1970), pp. 101–113.

27. Ibid., p. 101.

28. Engerman, "Antebellum South," p. 128, recognizes this point.

29. If growth of the export sector is considered crucial, there are two additional ways in which expansion of the cotton culture could have provided the impetus to western development during the period in question. First, the expansion of cotton production and

here, the cited studies do *not* test North's version of the antebellum interregional trade hypothesis although they successfully contradict the Callender–Schmidt version.

THE POTENTIAL SOUTHERN PORK MARKET: 1840, AND SOME CONJECTURAL ESTIMATES FOR 1810–1830

Grain and grain derivatives made up the vast bulk of western agricultural produce and exports in the antebellum period, with the derivatives predominating in exports because they were of higher value than bulk grains, relative to weight. Wheat was exported as flour, and corn as provisions (pork, lard, hams, bacon, etc.) and whiskey.[30] John E. Clark suggests that prior to 1825, flour was the most important single export (from the old Northwest), but that after 1825 provisions and whiskey together were probably of greater value.[31] Estimation of the potential southern market for western produce focuses here on one particular corn derivative: pork, which was an extremely efficient means of exporting western corn in terms of transport costs. Because of this efficiency, pork was undoubtedly the primary western agricultural export of the antebellum period, and it was certainly the major potential export to the South, where pork in its many forms was by all odds the most popular meat.[32] For this reason, tests of the trade hypothesis that rest solely on grain flows are inadequate for their task.

An immediate problem in analyzing southern food supply and demand is that of regional definition. In his statement of the trade hypothesis, Douglass North places Kentucky and Tennessee in the

---

associated rise in southern income could have led to an increase in southern imports from the Northeast. In turn, this would result in a rise in aggregate income in the Northeast—a food deficit area—and the Northeast's demand for food imports would increase. The West would be the natural source of supply. As is well known, in the earlier period goods moved from West to Northeast by way of the Mississippi River and New Orleans. The second possibility is that western exports rose in part by the mechanism just described and in part also as suggested by the traditional West–South focus of the antebellum interregional trade hypothesis. The latter seems more likely.

30. John E. Clark, *The Grain Trade in the Old Northwest* (Urbana: University of Illinois Press, 1966), p. 15.

31. Ibid.

32. See Sam Bowers Hilliard, *Hog Meat and Hoecake: Food Supply in the Old South, 1840–1860* (Carbondale and Edwardsville: Southern Illinois University Press, 1972), especially Chapter 5, "Pork: The South's First Choice," for an in-depth and entertaining discussion of this point.

West. Others class them as southern states and then proceed to test North's hypothesis.[33] Because both are substantial "surplus" states in terms of foodstuff production, this certainly biases the test against the trade hypothesis as stated by North and abets the conclusion of recent researchers that the South as a whole was self-sufficient in meat production in one or more of the census years 1840, 1850, and 1860.[34] In this chapter, for the empirical analysis of pork markets and production, the West is defined in two ways: (*a*) with Kentucky and Tennessee classed as western states, and (*b*) with the West being only the Old Northwest.

Any attempt to test the North hypothesis on its own grounds for the period between 1815 and 1845 confronts an immediate problem: The 1840 census was the first one to provide data on agricultural production and the inventory of swine. Until new research provides evidence that would allow reconstruction of the pattern of agricultural development before 1840, it is simply impossible to go much further into the matter than North himself did. Indeed, the lack of data before 1840 probably explains why North's critics focus on the later periods. Although understandable, their reliance on anachronistic data greatly weakens their criticism of the hypothesis.

Although we cannot reproduce the actual structure of agricultural production in either the South or the West prior to 1840, we can, by extrapolating the 1840 data on production backward in time, construct some boundaries on the range of possibilities that existed during the early period of North's analysis. To date, his critics have not done this. Although such extrapolations would be highly conjectural, and would not "prove" or "disprove" the North hypothesis on interregional trade, they should reveal whether or not his analysis is consistent with the evidence in 1840. As a step toward answering one aspect of this question, estimates of southern production and consumption of pork are presented for 1810, 1820, and 1830. The conjectural estimates presented here for 1810–1830 assume that per capita inventory was the same, by

33. Gallman, "Self-Sufficiency," Table 7, p. 22, apparently puts Tennessee in the South and Kentucky in the West.

34. See Engerman, "Antebellum South," Table 1, p. 1341. If Kentucky and Tennessee were excluded from the South, Engerman's calculations in the cited table would show a southern meat deficit rather than a surplus in both 1840 and 1850. The deficit already shown in 1860 would, of course, be smaller since Kentucky and Tennessee are shown as deficient in meat in 1860. Schmidt, "The Internal Grain Trade," p. 97, fn. 6, includes Kentucky in the West as a grain-growing state and Tennessee (p. 97, fn. 5) in the South. Thus, Gallman (see the preceding note) follows Schmidt in regional classification of these two states.

county, in 1810, 1820, and 1830 as it was when first reported with county-by-county data as of the June 1 inventory of swine in the 1840 census.[35]

Previous researchers have used diverse assumptions regarding the slaughter ratio, live weight, and dressed weight of hogs to arrive at pork output. At one extreme, Gallman assumed a slaughter ratio of .5 and average slaughter weight of 160 lbs. (120 net lbs.) but stated that the slaughter ratio was "probably a little too low."[36] At the other end of the spectrum, Richard Sutch (like Fogel and Engerman) estimated the slaughter ratio to have been .83.[37] Fogel and Engerman used the 160 lbs. live weight figure with a net weight of 120 lbs., but Sutch uses an average net weight of 144 lbs. (and implicitly a live weight of 192 lbs.) based on more than 17,000 slaughters in plantation records.[38] The values cited are used here to provide a range estimate for deficit southern counties: a low deficit with slaughter ratio of .83 and net weight of 144 lbs. and a high deficit with slaughter ratio of .5 and net weight of 120 lbs.

For the period 1810–1840, the low estimate is probably unrealistic, given the quality and treatment of southern swine, and the high estimate must be much nearer the mark.[39] On the other hand, given the improvement in quality and treatment of swine in the South in the later antebellum period, the low estimate is undoubtedly more accurate for 1860. The significant decline in swine per capita (from 1.9 to 1.65) for the total South as defined here provides evidence of improvement in the swine slaughter ratio and weight. The major two points that might contravene this seem unlikely: (*a*) that per capita pork consumption de-

35. The 1840 level of swine per capita reflects the 1840 influences of market specialization on product mix—what might be termed the "stage" of agricultural development. To the extent that southern counties became more specialized in staple production over the period 1810-1840, it is possible that they produced more foodstuffs per capita in the earlier years than we find in 1840. Thus, the conjectural estimates of pork deficit presented here for 1810-1830 may be "high." Still, the trend of this potential southern deficit relative to potential western surplus is of interest.

36. "Self-Sufficiency," pp. 14, 19.

37. Richard Sutch, "The Care and Feeding of Slaves," in Paul A. David *et al.*, *Reckoning with Slavery*, (New York: Oxford University Press, 1976), pp. 246–247; Robert W. Fogel and Stanley C. Engerman, *Time on the Cross: Evidence and Methods* (Boston: Little, Brown & Co., 1974), p. 95.

38. Sutch, "Care and Feeding," p. 246.

39. See Hilliard, *Hog Meat and Hoecake*, pp. 95–102, for a discussion of quality and treatment of southern swine. Hilliard reports an average net weight of 133 lbs. for 3949 slaughters from plantation records prior to 1845 and an average net weight of 153 lbs. for 7718 slaughters over the period 1841–1861 (p. 261, fn. 37).

clined proportionately and/or (*b*) that southern pork imports rose proportionately.

In subsequent tables, western production is estimated on the basis of a slaughter ratio of .83 and live weight of 192 lbs. (net weight 144 lbs.).[40] Sutch and Hilliard both place southern pork consumption per capita at 150 lbs., and this figure is used here.

The question to be examined is the magnitude of the potential southern and northeastern market (deficits) for pork relative to the potential western market production (surplus) of pork. On the basis of assumptions spelled out earlier, the southern pork deficit is calculated for those counties whose estimated production is less than their estimated consumption. Some considerable part of this deficit was undoubtedly rectified by purchase of southern rather than western pork, but the aim here is to estimate the size of the market regardless of the source of supply. Previous estimates based on state data do not provide this information but do allow for an altogether too facile satisfaction of southern deficits with southern surpluses. The deficit counties have one common characteristic: They are relatively available to transportation routes for imports from the West.[41] This is surely not coincidental, and it provides further evidence of a potential southern market for western pork. The question is, How large was that market and how does it compare to western output?

Table 4.1 lists low and high estimates of the potential southern pork market for the years 1810, 1820, 1830, and 1840 for the cotton South and the total South.[42] Arkansas, not included here, had no deficit counties in 1840. The estimated market doubles between 1810 and 1840, with the largest growth shown between 1820 and 1830.

Table 4.2 estimates (surplus) pork production in the West, based on state data, with a breakdown shown between the Old Northwest and the West as classified by North. This is a "high" surplus estimate based on a slaughter ratio of .83, a net weight per slaughter hog of 144 lbs., and per capita consumption of 150 lbs. Because the latter figure may be high for the Old Northwest, the estimated western surplus is most likely

40. Thomas S. Berry, *Western Prices before 1861* (Cambridge, Mass.: Harvard University Press, 1943), p. 231, cites an average live weight for "the hogs of a hundred years ago" of 200 lb.

41. See Hilliard, *Hog Meat and Hoecake,* pp. 104–110 for a discussion of this point. As Hilliard notes, "the relation between pork deficits and the availability of commercial meat is unmistakable [p. 110]."

42. Virginia has not been included in earlier estimates of southern self-sufficiency. It is interesting (and surprising) that Virginia's pork deficit, based on the assumptions based here, is so large.

TABLE 4.1
Range of Estimated Southern Pork Market (Deficit Counties)
(Millions of Pounds)

	1810		1820		1830		1840	
	Low	High	Low	High	Low	High	Low	High
North Carolina	2.7	15.2	2.9	17.8	3.4	20.1	3.4	21.1
South Carolina	11.0	26.6	12.4	31.2	15.2	37.6	14.7	37.5
Georgia	2.9	10.6	3.1	12.9	4.0	19.0	6.2	22.9
Alabama	—	—	1.3	3.3	3.0	7.9	4.8	14.7
Mississippi	.1	.6	1.5	2.7	1.8	4.0	2.4	6.5
Louisiana	6.6	7.9	10.8	13.6	16.1	21.8	26.0	34.3
Total (cotton South)	23.3	60.9	32.0	81.5	43.5	110.4	57.5	137.0
Virginia	11.6	56.3	12.5	59.4	14.8	67.1	15.0	69.1
Total	34.9	117.2	44.5	140.9	58.3	177.5	72.5	206.1

TABLE 4.2
Estimated Market (Surplus) Pork Production: The Old Northwest—Kentucky and Tennessee

	1840							
				Surplus production[a]		Surplus production (mil. lbs.)		
	Population	Swine (000)	Swine per capita	per capita pounds	total (mil. lbs.)	1810	1820	1830
Ohio	1,519,467	2,099,746	1.38	21.8	33.1	5.0	12.7	20.4
Indiana	685,866	1,623,608	2.37	145.1	99.5	3.6	21.4	49.8
Illinois	476,183	1,495,254	3.14	240.9	114.7	3.0	13.3	37.9
Michigan	212,267	295,890	1.39	23.1	4.9	.1	.2	.7
Wisconsin	30,945	51,383	1.66	56.7	1.8	.0	.0	.0
Iowa	43,112	104,899	2.43	152.5	6.6	.0	.0	.0
Missouri	383,702	1,271,161	3.31	262.1	100.6	5.5	17.5	36.8
Total					361.2	17.2	65.1	145.6
Kentucky	779,828	2,310,533	2.96	218.5	170.4	88.8	123.3	150.3
Tennessee	829,210	2,926,607	3.53	289.5	240.1	75.8	122.4	197.4
Total					410.5	164.6	245.7	347.7
Total					771.7	181.8	310.8	493.3

[a] Slaughter ratio to June 1 inventory assumed to be .83. Dressed weights assumed to be 150 lbs. Per capita consumption assumed to be 150 lbs.

biased downward. The values shown increase more than twentyfold from 1810 to 1840 for the Old Northwest and more than fourfold for North's West. Western production, as measured by the conjectural estimates here, grew far more rapidly than the potential southern market.

Table 4.3 includes estimates of the pork market (deficit) in the Northeast, based on state data, with a division between the New England and the Middle Atlantic regions.[43] The estimated magnitude of the Northeastern market expands almost 80% between 1810 and 1840. Other things equal, the growth of the southern pork market is much more rapid than that of the northeastern pork market. Of course, other things were not equal for western producers.

Table 4.4 lists the estimated pork markets in the South and the Northeast as percentages of estimated western pork production. The clear pattern is that both southern and northeastern markets declined in size over time relative to western output, however one defines the West, and the northeastern market was clearly larger than the southern relative to western production at all times. Of course, even if these conjectures on census-year size of market and market production are realistic, they tell us nothing about what happened between census years. Based on the high estimate, they do suggest that the potential southern market for pork was of significant size relative to potential western pork production through 1830: It represented about one-quarter to one-third of the estimated surplus pork production of North's West at the date. This fraction declined over time and by 1840 was down to, at most, about one-quarter of the potential output of his West. The estimates presented here indicate that through 1830 the southern pork market may have been a significant factor, although probably not *the* significant factor, for pork production in the West as defined by North. For the Old Northwest, however, given transportation difficulties, the southern pork market potentially was not only *a* significant factor but *the* significant market for pork producers through 1830 and especially in the teens and twenties.

Earlier it was suggested that the relative price of southern products and foodstuffs would have been an important determinant of southern demand for western products. Table 4.5 presents series of prices for cotton relative to hogs and of sugar relative to hogs for 1817–1840. By the North formulation (1974) these would indicate the southern demand for western products should have been highest in the early 1820s, although the relatives are also high in the teens compared to the whole time period. These relative price data, in conjunction with the relationship between

43. The estimated deficit is probably far too large for the New England region, where fish represented a much more significant part of the diet.

TABLE 4.3
Estimated Pork Market (Deficit) in the Northeast

	1840						Pork deficit (mil. lbs.)		
					Pork deficit				
	Population	Swine (000)	Swine per capita	Pork production per capita lbs.	Per capita lbs.	Total (mil. lbs.)	1810	1820	1830
Maine	501,793	117,386	.23	28.6	121.4	60.9	27.8	36.2	48.5
New Hampshire	284,574	121,671	.43	53.5	96.5	27.5	20.7	23.6	26.0
Vermont	291,948	203,800	.70	58.1	91.9	26.8	20.0	21.7	25.8
Massachusetts	737,699	142,221	.19	23.7	126.3	93.2	59.6	66.1	77.1
Rhode Island	108,830	30,659	.28	34.9	115.1	12.5	8.9	9.6	11.2
Connecticut	309,978	131,961	.43	53.5	96.5	29.9	25.3	26.6	28.7
New York	2,428,921	1,900,065	.78	97.1	52.9	128.5	50.7	72.6	101.5
New Jersey	373,306	261,443	.70	87.2	62.8	23.4	15.4	17.4	20.1
Pennsylvania	1,724,033	1,503,964	.87	108.3	41.7	71.9	33.8	43.8	26.2
Delaware	78,085	74,228	.95	118.3	31.7	2.5	2.3	2.3	2.4
Maryland	470,019	416,943	.89	110.3	39.2	18.4	14.9	16.0	17.5
New England						250.8	162.3	183.8	217.3
Middle Atlantic						244.7	117.1	152.1	197.7
Total						495.5	279.4	335.9	415.0

TABLE 4.4
Estimated Pork Markets Relative to Estimated Western Pork Production

	Cotton South[a]		Total South[b]		New England	Middle Atlantic	Total Northeastern
	Low	High	Low	High			
	Estimated pork market as percentage of Old Northwest pork production						
1810	135	354	203	681	944	681	1624
1820	49	125	68	216	282	234	516
1830	30	76	40	122	149	136	285
1840	16	38	20	57	69	68	137
	Estimated pork market as percentage of pork production in North's West[c]						
1810	13	33	19	64	89	64	154
1820	10	26	14	45	59	49	108
1830	9	22	12	36	44	40	84
1840	7	18	9	27	32	32	64

[a]North and South Carolina, Georgia, Alabama, Mississippi, and Louisiana (i.e., "Cotton South").
[b]Cotton South plus Virginia.
[c]The Old Northwest plus Kentucky and Tennessee.

the potential southern pork market and western production, suggest that the southern market probably had the greatest importance for the West before 1830. However, this may be misleading because census year estimates miss the large expansion in cotton production in 1832-1839. Thus, North's (1974) comment about increased regional specialization in years of high cotton prices remains unresolved.

TRANSPORTATION FEASIBILITY OF WEST–SOUTH PORK TRADE

A significant question with regard to the estimates developed here is whether, in terms of transportation, the producing region (the West) could efficiently have supplied the indicated (southern) market? The issue is examined here by determining the location of both the estimated 1840 southern pork deficit (counties) and the estimated 1840 western pork surplus (counties) with regard to water transportation. Figure 4.2 shows the southern deficit counties (gray) for the 1840 low-deficit estimates. Casual observation confirms that most of their counties are easily accessible to water transportation. Figure 4.3, giving the same information for the 1840 high-deficit estimate, shows that the deficit counties so accessible are a smaller proportion of total deficit counties than for the low–deficit estimate.

TABLE 4.5
Price Relatives: Southern Products and Hogs[a]

	Ratio of cotton price to hog price[b]	Ratio of sugar price to hog price[c]
1817	5.6	3.4
1818	5.1	2.6
1819	4.2	3.0
1820	3.4	5.5
1821	6.4	9.1
1822	11.5	7.0
1823	6.5	4.8
1824	5.9	5.1
1825	8.0	4.5
1826	5.9	4.2
1827	4.8	4.9
1828	5.9	3.3
1829	3.7	2.9
1830	3.8	2.8
1831	3.8	1.7
1832	2.7	2.0
1833	3.9	1.9
1834	3.4	2.0
1835	5.0	1.3
1836	2.8	1.3
1837	1.9	1.8
1838	2.6	1.6
1839	3.2	1.6
1840	2.0	1.6

Sources: Hog prices—Berry, Table 26, p. 570; cotton prices—*Historical Statistics of the United States* (Series E126); sugar prices—*Historical Statistics of the United States* (Series E125.

[a] Hog prices are for the winter pack season; thus, 1817 means the 1816–1817 winter pack season. Cotton and sugar prices are for the second year in the pack season; that is, where hog prices are for the 1816–1817 winter pack, cotton and sugar prices are for 1817 and the ratio is shown for 1817.

[b] Hog price is the mean price of live hogs at Cincinnati for the winter pack season (generally mid-November to mid-February). Cotton price is the average for the year for middling uplands for the New York market.

[c] Sugar price is the wholesale price at Philadelphia (1817–1825) and at New York (1826–1840).

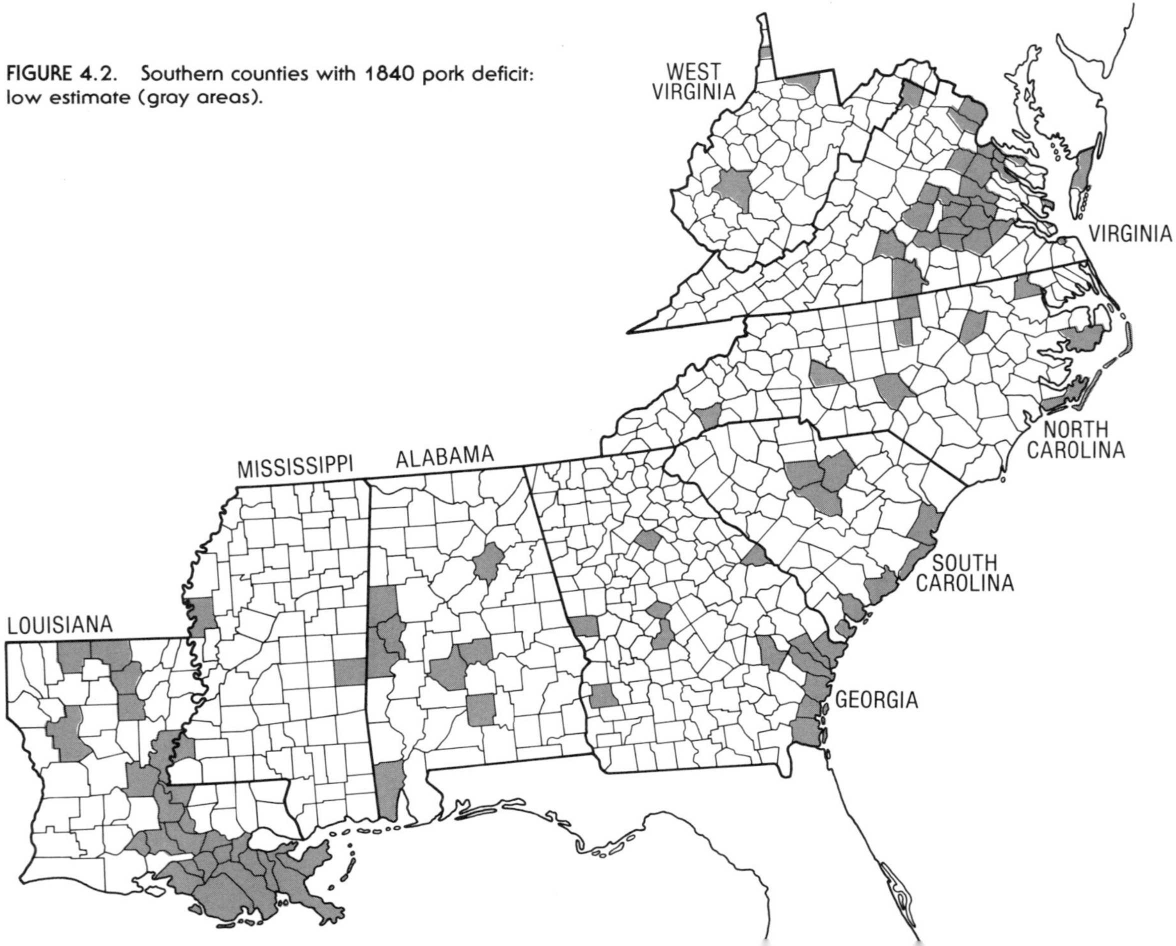

FIGURE 4.2. Southern counties with 1840 pork deficit: low estimate (gray areas).

FIGURE 4.3. Southern counties with 1840 pork deficit: high estimate (gray areas).

What is important here, however, is not the proportion of deficit *counties* accessible by water, but the share of the *deficit* itself that occurs in counties accessible by water.[44] Table 4.6 presents this information for the 1840 deficit. In general terms, 90% of the 1840 low deficit was in counties where water transportation was readily available (both the cotton South and the total South), and around 75% of the 1840 high-deficit estimate was in such counties. Clearly, the potential 1840 southern pork market estimated here was localized with respect to availability of water transportation.[45]

The location of pork specialization (production) in the Old Northwest also hinged on transportation (costs) in any potential West-South pork trade. For 1840, the pork surplus (which could be negative) is estimated as before for each county in the four Old Northwest states that could have produced a significant statewide surplus: Missouri, Illinois, Indiana, and Ohio. Figure 4.4 shows the location in those four states of counties that specialized in pork—defined here as those counties having a ratio of swine to population of 3.75 or larger (this being three times the number of swine per capita needed to break even on consumption, given the parameters used, or a pork surplus of 2 million lbs. or more).

Pork production was considerably localized in the Old Northwest in 1840. In Missouri, 34 out of 62 counties met the definition of specialization and produced almost 80% of the estimated net pork surplus of the state. Specialization in Illinois was somewhat less intense, with 60% of the net state surplus produced in 32 out of 87 counties. Indiana was even more specialized than Missouri, with only 26 out of 87 counties accounting for about 70% of the state's net surplus. Ohio, which had apparently moved to a broader base of agricultural development by 1840, showed by far the smallest net surplus of pork for the four major states while yet exhibiting the highest density of county specialization (as measured here), with 6 counties out of 79 producing 103% of the state's net surplus. In Ohio, 25 counties are estimated to have been deficient in pork

44. Information in George R. Taylor, *The Transportation Revolution* (New York: Holt, Rinehart and Winston, 1966), and Robert W. Fogel, *Railroads and American Economic Growth* (Baltimore: The Johns Hopkins Press, 1964), was used to determine water transportation accessibility in terms of rivers and canals. Fogel's estimate (pp. 75–79) for 1890 that the boundary of feasible agriculture would have been 40–50 miles from navigable water is used here.

45. The evidence presented here fits the hypothesis of interregional trade suggested earlier in this debate by Robert W. Fogel in "Discussion," pp. 337–389. Also, see his "American Interregional Trade in the Nineteenth Century," in Ralph Andreano, ed., *New Views on American Economic Development* (Cambridge, Mass.: Schenkman Publishing Company, 1965), pp. 201–209.

TABLE 4.6
Estimated 1840 Southern Pork-Deficit Counties Accessible to Water Transportation (Percentages)

State	Low W[a]	Low CW[b]	High W[a]	High CW[b]
Alabama	100.0	100.0	91.6	91.6
Georgia	65.5	71.9	40.2	46.1
Mississippi	81.0	81.0	76.3	76.3
Virginia	76.1	84.1	53.1	61.9
Louisiana	92.2	92.2	89.2	90.0
South Carolina	100.0	100.0	80.6	80.6
North Carolina	61.3	65.9	56.0	75.7
Cotton South	89.0	90.1	73.6	77.8
Total South	86.5	88.9	66.9	72.6

[a]Deficit in counties on water.
[b]Deficit in counties on water plus others contiguous.

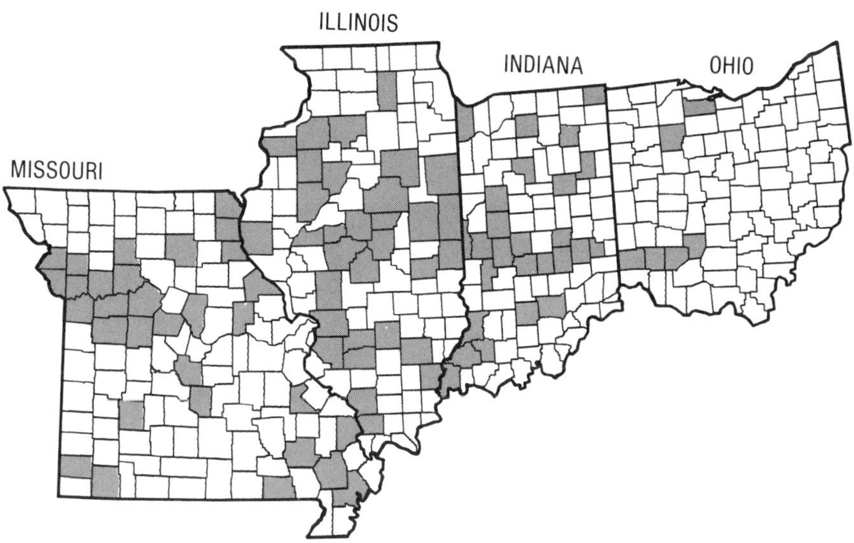

FIGURE 4.4. Pork-specialized counties: Missouri, Illinois, Indiana, and Ohio (gray areas).

production in 1840, as compared to 3 deficit counties in Missouri, 1 in Illinois, and 15 in Indiana. Specialized pork production in the Old Northwest of 1840 was greatest in the area's western reaches.

The location of pork-specialized counties in 1840 supports the potential for a significant trade in provisions to the South. In Ohio, 4 of the 6 adjoined each other in the southwest corner of the state, just north of the early pork-packing capital in Cincinnati. In western Indiana, 9 pork counties were within 40 miles or less of the Wabash River, and in the central and south-central part of the state, 10 other counties were within access of the equally navigable White River.[46] The Illinois River was within the same radius of 11 specialized pork counties in Illinois, where another 6 were similarly situated with respect to the Wabash River and another 9 with respect to the Mississippi River.[47] In Missouri, the pork-specialized counties clearly traced out the major rivers: 15 pork counties were within access of the Missouri and 11 of the Mississippi, and another navigable river, the Osage, served 3 more counties.

Thus the 1840 pork-specialized counties of the Old Northwest were heavily localized along navigable water and well situated for exportation of pork outside the region. Clearly producing far more pork than they could have consumed, they entered the market partly to meet deficits in other counties of the Old Northwest itself, but also in the export trade beyond the region. Each of the four states shows a significant 1840 net surplus of pork production. The three major potential export markets were the Northeast, the South, and overseas. We have seen that there was a significant market for pork in the South of that period (and most likely an even larger market before 1840, relative to Old Northwest pork production). Given the location of potential shipping (Old Northwest) and receiving (South) counties and the transportation realities of the time, it seems most likely that a West–South pork trade did exist in 1840 and earlier. Such a trade would certainly have played a positive role (at the margin) in western economic growth to at least 1840.

CONCLUSION

The estimates and examination of the antebellum interregional trade hypothesis in this paper suggest that the trade hypothesis, and particularly North's (1974) version appropriately qualified can be *a* meaningful

46. Fogel, *Railroads,* p. 252.

47. Clark, *The Grain Trade,* reports that with respect to grain, "as in previous decades, the grain trade of both Illinois and Indiana during the 1840's was predominately with the South [p. 147]." Clearly the same trade nexus existed for pork.

part of our explanation of antebellum economic growth—that is, while it cannot in itself be *the* explanation á la Callender-Schmidt it cannot be excluded from the explanation as recent critics would have us believe.

Callender and Schmidt's version implies an absolute dependence of the South on the West for foodstuffs. This is clearly nonsense. Unfortunately, in disproving this contention critics have gone too far—to the point of denying any significant West-South trade relationship. Surely this is equally wrong. It is wrong because what is important here is not the absolute (or average) relationship involved but, rather, the marginal relationship. North's versions of the trade hypothesis refer precisely to this aspect of the relationship by stating that *at the margin* southern demand for western products contributed significantly to western growth. Neither North nor his critics have data for the early years of the nineteenth century to fully document the magnitudes of the markets in which these trade flows took place. The estimates of this paper, based on available data from 1840, demonstrate the clear possibility that the southern demand for pork—whether or not the trade relied primarily on expansion of cotton—exerted a significant marginal impact on the growth of the West during the period from 1810–1845.

APPENDIX

Table 4A.1 lists three alternative formulations of the antebellum interregional trade hypothesis in the form of simple general equilibrium models. The models focus on the West and West-South trade because the trade hypothesis literature has been so largely

TABLE 4 A.1
Alternative Formulations of the Antebellum Interregional Trade Hypothesis

Callender-Schmidt	North (1961)	North (1974)
1) $Y_W = f(G_W, \mathbf{Z})$	(1) $Y_W = f(G_W, \mathbf{Z})$	(1) $Y_W = f(G_W, \mathbf{Z})$
2) $G_W = G_W^W + G_W^S + G_W^E + G_W^F$	(2) $G_W = G_W^W + G_N^S + G_W^E + G_W^F$	(2) $G_W = G_W^W + G_W^S + G_W^E + G_W^F$
3) $G^W = g(Y_W, N_W)$	(3) $G_W^W = g(Y_W, N_W, PG_W^W)$	(3) $G_W^W = g(Y_W, N_W, PG_W^W)$
4) $G_W^S = h(C)$	(4) $G_W^S = h(C, PG_W^S)$	(4) $G_W^S = h(PC_S/PG_S, PG_W^S)$
5) $G_W^E = i(Y_E, N_E)$	(5) $G_W^E = i(Y_E, N_E, PG_W^E)$	(5) $G_W^E = i(Y_E, N_E, PG_W^E)$
6) $G_W^F = j(FD - FS)$	(6) $G_W^F = j(FD - FS, PG_W^F)$	(6) $G_W^F = j(FD - FS, PG_W^F)$
7) $Y_E = k(\mathbf{Z}, Y_W, Y_S)$	(7) $Y_E = k(\mathbf{Z}, Y_W, Y_S)$	(7) $Y_E = k(\mathbf{Z}, Y_W, Y_S)$
8) $Y_S = l(\mathbf{Z}, R_S, C)$	(8) $Y_S = l(\mathbf{Z}, R_S, PC_S)$	(8) $Y_S = l(\mathbf{Z}, R_S, PC_S)$
	(9) $PG_W^i = m(R_W, G_W, TC_W^i)$	(9) $PG_W^i = m(R_W, G_W, TC_W^i)$

Note: Subscripts (and superscripts) W, S, E, and F refer to West, South, East, and Foreign; Y = income; G = grain (foodstuffs) output—subscripts refer to location (region) of production, superscripts to location of purchase; N = population; FD = foreign demand for foodstuffs; FS = foreign supply of foodstuffs; $\mathbf{Z}$ = a vector of exogenous factors; R = resources devoted to production; C = cotton output; TC = transportation costs; PC = price of cotton; PG = price of foodstuffs; and, i = region, i.e., W, S, E, and F.

preoccupied with the massive economic growth and transformation of the West during the antebellum period.

The crucial differences among the three models are illustrated by the alternative formulations of Eq. (4). The North models of 1961 and 1974 are identical except for the explicit inclusion of relative prices in Eq. (4) of the latter. This single difference is highly significant for the interpretation of the models. The important divergences between the North and the Callender–Schmidt versions are North's inclusion of prices as a determining factor and his explicit recognition of the role of transportation costs.

Viewed in this way, alternative versions of the trade hypothesis can easily be compared, thus facilitating an evaluation both of the trade hypothesis itself and of the various critiques that have been made.
cb/ Mercer

Lloyd Mercer received his Ph. D. from the University of Washington in 1967 for his thesis: "The Central Pacific System: An Estimate of Social and Private Rates of Return for a Land-Grant Aided Railroad System." He is best known for his work on evaluation of the land grants to the major transcontinental railroads. In this work Mercer pioneered the application of the New Economic History to estimation of the economic return from the policy of promoting railroad construction through land grants.

Mercer has been a member of the faculty in economics at the University of California, Santa Barbara since leaving Seattle. He is now a Professor of Economics and has served several terms as Chair of his department. His current work in economic history deals with the railroad reorganizations of 1890–1910 and the issues of productivity growth, capital utilization, and prices in the 1920s and 1930s.

Chapter 5

Staples and Eighteenth-Century Canadian Development: The Case of Newfoundland

James F. Shepherd

There are few exceptions to the essential initiating role of a successful export sector in the early stages of accelerated growth of market economies. The reason is that the domestic market has been small and scattered. These economies have been predominantly rural, with a high degree of individual self-sufficiency. Reflecting this aspect of the market, specialization and division of labor have been limited and rudimentary. An expanding external market has provided the means for an increase in the size of the domestic market, growth in money income, and the spread of specialization and division of labor

—Douglass C. North[1]

In his earlier work, Douglass North has drawn attention to the important role exports played in the economic development of the United States during its early national period. Exports and overseas trade may have been of even greater significance during the preceding American colonial period. Estimates from recent research on the eighteenth-century overseas and coastal trade of the British North American colonies suggest that various colonies had high exports relative to their population and to total output.[2] These same colonies later turned out to

1. *The Economic Growth of the United States, 1790–1860* (Englewood Cliffs, N.J.: Prentice-Hall, 1961), p. 2.

2. James F. Shepherd and Gary M. Walton, *Shipping, Maritime Trade, and the Economic*

EXPLORATIONS IN THE NEW ECONOMIC HISTORY

ISBN 0-12-580080-0

be those Canadian provinces and American states that came to have relatively low per capita incomes. In fact, it appears that there was roughly an inverse correlation between eighteenth-century exports and later "success."

Newfoundland, for which exports around 1770 were in the probable range of 12–15 pounds sterling, per capita, is the outstanding example, followed by South Carolina, for which per capita exports ranged from 3½ to 4 pounds sterling, as the best example in the present-day United States. Although considerably less than Newfoundland's, South Carolina's per capita exports ranked second to Newfoundland's among the North American continental colonies. Chiefly rice and indigo destined for West Indian, southern European, and British markets, the exports from South Carolina in great part had been produced by the labor of a large slave population. Since South Carolina appears to have been relatively self-sufficient in the production of foodstuffs (which would have been the main part of the subsistence income furnished to the slave labor force), it is a reasonable view that the colony's export earnings accrued only to the free population. On that basis, exports per free resident were considerably higher—more than 9 pounds sterling. To put these earnings into some perspective, it should be recalled that various guesses about colonial per capita output at this time center around 11–13 pounds sterling.[3] By this standard, per capita exports from both areas loom high indeed. The British West Indies represent another colonial region that conformed to the pattern of a high level of exports relative to total output, followed by slow growth in later years. Per capita exports for this area appear to have been in the range of 4–6 pounds sterling during the eighteenth century.

The question, of course, is whether this pattern was coincidental. It may well have been. Many other arguments have been advanced about the slower growth of these areas, especially for the American South and the West Indies. Nevertheless, this question of whether the seeds of slower growth were sown in earlier years by concentration in export production deserves exploration. Such a possibility is especially interesting because it seems to run counter to some of the statements and inferences about export-led growth in the literature of Canadian and United States economic history. The observation is more akin with the view sometimes expressed in the development literature that overconcentration in production for export tends to retard growth.

It is, of course, one thing to state the question, and quite another to

---

Development of Colonial North America (London: Cambridge University Press, 1972), pp. 44–48.

3. Ibid., pp. 27–31.

answer it. A complete answer would require examination of as many connections as possible between foreign trade and growth. A preliminary task would be to examine evidence on trade to see whether or not this inverse correlation between earlier trade and later growth does in fact exist. The question could then be asked: Was the growth of exports from these regions an exogenous disturbance (arising, for example, from an increase in foreign demand or from some domestic occurrence such as the discovery of a natural resource) rather than a result of an expansion of domestic capacity?[4] Following this, one could examine as many other links between trade and growth (both extensive and intensive) as would be possible with existing data.[5] Those data, though perhaps not wholly adequate, should undergird a preliminary comparison of levels of exports relative to population.

The purpose of this essay, then, is to begin such a project with the case of Newfoundland. Data on exports and population are compiled for Newfoundland and, for purposes of comparison, for those neighboring colonies which later became the Canadian provinces and for still others which had important staple exports. Newfoundland in its earlier history was characterized by very high exports relative to its population. If recent estimates of early per capita output are anywhere near the mark, the standard of living in the late eighteenth century would have been as high there as in any of the British North American colonies or in the newly formed United States (though several important qualifications are made to this statement in the following sections). Today, Newfoundland is the poorest province in Canada. Per capita income in recent years has been little more than half the national average; the province has had the highest rates of unemployment, and outmigration has been substantial. Somewhere along the line something happened—Newfoundland did not keep up.

To begin to examine when, and why, this happened, the following three sections respectively (*a*) survey the eighteenth-century history of Newfoundland's population and the bearing of its export trade on the area's economic development; (*b*) compare the economy of Newfoundland with that of other colonies profiting from staple exports; and (*c*) study the implications for Newfoundland's development of a conclusion reached in the second section. This conclusion, which seems somehow to have escaped attention in the mainstream of the literature, has to do

4. Richard E. Caves, "Export-Led Growth and the New Economic History," in Jagdish N. Bhagwati *et al.*, eds., *Trade, Balance of Payments, and Growth* (Amsterdam: North-Holland, 1971), pp. 425–427.

5. Ibid., pp. 427–438.

with the respective effects of the great early Canadian staples of fur and fish: Whereas in Quebec the originally vital fur trade dwindled in the course of the century to a relatively small part of the total output, in Newfoundland the cod fishery continued to form a dominant part of the total economic activity of the resident British population.

POPULATION, EXPORTS, AND ECONOMIC WELFARE

In assessing the role of exports in any economy, one would, of course, like to know their relative importance. The obvious comparison is that of exports to total output. Lacking any solidly based estimates of output for Newfoundland in the eighteenth and nineteenth centuries, we must as a second-best measure, compare export values to population. Early estimates of population for those British North American colonies which later became parts of Canada are discussed in the *Seventh Census of Canada.*[6] On the basis of this information for the seventeenth and eighteenth centuries, and from other sources for the nineteenth and twentieth centuries, estimates of Newfoundland's resident population are presented in Table 5.1.

Although the first permanent English settlement was established in Newfoundland in 1610, the resident population grew slowly through the rest of the century. Because West Country fishing interests in England viewed Newfoundland's activities as competitive, English gov-

6. Canada, Dominion Bureau of Statistics, *Seventh Census of Canada, 1931* (Ottawa, 1936), I: 133–153, "Chronological Summary of Population Growth in Canada, with Sources of Information, 1605–1931." According to statements about early Canadian population in this source, residents of European nativity or descent were fewer than 1000 in all of Quebec, Nova Scotia, and Newfoundland at the middle of the seventeenth century. By 1700 this number had risen to perhaps 20,000.

Quebec was the most populous at this date with about 15,000 persons. Over the century, Quebec's population increased to about 30,000 by 1725, to 50,000 around 1750, and to 75,000–80,000 around the time of the Conquest. After the Seven Years' War it declined to about 70,000 in 1765 but then began to increase again and was around 90,000 in 1775.

Newfoundland's British resident population grew from about 3500 at the beginning of the eighteenth century to 6000 by 1740, 13,000 by 1760, and 15,000 by 1765. After that time, it apparently began to decline slightly; by 1770 it was said to be about 11,500, by 1785 about 10,000. Newfoundland's smaller French resident population was in addition to these figures.

Nova Scotia's population is somewhat more difficult to approximate because of its French settlers; the number of Acadians is estimated at several thousand in 1700, increasing to 13,000 by the middle of the century at which time the British settlers consisted of perhaps 2500–3000 persons. An increasing British population was offset by the departure of some Acadians during and after the War; the British and French groups together totaled perhaps 20,000 to 25,000 in the late 1760s and early 1770s.

TABLE 5.1
Estimates of Newfoundland Resident Population, 1675–1951

Year	Population
1675	2,225
1700	3,500
1740	6,000
1760	13,000
1765	15,000
1770	11,500
1785	10,000
1789	18,000
1804	20,380
1806	26,505
1813	32,749
1816	52,672
1823	52,157
1825	55,719
1827	59,571
1828	60,088
1832	59,280
1836	73,705–75,094
1845	96,606–98,703
1857[a]	124,288
1869[a]	146,536
1874[a]	161,374
1884[a]	197,589
1891[a]	202,040
1911[a]	242,600
1945[a]	321,000
1951[a]	361,416

Sources: Canada, Dominion Bureau of Statistics, *Seventh Census of Canada, 1931* (Ottawa, 1936), I: pp. 133–153, "Chronological Summary of Population Growth in Canada, with Sources of Information, 1605–1931"; Richard E. Caves and Richard H. Holton, *The Canadian Economy; Prospect and Retrospect* (Cambridge, Mass.: Harvard University Press, 1959), p. 161; D. W. Prowse, *A History of Newfoundland from the English, Colonial, and Foreign Records* (London: Macmillan and Co., 1895), p. 702; United States, Congress, Senate, *Report on the Trade and Commerce of the British North American Colonies with the United States and Other Countries, 1829–1850,* Senate Ex. Doc. No. 23, 31st Cong., 2d Sess., 1851 (Washington, D.C.: Printers to the Senate, 1851), p. 775.

[a]Includes Labrador.

ernmental policies discouraged such growth. Perhaps only the threat of French encroachment restrained the English government from deporting the settlers around 1675. Nevertheless, after the first quarter of the eighteenth century Newfoundland's resident population increased rapidly until the 1760s and began to rise as a proportion of the total population, which was at its peak during the summers. Thus we may presume that an increasing share of output was produced by the resident population, and that economic activity was more and more dominated by it. All contemporary accounts support this assertion.[7] The American Revolution halted this growth, and the resident population may even have fallen somewhat as fishermen volunteered or were impressed into the navy. At this time natural increase could not have been a large source of population increase: Women made up only 10% of the population in the 1760s and 1770s, as against 60–70% adult male.[8] The migratory fishery fell off substantially during the war, so that the relative importance of the resident population in overall economic activity increased sharply, though temporarily. After 1783, rapid growth in both the sedentary and the migratory fisheries is evidenced by the rapid increase of the resident population as shown in Table 5.1. With the beginning of the Napoleonic wars in 1793, the migratory fishery once again fell off, and by the end of the century nearly 90% of the total summer population had become resident.[9] "By the first decade of the nineteenth century, too, the commercial production of the island was coming very nearly exclusively from the year-round inhabitants."[10]

The prosperity during the Napoleonic wars brought increased migration, and there was rapid growth of the population from the mid-1780s to 1815. In 1815 alone, some 7000 immigrants were said to have come from Ireland.[11] When depression followed the end of the war, the population stagnated until Irish immigration began to increase again in the 1820s and early 1830s.[12] From that time through the remainder of the nineteenth century and into the twentieth, Newfoundland's population grew rapidly, though at rates that began to decline in the second half of the nineteenth century.

Because American customs records purportedly comprise the only

7. See C. Grant Head, *Eighteenth Century Newfoundland: A Geographer's Perspective* (Toronto: McClelland and Stewart, 1976), Chapters 7–11.

8. Ibid., p. 145.

9. Ibid., p. 82.

10. Ibid., p. 232.

11. Ibid., p. 237.

12. St. John Chadwick, *Newfoundland: Island into Province* (London: Cambridge University Press, 1967) pp. 14–15.

complete source for the legal commodity trade of the British North American colonies for any years in the eighteenth century,[13] this is the logical starting place for assembling the evidence on exports. These records list the quantities of all commodities legally exported from and imported into the British North American colonies for the period January 5, 1768–January 5, 1773; the figures are given by port district. Quantities of exports and imports in the coastal trade are also listed. Exceptions are that colonial-owned ships sold abroad were not recorded, and imports from Great Britain and Ireland were recorded for only 3 years, 1769–1771. Other items such as the number and tonnage of ships entering and clearing these colonial port districts and the duties collected on dutiable imports, were also recorded; but no values were given for any commodities except entries called "sundries," which were not of significant magnitudes.

For purposes of comparison, Table 5.2 shows exports from those colonies which later became part of the Canadian nation. Prince Edward Island (listed as the Island of St. Johns) was given separately in the records for 1771 and 1772, but because its trade was relatively small, its exports have been included with those of Nova Scotia in Table 5.2. Using the quantities from this source, and those prices which could be obtained from price histories or from other sources, values were calculated for those commodities for which price data were available.[14] Annual average quantities and estimated values of commodity exports (principally on the basis of Boston and Philadelphia prices) are given in Table 5.2.

A number of important qualifications must be made concerning the estimates of values in Table 5.2. Among the more important are that exports of furs were not valued because of the lack of accurate price data and the failure of the records to distinguish between the more expensive *castor gras* and the cheaper *castor sec*.[15] A number of other exports, of less importance than furs, could similarly not be valued due to lack of price

13. Great Britain, Public Record Office, *Customs 16/1*, the American Inspector-General's Ledger. For a discussion of the nature and validity of these records, see James F. Shepherd, "Commodity Exports from the British North American Colonies to Overseas Areas, 1768–1772: Magnitudes and Patterns of Trade," *Explorations in Economic History* 8 (1970), pp. 5–76.

14. For the details of these calculations, and the sources of the prices used, see Shepherd, "Commodity Exports."

15. The American customs records did not distinguish between different kinds of furs for 1768. They stated 268,224 furs (of all types) were exported to Great Britain in this year. For the years 1769–1772, exports of beaver skins to Great Britain averaged 98,261 (in number) and an additional 2830 lbs. (in weight).

TABLE 5.2
Annual Average Quantities and Estimated Values of Selected Exports from Newfoundland, Quebec, and Nova Scotia, 1768–1772 (Values in Pounds Sterling)[a]

	Destination									
	Great Britain		Ireland		So. Europe		West Indies		Total	
Commodity (unit)	Quantity	Value	Quantity	Value	Quantity	Value	Quantity	Value	Quantity	Value
				Newfoundland[b]						
Dried fish (quin.)	12,680	6,323	2,438	1,220	208,727	104,819	12,311	6,157	236,156	118,519
Flaxseed (bu.)			908	150					908	150
Oil, train (tons)	710	8,517	59	707	209	2,513	5	64	983	11,801
Wood products										
Pine boards (1000 ft.)	89	134	4	5			9	15	102	154
Staves & headings (thousands)	35	97	19	53	2	5	2	6	58	161
Total, Newfoundland		15,071		2,135		107,337		6,242		130,785
				Quebec						
Bread and flour (tons)					10	123	41	454	51	577
Deerskins (1000 lbs.)	140	13,793							140	13,793
Dried fish (quin.)					9,525	4,754	1,980	983	11,505	5,737
Oil, train (tons)	285	3,423			11	133	3	40	299	3,596
Pig iron (tons)	77	383							77	383
Potash (tons)	37	936							37	936
Wheat (bu.)	1,213	294	10,697	2,421	55,614	12,881	240	54	67,764	15,650

Wood products									
Pine boards (1000 ft.)	42	63		37	57	43	68	122	188
Staves & headings (thousands)	192	557		3	8	1	2	196	567
Total, Quebec		19,449	2,421		17,956		1,601		41,427
Nova Scotia[c]									
Dried Fish (quin.)	401	201		12,096	6,048	4,523	2,260	17,020	8,509
Horses (number)						23	234	23	234
Oil, train (tons)	20	243		4	47	3	31	27	321
Wood products									
Pine boards (1000 ft.)	77	119		1	1	125	190	203	310
Staves & headings (thousands)	4	12		1	4	1	3	6	19
Total, Nova Scotia		575			6,100		2,718		9,393
Total, all colonies		35,095	4,556		131,393		10,561		181,605

Source: James F. Shepherd, "Commodity Exports from the British North American Colonies to Overseas Areas, 1768–1772: Magnitudes and Patterns of Trade," *Explorations in Economic History* 8 (1970), pp. 5–76. The original source of the quantity data is the American Inspector-General's Ledgers (London, Public Record Office, *Customs 16/1*).

[a]Commodities were selected for this table on the basis of the availability of price data and those exports for which the total estimated value of the commodity was over 100 pounds sterling. Values were computed using principally Boston and Philadelphia prices (see the source for details). Furs were not valued because of the lack of price data and information about quality.

[b]St. Johns only.

[c]Nova Scotia includes Prince Edward Island for 1771 and 1772, which was listed separately in the American Inspector-General's Ledgers for these 2 years. The exports from Nova Scotia may have been exports from Halifax only (see text).

data. Moreover, the records themselves indicate less than complete coverage for Newfoundland and Nova Scotia.[16] Smuggling may have contributed to an understatement of trade values in Table 5.2[17] as may also the fact that Boston prices were used in evaluating exports of dried cod.[18]

Newfoundland presents a further unique question: how to deal with

16. The records state that the data for Newfoundland for some years were for exports from St. Johns only; the rest of Newfoundland apparently was not included. There is also the likelihood that the exports of Nova Scotia as given in Table 5.2 may have only been from Halifax. This is not specifically stated in the records, but exports for some years were listed as being from Halifax, and for other years as being from Nova Scotia.

The importance of this omission of the remainder of Newfoundland's exports is indicated by some figures cited by Harold A. Innis, *The Cod Fisheries: The History of an International Economy* (Toronto: Ryerson Press, 1940), p. 195. Imports into Newfoundland from New England were said to have been 102,304 pounds sterling, but only 38,035 pounds sterling of these imports (37%) were destined for St. Johns. The accuracy of these figures is questionable, but they do point out that the trade of St. Johns was only a part of the whole of Newfoundland's external trade. The naval officers' returns from Newfoundland, which will be examined in what follows, indicated considerably more exports for all of Newfoundland than Table 5.2 lists for St. Johns.

17. Except for the enumerated goods, and the prohibition of direct trade with northern Europe (above Cape Finisterre), there were no restrictions on exports. The important market for cod was southern Europe, as is indicated by Tables 5.2 and 5.4. Beaver skins and other furs were enumerated goods, and, after the Conquest, Quebec's furs could be exported legally only to Great Britain. That they in fact did go there seems likely because before the Seven Years' War the most important destination of the contraband trade in French furs was the English colonies. See Harold A. Innis, *The Fur Trade in Canada*, revised ed. (Toronto: Toronto University Press, 1956), especially pp. 77–81; and Alice J. E. Lunn, "Economic Development in French Canada, 1740–1760" (unpublished M.A. thesis, McGill University, 1934), pp. 166–170.

Others have said that smuggling was not important in the fur trade, especially in the English trade. See Murray G. Lawson, *Fur: A Study in English Mercantilism, 1700–1775* (Toronto: University of Toronto Press, 1943), p. 77. Charles M. Andrews states with regard to the English trade: "Very little illicit trade in furs is recorded." See his *Colonial Period of American History* (New Haven: Yale University Press, 1938), 4: 105. For a general discussion of the extent of colonial smuggling, see Lawrence A. Harper, *The English Navigation Laws* (New York: Columbia University Press, 1939), pp. 256–271.

18. Much of the fish exported from Boston was destined for the West Indies, and it was said to be of lower quality than the fish exported from Newfoundland to southern Europe. It is not surprising, then, to find evidence that Boston prices averaged only about 10s. sterling per quintal compared with a range of 8s. 6d. to 16s. for Newfoundland prices, the midpoint of this range being about 12s. per quintal. The Boston prices are taken from Arthur H. Cole, *Wholesale Commodity Prices in the United States, 1700–1861: Statistical Supplement* (Cambridge, Mass.: Harvard University Press, 1938). The Newfoundland prices are cited in D. W. Prowse, *A History of Newfoundland* (London: Macmillan, 1895), p. 694. Prowse's source was apparently Great Britain, Parliament, *Parliamentary Papers* (House of Commons), 1731–1800, Vol. 35 (*Accounts and Papers*, no. 761), "State of the Newfoundland Fishery in Various Years from 1699 to 1791; Taken from the Returns of Admirals Who Commanded That Station." If average Newfoundland prices were around 12s. sterling per

the floating population of that colony. Recorded exports of codfish, for example, surely represent the catch not only of the British year-round inhabitants, but of the West Country fishing boats and the byeboatkeepers as well.[19] If we wish to compare the estimates of the resident population in Table 5.1 to exports, then the exports should represent those produced by the permanent inhabitants. Finally, if we are to rely upon export data to indicate the extent of certain types of economic activities, and the respective importance of those activities to the various colonies, then exports to the other continental colonies in the coastal trade should be considered as well as the exports to overseas areas. Was the coastal trade a significant outlet for Newfoundland goods? On the basis of evidence from American customs records regarding the composition and magnitudes of the coastal trade, it would appear that the answer to this question is negative: Markets in other colonies were of small consequence for Newfoundland.[20]

---

quintal, then Newfoundland exports for this reason are understated by about 20% in the estimated values shown in Table 5.2.

19. The American customs records themselves are not clear about this point, but probably exports of codfish did represent the catch of all three groups if for no other reason than the cod was taken ashore and dried, and then packed and exported. Exports of the French fishery were not included; for those statistics see Prowse, *History of Newfoundland*, p. 696.

20. The general picture of the coastal trade of Newfoundland was one of sizable imports and few exports (relative to the overseas trade). See James F. Shepherd and Samuel H. Williamson, "The Coastal Trade of the British North American Colonies, 1768–1772," *Journal of Economic History* 32 (1972), p. 808. Judging from evidence in the American customs records, the values of trade between Newfoundland and New England cited by Innis (see Note 16) are far too large. Newfoundland was importing foodstuffs, wood products, and West Indian goods from New England but exporting little to these or other continental colonies. According to Innis, the deficit in Newfoundland's trade with New England was paid principally by bills of exchange on England (*The Cod Fisheries*, p. 195, where Innis is quoting Prowse, *History of Newfoundland*). The value of coastal exports averaged 2400 pounds sterling annually from St. Johns for 1768–1772 (compared with £6700 from Quebec, £14,000 from Nova Scotia, and £3600 from Prince Edward Island—the latter for 1771–1772; see Shepherd and Williamson, "The Coastal Trade," p. 808).

It would appear that the Nova Scotian coastal trade was more evenly balanced and that exports were substantially larger than for either Newfoundland or Quebec. One of the more important commodities in the coastal trade, as in the overseas trade, was dried codfish. Annual average exports for the period 1768–1772 (1771–1772 for Prince Edward Island) were given as

Newfoundland (St. Johns only)	6,999 quintals
Quebec	6,451 quintals
Nova Scotia	25,505 quintals
Prince Edward Island	6,413 quintals

One might note that the figure for exports of dried codfish from Nova Scotia is very close to that given by Innis (*The Cod Fisheries*, p. 189). Not only did Nova Scotia export more codfish than Newfoundland to the other continental colonies, but it exported more beaver

After viewing the evidence from the American customs records, what can we conclude, at least for this limited 5-year period? The most striking point to emerge from the evidence and discussion is the overwhelming preponderance of cod destined for southern European markets. In addition, most of the qualifications concerning Newfoundland's cod exports would suggest that the estimated values in Table 5.2 *understate* the true values.

Fortunately, there are several other sources to which one may turn for statistical evidence on the eighteenth-century export trade of Newfoundland. Two reports published in Great Britain's *Parliamentary Papers* provide much of our statistical evidence for the British fishery in Newfoundland waters in the eighteenth century.[21] These reports, based upon the returns of Newfoundland naval officers, are summarized in Tables 5.3 and 5.4. Once more, these data are open to serious question, since they rely on the validity of returns prepared by those officers over the century. Few comparisons can be made with other records.[22] Because the cod trade was unrestricted, we would expect that smuggling would have been of little consequence. Thus, the expectation is that this evidence gives us a reasonable approximation of cod exports. Values in Table 5.3 were estimated using the price data usually given in the source as a range for each of the years included in Table 5.3. The midpoint of the range was taken as an average price for the year, and these midpoints were then averaged for each of the periods shown in the table. The resulting simple average was used to value the annual average quantities exported. These were presumably Newfoundland prices, thus they were f.o.b. and the resultant values would not reflect shipping and

---

skins in the coastal trade than Quebec (6019 lbs. compared with 2046 lbs.), more pickled fish (an annual average of 5698 barrels as opposed to negligible amounts from the other colonies), and far more wood products than the others. The figures for beaver skins are an average of the 4 years, 1769–1772; they were not distinguished from other furs in the records for 1768 (see Note 15). The value of coastal exports cited for Quebec did not include furs (which also were excluded in the overseas trade of Quebec presented in Table 5.2). The small quantities recorded would not have been of significant value, however.

21. Great Britain, Parliament, *Parliamentary Papers* (House of Commons), 1731–1800, Vol. 35 (*Accounts and Papers*, no. 760, "An Account of the Shipping and Trade of Newfoundland, 1787–1791"); and "State of the Newfoundland Fishery in Various Years . . . ," cited in Note 18.

22. One comparison might be to rank the figures of codfish exports to Great Britain and Ireland from the Naval Office lists (as given in Table 5.4) against the British and Irish customs statistics of imports (Great Britain, Public Record Office, *Customs 15* [Ireland] and *Customs 17* [Great Britain]). Another possible comparison would be with the American customs records (*Customs 16/1*); but since, as noted earlier, these records most likely pertain only to St. Johns, this check would be of little value.

TABLE 5.3
Annual Average Quantities of Dried Codfish Produced, and Quantities and Estimated Values of Codfish Exported, by the British Fishery in Newfoundland, for Various Years, 1699–1791

	Production (quintals)			Exports	
Period	Total[a]	By inhabitants	By all others[b]	Quantity (quin.)	Value[c] (£ sterling)
1699–1701	216,320	136,500	79,820	154,370	—
1714–1716	97,730	38,120	59,577	102,363	—
1749–1751	432,318	222,062	—	422,116	266,000
1764–1774	626,276	295,141	—	514,296	308,000
1784–1791	641,915	300,434	—	643,321	413,000

Source: Great Britain, Parliament, *Parliamentary Papers* (House of Commons), 1731–1800, Vol. 35 (*Accounts and Papers,* no. 761), "State of the Newfoundland Fishery in Various Years from 1699 to 1791; Taken from the Returns of Admirals Who Commanded That Station."

[a]The discrepancy between total and components for 1714–1716 was in the source. Other small discrepancies existed between the averages given in the source and the figures given for the individual years. Discrepancies also exist between the source and D. W. Prowse, *A History of Newfoundland* (London: Macmillan, 1895), pp. 694–696.

[b]Includes codfish caught by British fishing ships, byeboatmen, and ships from other British colonies. These data were not given separately by the source for the last three periods.

[c]Values were estimated using average prices given in the source.

TABLE 5.4
Quantities of Dried Codfish Exported from the British Fishery in Newfoundland, by Destination, 1787–1791 (Quintals)

		Destination			
Year[a]	Total	Great Britain and Ireland[b]	Southern Europe[c]	West Indies	Other British North American colonies[d]
1787	692,554	15,997	640,725	35,432	400
1788	764,069	22,564	717,808	23,582	115
1789	894,587	24,798	807,927	61,862	—
1790	738,976	25,394	661,441	51,287	854
1791	751,296	29,717	664,402	57,177	—

Source: Great Britain, Parliament, *Parliamentary Papers* (House of Commons), 1731–1800, Vol. 35 (*Accounts and Papers,* no. 760), "An Account of Shipping and Trade Outwards at Newfoundland; Taken from the Naval Officer's Returns, for the Years, 1787 . . . 1791."

[a]October 1 of preceding year to October 1 of stated year.

[b]Includes the Channel Islands.

[c]Spain, Portugal, Italy, and Madeira.

[d]Quebec, Nova Scotia, and New Brunswick. No exports went to the United States.

other costs of distribution. Over the eighteenth century southern Europe remained the major market for Newfoundland cod. As can be seen in Table 5.4, exports to all other areas were relatively small.

The quantities and estimated values in Table 5.3 strongly suggest that the values of cod exports were significantly greater than those shown in Table 5.2. The production of dried cod, and the exports of the British fishery from Newfoundland, grew gradually over the eighteenth century. Although lack of price data in the source precludes an estimation of values for the earlier years, the quantities exported support the view that even at the beginning of the eighteenth century, dried codfish was a very valuable export.

Table 5.5 shows per capita export values for Newfoundland based on the resident population shown in Table 5.1 and calculated for the eighteenth century from the export values shown in Table 5.3 and for the nineteenth century from Prowse. The export values for the second half of the eighteenth century are given for the entire British fishery, and that part of those exports produced by residents has been estimated (based upon the reported production of dried cod by inhabitants to total production in the British fishery). After 1793, the overwhelming bulk of exports was produced by the resident population. Hence, in regard to Table 5.5 we safely may presume that exports were produced almost wholly by residents after 1800, and that the previous distinction between residents and migratory fishermen is now unnecessary. Exports per capita thus reflect the contribution of the resident population.

The question remains, however: How important were exports to total economic activity, and how did they change in the course of Newfoundland's development? The simple comparison in Table 5.5 gives some idea of this. Per capita exports appear to be very high for the eighteenth century, if the earlier suggested estimates of 11–13 pounds sterling as the per capita output of other North American colonies are anywhere near the mark. However, once again, several qualifications need be noted—in this case, before making any conclusions about economic welfare. One is that prices of foodstuffs were almost surely higher in Newfoundland than in the other colonies. In all likelihood, Newfoundland imported a high proportion of its food requirements, originally from England and Ireland, but increasingly, during the eighteenth century, from the American colonies. After the Revolution, Quebec became a major supplier. With food representing a large proportion of a household's spending, the high prices of imports would almost surely have resulted in a much higher cost of living in Newfoundland. The monetary value of per capita exports in Table 5.5, therefore, may overstate the real purchasing power if compared with the other colonies. Another point to be

TABLE 5.5
Annual Average Values of Exports, and Per Capita Exports, from Newfoundland, for Various Years, 1749–1893 (Exports in Thousands of Pounds Sterling, Per Capita Exports in Pounds Sterling)

	Exports[a]			
Period	British fishery		Residents[b]	Exports per capita[c]
1749–1751	266		137	14.4
1764–1774	308		145	12.6
1784–1791	413		193	13.8
1805		590		25.2
1810		763		25.4
1815		1184		25.7
1820		967		18.5
1822–1823, 1826		708		13.1
1835–1840		873		11.2
1841, 1843–1850		888		9.1
1851–1860		1220		10.1
1861–1870		1145		8.2
1871–1880		1310		7.9
1881–1890		1282		6.5
1891–1893		1345		6.6

Sources: D. W. Prowse, *A History of Newfoundland from the English, Colonial, and Foreign Records* (London: Macmillan and Co., 1895), pp. 692–693, for nineteenth-century exports. Export values for the eighteenth century are developed in Table 5.3.

[a]Of the years 1805, 1810, 1815, and 1820, one source (Prowse) states that "the returns do not furnish the *value* of the goods imported or exported, only the quantities of each article; so that the sterling amount for either the imports or exports is only an approximation, being based upon the prices paid and given for the various articles at the present time."

[b]These figures are calculated from total exports using the proportion of dried cod produced by the inhabitants to total output of dried cod.

[c]Exports per capita were computed from the population given in Table 5.1, and interpolating between the figures given for the two closest years.

considered is the participation rate. In the modern world, other things equal, higher per capita incomes result from higher participation rates. Since 60–70% of Newfoundland's population was comprised of adult males, the participation rate must have been high indeed. It should be noted, nonetheless, that all the other colonies were heavily agricultural, with wives and children also participating in productive activities. However, one might suppose that adult males were generally more productive than women and children; if they were, then the difference in Newfoundland's participation rates would have mattered.

If exports were a major proportion of total output, the estimates suggest that economic activity in Newfoundland was nearly completely specialized in the cod fishery and related types of economic activities. The composition of exports gives some clue to the relative importance of these different economic activities. For the first decade of the nineteenth century when the resident fishery was flourishing, the composition of exports was roughly:

dried cod (from the inshore fishery)	70%
offshore cod fishery	12%
seal oil and skins	8%
cod-liver oil	7%
salmon	1%
furs and other	<1%[23]

The seal "fishery" and exports of river-run salmon began early in the eighteenth century, and one hundred years later these activities were of some importance. However, the cod fishery obviously dominated production for export with a total close to 90%, if the figures presented here are accurate.

Did it similarly dominate overall activity? Unfortunately, we have no good statistical evidence relating to other economic activities. Agricultural production would be the most important sector. However, the fact noted earlier—that Newfoundland probably imported a high proportion of its food requirements—suggests that agriculture was of little consequence in the colony. For 1775 it has been said that "there was no agriculture on the island beyond small vegetable gardens, so that the settlers were completely dependent on imports."[24] This may be a slight exaggeration, but probably not much of one. During the American Revolution food imports were sharply reduced, and the island found itself under great stress. At such times local agriculture was encouraged, but the degree of progress is uncertain. The potato had been introduced sometime around the mid-eighteenth century, and this, with other vegetables, was the major crop. Some success is indicated by Governor Edwards's remark in 1779 that "the Ground which is cultivated produces vast quantities of (and very fine) Potatoes and other Vegitables [*sic*]."[25] The area of cultivated land during the War rose from 1700 acres to 6000, but much of the increase was due to the military, who attempted to produce some of their own food requirements while stationed at Newfoundland.[26]

23. Head, *Eighteenth Century Newfoundland,* p. 233.

24. W. T. Easterbrook and Hugh G. J. Aitken, *Canadian Economic History* (Toronto: Macmillan Company of Canada, 1956), p. 139.

25. Quoted from Head, *Eighteenth Century Newfoundland,* p. 199.

26. Ibid.

Reports say that by 1779 food was so scarce in Conception Bay that it could not be obtained at any price, and the people were reduced to eating the fish they caught.[27] Settlement then, as now, remained tied to the coast, and no one pushed inland to cultivate the land that did have agricultural potential. The consensus is stated by Head, speaking of the end of the eighteenth century: "Despite an increasing use of the soil in Newfoundland, the island remained strongly tied to outside sources of supply for most of her major foodstuffs. Fish, some of the potato needs, and salad greens were, essentially, the few home-grown goods."[28]

Unique among the colonies, then, Newfoundland specialized its economy almost completely around the fishery. Lacking an agricultural base, subsistence production must have been small. Most production was for export markets, making Newfoundland's economy perhaps the most commercialized of all the British colonies.

If the export figures in Table 5.5 are correct, the years of the Napoleonic wars were a period of prosperity. Chadwick says that it was a golden period: The resident fishery was dominant; and both the import–export and the domestic trade were in the hands of local merchants.[29] Prices of cod were high, and these were years of generally good yields. Other accounts have not been so glowing, however. Though describing the period as one of prosperity, A. H. McLintock notes the "appalling poverty and misery which existed almost unrecognized in the island's scattered settlements."[30] W. S. MacNutt stresses the good times, but notes "poverty flouished amid great riches."[31] Head states that "if there was a prosperity at all, it was one that in no real terms affected the bulk of the inhabitants."[32] The answer to this seeming contradiction probably lies in the movement of both export and import prices. If we had an acceptable index with which to deflate the export values in Table 5.5 for the years through 1815, real exports and per capita exports would presumably look a good deal different from those shown. For example, normal prices for dried cod, which before the American Revolution had been 12s. sterling per quintal, were in some years after

27. Ibid., p. 198.

28. Ibid., p. 233.

29. Chadwick, *Newfoundland,* p. 14.

30. *The Establishment of Constitutional Government in Newfoundland, 1783 1832* (London: Longmans Green, 1941), p. 121; quoted from Head, *Eighteenth Century Newfoundland,* p. 220.

31. *The Atlantic Provinces: The Emergence of Colonial Society, 1712–1857* (Toronto: McClelland and Stewart, 1965), p. 141; quoted from Head, *Eighteenth Century Newfoundland,* p. 220.

32. Head, *Eighteenth Century Newfoundland,* p. 220.

1793 more than double that figure.[33] On the other hand, the prices of foodstuffs generally doubled between the 1760s and the years of the Napoleonic wars, probably due in part to the prohibition of American shipping from Newfoundland after 1783 and to the scarcity of British shipping after 1793. Again, the higher cost of living almost certainly undercut the higher money incomes of Newfoundlanders during these years.

After 1815 the trend in per capita exports was downward through the remainder of the century. Given the qualification that export values in Table 5.5 should be deflated, it would appear that the period of the Napoleonic wars was the high point for the Newfoundland fishery. What followed was near stagnation, or even decline, if exports are viewed relative to population. Over the nineteenth century few alternative sources of employment appeared for Newfoundlanders: In 1911, about 84% of the labor force was still employed in fishing and hunting.[34] As late as the 1870s, 97% of exports had been fishery and marine products.[35] This dropped by the end of the century to 87%, as exports of iron ore from Bell Island began to be of some importance, and by 1915 to 74% following the introduction of pulp and paper production in 1909. Not until the twentieth century, then, did Newfoundland's economy begin to diversify. Through the nineteenth century, it had remained tied to exports from the fishery, which almost certainly constituted a large part of total output.

COD AND THE OTHER STAPLES: A COMPARATIVE VIEW

The most striking feature of the estimates of exports of cod and cod fishery products derived in the preceding section is their large magnitudes relative to Newfoundland's population. None of this is surprising: That cod was the first great staple is a well-acknowledged part of Canadian and American economic history, thanks to Innis. But how did cod compare with that other great Canadian staple—fur—and with other important staple exports from British American colonies?

The greatest difficulty in answering this question pertains to exports of furs. Exports from Quebec for 1768–1772 were presented in Table 5.2. Though quantities of furs were listed in the American customs records, their values are not estimated in the table because of the difficulties

33. This and the following references to prices are from ibid., pp. 218–219.

34. Richard E. Caves and Richard H. Holton, *The Canadian Economy: Prospect and Retrospect* (Cambridge, Mass.: Harvard University Press, 1959), p. 162.

35. This and the following percentages are from ibid., p. 156.

mentioned earlier. All statistical evidence on export of furs tends to be more disjointed, and less satisfactory, than for cod or some of the other staple commodities such as sugar, tobacco, and rice. This is partly due to the fact that for more than half the century the major fur-producing colony was French rather than English. Not only is the evidence thus divided between two languages and two national series of records, but furthermore a case might be made that during the eighteenth century the British government compiled more comprehensive statistical records on colonial trade than did the French government. Moreover, furs varied widely in kind and quality, making an evaluation highly difficult.

Despite such problems much fragmentary evidence has survived, and estimates of fur exports have been constructed by various scholars. Enough of this evidence exists to get at least the rough notion of the magnitudes of the trade as presented in Tables 5.6, 5.7, and 5.8. Because our concern is with the long-term trends in these exports over the

TABLE 5.6
Annual Average Quantities of Beaver Skins Exported from Quebec for Various Years during the Eighteenth Century[a] (in Pounds Weight)

	(1)		(2)
1706–1714	70,000	1701	75,993
1715, 1717	120,945	1712, 1717	109,886
1721–1722, 1725–1730	116,480	1722–1723, 1725–1726, 1728–1730	123,230
1732–1740	162,905	1732–1740	149,228
1742–1748	154,571	1742–1748	165,394
		1754–1755	140,725
			(3)
		1769–1772	134,000[b]
			(4)
		1793–1808[c]	170,000[b]

Sources: (1) Alice J. E. Lunn, "Economic Development in New France, 1713–1760" (unpublished Ph.D. dissertation, McGill University, 1942), p. 456; (2) Murray G. Lawson, *Fur: A Study in English Mercantilism, 1700–1775* (Toronto: University of Toronto Press, 1943), p. 136; (3) Great Britain, Public Record Office, *Customs 16/1,* "The American Inspector-General's Ledger"; (4) Harold A. Innis, *The Fur Trade in Canada,* revised ed. (Toronto: University of Toronto Press, 1956), p. 265.

[a] Exports from 1701 through 1755 were to France. Exports for 1769–1772 were to Great Britain. The destination of exports for 1793–1808 is not given by the source, but it was presumably Great Britain.

[b] Converted from number of skins to pounds assuming one beaver skin equaled 1⅓ lbs. (Innis, *The Fur Trade,* p. 267). Had these figures been converted on a ratio of 1 to 1½ (Lawson, *Fur: A Study in English Mercantilism,* p. 136) they would have been somewhat larger.

[c] The average for these years does not include exports of beaver skins to the United States after 1798. In 1798 this amounted to 19,283 lbs. of beaver skins, and 29,115 lbs. in 1805 (Innis, *The Fur Trade,* p. 265).

TABLE 5.7
Annual Average Estimated Values of All Furs Imported into La Rochelle, France, 1718–1761 (in Thousands of *Livres*)

	Beaver	Other	Total
1718–1720	274	220	494
1721–1730	499	419	918
1731–1740	431	628	1059
1741, 1744, 1746–1750	339	910	1249
1751–1754, 1756–1760	427	904	1331
1761	22	511	533

Source: Alice J. E. Lunn, "Economic Development in New France, 1713–1760" (unpublished Ph.D. dissertation, McGill University, 1942), pp. 464–465.

eighteenth and early nineteenth centuries, and not with year-to-year fluctuations, broad averages have been computed. In Tables 5.6 and 5.7, decadal averages were calculated, using any of the years within a decade for which data existed. Each of the three tables shows either annual average figures for a period of years or annual exports for specific years.

Table 5.6 shows estimates of quantities of beaver skins exported over the eighteenth century. Early in the century beaver provided more than half the value of furs exported, but its importance relative to other furs declined over the century.[36] Innis states that its share was about one-third of the total value of furs exported near the end of the eighteenth century.[37] Table 5.6 shows two different series for the first half of the century. Series 1 was taken from Lunn,[38] who depended largely upon correspondence between government officials in Quebec and in France (this correspondence is deposited in the Dominion Archives). Series 2 was taken from Lawson, who in turn had taken it from Innis.[39] Innis, like Lunn, derived these figures from correspondence in the Dominion Archives. Some of their estimates apparently came from the same sources, because figures for some years are identical. The differences between the Lunn and Innis estimates, in general, are relatively small. In order to give a longer picture, annual averages were computed from

36. Innis, *The Fur Trade,* pp. 264–265, lists the more important furs and skins exported in the late eighteenth century as being deerskins, otter, bear, raccoon, and marten.

37. Ibid., p. 264.

38. Alice J. E. Lunn, "Economic Development in New France, 1713–1760" (unpublished Ph.D. dissertation, McGill University, 1942), p. 456.

39. Lawson, *Fur; A Study in English Mercantilism,* p. 136. Lawson's reference to Innis is to the first edition of *The Fur Trade in Canada* (New Haven: Yale University Press, 1930), Appendix A.

TABLE 5.8
Official Values of All Furs Imported into England from North America, Quinquennial Years, 1760–1775 (in Pounds Sterling)

Year	Quebec	Hudson's Bay	All other continental colonies	Total
1760	1,930	8,321	4,386	14,637
1765	24,512	9,770	11,643	45,925
1770	28,433	9,213	6,748	44,394
1775	34,486	5,640	10,932	51,058

Source: Murray G. Lawson, *Fur: A Study in English Mercantilism, 1700–1775* (Toronto: University of Toronto Press, 1943), p. 108.

the American Inspector-General's Ledger for 1769–1772 (Series 3) and from Innis for the 16-year period 1793–1808 (Series 4).

From Table 5.6 it appears that exports of beaver skins from French Canada hit a peak around mid-century, then declined until later in the century, when they rose to new high levels as the Northwest Company pushed into new western areas. Thereafter they must have decreased; according to Innis, "the decline in total exports [of beaver] after 1800 was unmistakable."[40] The overall trend, then, was one of gradual growth to mid-century, a decline during the Seven Years' War, a gradual increase again from the Conquest to the end of the century, then once again decline. Because beaver declined in importance relative to other furs, exports of all furs must have grown somewhat more rapidly over the century than did the exports of beaver shown in Table 5.6.

Tables 5.7 and 5.8 present some estimates of values of furs exported from the colonies. Table 5.7 shows Lunn's estimated values (based on French records) of beaver and all other furs imported into the French entrepôt for the fur trade—La Rochelle—during the eighteenth century before the Conquest. Presumably the furs imported there were principally, if not entirely, from Quebec. Note that the values shown in Table 5.7 are based upon French prices, and if the underlying data are accurate, these values would tend to *overstate* the amount received by Quebec residents for these exports.[41]

40. *The Fur Trade,* p. 268.

41. Innis, in *The Fur Trade,* p. 240, cites an example of 1400 bundles of furs received at Grand Portage by the Northwest Company (presumably in 1805 or 1806). These furs cost the Northwest Company a total of 16,000 pounds sterling; they sold in Montreal for £56,000 and sold again in London for £88,000. This example may be exaggerated, but it does illustrate that the difference between Canadian and European values of furs could be sizable.

For those who may wish to compare these values to the values of cod exports and the value of English imports of furs (Table 5.8), both shown in pounds sterling, the exchange rate between the French *livre tournois* and the English pound sterling was 24 to 1 in Montreal in 1777.[42] Provided this exchange rate is applicable to earlier years, this would mean the French values, equivalent to approximately 55,000 pounds sterling at the peak of the French trade in the 1750s, would have risen from about 20,000 pounds sterling earlier in the century. Remembering that these are French values, and that the estimates are subject to all the qualifications mentioned above, the value of fur exports in Quebec must have been somewhat lower, and possibly substantially less than 55,000 pounds sterling. The English records following the Conquest do indicate lower values. As given in Table 5.8, these are the so-called "official values" from the English customs records, computed from the quantities of goods imported into England and from standard rates which had been set around the beginning of the eighteenth century.[43] If these rates were at all close to market prices, then the official values provide a rough idea about the value of furs imported from Quebec after the Conquest.[44] For purposes of illustration the value of furs imported into England by the Hudson's Bay Company and from all other American continental colonies also is given in Table 5.8. As the fur trade in Quebec recovered from the Seven Years' War and passed into the hands of British merchants in Montreal, it quickly regained its dominance over the trade of the Hudson's Bay Company and the other colonies. Even so, the foregoing evidence suggests the fur trade never achieved anything like the value of codfish exports from Newfoundland.[45] One must grant that the statistical evidence would have to be completely out of line, however, to invalidate

42. Twenty-four French *livres tournois* equaled one pound sterling (see R. Craig McIvor, *Canadian Monetary, Banking, and Fiscal Development* [Toronto: Macmillan, 1958], p. 14). One *livre* (Quebec) was approximately the equivalent of one shilling sterling between 1729 and 1758 (see William L. Marr and Donald G. Paterson, *Canada: An Economic History* [Toronto: Macmillan of Canada, 1980], p. 81).

43. Great Britain, Public Record Office, *Customs* 3. See Lawson, *Fur: A Study in English Mercantilism*, p. 78, for a discussion of these values. Also, see Shepherd and Walton, *Shipping, Maritime Trade*, Appendix II, for a general discussion of the relation between official values and market values.

44. Note that these values are taken from the English customs records and consequently do not include any possible imports of furs into Scotland from Quebec. Any such imports should be recorded in the Scottish customs records (Great Britain, Public Record Office, *Customs 14*). It seems doubtful, however, that exports of furs to Scotland from Quebec would have been significant; London was the center for the British fur trade.

45. Innis, *The Fur Trade*, pp. 266–267, seems to dispute this evidence, citing some values for furs exported from Quebec as being £236,418 in 1784, £258,970 in 1788, and £371,140 in 1801. He does not state, however, whether these were sterling values. If they were pounds of Quebec currency, they would have been less in terms of sterling values (see Note 42).

the conclusion that the value of cod exports were many times the value of exports of furs from Canada during the eighteenth century.

How did cod compare with the staple exports from the other British colonies? Of all the colonial staples produced elsewhere in the Empire, probably only sugar from the West Indies and tobacco from Maryland and Virginia exceeded it in terms of value of individual commodity exports early in the eighteenth century. Total and per capita exports for these areas (based upon the official values of the British custom records) are given in Table 5.9.[46] These understate the value of total and per capita exports from these colonies because exports to overseas areas other than Great Britain are not included. During 1768–1772, for example, per capita exports to all overseas areas from Virginia and Maryland averaged annually 1.8 pounds sterling, or nearly 3 pounds sterling per

TABLE 5.9
Official Values of Exports to Great Britain from the British West Indies, and from Virginia and Maryland, 1710–1822[a] (Annual Averages; Exports in Thousands of Pounds Sterling; Per Capita Exports in Pounds Sterling)

	British West Indies		Virginia and Maryland	
	Total	Per capita	Total	Per capita
1710–1714	725	4.1	249	2.1
1715–1724	1022	4.8	294	1.9
1725–1734	1351	5.2	360	1.8
1735–1744	1324	4.6	441	1.5
1745–1754	1398	4.2	625	1.7
1755–1764	1976	5.2	593	1.2
1765–1774	2999	6.3	696	1.1
1775–1784	2883	5.4	—	—
1785–1794	4051	—	532[b]	0.5[b]
1795–1804	6211	—	—	—
1805–1814	8077	—	—	—
1815–1822	8001	9.9[c]	—	—

Sources: Stanley L. Engerman, "Notes on the Patterns of Economic Growth in the British North American Colonies in the Seventeenth, Eighteenth, and Nineteenth Centuries," in Paul Bairoch and Maurice Lévy-Leboyer, eds., *Disparities in Economic Development since the Industrial Revolution* (London: Macmillan, 1981), p. 48 (the estimates are based upon population data from J.J. McCusker, "The Rum Trade and the Balance of Payments of the Thirteen Continental Colonies," unpublished Ph.D. dissertation, University of Pittsburgh, 1970, p. 712), for the West Indies; U.S. Bureau of the Census, *Historical Statistics of the United States, Colonial Times to 1970, Bicentennial Edition, Parts 1 and 2* (Washington, D.C.: U.S. Government Printing Office, 1975), pp. 29, 36, 1168, 1176–1178, for Virginia and Maryland.

[a]For the West Indies, data cover exports to England and Wales until 1754 and to Great Britain thereafter; for Virginia and Maryland, the destinations were England and Wales until 1744 and England, Wales, and Scotland thereafter.

[b]1785–1791.

[c]Based upon population in 1830.

white resident.[47] Over the eighteenth century only flour from the middle colonies and rice from South Carolina and Georgia challenged exports of cod. In 1768–1772, annual average per capita exports from South Carolina reached a value of 3.7 pounds sterling, or 9.4 pounds sterling per white resident.[48] In this same period per capita exports from the middle colonies (the major flour-producing regions) were slightly over 1 pound sterling.[49] In 1768–1772, dried codfish exports ranked fourth behind tobacco, bread and flour, and rice in terms of total value of exports from the continental colonies.[50]

From this discussion, and from the evidence in Table 5.9, it is clear that the total value of exports of sugar from the West Indies and tobacco from Virginia and Maryland was larger than that of cod exports from Newfoundland early in the eighteenth century. As the century progressed, flour and rice surpassed cod in total value. Yet, the fascinating point remains that Newfoundland's exports relative to its population were far greater than for most of the other British American colonies. Even the British West Indies, which came closest, were outclassed by Newfoundland in per capita export values by a factor of two or three during the eighteenth century. For those colonies which later became Canadian provinces—Quebec and Nova Scotia—per capita export values were likely in the range of 1 to 2 pounds sterling (including coastal exports), even with Quebec's important fur trade. This vast difference between the relative importance of the fishery to Newfoundland and the fur trade to Quebec has not been properly stressed in the literature of Canadian economic history.

In the literature of American colonial economic history, an equally slighted fact has been that every British North American colony save Newfoundland had a strong agricultural base which made it self-sufficient in the production of foodstuffs.[51] For those other colonies, it seems likely that more than half of total output, and perhaps three-quarters, was subsistence production, a large part of this being home-grown and home-prepared food. Lunn's statement about the dependence of Quebec on agriculture rather than furs might profitably be repeated here.

46. See Note 43 regarding the relation between official values and market values.

47. Shepherd and Walton, *Shipping, Maritime Trade,* p. 47. The figures in Table 5.9 include commodity exports other than sugar and tobacco, though these two enumerated goods would have dominated exports to Great Britain.

48. Ibid.

49. Ibid.

50. Ibid., p. 98.

51. The West Indies were not self-sufficient in the production of foodstuffs during the eighteenth century, though they probably could have been had they not been so heavily specialized in the production of sugar for export markets.

> But, however important the fur trade was it had less to do with determining the general condition of the colony than agriculture had. By 1740 at least, the fur trade, no matter what it might have been earlier, was not the economic basis of the colony. A great many more people were gaining a livelihood from farming than there were from the fur trade, large as the number of individuals engaged in the exploitation of the up country was. We have seen the effect on the colony of a poor harvest. A falling off in peltry returns had no such widespread result.[52]

No such statement could be made about Newfoundland and the cod fishery. As we have seen in the preceding section, Newfoundland had virtually no agricultural base. How did its consequent nearly complete dependence upon exports affect Newfoundland's subsequent economic development? To this question we turn in conclusion.

THE STAPLE THEORY: IMPLICATIONS FOR NEWFOUNDLAND'S DEVELOPMENT

What is the answer to the question originally posed: Did Newfoundland's high level of exports lead to slower growth in later years? Was Newfoundland a case of export-led growth? Of export-led decline? The answers to the last two questions are relatively easy. Newfoundland's earlier growth clearly was "led" by exports from the cod fishery, in the sense that exports dominated overall economic activity. Its decline in the nineteenth century seems due to the fact that its fate was tied inextricably to the fishery. The interesting question is: Why was it so tied? Watkins, in his discussion of the staple theory, seems to have had this problem in mind when he stated that "growth, if it is to be sustained, requires an ability to shift resources that may be hindered by excessive reliance on exports in general, and, in particular, on a small number of staple exports."[53]

The answer to the first question is not so easy. Newfoundland's decline (in the sense of not keeping up with other areas in which per capita output was growing more rapidly) was due to the fact that productivity in the cod fishery did not continuously expand over the nineteenth century. All evidence points to this. Lacking technological developments in fishing to raise this productivity, the possibilities for growth were severely limited. With an expanding population such as Newfoundland had during the nineteenth century and with a fixed natural resource base—the fishery—the only route to growth was for other sectors with growing productivity to absorb labor released from the fishery

52. Lunn, "Economic Development in French Canada, 1740–1760," p. 184.

53. Melville H. Watkins, "A Staple Theory of Economic Growth," *The Canadian Journal of Economics and Political Science* 29 (1963), p. 144.

or for a net emigration of labor to other regions. Neither event seems to have happened in Newfoundland. Some recent literature on retardation in the American South after the Civil War has been addressing similar questions. The following excerpt from Ransom and Sutch is directly relevant.

> Such an extractive economy has its natural limits. Increasing the quantity of land per worker is necessary if the productivity of agricultural labor is to be continuously expanded. Yet, with a constant or growing population, the land–labor ratio can be increased (once all the arable land is taken up) only by removing labor from agriculture. In other words, if an agricultural economy is to grow continuously, it must either have a growing industrial sector to absorb the released labor or a continuing outmigration of labor to some other region. The South of the late nineteenth century was without a growing industrial sector and without significant outmigration. There were no employment opportunities for those who would be displaced by agricultural productivity advances.[54]

Substitute the "natural resource of cod" for "land," and "fishery" for "agriculture," and the statement is directly applicable to Newfoundland.

The interesting question then becomes: Why was it that mobile resources did not shift into other and more productive activities, in Newfoundland or elsewhere? Here the ideas of Innis about the character of staple production surely have some application. The pattern of settlement of relatively isolated, small coastal communities in Newfoundland was not conducive to the mobility of resources. Even when the technology became available, there was no incentive, as in agricultural areas, to break through the barrier of high inland transport costs by investing in advanced transportation systems. Communication must have been poor; hence, information about alternatives, especially in the outside world, was not easily and readily attainable. Educational opportunities and incentives were also restricted.

One could go on with the same familiar arguments. If, for plausible reasons, no alternative activities leading to growth developed in Newfoundland, why did not the usual regional model apply? Why did people stay there? The model, based upon standard neoclassical microeconomic theory states that "incomes per capita should tend toward equality among regions."[55] Persistent regional income differentials (which are observed in the real world) must then be explained by: (*a*)

54. Roger L. Ransom and Richard Sutch, *One Kind of Freedom: the Economic Consequences of Emancipation* (London: Cambridge University Press, 1977), pp. 192–193.

55. Caves and Holton, *The Canadian Economy*, p. 165.

differences in regional participation rates; (*b*) differences in skills or training (quality of labor) on the part of the typical worker; (*c*) differences in property income per capita; (*d*) the deterrent of relocation costs, lack of information about alternatives available, or other sorts of imperfections in the labor market; or finally, (*e*) differences between money income and psychic income.[56] Perhaps all apply in some degree to Newfoundland. One is struck by the likely importance of (*d*). In any event, once the facts are known, the original questions about the role of exports in growth become less interesting than these tantalizing other questions to which they lead.

One important comment should be made about the expectation of net emigration from a "declining" region such as Newfoundland. Newfoundland has always experienced substantial outmigration. Note Head's statement:

> From the late seventeenth century onwards it became a temporary resevoir of manpower almost continuously tapped by the continental colonies. The flow is impossible to trace in any detail, but we know that migration from the island was nearly continuous. We suspect that the Irish derivation of so much of the population of Halifax and of coastal eastern Nova Scotia was by way of Newfoundland.[57]

In the language of the economist, this hints of a "disequilibrium" situation. To what extent have Newfoundland's difficulties been due to a "disequilibrium" situation, rather than to the "static equilibrium" kind of argument put forth earlier in the context of the regional adjustment model? The lack of good evidence prohibits any definitive answers. This paper does, however, raise the question for future research.

In conclusion, the problem of Newfoundland's decline, or stagnation, offers one important contrast with much of the recent (and not so recent) literature on retardation of growth in the American South and in the West Indies. For some time now, slavery has been made the culprit. Earlier, the general argument made by Baldwin, and applied by North to the American South, was that the retardation of the southern United States resulted from the lack of investment in human capital.[58] Recently, Stanley Engerman has argued that it was not slavery per se but rather its abolition which retarded growth in regions in which an agricultural

56. Ibid., pp. 165–166.

57. Head, *Eighteenth Century Newfoundland*, p. 248.

58. Robert E. Baldwin, "Patterns of Development in Newly Settled Regions," *The Manchester School of Economic and Social Studies* 34 (1956), pp. 161–179; North, *Economic Growth of the United States*, pp. 133–134.

system based upon the use of slave labor had dominated.[59] Obviously, there are many reasons for "decline," but it should be emphasized strongly that Newfoundland represents a refreshingly different case: Slavery never existed there. Hence we must look at other factors to fix the blame for Newfoundland's slackening development through the years.

ACKNOWLEDGMENTS

This essay draws upon two papers presented by the author at the Fifth and Ninth Conferences on Quantitative Methods in Canadian Economic History: "Staples and Eighteenth-Century Canadian Development: A Comparative Study," at Laval University, Quebec City, Quebec, March 24, 1972; and "Newfoundland and the Staple Theory: Export-Led Growth or Decline?" the University of Western Ontario, London, Ontario, March 17, 1978. The author is indebted to participants of the conferences for comments. He wishes to acknowledge, with thanks, financial assistance on the second paper from the Regional Economic History Research Center, Eleutherian Mills–Hagley Foundation, Greenville, Delaware.

James Shepherd's dissertation in 1966 was the first attempt to construct a comprehensive balance of payments account for the American Colonies. Based on extensive archival research, it still stands as the definitive work on that subject. Shepherd began a long and fruitful collaboration with another North student, Gary Walton, while the two of them were graduate students at the University of Washington. That collaboration eventually resulted in **Shipping, Maritime Trade, and the Economic Development of Colonial North America** (1972), and **The Economic Rise of Early America** (1979). Shepherd also has collaborated with another contributor to this volume, Philip Coelho, in an important study of regional wages and prices in the nineteenth-century United States. An area of further interest and publication has been the agricultural history of the Pacific Northwest.

Shepherd was coeditor with Gary Walton of **Explorations in Economic History** in 1979 and 1980 until he assumed full editorship in 1981. He taught at the University of British Columbia, Purdue University, and the University of California at Berkeley before returning to his hometown in 1971 to assume a position at Whitman College in Walla Walla, Washington.

59. Stanley L. Engerman, "Notes on the Patterns of Economic Growth in the British North American Colonies in the Seventeenth, Eighteenth, and Nineteenth Centuries," in Paul Bairoch and Maurice Lévy-Leboyer, eds., *Disparities in Economic Development since the Industrial Revolution* (London: Macmillan, 1981), pp. 46–57.

Chapter 6

In Search of Security: The Growth of Government Spending in the United States, 1902–1970

Roger L. Ransom

The cliometric revolution in economic history has wedded neoclassical economics and quantitative methods in order to describe and explain the performance of economies in the past. . . .

The nineteenth century was perhaps the most dramatic period of market expansion in history. It has been chronicled as part and parcel of the extraordinary economic growth of that century. But there has been less attention paid to its disruptive consequences as a result of the replacement of self-sufficiency and personal relationships with impersonal contracts.

—Douglass C. North[1]

The marriage to which Douglass North refers has just passed its silver anniversary.[2] During that quarter century cliometricians have produced an impressive body of research on the nineteenth-century growth and development of the American economy. The United States provided an

1. "Structure and Performance: The Task of Economic History," *Journal of Economic Literature* 16 (September 1978), pp. 963, 970–971.

2. Because no records are kept for such marriages, the precise date of the wedding is unknown. One can conjecture that it must have taken place sometime in the late 1950s; however, the public announcement of the event was withheld for several years. On the origins of the term "cliometrics," see J. R. T. Hughes, "A Note in Defense of Clio," *Explorations in Entrepreneurial History*, 2d ser., 2 (Winter 1965), p. 154.

ISBN 0-12-580080-0

ideal setting for the functioning of a neoclassical economy: an environment in which market transactions could take place with a minimum of interference and uncertainty. Messrs. Jefferson, Adams, Madison, and friends were sufficiently suspicious of the capability of governments to create mischief in the economic system that they deliberately placed checks on governmental interference in the right to hold property and to enforce contracts.

During the first century of the United States' existence, the formula devised by the founding fathers worked very well indeed. After a rocky start, the American economy took off into a prolonged growth that was to last (with some interruptions) for more than a century. From 1840 to 1899, gross national product (GNP) multiplied almost tenfold, growing just over 4% annually.[3] America was transformed in that period from a rural, agrarian society into an urban, industrial society. Yet, despite these momentous changes in the economic and social structure, the government remained only a passive participant in the exchange of goods and services. What evidence we have suggests that, at the end of the nineteenth century, government expenditures as a proportion of total output in the economy accounted for only about 8% of GNP and had been falling slightly over the final two decades.[4]

In the twentieth century real output continued to rise (by a factor of eight between 1900 and 1970), although economic growth was much more erratic.[5] But in that time the role of government has changed dramatically. Total spending by the government has risen almost two-hundred-fold: from $1.7 billion in 1902 to $333 billion in 1970. A significant portion of that increase, of course, reflects the more than quadrupling of prices in the American economy in the same period. Yet, even adjusted to reflect this inflation of prices, government expenditures in the public sector rose from $6.7 billion to $246.3 billion.[6]

3. The most reliable income estimates for the nineteenth century are those presented by Robert Gallman, "Gross National Product in the United States, 1834–1909," in *Output, Employment, and Productivity in the United States After 1800,* National Bureau of Economic Research, Studies in Income and Wealth, Vol. 30 (New York: Columbia University Press, 1966).

4. There are very few data on government expenditures, other than federal spending, before the Civil War. The most comprehensive estimates are those of Lance Davis and John Legler, "The Government in the American Economy, 1815–1902: A Quantitative Study," *Journal of Economic History* 26 (December 1966, pp. 514–552. Thomas Borcherding has incorporated the Davis–Legler estimates after 1870 into his study, "One Hundred Years of Public Spending, 1870–1970," in Borcherding, ed., *Budgets and Bureaucrats: The Sources of Government Growth* (Durham, N.C.: Duke University Press, 1977), pp. 19–44.

5. U.S. Bureau of the Census, *Historical Statistics of the United States, Colonial Times to 1970,* Bicentennial Edition, 2 parts (Washington, D.C.: G.P.O., 1976), Series F 1–5, p. 224.

6. Although the adjustment for price changes substantially lessens the magnitude of the

This growth has been examined in great detail by economists who have developed theories of public choice and market failure, by cliometricians and statisticians who have collected data on government activity, and by historians who have documented the various changes in specific areas of government activities. Despite all of this effort, we still do not have an adequate explanation. The statistics leave no doubt that government in the United States *has* expanded enormously, but by themselves they do not say *why*. Economic theories which explain why we need public goods have been much less insightful in explaining the observed level of public spending.

Obviously, these elements cannot all be integrated into a unified theory in this essay. Our more modest aim will be to show that, although no single theory of government explains the extent of the increase in government spending, an examination of the available data does reveal some dominant factors which seem to be present throughout the period since 1900—and particularly since 1930. Our discussion will center on the following "causes" of growth in government spending:

1. National security, both as the objective of increased public expenditures and as a factor leading to increased revenues.
2. The increased need for public goods (government services) in an industrial society.
3. Changes in the tax system as an impetus to government spending, particularly after World War II.
4. The perceived threat to economic security posed by adjustments of market forces in an industrial economy, and the resultant pressures both for direct government expenditures and for transfer payments.

THE PATTERN OF GOVERNMENT SPENDING: 1902–1970

We have reasonably complete data for the expenditures and revenues of federal, state, and local governments for selected years between 1902 and 1970. Table 6.1, presenting data for all government expenditures for 1902, 1913, 1927, 1940, 1950, 1960, and 1970, identifies those functions which have contributed most to the growth of government spending

---

increase in government spending, it does not alter the *relative* share of government to total spending in the economy, nor does it affect our estimates of the importance of particular components of government spending which are the focus of this paper. This being so, and in view of the problems associated with determining an appropriate index with which to deflate the figures, the analysis of this paper will be carried out using current prices. The figures for real government expenditures given in the text were computed using the GNP deflator with 1958 = 100 (*Historical Statistics,* Series F-5, p. 224).

TABLE 6.1
Government Expenditures by Function, 1902–1970

Year	Total spending	Defense[a]	Debt interest	Public welfare[b]	Social security	Education	Health	Other
			1. Gross expenditures in billions of dollars					
1902	1.66	.30	.10	.04	.00	.26	.06	.90
1913	3.22	.43	.17	.06	.00	.58	.11	1.87
1927	11.22	1.20	1.35	.16	.00	2.24	.43	5.48
1940	20.42	2.09	1.55	2.52	.02	2.83	.73	10.68
1950	70.33	21.61	4.86	7.66	.73	9.65	2.71	23.11
1960	151.29	52.72	9.33	10.53	10.80	19.40	5.24	43.28
1970	332.99	89.71	18.41	24.59	35.83	55.77	13.59	95.09
			2. Expenditures as a percentage of total government spending; total government spending as a percentage of GNP					
1902	7.7	18.1	6.0	2.4	.0	15.7	3.6	54.2
1913	8.1	13.4	5.3	1.9	.0	18.0	3.4	58.1
1927	11.8	10.7	12.0	1.4	.0	20.0	3.8	52.1
1940	20.5	10.2	7.6	12.3	.1	13.9	3.6	52.3
1950	24.7	30.7	6.9	10.9	1.0	13.7	3.9	32.9
1960	30.0	34.8	6.2	6.9	7.1	12.8	3.5	28.6
1970	34.1	26.9	5.5	7.4	10.8	16.8	4.1	25.6

Source: U.S. Bureau of the Census, *Historical Statistics of the United States, Colonial Times to 1970*, Bicentennial Edition, part 2, Series Y-566, pp. 1120–1121.

[a] *Defense expenditures* include payments to veterans not elsewhere classified.

[b] *Public welfare expenditures* include payments for farm subsidies and payments for unemployment compensation.

over the interval 1902–1970. Table 6.2 shows the annual rates of growth in government activity by function for four periods. Table 6.3 presents the fraction of total increase in expenditures which can be attributed to each function over the same intervals. The tables fully confirm the extent to which government has expanded over the past 68 years, and examination of the data reveals several significant features of government spending which are pertinent to our analysis of the public sector.

Perhaps the most surprising conclusion from the data is that government expansion has proceeded at an exceptionally high rate *throughout* the period. According to the estimates of Table 6.2, the annual rate of increase in total expenditures was 8.11% per year for the entire period and was approximately that level in each of the three subperiods. The growth rates shown in Table 6.2 also reveal that, although there was a wide variation in expenditures on various functions, *all* expenditures increased at rates significantly above the rate of increase in GNP. For only two cells in Table 6.2 (defense and public welfare between 1902 and

TABLE 6.2
Annual Compound Rates of Growth in Government Expenditures for Selected Years from 1902–1970

Years	GNP	Total spending	Defense	Debt interest	Public welfare[a]	Health–education	Other
1902–1927	6.10	7.94	5.70	10.97	5.70	8.20	6.16
1927–1950	4.89	8.31	13.39	5.73	18.79	6.89	7.77
1950–1970	6.36	8.01	7.38	6.89	10.38	9.01	7.33
1902–1970	5.77	8.11	8.74	9.79	11.37	8.23	7.09

Source: Table 6.1
[a]*Public welfare expenditures* include social security and unemployment compensation payments after 1940.

1927) was the rate of increase in government spending less than the rate of increase in GNP. Finally, the data show that the expansion of government spending proceeded at a fairly constant pace even during periods when total output in the private sector slowed markedly. This is most evident, of course, in the period 1927–1940, when GNP grew very little while government spending almost doubled. Not surprisingly, government spending as a fraction of GNP made its most notable jump during the 1930s.

A second point emphasized by the data is the dominance of defense spending throughout the twentieth century. The calculations of Table 6.3 reveal that defense expenditures alone contributed more than one-fourth of the total increase in government spending between 1902 and 1970. What is not often stressed is the comparative importance of defense spending early in the century; in 1902 it already represented 18% of total government outlays. In fact, the figures for national defense in Tables 6.1–6.3 understate the actual impact of military expenditures by

TABLE 6.3
Sources of Increases in Government Spending; 1902–1970

	Percentage of total increase in spending by area				
Years	Defense	Debt interest	Public welfare	Health–education	Other
1902–1927	9.41	13.08	1.30	24.58	51.24
1927–1950	34.53	5.94	13.92	16.39	29.22
1950–1970	25.93	5.16	19.18	21.70	27.40
1902–1970	26.99	5.33	18.24	20.83	28.43

Source: Table 6.1.

failing to include the increased interest costs on debts accumulated during wartime. The federal debt in 1902 was attributable in large part to the Civil and Spanish-American Wars, and the vast increases in debt interest between 1913 and 1927, and between 1940 and 1950, clearly reflect the increased federal debt incurred during World Wars I and II respectively. For 1927, therefore, a sizable portion of the interest paid by government should be attributed to its defense function. Indeed, it is not unreasonable to claim that defense accounted for almost one-fifth of all government expenditures in the years before World War I, and the costs from that war meant that defense-related expenditures remained significant through the 1920s, despite a substantial reduction of the war debt during that decade.[7] The additional jumps in defense spending during World War II made an already considerable item larger still. The conclusion is inescapable: A major reason for the expansion of government in the twentieth century has been our proclivity for waging war.

A final point which emerges from an examination of the data is that, despite the relative constancy of the rate of increase in government spending, the *source* of that increase was not the same in each period. Prior to 1927, the major impetus for government spending came in the areas of defense, education, and the financing and operating of government enterprises—all very "traditional" functions of government. In the 1930s and 1940s this pattern changed drastically, as an increasing share of government services took the form of transfer payments rather than purchases of goods and services in the economy. Though Table 6.1 does not distinguish between direct expenditures and transfer payments, the effect can be seen in the increased importance of social security payments (transfers) and in public welfare expenditures (which include, in addition to direct welfare transfers, payments of unemployment compensation and payments for farm price supports). Designed specifically to redistribute income among various groups, such transfers break sharply with former concepts of public spending. It is this change—a change representing a major revision in the American view of the function of government—which gives a focal point for this paper.

One would expect, of course, a considerable increase in government spending due simply to the growth of the economy itself. But, as we noted, GNP has been growing at a far slower rate than government spending—so much so that the public sector, which represented less

7. If interest payments by the federal government are added to defense expenditures, then the upper bound estimate of defense spending in 1902 would be 19.9% of total government outlays, and in 1927 the estimate would be 17.5%. Note that payments to veterans not elsewhere classified have been included in the defense expenditures reported in Table 6.1.

than 10% of GNP in 1902, had risen to 34% by 1970. Can this be explained by a larger, more affluent economy? It seems unlikely that rising incomes alone could account for it. In a recent study of the sources of government expenditure, Thomas Borcherding identified four economic factors that might affect the level of government spending over time: (*a*) population increase, (*b*) increases in real income, (*c*) changes in the price elasticity of demand for government services, (*d*) the presence of "interdependencies . . . that are not well handled by markets."[8]

According to Borcherding, the first three of these factors (those associated with the expansion of the economic system generally) account for only about one-half the total increase in government, and the fourth variable, interdependencies, added only a small increment. Thus, he concludes, "The evidence suggests that the growth of government has been 40 to 50 percent faster than would be predicted on the basis of changes in relative prices, incomes, population, and indices of interdependence."[9] That leaves much to be explained. Can we locate the source of the additional increase? Let us consider the explanations that have been advanced for government expenditures required in a market society.

PUBLIC GOODS, PUBLIC CHOICE, AND PUBLIC SPENDING

Economists have been aware for some time that markets cannot deal adequately with a situation where "interdependencies" or "externalities" occur among consumers or producers. Instances of such relationships abound in even a simple economy; in an industrial society they are everywhere. Many of these either are trivial, involving only a very few people, or are related to ambiguities of property rights which can be resolved through agreements between individuals or groups. One type of interdependency particularly pertinent to the issue of public spending is the so-called free rider problem. Economists use the term "public goods" in referring to a certain class of goods which, once produced, become available to all users. People who cannot be excluded from enjoying the benefits of the goods then become "free riders," and the producers of the goods cannot recoup their costs.[10]

The need for such goods thus provides a powerful rationale for government expenditures. In Table 6.4, government expenditures have

8. "The Sources of Growth of Public Expenditures in the United States, 1902–1970," in Borcherding, *Budgets and Bureaucrats*, pp. 46–56.

9. Ibid., p. 64.

10. The case of a pure public good is a situation where there is no feasible way to

been grouped into three categories according to the degree to which they satisfy the definition of a "public good." Table 6.5 allocates government expenditures according to these three classifications.

The importance of public goods throughout our period of analysis is immediately apparent. In 1902, public goods ("pure" and "quasi") accounted for 57% of all government spending, a proportion that still held 25 years later. Thereafter, public goods steadily gained dominance to the point where, by the end of the 1970s, they accounted for almost three-fourths of government budgets. Put another way, 74% of the total increase in public spending was due to the increased provision of public goods. At the same time, the share of expenditures on public enterprises declined by nearly 50%, a reflection of the changes in government programs beginning with the New Deal of the 1930s.[11]

These statistics would indicate that interdependencies and the demand for public goods were far more important than is suggested in Borcherding's analysis.[12] This is not surprising; we have already seen that national defense—a public good so "pure" that even Adam Smith conceded it must be provided by the government—by itself necessitated an enormous increase in the public sector. Moreover, the data of Table

---

prevent free riders from enjoying all the benefits of the good. There are, of course, many other goods which have some degree of joint consumption (see, for example, the classification of goods listed in Table 6.4). We might also note that the free rider problem is not the only rationale for public intervention in the marketplace; other interdependencies can justify governmental rather than private production. On the problem of "market failure" and the general case for government intervention, see Francis Bator, "The Anatomy of Market Failure," *Quarterly Journal of Economics* (August 1958), pp. 351–379. On the free rider problem specifically, see Mancur Olsen, *The Logic of Collective Action* (Cambridge, Mass.: Harvard University Press, 1964). For a mathematical definition of a public good, see Paul Samuelson, "The Pure Theory of Public Expenditure," in Joseph Stiglitz, ed., *The Collected Scientific Papers of Paul A. Samuelson,* Vol. 2 (Cambridge, Mass.: MIT Press, 1966).

11. The declining importance of public enterprise was not due to an absolute decline in spending on such endeavors; expenditures on public enterprises grew at a rate of just over 7%. We might note, however, that the contrast between expenditures for public goods and those for public enterprise would have been even more marked had expenditures on hospitals been counted as a "quasi" public good rather than a public enterprise. Expenditures on public enterprises other than hospitals grew at an annual rate of 6.78%.

12. Borcherding did not try to identify any specific interdependencies in his analysis. He assumed that most of their effects would be reflected in the other three factors included in his analysis. To the extent that he did consider the question, his analysis was biased strongly against the presence of interdependencies. Thus, for example, his analysis of the effect of rising income (the most significant factor, according to his results) assumed that the income elasticity for government services was only .75. This is tantamount to assuming that the role of government should decline as the economy expands. He found no relation between government spending and urbanization, and the only other variable considered in his analysis was a measure of the possible effects of benefits from one governmental unit spilling over to another.

TABLE 6.4
Classes of Government Expenditures

1. "Pure" public goods and services[a]
   - National defense
   - Highways
   - Police
   - Fire protection
2. "Quasi" public goods[b]
   - Education
   - Public welfare and assistance
   - Health
   - Housing and urban renewal
   - Parks and recreation
   - Natural resources
   - Unemployment compensation
   - Social security payments
3. Public enterprises[c]
   - Post office
   - Local sanitation services
   - Utilities and liquor operations
   - Hospitals
   - Air and sea terminals
4. Other
   - Interest on public debt
   - Financial control and administration
   - Other not elsewhere classified

[a] Includes those goods, services, or transfer payments which involve such a strong interdependency that the private market is unable to supply the demand.

[b] Includes those goods, services, or transfer payments which involve some degree of interdependence, but which can be provided by both government and private producers.

[c] Includes those goods or services which have traditionally been supplied by the government, even though private production might be feasible.

6.5 reveal that, quite apart from defense, the production of both "pure" and "quasi" public goods also grew at annual rates (8.09 and 9.01, respectively) far above that for GNP.

The theory of public expenditure identifies circumstances where governments must intervene in the marketplace to provide services, and the statistics on government spending suggest that the government has, in fact, grown in precisely those areas which exhibit the characteristics of a "public good." Unfortunately, however, there is a problem in using the demand for public goods as an explanation of the impetus for government spending: In a democratic society, consumers tend to understate

TABLE 6.5
Government Expenditures by Type of Good or Service, 1902–1970

Year	"Pure" public good	"Quasi" public good	Public enterprise	Other
	1. Government expenditures in billions of dollars			
1902	0.57	0.37	0.33	0.39
1927	3.51	2.84	2.00	2.87
1950	26.83	21.86	8.51	13.13
1970	113.38	132.39	34.24	52.98
	2. Expenditure as a percentage of total government spending			
1902	34.3	22.3	19.9	23.5
1927	31.3	25.3	17.8	25.6
1950	38.1	31.1	12.1	18.7
1970	34.1	39.8	10.3	15.9

Source: Data from Table 6.1; classification of expenditure from Table 6.4.

their preferences for public services until the good is actually produced by someone else. Public expenditure theory is not inconsistent with a growing public sector, but it fails to explain adequately the phenomenal growth in government services since 1900—and certainly does not account for the explosion of services and transfer payments since the 1930s.[13] In fact, on the basis of the theory itself, some economists insisted that the government sector was being "starved" during the 1950s and 1960s, and that social needs were being ignored in favor of private production. There was, they claimed, a "social imbalance" between private and social needs.[14] An imbalance in that direction is hardly evident in the data that has been presented here. Thus, although the theory of public expenditure developed by economists in the last quarter century explains the *need* for government action, some further probing is required to explain why the *level* is, in fact, so high.

Enter the Politician. In recent years, economists—particularly those who style themselves "new political economists"—have been focusing

13. The strong tendency of consumers to disguise their preferences for public goods was demonstrated by Paul Samuelson in his paper cited earlier, "The Pure Theory of Public Expenditure" and elaborated in a subsequent paper, "Pure Theory of Public Expenditure and Taxation," in Robert C. Merton, ed., *The Collected Papers of Paul A. Samuelson*, Vol. 3 (Cambridge, Mass.: MIT Press, 1972), pp. 492–517. On the reluctance of voters in a democratic society to support public services, see Anthony Downs, "Why the Government Budget in a Democracy is Too Small," *World Politics* (June 1960).

14. Probably the most outspoken advocate of this thesis was John Kenneth Galbraith in his book, *The Affluent Society* (New York: Houghton Mifflin, 1966). Alvin Hansen also argued the case in his book, *Economic Issues of the 1960s* (New York: McGraw-Hill, 1960).

their attention on the extent to which government, far from being a disinterested party serving the needs of others, has grown into an entity with its own goals and objectives. As James Buchanan has noted:

> Politicians are politicians because they want to be. They are no more robots than other men. . . . They seek office because they seek "profit" in the form of "political income," which will normally be obtained only if their behavior is not fully in accord with the desires of electoral majorities.[15]

Buchanan's statement carries two implications. First, politicians maximize their own "objective function" in running the government. Second, they will be influenced by groups who are willing to provide "political income" to the individual politician. That politicians, together with bureaucrats, have incentives to expand their political and/or economic power is not really subject to dispute. Most people do not question "Parkinson's Law":

> Work expands so as to fill the time available for its completion. . . . This fact is widely recognized, but less attention has been paid to its wider implications, more especially in the field of public administration. Politicians and taxpayers have assumed (with occasional phases of doubt) that a rising total in the number of civil servants must reflect a growing volume of work to be done. . . . The fact is that the number of the officals and the quantity of the work are not related to each other at all.[16]

Recent research has refined this conclusion somewhat, without seriously undermining Parkinson's thesis.[17]

Ironically, the logic of the theory of public expenditure which implies that consumers will conceal their preferences for public goods also suggests that the voting habits of the electorate will reinforce the tendency of politicians to cater to particular interests in the provision of public services. In a large group, each person has little incentive to vote, realizing that a single vote is unlikely to affect the outcome. Even if people do vote, they are not likely to invest much effort in acquiring the information needed to vote "wisely."[18] Thus, the goals of special inter-

15. James M. Buchanan, "Why Does Government Grow?" in Borcherding, *Budgets and Bureaucrats*, p. 13.

16. C. Northcote Parkinson, *Parkinson's Law and Other Studies in Administration* (Boston: Houghton Mifflin, 1957), pp. 2–4.

17. An example of such work, by an avowed advocate of the "new political economy" which strongly supports the notion that governments promote their own expansion, is William Niskannen, Jr., *Bureaucracy and Representative Government* (Chicago: Aldine, 1971).

18. Anthony Downs was one of the earliest writers to emphasize this point; see *An Economic Theory of Democracy* (New York: Harper and Row, 1957). Lance Davis and Douglass North, in their treatment of institutional change, also stress the importance of

est groups and of the politician are unduly represented in subsequent governmental decisions.

There is, however, a serious omission in the argument that increased government spending results primarily from the sort of "bureaucratic imperialism" described by Buchanan. Even if we grant that bureaucrats and politicians will seek to maximize their political "income," the nagging question remains: Where do they get the resources with which to fund their expanded programs? Constituents may be reluctant to wage costly and time-consuming campaigns to block specific projects backed by interest groups, but what happens when voters get the bill? One of the most effective checks on government expansion has always been the resistance to taxation.

The tax system that provided governments with revenues through 1900 relied on types of taxes that had been levied for years: property, sales, and excise taxes, as well as tariffs—all supplemented by an occasional experiment with taxes on wealth or income.[19] Though sufficient to meet the "normal" demands of government up to that point, such measures clearly could never have funded the bursting expansion of governmental spending during the first three quarters of the twentieth century. Tables 6.6, 6.7, and 6.8, which detail the sources of government revenues over the period 1902–1970, reveal the extent to which the system of revenues was altered. Indeed, these tables suggest that the changes in the sources of government revenue have been nearly as radical as the shifts in expenditures noted earlier.

As might be expected from our data on expenditures, the revenues have persistently been on the increase over the entire period. The source of increased revenues is obvious enough: Governments had found a new tax base to exploit. Ratification of the Sixteenth Amendment to the Constitution in 1913 meant that:

> The Congress shall have power to lay and collect taxes on incomes, from whatever source derived, without apportionment among the several States, and without regard to any census or enumeration.[20]

---

information—and the costs of acquiring reliable information; see *Institutional Change and American Economic Growth* (New York: Cambridge University Press, 1971).

19. An income tax was levied during the Civil War when the pressures of defense spending were extreme and again in 1894 when revenues from the tariff slumped. States were also beginning to experiment with income taxes towards the end of the century.

20. A constitutional amendment was required before a federal tax could be imposed on incomes because the Constitution provided that all federal taxes must be levied proportionately among the states. The Supreme Court had ruled in 1894 that an income tax law was not proportional, and was therefore unconstitutional.

TABLE 6.6
Government Revenues by Source, 1902–1970

Year	Total revenue	Tax revenues: Personal income	Corporate income	Sales–property	Other	Unemployment–social security	All other revenues
		1. Tax revenues in billions of dollars					
1902	1.69	.00	.00	1.23	.15	.00	.31
1913	2.98	.00	.04	2.00	.23	.00	.71
1927	12.19	.95	1.35	6.29	.86	.00	2.74
1940	17.80	1.18	1.28	8.54	1.69	1.47	3.64
1950	66.68	16.53	11.08	20.35	3.14	3.30	12.28
1960	153.10	43.18	22.67	10.86	6.41	13.13	26.85
1970	333.18	101.22	36.57	82.67	12.41	41.71	59.22
		2. Revenues by source as a percentage of total revenues; total tax revenues as a percentage of total revenues					
1902	81.1	.0	.0	72.8	8.9	.0	18.3
1913	76.2	.0	1.3	67.1	7.7	.0	23.8
1927	77.5	7.8	11.1	51.6	7.1	.0	22.5
1940	71.3	6.6	7.2	48.0	9.5	8.3	20.5
1950	76.6	24.8	16.6	30.5	4.7	5.0	18.4
1960	73.9	28.2	14.8	26.7	4.2	8.6	17.4
1970	69.7	30.3	11.0	24.8	3.7	12.5	17.7

Source: Bureau of the Census, *Historical Statistics of the United States, Colonial Times to 1970,* Bicentennial Edition, 2 vols. (Washington, D.C.: GPO, 1976), Series Y505–521, p. 1119.

TABLE 6.7
Percentage Distribution of Tax Revenues, by Type of Tax

Year	Personal income	Corporate income	Sales	Property	Other
1902	.0	.0	37.7	51.4	10.9
1913	.0	1.8	29.5	58.6	10.1
1927	10.1	14.3	16.5	50.1	9.1
1940	9.3	10.1	32.4	34.9	13.3
1950	32.3	21.7	25.4	14.4	6.1
1960	38.2	20.0	21.6	14.5	5.7
1970	43.5	15.7	20.9	14.6	5.3

Source: Table 6.6.

TABLE 6.8
Annual Rates of Growth in Government Revenues, 1902–1970

Years	GNP	Total revenue	Tax revenue	Personal income taxes	Corporate income taxes	Sales taxes	Property taxes
1902–1927	6.10	8.22	8.00	—	—	4.49	7.88
1927–1950	4.89	7.67	7.61	13.22	9.84	9.66	1.93
1950–1970	6.36	8.39	7.88	9.48	6.15	6.82	7.97
1902–1950	5.57	8.00	7.74	11.47	7.97	8.33	4.70
1902–1970	5.77	8.08	7.83	—	—	6.90	5.86

Source: Table 6.6.

Initially the new power was used sparingly. In 1913 the total contribution of income taxes amounted to only 1.3% of all government revenues. Income taxes were increased temporarily during World War I but quickly fell back during the 1920s. In 1927, taxes on corporate and individual incomes totaled $2.3 billion, or just under 20% of all revenues. Income taxes had become a robust source of revenue, but they were still levied primarily on the wealthy and on corporations.[21]

Then came World War II. By 1945 almost 50 million Americans—36% of the population—were filing income tax returns. In the space of a few years, this had become the most important single source of tax revenues to the government. Once again, peace brought some reductions in taxes, but the drastically altered rates and structure had become firmly embedded in the tax system. In 1950, taxes on personal income generated almost one-third of all tax revenues; corporate and personal income taxes together contributed 54%. This means that between 1927 and 1950 revenues from personal income taxes had grown by an average of 11.5% per year. Of the total increase in tax revenue over that period, the personal income tax alone accounted for 44% and corporate and personal income taxes together for 59%. National security had provided not only an irresistible push toward increased public expenditures but also a rationale for continually expanding tax rates.

In the case of the personal income tax, exemption allowances were cut

21. The rates on individual incomes remained low except for a brief period during World War I, and the exemptions allowed were fairly liberal. In 1927, only 4.1 million individuals, representing 3.5% of the population, filed personal income tax returns. The fraction fell to less than 3% in 1931 before increasing again in the late 1930s. Statistics on income tax returns and revenues are from *Historical Statistics,* Vol. 2, Series Y-343 and Y-402, p. 1110.

drastically (to only $500 per person), and the rates on marginal income were increased to a point where the highest bracket was 90%. Although reduced somewhat after the war, both the marginal rates and the number of incomes taxed remained far above prewar levels. The change in the rate structure was accompanied by a change in the collection system: Personal income taxes were now withheld on a "pay-as-you-earn" basis before the income was delivered to the wage earner. The new method did not affect the level of taxation. It did, however, make the collection of taxes far more efficient, and it greatly reduced the opportunity for evasion. It also subtly changed the way wage earners viewed the relationship between taxes and earnings. Because taxes had already been "netted out" of the paycheck, people now tended to overlook them entirely, focusing instead on "take home" pay as their actual earnings. With payroll deduction, the increased burden of personal taxes was spread over the year and made much less visible.[22]

The significance of this sudden influx of revenues can hardly be overstated. The tax system spawned by wartime emergency was now generating greatly increased peacetime revenues for government without any increase in the tax *rate*. (Indeed, the rates could be *lowered*.) Moreover, because the structure of tax rates was progressive, as income rose, tax revenues were rising even faster. Thus, even though the tax rate on individual incomes was lowered substantially between 1950 and 1970, the share of the personal income tax as a source of revenue increased markedly. By 1970, revenues from personal income taxes alone accounted for over 30% of *all* government revenues and for 43% of all tax revenues. Taxes on all forms of income accounted for nearly 60% of tax revenues.[23]

Clearly, the introduction of taxes that spiraled upward with a rising level of economic activity nullified the role of taxation as a constraint on governmental spending. The structure of the revenue system now virtually guaranteed that the income of the government would not only increase, but would increase more rapidly than production in the private

22. J. R. T. Hughes emphasizes that this change in tax collection was a major reason why governments were able to shift so much of the burden of taxes onto individuals and to increase the level of taxation in the process. See his book, *The Governmental Habit: Economic Controls from Colonial Times to the Present* (New York: Basic Books, 1977), pp. 207–211.

23. Though the income elasticity of the tax structure is most obvious in the case of the income tax, it should be noted that the sales tax revenues also more than kept pace with the increase in GNP. The figures presented in Table 6.6 suggest an income elasticity of 1.5 for the tax revenues as a whole; 2.1 for the individual income tax; 1.26 for property and sales taxes. These figures overstate the elasticity of sales and property relative to income, since the rates on those taxes rose, while income tax rates declined.

sector. In line with an argument that the determining variable for government activity is the available revenue, most of the expansion of government since 1913 could be attributed to the passage of the Sixteenth Amendment and to the income tax revenues which that change introduced. As Professors Parkinson and Buchanan might argue, the bureaucracy has created work to absorb the full measure of each dollar taken in as taxes.

There is doubtless a sizable grain of truth in this observation. However, such a simple explanation does not consider two anomalies in the enormous expansion of government spending documented in Table 6.1. First, it ignores the fact that virtually all of the increases in revenues occurred during wartime, when the higher tax rates were necessitated by a pressing *external* demand for government services—the military effort to defeat a foreign enemy. During neither of the two world wars was the expansion in sources of revenue attributable to pressures for bureaucratic growth. The argument also has trouble explaining the conflicting behavior of taxes after the wars. The level of taxation after 1919 was reduced substantially, yet tax rates after World War II remained at levels far above those of the 1920s or 1930s. Why? People were presumably no fonder of high taxes in 1945 than they were in 1920, yet they accepted a higher level of taxation. Is it possible that people *wanted* more government services and were willing to say so?

THE SEARCH FOR ECONOMIC SECURITY

Douglass North provides a perceptive insight as to why neoclassical economics has so much difficulty explaining the increase in government spending:

> Neoclassical theory simply ignores the losers. In a general equilibrium model they are costlessly reabsorbed into the economic system. In fact, there are losers—both relative and absolute—in a dynamic economic system, and those participants attempt to avoid the costs associated with being losers.[24]

This is not merely a shortcoming in the theoretical models; the costs associated with "losers" in a market system are very real and, as North points out, adjustments to a market situation can be quite disruptive. The expansion of market activity has meant that an increasing fraction of the population has been subjected to adjustments demanded by the

24. North, "The Task of Economic History," p. 970. See also his comments on neoclassical theory and the state in "A framework for Analyzing the State in Economic History," *Explorations in Economic History* 16 (July 1979), pp. 249–250.

price system. In many cases these have imposed costs that have threatened the very economic security of such people.

In the agrarian society of nineteenth-century America, the insecurity posed by market pressures was countered in two ways: The farmer sought to maintain a degree of self-sufficiency in agricultural production which would ensure some minimum level of income irrespective of the current level of prices; and, over a longer period of time, he sought to acquire and improve enough land to ensure the security of his family. Land could provide income, and it also could serve as a basis for capital accumulation in the form of labor effort toward farm improvements. This process achieved almost half the total capital formation in agriculture in the early nineteenth century.

In other words, economic security was maintained by keeping some fraction of economic activity outside the influence of market forces, as a form of "insurance" against market fluctuations. But as the nineteenth century wore on, farmers found that the opportunity costs of this insurance were oppressive. When times were "good," the gains from specialization and market involvement proved too tempting to resist. Most farmers chose to become more involved with the market despite the resultant uncertainties. However, once they abandoned their self-sufficient production, farmers could not easily back away from commercial production. Market obligations, which required money payments in most cases, made withdrawal from the marketplace impossible. When "hard times" hit, the farmers found themselves unable to cope with the situation through individual actions and turned to the government for aid.

An obvious solution to the problem of fluctuating prices was the intervention of government in commodity markets. Farm prosperity in the first two decades of the twentieth century deferred serious consideration of such ideas for a time; however, the problems in farm markets following World War I brought renewed presssures for assistance. By the late 1920s, the concept of commodity stabilization boards had become a reality. With the collapse of farm prices in the 1930s the stabilization boards gave way to the outright purchase of selected crops by the government to maintain agricultural prices at some parity level. This policy was pursued with so much vigor that by 1940 about $700 million was being spent on the stabilization of farm prices. Ten years later that figure had risen to $2.7 billion, and by the mid-1960s it had more than doubled again.[25]

25. The expenditures for stabilization of farm income are from *Historical Statistics,* Series Y-553, p. 1121. Price stabilization was not the only aid farmers received, of course. Gov-

Though it has been a very small fraction (about 2.3%) of total government spending, the money spent for support of agricultural prices provides a revealing index of the willingness of people to accept government expenditures as a means of protecting their economic security. When farmers first received cash payments to alleviate the pressures of economic forces, an important step was taken toward the overall acceptance of "income maintenance" programs. Farm families are, after all, not the only group exposed to risk through the expansion of the market system. In fact, they are in a better position to withstand the pressures and risks from market prices than are many urban families. The transformation of the United States from a rural agrarian society to an urban industrial society not only has produced many losers, it also has increased the possibility that, at any given time, anyone may become a loser. It is this potential loss—the risk of unemployment and loss of income from market forces—that creates the plight of wage earners in an industrial system: Without their job, they have no means of support. And, like the farmers who become dependent on a "cash crop" to provide money income, the workers who offer their labor in return for a cash wage cannot readily abandon their dependence on the marketplace. These groups have sought some form of "social insurance" just as the farmers eventually have come to lobby for price supports for their crops.

The market offers two ways for a wage earner to combat the risk of temporary unemployment: building up savings during period of employment or purchasing some form of insurance against such an event.[26] Either method will be effective for those who can afford it, and for workers whose incomes are high enough, self-insurance (saving when times are good) is feasible. But the incidence of unemployment falls most heavily on the less skilled, lower income members of the labor force; for these people, the market offers no effective hedge against the risk of unemployment. First, their incomes are too low to generate adequate savings, particularly in the face of frequent periods of unemployment. And second, any private system of unemployment insurance is precluded by the certainty of adverse selection: The demand would be greatest among those who represent the highest risk to the insurer. Only

ernment expenditures on agricultural research, on mortgage assistance, and on irrigation and water projects also benefit farmers, and many of these projects date back to the nineteenth century.

26. Throughout this discussion I refer to the wage earner as the person who bears the risk in the labor market. It should be obvious that many self-employed persons also bear substantial risks from potential changes in prices and market demand and their need for economic security is equally reflected in the sorts of programs discussed in the text.

by making such insurance mandatory for all workers has the government been able to create a system financed through contributions from workers and employers. Though expenditures for unemployment compensation totaled just under 3% of all government expenditures in 1970, this represented a very important response to the need for protection against unemployment.

Simultaneously, the government was taking steps to provide security for another group: the retired older worker. Historically, the market had relied on the frugality of the worker himself to save enough for his retirement. This option had done well enough for those able to maintain steady employment as part of a large group; for them, the setting up of a personal retirement scheme had been practical. Others, however, had been baffled in their attempts to set up viable pension funds: Some had faced costly periods of unemployment; others had difficulty establishing individual pension trusts because the capital market in the 1930s was not geared to the needs of the very small investor. By 1933 the problem was acute; those who had followed the market dictates and invested their savings had lost them in the shattering decline in asset prices. Almost a third of the labor force had endured unemployment, and the reduced earnings of those still employed made the prospect for future savings bleak indeed.

Against this background, Old Age Survivors Insurance, or "social security," emerged in 1935 to provide a minimum level of economic security for older workers. The commitment to fund a program of social insurance for the elderly—initially at very modest levels of expenditure—was to have far-reaching implications on the levels of government spending in years to come. For, as we have noted, social security and unemployment insurance cannot be managed as voluntary insurance plans. Only if everyone participates (willingly or not) can such "insurance" plans fund themselves. And, even where the premiums (or taxes) are set at a level to cover outlays, a strong element of redistribution of income is inherent in social insurance. Benefits to those with relatively low risks of poverty and unemployment are less (relative to the premium paid) than are benefits to those with high risk of unemployment or poverty. These risks are not randomly spread through the system; thus only the government's power to mandate participation makes possible a public program, in a situation where private insurers would be unable to operate.[27] The same feature makes such programs

27. At the time social security was enacted, it was argued that these factors also explained why *federal*, rather than state or local, government must assume responsibility for this function. Hughes points out that the truly "revolutionary" feature of social security

highly controversial should the costs become burdensome to those who do not receive net benefits from the system.

In the case of unemployment insurance, the plan has worked fairly well. Coverage is comprehensive, and income from the premiums levied on employers and workers has consistently funded the benefits paid out. Such has not been the case with social security. Through the 1950s, the large numbers of young workers entering the labor force generated sufficient funds to cover an increase in the number of workers insured, as well as higher levels of benefits. Since the age composition of the population began to shift in the 1970s, this has been changing. By the end of that decade, the costs of social security (now expanded to include substantial benefits for health as well as old age) had grown to the point where these expenditures alone accounted for over 20% of total federal expenditures; and today "income security" payments of all varieties compose more than one-third of all federal spending.[28] According to the data of Table 6.3, expenditures on "public welfare," which include farm subsidies as well as social security and other income-maintenance programs, accounted for 20% of the increase in government spending between 1902 and 1970. Viewed from another perspective, these expenditures went from about $40 million in 1902 (2.4% of all expenditures) to just over $60 billion (18.2% of all expenditures) by 1970.

There is, of course, another way in which the risk of unemployment and the problems of saving for retirement can be alleviated: Steps can be taken to ensure that the labor market offers a job for everyone. For many years, economists insisted this would be accomplished through normal adjustments in the labor market; unemployment was only "frictional." However, the 1930s showed dramatically that full employment simply cannot be taken for granted as a gift from the market system. The confidence of the American wage earner was badly shaken during a 10-year interval in which a share of the labor force ranging from 10 to 35% could not find work to do. Since that time, unemployment insurance has helped. But a more optimistic response to the challenge has been the setting of full employment as an explicit goal of government policy.

The most practical way to accomplish this objective, it was determined, was to maintain a level of government spending sufficient to

was the shifting of this burden onto the federal government (see *The Governmental Habit*, pp. 189–193). Social security was not, in fact, made mandatory in 1935, and the exclusion of all federal employees and many state employees has proven troublesome in later years, when the costs of the program have risen sharply.

28. Figures for the 1980 federal budget are from Joseph Pechman, ed., *Setting National Priorities: The 1980 Budget* (Washington, D.C.: The Brookings Institution, 1979), p. 48.

increased to make some minimal level of these services available to everyone in the society at a cost which even the poorest segment of society could afford. The argument is frequently made that society as a whole will benefit through the public provision of health and education services. Unfortunately, the marketplace will not find the combination of services and prices profitable. Here again, then, the pressures for security involve a redistribution of income in favor of one group (those who cannot afford minimal levels of health or educational services) at the expense of another group (those who could "more efficiently" obtain the services they desire through the market).

The effects of the search for security are not confined to the areas of government expenditure just discussed. Its pervasive presence indirectly influences spending in both the public and the private sector. For that reason it is not easy to quantify the impact that insecurity has had on the pattern of government expenditures. At a minimum, it can be argued that the efforts to provide public welfare—including social security, unemployment compensation, and farm stabilization programs—were prompted in large measure by the demands for greater economic security. Those programs have, by themselves, accounted for about one-fifth of the growth in government in the postwar years. If we expand our consideration to include the many areas of health and education that are also related to the problem of security, the figure would be much larger; perhaps as much as 40%. If the indirect effects of pressures to maintain full employment are taken into account, the search for economic security emerges as the single most important factor leading to the expansion of government spending.

CONCLUSION

This essay began by asking why government expenditures have grown so much over the past 75 years, and particularly during the half century since the Great Depression.

It is evident that no single factor can provide a complete answer for

belief that these goods should be made available to each member of society at some minimal cost, presumably below that which would prevail if private producers were left to determine the price. As with the definition of the public good, the distinctions become blurred when actual cases are considered. Both education and health services have characteristics of a "public good," but their production by the government is frequently defended on grounds that everyone is *entitled* to some minimal education and health service.

the phenomenal growth of the public sector; yet each of the approaches discussed in this paper tends to complement, rather than to negate, the others. The theory of public expenditures does provide insights regarding which types of goods and services government will have to produce. Certainly many of the areas where public spending has increased dramatically are in consonance with the model. The other factors we have discussed (internal pressures for bureaucratic expansion, the creation of a highly income elastic tax structure, and the demand for full employment) have all served a permissive end, removing constraints which might otherwise have curbed the growth of governmental programs. In the context of the major historical events of the twentieth century, particularly World War II and the Great Depression, each of the explanations adds some insight as to the expansion of government spending.

Nevertheless, although each factor has played an important role, it seems to be the search for security—both national security and economic security—that has been the dominant factor determining the level of public spending. The perils to our national security, whether real or exaggerated, are well known. The emergence of the United States as a world power by the end of the nineteenth century brought with it a need to maintain a military establishment which at its peak (1943–1945) absorbed almost half the total GNP. The perils to economic security are more subtle but have exerted an equally profound effect on the size and role of government in our society. The 1930s, which seemed at the time to be much longer than a mere decade, brought home with particular force just how fragile the economic security of an individual in a modern industrial society really can be. Out of that frightening historical experience came the comforting acceptance, and then the expansion, of social insurance.

Unfortunately for those of us who are economists, "social insurance" does not readily fit the categories of either a private good or a public good. The combination of adverse selection and costs precludes any comprehensive offering of coverage by a private insurance plan, while the differential distribution of benefits poses problems for the consideration of social insurance as a public service.

Equally unfortunately, the problem will not simply go away. People continue to demand that the government provide them with economic security. At the same time, they become disillusioned by the difficulties inherent in public programs which purport to address the manifold problems of "income maintenance."

So the search for economic security goes on, with no clear answer in sight.

Roger Ransom studied with Douglass North at the University of Washington from 1961 to 1963, when he received his Ph.D. At North's suggestion, Ransom focused his research on the government's promotion of canal development in the early antebellum era. In his thesis and several journal articles on this topic, Ransom employed the theory of rent to estimate the returns to investment in public transportation.

After 4 years on the faculty of the University of Virginia, Ransom moved west in 1967 and, with Richard Sutch, established the Southern Economic History Project. Ransom and Sutch have coauthored numerous articles on the post-bellum American South. In 1977 their book, **One Kind of Freedom: The Economic Consequences of Emancipation,** was published.

Ransom has taught at the University of California Riverside since 1968 and is currently chair of his Department. The paper he has contributed to this volume is a part of his ongoing research into the problems of economic insecurity in a modern economy. His most recent book, **Coping with Capitalism: The Transformation of the American Economy 1776–1970,** was published in 1981.

Chapter 7

The Historical Analysis of National Welfare Systems

Gaston V. Rimlinger

Modern welfare policies have created secondary systems of income distribution which are superimposed on the market in market economies or are integrated with the plan in centrally planned economies. Historically, the reason for the introduction of this secondary system, which provides services as well as cash incomes, is the failure of the free market to distribute and sustain incomes in a politically acceptable manner. In dynamic economies, the free market generates insecurity and inequality, which may be considered social costs of the system. Those who have to bear the burden of these costs act only rationally when they seek to protect themselves against them.

An important difference between modern and preindustrial societies is that in the latter most of the costs of insecurity are internalized. A production process based on peasant or artisan households normally provides for the cost of maintaining the household over its life cycle. Intertemporal distribution is resolved within the production unit, while inequality is legitimized by tradition and therefore not identified as a burden. The function of social policy under both capitalism and socialism is to define the institutional means for handling these inherent costs, which increase as markets become more impersonal and the population more mobile. Although welfare policy may appear to be primarily a distributional question, in the institutional sense it is a political validation of economic claims which assumes a respecification of private property rights.

EXPLORATIONS IN THE NEW ECONOMIC HISTORY

ISBN 0-12-580080-0

The task of this paper is to initiate a comparative historical analysis of national welfare systems—a term that comprises both the institutional structure of a country's welfare programs and, more specifically, their rules and objectives. The reason for stressing a comparative approach is to enhance our understanding of those forces which have shaped past institutional change. Particularly useful in dealing with complex phenomena which result from many interacting forces, systematic comparison requires that there be both common and disparate elements in the situations to be compared. Similarities and differences between countries enable the historian to make judgments about the relative causal significance of specific factors and about the circumstances that tend to support or to counteract certain forces at work.

The first three sections of this paper explore these historical similarities and differences between countries, mainly to illustrate the kind of insight one can gain from a comparative approach, rather than to generate historical generalizations. Nevertheless, an analytical approach requires that some theoretical notions about underlying causal factors be suggested. The final section of the paper examines these underlying theoretical implications.

To construct a comparative framework which brings out similarities and differences between countries, this paper follows a rather simple scheme, focusing on three fundamental questions. The first question is, How did the welfare system begin? In other words, What were the forces and circumstances that led to the recognition that the prevailing economic system, supplemented by traditional methods of relief, was in some sense "unacceptable," and what forces helped usher in the needed modifications? The second question is, What were the objectives of those who shaped welfare policies and how did these evolve over time? How did the policymakers view the role of the welfare system? The promotion of the welfare of certain groups, either by themselves or by others, is never unambiguous and hardly ever an end in itself. It always rests on power and influence and therefore is intertwined with other interests and policy considerations. The third question is, What means were selected for implementing the welfare objectives? This question explores the role of historical forces in determining the structure of the welfare system: who is to be protected, how much, against what risks, on what conditions, at whose expense, and by what administrative procedures. It is evident that this paper cannot attempt to answer these highly complex questions but can merely illustrate their role in a comparative historical approach.

THE INTRODUCTION OF THE WELFARE SYSTEM

The forces leading to modern welfare systems are extremely complex. The roots of change reach deep into the past and over a wide area. Let me begin with the general proposition that the drive for protection, of which social policy is a major component, is an inevitable and spontaneous reaction to industrial capitalism. Perhaps the best known version of this proposition was advanced by Karl Polanyi in *The Great Transformation.* In Polanyi's own words:

> If market economy was a threat to the human and natural components of the social fabric, as we insisted, what else would one expect than an urge on the part of a great variety of people to press for some sort of protection? This is what we have found. Also, one would expect this to happen without any theoretical or intellectual preconceptions on their part, and irrespective of their attitudes towards the principles underlying a market economy. Again this was the case.[2]

Polanyi emphasized the element of threat or risk to the social fabric inherent in laissez-faire capitalism. Insecurity under this system was generated not only by the uncontrolled forces of the free market—Polanyi indicated also the impersonal social relations which under laissez-faire capitalism replaced the more personal forms of social attachment and allegiance observed in preindistrial societies. Although he overstated the case by juxtaposition of extremes, it is worth noting that there is a social as well as an economic basis for insecurity in modern society.

The emphasis on threat as a key factor in the quest for protection is flatly rejected by John Kenneth Galbraith. In Galbraith's view, "the notion so sanctified by conventional wisdom, that the modern concern for security is the reaction to the peculiar hazards of modern life, could be scarcely more in error."[3] He sees the concern for security as a conse-

1. See, for instance, Maurice Bruce, *The Coming of the Welfare State* (London: B. T. Batsford, 1961); Bentley B. Gilbert, *The Evolution of National Insurance in Great Britain* (London: Michael Joseph, 1966); H. Hatzfeld, *Du paupérisme à la sécurité sociale* (Paris: A. Colin, 1971); J. R. Hay, *The Origins of the Liberal Welfare Reforms* (London: Macmillan, 1975); Hugh Heclo, *Modern Social Politics in Britain and Sweden* (New Haven: Yale University Press, 1974); Samuel Mencher, *Poor Law to Poverty Program* (Pittsburgh: University of Pittsburgh Press, 1967); Gaston V. Rimlinger, *Welfare Policy and Industrialization in Europe, America, and Russia* (New York: Wiley, 1971); H. S. Tishler, *Self-Reliance and Social Security, 1870–1917* (Port Washington, N.Y.: Kennikat Press, 1971); Walter Vogel, *Bismarck's Arbeiterversicherung* (Braunschweig: G. Westerman, 1951).
2. Karl Polanyi, *The Great Transformation* (New York: Rinehart, 1944), p. 150.
3. John Kenneth Galbraith, *The Affluent Society* (Boston: Houghton Mifflin, 1958), p. 109.

quence of rising affluence, but not in the sense suggested by some writers, that affluent countries are more able to afford the cost of protection. Galbraith argues that "with increased well-being all people become aware sooner or later that they have something to protect."[4] For him, the demand for protection arises, not from any lack of wealth or income, but rather from the possession of wealth, or the achievement of a certain level of income, and the potential danger of losing either. This is a quite different perception from Polanyi's and one perhaps more relevant for wealthy countries like the United States. One difference between Polanyi and Galbraith is that they were thinking of different stages of the industrialization process.

Concurrently with the new kinds of risks presented by industrial society, a new attitude toward risk emerged, which made preindustrial methods of social protection obsolete. In part this was a consequence of the greater numbers now exposed to economic insecurity. In the preindustrial society, those likely to depend on poor relief were relatively few and were the marginal elements. In the industrial society, potential loss of livelihood became a reality for the mass of the population. The need for protection was no longer limited to more or less chronic paupers but faced large numbers who were normally self-supporting throughout most of their productive lives. It was for them that lifetime maintenance somehow had to be incorporated into the aggregate production cost. For economic as well as for social and political reasons, such people could not be treated like traditional paupers, nor would they be satisfied with dependence on charity.

This aspect of the pressure for new forms of protection was noted with great insight by John Stuart Mill. Mill argued that the laboring classes in an industrial society would no longer accept the old idea of dependence on the ruling classes, based on authority and protection from above and obedience and deference from below. The industrial laboring classes were going to take the protection of their welfare into their own hands; they were going to insist on adequate measures to secure their livelihood. This issue, Mill wrote,

> was decided when they were taught to read, and allowed access to newspapers and political tracts. It was decided when dissenting preachers were allowed to go among them, and appeal to their faculties and feelings in opposition to the creeds professed and countenanced by their superiors. It was decided when they were brought together in numbers, to work socially under the same roof. It was decided when

4. Ibid., p. 107.

> railways enabled them to shift from place to place, and change their employers as easily as their coats.[5]

Mill was describing a fundamental factor in the development of modern welfare policy—the rising aspirations of the working classes and their growing ability to enforce their demands.

It is left to the historian to establish the merits of the conjectures of Polanyi, Galbraith, and Mill. But the historian must also account for the timing, the manner, and the agents by which the conjectured forces have been translated into varying national policies. How do policymaking elites come to recognize that the costs of industrialism are not acceptably allocated? In most countries, welfare policies seem to emerge as a response to some combination of pressures from below and changed attitudes from above. The historian finds it very difficult if not impossible to disentangle these two kinds of forces, but he can look behind them to explore the ideas and motivations of the various parties involved.

Historians of welfare policies in Britain, for instance, have emphasized the second factor, a change in ruling class attitudes toward the laboring classes as an important element in the introduction of welfare policies in the decade preceding World War I.[6] Early in the nineteenth century, there was widespread acceptance of the Malthusian view that the poor were responsible for their own misery. By the end of the century, a new social climate had become apparent. Largely as a result of new intellectual and ideological insights based on detailed scientific information about social conditions, it was now widely felt that the lower classes were actually victims of the economic system. Major investigations into the living conditions of the poor, and revelations about the deteriorated physical condition of the working population in general, had a strong impact on the conscience of the late Victorian ruling classes. Evidently, the elites had been intellectually prepared to feel vulnerable to this kind of information and had become insecure in their traditional laissez-faire attitudes.

It is interesting to explore whether similar revelations about the conditions of the laboring classes had a comparable impact in other countries. In the United States, for instance, around the turn of the century there were important revelations concerning the failings of capitalism and the burdens it imposed on the laboring population. Scholars and philanthropists were calling for social and economic reforms, and one of the

5. John Stuart Mill, *Principles of Political Economy* (London, 1848), 2:317.

6. For a recent discussion of this view, see E. P. Hennock, "Poverty and Social Theory in England: The Experience of the Eighteen-Eighties," *Social History* 1 (1976), pp. 67–91.

country's leading economists, Irving Fisher, calculated that the preventable loss from illness and premature death was, in 1910, on the order of 5% of national income.[7] None of these claims shook the dominant faith in laissez-faire capitalism. Only an economic catastrophe of the dimensions of the Great Depression of the 1930s could generate the change in social climate, the pressure from below and the change in attitude from above, essential to the inauguration of a genuine national welfare policy.

The classic case of social policy as a response to threat was no doubt the Bismarckian social insurance program. Without denying the patrimonial-state tradition in Bismarck's thinking, and without belittling his Christian charity, one must recognize that it was primarily the rumblings of revolution, threatening to obstruct his nation-building ambitions, that spurred him to action. Believing that it was the workers' sense of insecurity that made them receptive to the revolutionary doctrines of the Social Democrats, Bismarck hoped that social insurance benefits, especially pensions, would give them a countervailing stake in the survival of the social order.

Obviously, political pressure from below does not automatically generate social policies; it may merely generate repression—or a combination of the two, as was the case in Germany. There, it was not merely pressure from below but the whole German setting that explained Bismarck's welfare policy response. In the United States, until the 1930s, a perception that welfare policy would undercut individual freedom, initiative, and willingness to work always loomed larger than any potential gains from such programs. In France before World War I, neither claims that the working class was a victim of capitalist exploitation nor the threat to social stability posed by revolutionary syndicalism could succeed in generating a significant program. The French labor movement of those days neither sufficiently frightened, nor sufficiently cooperated with, the bourgeois government to promote social legislation.

Thus, beyond the role of ideologies and attitudes, one has to examine the organization and activities of interest groups in the introduction of social reforms. Which groups demand reforms, and which groups oppose them? Contrary to what one might expect, in most of the old industrialized countries the top leadership of the labor movement generally opposed the introduction of modern welfare policies. The opposition of the German Social Democrats to Bismarck's social insurance program is well known,[8] although their objection was less to social

7. *National Vitality: Its Wastes and Conservation* (Washington: GPO, 1910), p. 634.

8. See, for instance, Herta Wolff, *Die Stellung der Sozialdemokratie zur deutschen Arbeiterversicherungsgesetzegebung* (Freiburg: University of Freiburg, 1933).

insurance as such than to the uses Bismarck intented to make of it. In France the *Confédération Générale du Travail* and most of the Socialists in government bitterly fought against the 1910 pension law and helped to sabotage it after it was enacted. In the 1920s, the communist *Confédération Générale du Travail Unitaire* continued the old battle, this time against health insurance, of which the C.G.T. was now the chief proponent. Under Lenin's leadership, the 1912 Prague Conference of the Russian Social Democrats declared that the health insurance bill then being considered by the Duma was "a means of putting new chains and a yoke upon the proletariat."[9] In the United States, the leader of the largest labor organization, Samuel Gompers, President of the American Federation of Labor, expressed his opposition to social insurance in even more dramatic terms. "As long as there is one spark of life in me," he wrote, "I will help in crystallizing the spirit and sentiment of our workers against the attempt to enslave them by the well-meaning siren songs of philosophers, statisticians and politicians."[10] Why would labor leaders from such different ideological camps have such a common hostility to the emergence of social security?

The question would seem to deserve more than casual inquiry. My guess is that in each case not social security, but worker support and loyalty, was the crux of the matter. Social security was perceived by labor leaders as a serious threat to the solidarity of the labor movement, which was of course also Bismarck's view. Even in England the trade unions and the allied friendly societies feared the competition of state welfare schemes. Eventually, despite residual differences among labor groups, the labor movement itself became the chief proponent of welfare policy. The hypothesis suggested here is that so long as a labor movement is insecure and fighting for its survival, it cannot be counted on to press for policies that might appear to make the government the chief protector of the workers. Revolutionary labor movements find it particularly difficult to support measures that might strengthen the existing order by promoting stability and by weakening the workers' revolutionary ardor.

Given that employers are generally called upon to bear a major share of the cost of welfare policies, one might expect them to be the leading source of opposition. In actual fact, this was generally not the case, or at least employers have been divided. In Germany, the staunchest support for Bismarck's social insurance program came from leaders of heavy

9. V. I. Lenin, *Collected Works* (Moscow: Foreign Languages Publishing House, 1963), 17: 478.

10. Samuel Gompers, *Labor and the Employer* (New York: E. P. Dutton, 1920), p. 149.

industry, from coal and steel magnates like Ludwig Baare and Freiherr von Stumm-Halberg. Small employers, on the other hand, were generally opposed to compulsory measures and favored voluntary programs. A similar cleavage in the attitudes of large and small employers has been aptly described by Henri Hatzfeld in his history of the origins of social security in France.[11] In the United States, the introduction of social insurance in the form of workmen's compensation programs before the First World War was supported by the National Association of Manufacturers, the National Founders Association, and the National Metal Trades Association, all of which represented mainly large employers. Support from large employers was significant also in the development of British welfare legislation between 1905 and 1914, as Mr. Hay has shown.[12]

More research is needed to establish precisely the roles of employer groups in different countries. Attitudes varied according to the type of program under consideration, but it is not difficult to think of reasons why larger employers took a more positive view than did smaller employers, with regard both to welfare policy and to factory legislation. Large enterprises typically were more able to bear or to pass on their share of the welfare costs, as well as to perceive clearer potential benefits in terms of higher productivity and greater stability. Why large employers often favored compulsory over voluntary programs was, in some instances, a question of competition: Those who had started voluntary programs wanted to impose the same costs on all. The French history of family allowance programs would seem to stand as a case in point.

The role of political organization in the emergence of welfare policy is highly complex. Whether autocratic or representative government is more favorable to its inception seems to depend on the historical setting. The autocratic regime of Imperial Germany favored social insurance but not factory legislation. The former was perceived as strengthening the authority of the state, and to some extent it provided social rights as a substitute for wider political rights. In Britain, on the other hand, the democratization of political power certainly contributed to the birth of the welfare state, although with some delay; social rights came as a consequence of political rights, not a substitute for them. In neither the United States nor France did political democracy contribute to the early development of a welfare system. For this to happen, it would seem, the

11. *Du paupérisme,* pp. 136ff.

12. J. R. Hay, "Employers and Social Policy in Britain: The Evolution of Welfare Legislation, 1905–14," *Social History* 4 (1977), pp. 435–455.

democratic institution must foster a sense of social solidarity which both pervades and transcends the laboring classes. Around the turn of the century this awareness had been achieved in Britain to a much higher degree than in either France or the United States.

The social structure of a country must also be taken into account in any explanation of that country's introduction of a welfare system. An aristocratic, agrarian-based upper class with a sense of social responsibility may view the working class as an ally against the political power of the industrial elite. On the other hand, a large class of small property owners may obstruct the development of social welfare policy. For example, with regard to France, Hatzfeld has noted that this group and its liberal allies viewed compulsory social insurance programs as a hindrance to private saving and an impediment to the acquisition of private property. Small property owners were considered the backbone of the body politic and access to small properties the chief road of social ascent for the thrifty French artisan and peasant. Hatzfeld has observed that "to opt for social insurance was to call into question a given social order based on the middle classes."[13] The individualism of these classes made them particularly prickly to the bureaucratic formalism of welfare officials (*le guichetier qui vous fait revenir trois fois*). The French situation suggests that social security is not fully acceptable to a population that does not foresee that it must depend, lifelong, on earnings from its hired-out labor. Social security implies acceptance of a social and economic order based on wage dependence. It is no coincidence that farmers and self-employed professionals and artisans are usually the last groups to be covered by social security programs.

THE GOALS OF WELFARE POLICY

In discussing the origins of the welfare system, I have several times touched upon certain implicit objectives. I now want to examine these in some detail in their relation to historical development. The primary goal of the welfare system is presumably to protect the average citizen against economic risks and to improve his or her chances for personal development. The exact meaning of this goal is not self-evident and has evolved over time in response to changing economic, social, and political conditions. In addition, certain secondary goals have appeared, varying over time and from country to country; as factors in the development of the welfare systems, these relate to the political, economic, social, and demographic objectives of the policymakers. With regard to these sec-

13. *Du paupérisme*, p. 308.

ondary objectives, the welfare system is essentially a means to a different kind of end. I shall try to illustrate briefly what I mean.

In most advanced capitalist countries the welfare system evolved from some form of social protection based on poor laws. The objective of these public charity programs had been not to relieve poverty but to relieve acute distress. Although the new welfare system was very different in its spirit and practical administration, the economic relief it provided still aimed essentially at the prevention of critical hardship. Bismarck was thinking of social insurance as a means of helping workers avoid destitution. In both France and Germany the low level of protection offered made the early programs an easy target for attacks by the Socialists. The minimal benefit philosophy was still dominant in the United States in the 1930s when the Social Security Act was worked out, except that by then social insurance was explicitly conceived as a floor upon which the worker and his employer were to erect a differential private system of protection.

The Beveridge Report of 1942 represents a fundamental shift in the income protection objective.[14] The state was now to be fully responsible for a level of protection designed in itself to prevent economic hardship. Beveridge formalized the concept of a state-guaranteed uniform national minimum at a level representing "freedom from want." This ideal of a socially adequate minimum, which was shaped by Britain's war-conditioned solidarity and sharing of sacrifice, became an internationally accepted standard after World War II. It signified that new definitions of poverty and want were being adopted, at least in the more developed countries.

With the progress of reconstruction and the return to greater affluence during the 1950s, the income security objective began to shift away from the mere assurance of an adequate national minimum toward maintenance of a higher economic status. The new ideal was to protect the differential standards of living individuals had achieved rather than any basic national minimum. These conceptual changes were carefully noted by the Minister of Labor of the German Federal Republic in his statement in 1955 on the principles of pension reform then being debated:

> Originally pensions had the objective of providing merely a supplement toward subsistence, not even an existence minimum, and much less a guarantee for a standard of living. All those concerned, the Government, the insured, the pensioners, and their families were thinking only in terms of such a supplement. In part this was related to the prevailing conditions under which the pensioner was more closely tied

14. Sir William Beveridge, *Social Insurance and Allied Services* (New York: Macmillan, 1942).

> to his family; the family provided for the subsistence of its aged members. It was simply seen as desirable and necessary not to let the family bear the whole burden of the aged and to offer it a supplement from another source to lighten its load. This conception of the old age pension has undergone substantial change, not only here but in the entire world. Today the task of old-age pensions is to safeguard for those no longer at work, and under their special conditions, the standard of living they had earned through a lifetime of labor.[15]

There is an important difference between the egalitarian notion of a state-protected common minimum and the idea of using the state to protect what amounts to income inequality. There has been a growing recognition since World War II of the practical difficulties of combining high levels of protection with equal protection for all.

Let me now turn briefly to some of the nonwelfare goals of the welfare system. Social welfare programs have, or often are perceived to have, an important influence on social and political behavior, and on relationships between social classes and between individuals and the state. Welfare policies have served as a means of social and political control, in both capitalist and socialist societies. Not only in Imperial Germany, but also in Britain, in the United States, and in other capitalist countries, the introduction of welfare policies has been motivated at least in part by the desire to preserve the existing social order. By meeting basic needs, welfare programs have thus protected, not only those at the lower end of the economic scale, but also those at the higher end against pressures from below. In most capitalist societies, however, welfare policies, including education and housing policies, became eventually a tool for restructuring social and economic relations, mainly in the sense of eliminating extremes of economic inequality and uplifting those at the lower levels.

In socialist societies the welfare system has played a similar social and political role. In the Soviet Union, for instance, social welfare benefits have always been an integral part of the ideological legitimization of the prevailing system. The head of the Soviet trade unions, N. M. Shvernik, told the workers in 1938 that "every figure in the state social insurance budget . . . breathes the warmth and paternal care which our leader and teacher Comrade Stalin manifests daily and hourly toward all people, great and small."[16] Officially, Soviet welfare policy is treated as an

15. "Grundgedanken zur Gesamtreform der sozialen Leistungen—Kabinettsvorlage des Bundesminister fur Arbeit," in Max Richter, *Die Sozialreform.* Quoted in Rimlinger, *Welfare Policy,* pp. 170–171.

16. Quoted in G. V. Rimlinger, "Social Security, Incentives, and Controls in the U.S. and U.S.S.R.," *Comparative Studies in Society and History* 4 (1961), p. 112.

expression of socialist humanism and state benevolence, as well as a historic achievement of the Great October Revolution for which citizens are reminded to be grateful. A ruling party is, in fact, in an even better position than a ruling class to use welfare policy for political ends.

With regard to the economic goals of a welfare system, one may distinguish between the fiscal and the manpower aspects. Historically, the manpower aspect has been the more important, in the sense that welfare policy has generally aimed at raising the quality of the work force together with the quality of the worker's life. In Great Britain, and to a lesser extent in the United States, national efficiency has been an important consideration in the development of welfare policy. Poor health in the industrial working population is seen as not only an economic but also military weakness, and in this area welfare policy goals overlap with those of factory legislation regulating safety and the work of women and children. It is a problem which was already of concern to Adam Smith and Robert Owen, and which confronts pioneers of child labor laws in all countries.

In a fairly advanced industrial society, however, the climate of industrial relations becomes an even more pressing determinant of productivity. As labor becomes more scarce in relation to capital and therefore increases in relative value, employers become more conscious of the value of good will and zeal on the part of the workers. Certain characteristics of modern industry—such as the control problems of large-scale enterprises, the high cost of production interruptions, the high cost of training, and the high cost of absenteeism and turnover—increase the value of worker loyalty and of spontaneous cooperation. In capitalist countries, the productivity incentive depends in varying degree on the development of private welfare schemes. But even the employer primarily interested in the welfare of his own employees may find it most effective to integrate his plan with the overall public system.

Socialist countries holding complete control over the remuneration of the worker have a much stronger tool than capitalist countries for shaping welfare policy to achieve productivity objectives. Perhaps the most determined effort in this direction was carried out in the Soviet Union during the 1930s, when social insurance and related benefits were consciously transformed into instruments of industrial discipline and manpower development. This transformation has been described by one Soviet writer as follows:

> The first five-year plan opens a new era in the history of Soviet Social Insurance. Already in 1929 the social insurance organs were fully confronted with the task of reorganizing their work to achieve every possible support to the growth of labor

productivity and every encouragement to shock work and socialist competition, to heighten the struggle against absenteeism and labor turnover, and to aid in the formation of cadres and the strengthening of labor discipline.[17]

It should be noted that this rather extreme attempt to exploit the productivity potential of welfare policy occurred during a period that approached a national emergency. In other countries as well, especially during wartime, welfare policy has been used to stimulate greater effort. In his essay on "War and Social Policy," Richard Titmus has shown how in Britain during World War II social policy was called upon to stimulate greater social discipline and a heightened commitment to a common purpose.[18]

The demographic goal of welfare policy can be mentioned only in passing. In some countries, particularly in France, low birth rates over long periods led to welfare programs such as family allowances and marriage and birth premia to stimulate population growth. One could also imagine welfare policies designed to reduce population growth. In developing countries, old age pensions might reduce the perceived need for relying on one's children in old age and thus contribute toward lower birth rates over time.

THE MEANS OF THE WELFARE SYSTEM

I have so far discussed the historical interpretation of welfare systems with regard to the forces involved in their introduction and with regard to certain basic objectives. Much historical insight can be gained also by looking at the various means of employed to achieve the welfare goals—such aspects as coverage, conditions of eligibility, benefit structures, and methods of financing and administration. To some extent these are technical issues, but historical analysis often reveals that the manner in which technical issues are resolved is a reflection of underlying economic and ideological motivation.

How do countries resolve such questions as who should be protected, on what conditions, and against what risks? Another way of putting this question would be, How do countries determine the nature or extent of an individual's right to protection? Under the poor laws of most countries the individual did not have a right to protection; the community

17. L. Ia. Gintsburg, *Trudovoi Stazh Rabochikh i Sluzhashchikh* (Moscow: Akademii Nauk, 1958), p. 66.

18. Richard M. Titmus, *Essays on the Welfare State* (London: Allen and Unwin, 1958), Chapter 4.

merely imposed upon itself a more or less definite obligation to relieve distress. The recipient was considered a failure and usually penalized in one way or another. If the motivation of the community was partly humanitarian, the methods of protection reflected a concern with order, discipline, and industriousness.[19]

The modern welfare system has eliminated the punitive intent and established claims to benefits and services as a matter of individual right. But that right is defined by rules of coverage and eligibility, and often by source of risk, and historically it has undergone important changes. In the early stage of modern welfare policy in capitalist countries, the right to income protection was often restricted to manual workers in industrial enterprises of a certain size. This was the group that Bismarck was most interested in protecting. In many countries, especially in France and in Latin America, income protection was initially restricted to specific industries or occupations, such as mining, railroads, seafaring, and government employment. Given that many countries excluded from coverage persons above a specified level of income, it may appear that presumed need was the criterion for protection, but this would be at best a partial explanation, because in most cases the people with the greatest need were excluded. Initially, the new right to protection in capitalist countries was granted primarily to those groups which were well enough organized or had sufficient strategic importance to pose an economic or political threat to the prevailing order.

In the Soviet Union, the system of state social insurance applied for a long time only to persons working for wages or salaries, although the Constitution of 1936 guaranteed the right to protection to all citizens. Partly for ideological reasons, collective farmers were not covered, but this largest of the excluded groups finally became part of the state system in 1964. In the United States, also, farmers and self-employed persons were initially excluded from the social security system, but the policymakers were explicit in their refusal to tie the right to protection to social class considerations; protection was intended for all citizens regardless of income, with the exception only of certain occupations whose members mostly wished to be excluded.

Two fundamental principles of the Beveridge report had been the equal eligibility of all citizens for benefits and services, and the comprehensiveness of the risks to be covered. Following World War II, most countries were endorsing those principles and moving in the direction of liberalizing the rules. But then something happened. In spite of rising

19. See, for instance, E. S. Furniss, *The Position of the Laborer in a System of Nationalism* (Boston: Houghton Mifflin, 1920).

prosperity during the 1950s and 1960s, it became evident that welfare policies based on equal rights left substantial minorities without a meaningful share in the prevailing affluence. The problem became particularly apparent among the racial and regional (e.g., Appalachia) minorities of the United States, but it arose also in other countries. The aim of an egalitarian and integrated society, which had inspired the universalist approach, now was seen to require an unequal approach: Discriminatory action in favor of underprivileged groups now had to be built into social policy. The real challenge for the affluent society, as Richard Titmus has noted, is to develop acceptable selective services as social rights around an infrastructure of universalist services.[20] This demand for a differentiated approach is not directly related to the demand for differentiated benefits noted earlier, but both developments illustrate the complexity of the drive for greater equality. There are clearly limits in the extent to which inequality may be considered a social cost; certain formal inequalities may be required to achieve egalitarian objectives.

The basis on which the right to protection is granted has important implications for methods of financing and levels of benefit. Specifically, it matters whether a certain level of protection is seen as a right that has to be earned personally by the beneficiary, or as a right inherent in citizenship. The most striking contrast in this regard may be found in the American and the Soviet approaches to social insurance. When the social security system was developed in the 1930s in the United States, it faced a formidable ideological obstacle in the historic American individualism. To counteract the argument of opponents that social security would rob the individual of his freedom by making him dependent on the state, the official literature and spokesmen stressed that benefits would not be based on any act of governmental benevolence but would be in the nature of an earned contractual right. Secretary of Labor Francis Perkins explained in a pamphlet for general distribution that in America protection against unemployment was similarly "a matter of contractual right."[21] Professor J. Douglas Brown, one of the architects of the Social Security Act, testified before Congress that "by contributing the individual worker established an earned contractual right to his annuity."[22] Somehow benefits were to be a matter of law and actuarial

20. Richard M. Titmus, "Universal and Selective Social Services," *New Statesman* (1967) reprinted in idem, *Commitment to Welfare* (London: Allen and Unwin, 1968), pp. 113–123.

21. U.S. Congress, Committee on Economic Security, *Security* (Washington, D.C.: GPO, 1934), p. 6.

22. U.S. Congress, *Hearings before the Committee on Ways and Means on H. R. 4120* (January 21, 1935), (Washington, D.C.: GPO, 1935), p. 241.

computation, protected from political decision. To be sure, the authors of the American system were well aware of the paradox inherent in basing social rights on individualistic principles. The original system, with its close similarity to private insurance, was not tenable for very long. It has been modified many times, but mainly on the benefit side. The original principle of individualistic financing without governmental contributions is still largely intact despite severe pressure.

The Soviet social insurance system has always been based on the opposite principle, that all benefits are a gift of a benevolent state, without any kind of contractual right earned by the individual. Soviet legal experts maintain that there is no "mutuality and reciprocity" and no contractual relationship in their social insurance; only the state has an obligation, not the worker.[23] They are certainly correct in claiming that the right of Soviet workers to protection has nothing to do with contributions to insurance funds, but the notion of a gift from the state is difficult to grasp, especially where all incomes are state controlled.

THEORETICAL IMPLICATIONS

There have been numerous attempts in recent years to develop theoretical generalizations on the basis of comparative welfare policy experience.[24] Most of these studies have explored quantitative relation-

23. A. S. Krasnopol'skii, "On the Nature of Soviet State Social Insurance," *Current Digest of the Soviet Press* (December 29, 1951), p. 6. For a more extensive discussion, see his *Osnovnye Printsipy Sovetskogo Sotsial'nogo Strakhovaniia* (Moscow: Akademii Nauk, 1951).

24. Included among these studies are the following: Henry J. Aaron, "Social Security: International Comparisons," in Otto Eckstein, ed., *Studies in the Economics of Income Maintenance* (Washington, D.C.: The Brookings Institution, 1967), pp. 13–48; Phillips Cutright, "Political Structure, Economic Development, and National Security Programs," *American Journal of Sociology* 70 (1965), pp. 537–550; idem, "Income Redistribution: A Cross-National Analysis," *Social Forces* 46 (1967), pp. 180–190; Peter Flora, Jens Alber, and Jürgen Kohl, "Zur Entwicklung der Westeuropäischen Wohlfahrtsstaaten," *Politische Vierteljahresschrift* 18 (1977); pp. 707–772; Phillis M. Frakt, "Democracy, Political Activity, Economic Development, and Governmental Responsiveness: The Case of Labor Policy," *Comparative Political Studies* 10 (1977), pp. 177–212; Walter Galenson, "Social Security and Economic Development," *Industrial and Labor Relations Review* 21 (1968), pp. 559–569; Margaret S. Gordon, *The Economics of Welfare Policies* (New York: Columbia University Press, 1963); Jerald Hage and Robert Hanneman, "The Growth of the Welfare State in Four Western European Societies: A Comparison of Three Paradigms" (paper presented at the second annual meeting of the Social Science History Association, Ann Arbor, Michigan, 1977); Hugh Heclo, "Income Maintenance: Patterns and Priorities," in A. J. Heidenheimer, H. Heclo, and C. T. Adams, eds., *Comparative Public Policy* (New York: St. Martin's Press, 1975), pp. 187–226; Robert W. Jackman, "Socialist Parties and Income Inequality in Western Industrial Societies," *Journal of Politics* 42 (1980), pp. 135–149; Stein Kuhnle, "The

ships between welfare policy and economic, political, and social variables. They have been primarily concerned with preconditions for the initiation of welfare policies and with determinants of the levels and rates of growth of welfare expenditures. One study in particular has concentrated on the international geographic diffusion of welfare programs.[25] On the whole, as Jens Alber has shown, these studies have established certain broad relationships, but the statistical results are often either inconsistent or weak.[26] In addition, they do not provide the kind of theoretical framework that would be helpful in analyzing the growth of *welfare systems* as institutional developments with their own rules and goals. This type of structural and organizational change has been the underlying concern of this paper, which has explored some of the historical differences between countries in the timing and in the choice of goals and methods.[27] An attempt will be made now to analyze the forces underlying the observed patterns in more generalized theoretical terms. The institutional changes that are the subject of discussion have as their objective the shifting of income risks for the mass of the population from the private market to the government. This shift, extending the protective functions of government into the economic sphere, implies a nonmarket redistribution which in turn requires a

---

Beginnings of the Nordic Welfare States: Similarities and Differences" (paper presented at the Ninth World Congress of Sociology, Uppsala, 1978); Felix Paukert, "Social Security and Income Redistribution: Comparative Experience," in E. M. Kassalow, ed., *The Role of Social Security in Economic Development* (Washington, D.C.: GPO, 1968), pp. 101–127; Guy Peters, "Economic and Political Effects on the Development of Social Expenditures in France, Sweden, and the United Kingdom," *Midwest Journal of Political Science* 16 (1972), pp. 225–238; Frederick L. Pryor, *Public Expenditures in Communist and Capitalist Nations* (Homewood, Ill.: Irwin, 1968); Koji Taira and Peter Kilby, "Differences in Social Security Development in Selected Countries," *International Social Security Review* 22:2 (1969), 139–153; Harold L. WIlensky, *The Welfare State and Equality* (Berkeley: University of California Press, 1975).

25. David Collier and Richard E. Messick, "Prerequisites Versus Diffusion: Testing Alternative Explanations of Social Security Adoption," *American Political Science Review* 69 (1975), pp. 1299–1315.

26. See Jens Alber, "Die Entwicklung sozialer Sicherungssysteme im Lichte empirischer Analysen," to appear in Hans F. Zacher, ed., *Bedingungen für die Entstehuing und Entwicklung von Sozialversicherung* (Berlin: Bunker & Humbolt).

27. Earlier studies of the subject by this author include those cited in Notes 1 and 16—*Welfare Policy* (1971) and "Social Security, Incentives, and Controls" (1961)—as well as "Social Change and Social Security in Germany," *Journal of Human Resources* 3 (1968), pp. 409–421; "Social Security and Society: An East–West Comparison," *Social Science Quarterly* 50 (1969), pp. 494–506; "American Social Security in a European Perspective," in W. G. Bowen, ed., *The American System of Social Insurance* (New York: McGraw-Hill, 1968); and "Welfare Policy and Economic Development: A Comparative Historical Perspective," *Journal of Economic History* 26 (1966), pp. 556–571.

redefinition of property rights. It involves "using the political system to alter the market structure," to borrows Douglass North's phrase.[28]

Underlying the differences between countries noted in this essay are two basic elements: one is interactions—coalitions and confrontations—between groups with competing goals; the other is interplay of rival ideologies. These are the basic elements of the proposed analytical framework. The relevant groups include organized labor, business, and other economic and professional groupings, as well as political parties, ruling coalitions, and governmental bureaucracies. The goals involved are shaped by economic interests and by ideologies. It is assumed for analytical purposes that groups seek to maximize their economic interests within existing structural and ideological constraints. One important structural constraint is power and authority relationships, particularly within governments.[29] Groups will seek those coalitions of forces which yield them greatest control over the redistributive actions of the state. It has to be kept in mind, however, that interests are perceived through an ideological prism and that the actions of groups have to be carried out by agents. Agents act in their own interest, which is not necessarily identical with that of the group they represent. This is why labor or political leaders may oppose welfare policies that might benefit their constituents but would also give a strategic advantage to a rival—which may be the government. The interests of different groups may coincide without being identical. Under Bismarck, the interest of the German bureaucracy in social insurance was far from identical with that of the Kaiser. Employers may support workers seeking a particular program primarily for reasons of productivity rather than of welfare. Opportunities for coalitions are conditioned by the historical relationships between groups and by institutional traditions.

The role of ideology has been largely overlooked by economic historians. They tend to view ideologies as other economists do, merely as given preferences. Or they may see ideologies simply as rationalizations, lacking any analytical relevance. Yet in explaining institutional changes

28. "Structure and Performance: The Task of Economic History," *Journal of Economic Literature* 16 (1978), p. 971. The discussion in the remainder of this section is indebted to ideas developed by Professor North in an economic history seminar which he taught at Rice University in the autumn of 1979 as Visiting Peterkin Professor of Political Economy. See also his articles: "A Framework for Analyzing the State in Economic History," *Explorations in Economic History* 16 (1979), pp. 249–259; "The New Economic History after Twenty Years," *American Behavioral Scientist* 21 (1977), pp. 187–199; "Markets and Other Allocation Systems in History: The Challenge of Karl Polanyi," *Journal of European Economic History* 6 (1977), pp. 703–716.

29. For a recent discussion of this aspect of governments, see Paul M. Sacks, "State Structure and the Asymmetrical Society," *Comparative Politics* 12 (1980), pp. 349–376.

an approach that overlooks the role of ideology is seriously deficient. Ideologies have to be seen as ideas or systems of ideas which are used to justify and to facilitate actions. In that sense, ideologies orient, as well as constrain, the actions and goals of groups. Their impact has two important and economically relevant dimensions. First, when used to identify the interest of the individual with that of the group, ideologies help to overcome the free rider problem. Second, ideologies serve to lower resistance to, or induce cooperation for, certain actions. They thereby lower the cost of using the political system—that is, the transaction costs of political action. Alternatively, any group that is able to utilize widely shared beliefs and values to facilitate, glorify, or legitimate its own actions has a cost advantage over other groups competing for use of the political system. Of course, groups do not ordinarily invent ideologies; that is mainly a function of intellectuals, and the process is part of the historical setting. But groups selectively adopt and nurture ideologies which suit their interests or lower their political transaction costs. Once embraced, even obsolescent ideologies may persist because of material as well as psychic costs in discarding them over a short period of time.

The task of comparative welfare-policy history, as conceived in this paper, is thus to explain the development of national welfare systems by focusing on similarities and differences between countries. The argument has been advanced here that such similarities and differences can be explained in terms of the interactions of groups and the interplay of ideologies as these emerge over time and in different places. A framework has been suggested within which to explore development patterns and to formulate testable historical hypotheses.

Gaston Rimlinger was introduced to Douglass North as a senior at the University of Washington. He took North's seminar in American Economic History in the Fall of 1950 and graduated from the University in 1951. He then left for North's own alma mater, the University of California, where he received his Ph.D. in 1956. Rimlinger has been at Rice University since 1960 and now is the Reginald Henry Hargrove Professor of Economics.

Rimlinger is known for his book, **Welfare Policy and Industrialization in Europe, America, and Russia**, which appeared in 1971, but his interests are not confined to economic history; from 1969 to 1972 he was with the Ford Foundation in West Africa.

Chapter 8

A Theory of Regenerative Growth and the Experience of Post-World War II West Germany

Donald F. Gordon and Gary M. Walton

The rapid recovery of war-destroyed Western Europe after World War II was then, and has since been, the subject of widespread discussion among scholars, laymen, government officials, and policymakers. Firm evidence on the degree of destruction and the subsequent rates of recovery, particularly in the years immediately following the cessation of hostilities, is difficult to obtain. Though somewhat imperfect, the indices in Table 8.1 provide rough contours of the degrees of destruction for selected nations as reflected in terms of per capita income. The table also permits some comparison of the alternative rates of growth in the early postwar years.

This rough sketch of pre-World War II and post-World War II economic conditions suggests that West Germany suffered the greatest degree of economic destruction, with Austria, Greece, Italy, France, and the Netherlands also experiencing an absolute fall in per capita income in the period from 1938 through 1947. These countries also shared a common experience of rapid recovery and high growth rates which later declined.

Of particular interest is the growth record of West Germany between 1945 and 1960. Few other nations, rich or poor, matched its performance during that period despite its earlier cataclysmic devastation. In fact, the exceptionally high growth rate achieved by West Germany after 1945 has been regarded by many as a phenomenon—a *wirtschaftswunder*, or economic miracle.

So many attempts have been made to explain the rapid West German

EXPLORATIONS IN THE NEW ECONOMIC HISTORY

ISBN 0-12-580080-0

TABLE 8.1
Indices of Real Per Capita Gross National Product[a] (1953 = 100)

	1938	1947	1948	1949	1950	1951	1952	1953	1954	1955
Austria	[76][b]	[47]	66	79	88	97	98	100	109	121
Belgium	[77]	[83]	87	88	92	97	98	100	102	107
Denmark	83	86	88	90	97	96	95	100	102	101
France	[79]	[72]	[78]	88	94	97	99	100	104	(111)
Germany (F.R.)	[101]	[50]	[58]	66	77	89	94	100	107	117
Greece	[118]	[77]	72	82	82	89	90	100	102	108
Ireland	83	83	88	92	94	95	98	100	101	104
Italy	89	75	77	81	86	93	94	100	104	111
Luxembourg	[87]	—	—	101	107	100	99	100	104	107
Netherlands	[84]	[78]	84	90	92	91	93	100	104	110
Norway	75	84	88	89	93	96	98	100	103	106
Portugal	(78)	(85)	(88)	(89)	(96)	96	95	100	105	105
Sweden	77[c]	84	89	92	96	95	97	100	105	107
Switzerland	[86]	[94]	[95]	[92]	[96]	[99]	[98]	100	[105]	[107]
United Kingdom	(88)	87	89	92	95	97	96	100	104	107

Source: OEEC, *Statistics of National Product and Expenditure, No. 2, 1938 and 1947 to 1955* (Paris, 1957).

[a] Brackets are used in this table to indicate rough estimates prepared by the Secretariat. These must be considered as subject to a rather important margin of error in most cases, but are indicators of the approximate orders of magnitude involved if their limitations are borne in mind.

Parentheses indicate cases where certain rather arbitrary standard estimating assumptions have been used by the Secretariat. In most cases it appears that the margin of error in the resultant figures is relatively small. The standard cases where parentheses have been used are (*a*) in connection with linking an older series to a revised series; (*b*) in assuming that defense and civil public expenditure follow the same price development as total public consumption; (*c*) in assuming that the gross national product at factor cost follows the same volume development as the gross national product at market prices. (See above source, p. 49.)

[b] 1937.

[c] 1938–1939.

recovery that merely to catalog them and to consider their supporting logic and evidence would be overly burdensome here. Of these attempts, none has been supported adequately with economic theory or empirical tests, and some actually contradict conventional theory. Typically they stress the unique institutions, culture, occupation policies, and other special features of early postwar Germany.[1]

1. Examples are legion. Among others, see A. K. Cairncross, "The Economic Recovery of Western Germany," *Lloyds Bank Review* Vol. 22 (1951): 30; Ferenc Janossy, *The End of the Economic Miracle* (White Plains, N.Y.: International Arts and Sciences Press, 1971); Rolf Krengel, "Some Reasons for the Rapid Economic Growth of the German Federal Republic," *Banca Nationale del Lavoro Quarterly Review* (Rome) 16 (1963), pp. 121–144; Horst Mendershausen, *Two Postwar Recoveries of the German Economy* (Amsterdam: North Holland, 1955); H. C. Wallich, *Mainspring of the German Revival* (New Haven: Yale University Press, 1955). There is also a series launched by Egon Sohmen, "Competition and Growth: West Germany," *American Economic Review* 49 (1959): 896–1003, followed by various comments

It would seem apparent, however, especially in light of the same tendency recorded by Japan, the Soviet Union, and some lesser cases as well,that what West Germany was experiencing was normal and predictable—a period of unnaturally high growth emerging from destruction, or what we here term "regenerative growth." In fact the "economic miracle" so admired in the case of West Germany was treated as a commonplace manifestation in the most influential economic textbook of the nineteenth century:

> The great rapidity with which countries recover from a state of devastation . . . has so often excited wonder. . . . An enemy lays waste a country by fire and sword, and destroys or carries away nearly all the moveable wealth existing in it: all the inhabitants are ruined, and yet in a few years after, everything is much as it was before. This *vis medicatrix naturae* has been a subject of sterile astonishment. . . . There is nothing at all wonderful in the matter.[2]

Despite the number of economists who reacted to post-World War II recovery with a repetition of Mill's "sterile astonishment," others did note the plausibility of spontaneous rapid growth succeeding massive destruction, and Clark, Friedman, and others reported the eventual slowing of such spurts to "normal" growth trends.[3]

---

and his reply, as follows: Alastair I. MacBean and W. Geoffrey Shepherd, "Competition and Growth—the Lesson of West Germany: Comment," *American Economic Review* 50 (1960), pp. 1018–1021; Roger G. Opie, "Comment," ibid., pp. 1022–1025; Karl W. Roskamp, "Comment," ibid., pp. 1015–1018; and finally Sohmen, "Reply," ibid., pp. 1025–1031.

A few explanations proffered for the German post-World War II "miracle" include the Marshall Plan, the Korean War boom, the pro-business political leadership, the investment incentives of the tax program, the "German national character," the monetary reform and freeing of the price system in 1948, the policies of the occupation authorities, the general policy of free enterprise, the low wages (a result, allegedly, of a combination of docility on the part of trade union leaders, a "probusiness" leadership, and other aspects of national character) leading to high profits and hence high saving and investment, and the alleged German propensity for hard work. Some accounts list a whole series of these and other factors, which of course constitute no explanation at all.

2. J. S. Mill, *Principles of Political Economy*, Book I, Chapter 5, Section 7. Mill's explanation seems to involve the propositions that (*a*) capital is created and destroyed in a very short period at all times (reminiscent of a wages fund); (*b*) land and food production are assumed to be left intact by the destruction; and (*c*) capital is created solely by labor (as opposed to a combination of labor and capital). He adds the puzzling comment that the saving involved is "involuntary privation." He attributes the theory to Thomas Chalmers who, however, had indicated specifically that under the stimulus of higher than ordinary gains "capital . . . would be fully restored . . . by the privations of a few successive seasons." Thomas Chalmers, *Works*, Vol. 19, *On Political Economy* . . . (Glasgow: 1836–1842), Chapter iv, section 13, pp. 140–142. This view anticipates the theme of this paper.

3. The idea that after destruction an economy may experience "natural" rapid regenerative growth until it returns to a "normal" growth trend is not new in this paper, even as

The goal of this paper is to analyze more precisely the mechanisms of regenerative growth within the framework of accepted economic theory. Regenerative growth, the phenomenon to be explained, is rapid recovery from economic destruction followed by a slowing of growth. Consider the output per capita of a hypothetical war-torn economy on the eve of peace, as illustrated abstractly in Figure 8.1. We may suppose its level to be at some point *C*, below some higher level, say *C*′, which would have prevailed if destruction had not been suffered. The growth trends, *AB* (prewar) and *DE* (postrecovery), reflect the "normal" long-run trend rate of growth, and *CD* indicates the more rapid rate during the period of recovery.[4] What must be explained is why the growth rate surpasses "normal" during the period of recovery and why it then slows to "normal" in the long run.

It should be stressed at the outset that the following analysis attempts to explain, not the long-run aspects of growth, but rather the factors that raise the postwar recovery rate above the normal long-run trend rate.

Models based on a theory of regenerative growth are presented in the second section. Their implications are tested in the third section with data on West Germany. The fourth section briefly considers human capital as a source of regenerative growth, and the fifth section sums up our findings.

THE THEORETICAL FRAMEWORK[5]

The Traditional Case

To begin, we assume an aggregate production function for an economy with the traditional factors of land, labor, and capital, all homogeneous.[6] Because all factors are included, the function is viewed

---

applied to a postwar period. The idea first was stated in this specific way in the West by Colin Clark in "The Myth of Soviet Productivity," *Fortune*, March 1960; it was attributed to Friedman by Lawrence Klein in "A Model of Japanese Economic Growth, 1878–1937," *Econometrics* 29 (1961), pp. 277–292. Also of interest are statements by B. Bazarov quoted in Nicholas Spulber, *Soviet Strategy for Economic Growth* (Bloomington: Indiana University Press, 1964). Nevertheless, the acknowledgment of this process was not accompanied by any explicit theoretical explanation.

4. Although the postwar trend rate of growth is not expected to equal the historical trend exactly, the two trends are expected to be approximately the same and distinctly lower than the rate of growth during the recovery period.

5. Major portions of this section stem from Donald F. Gordon, "A Theory of Regenerative Growth," Working Paper #7023, Graduate School of Management, University of Rochester (presented to the annual meeting of the Western Economic Association, University of California, Davis, August, 1970).

6. Aggregation does not require that we think of a one-product economy; it requires

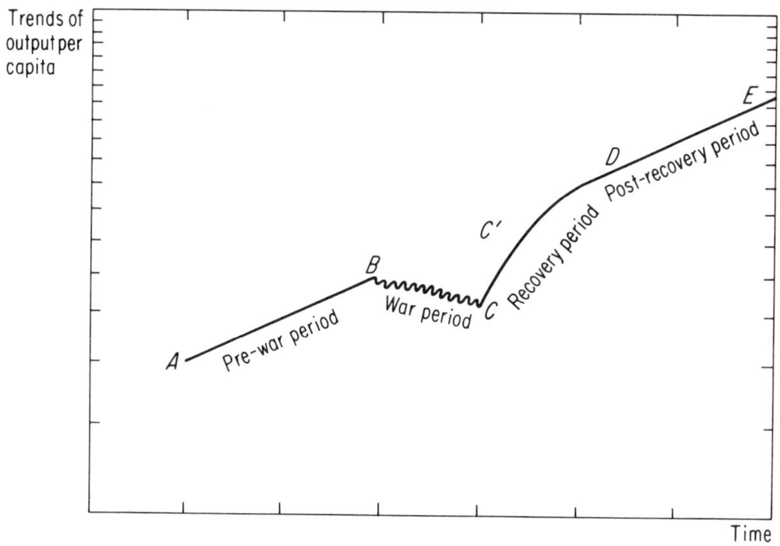

FIGURE 8.1. Illustration of regeneration: output per capita trends.

as linear and homogeneous. For the present, we also assume that the economy is closed[7] and that technology is constant and uniform across countries. Isoquants from such a production function are shown in Figure 8.2, where capital is measured along one axis and composite bundles of the other (constant) factors are measured on the other.

A notable feature common to the destroyed economies was a drastic decline in the quantity of capital relative to other factors. Let *FA* represent the predestruction quantity and *FB* the postwar quantity. With the same quantity of other factors the marginal efficiency of investment will

---

that we assume that the production of each commodity demands the same ratio of the factors of production at any set of price ratios. With a suitable unit of measurement this gives identical isoquants.

7. Once aggregation is assumed this further assumption is immaterial as far as balanced trade in commodities is concerned. In principle it would be a bad assumption to exclude net capital flows, since under the circumstances envisaged in the subsequent models one would expect a sharp influx of capital provoked by higher than normal rates of return. In fact, even with the Marshall Plan, only a small influx occurred in West Germany in the regenerative period and almost none in the earlier postwar period of greatest capital scarcity, perhaps because of fears of political insecurity. Total credit from the Economic Recovery Plan as a percentage of gross investment was in fact less than 3%, 1949–1956. See Egon R. Baumgart, *Investitionin und ERP-Finanzierung* (Berlin: 1961), p. 125; or Wallich, *Mainspring*, p. 126. Moreover, the economic theory of the gift would suggest that such donations contributed even less in percentage terms to capital formation; therefore foreign capital will be excluded from consideration in the rest of the paper.

be higher at B than at A;[8] and this added because this incentive to save will lead to a higher savings fraction;[9] therefore an economy at B should be expected to grow faster than at A.

Yet this is not very satisfactory as an explanation of regenerative growth. It is true that a destroyed economy such as postwar West Germany should grow faster at B than it would at A. However, the model suggests that it should also grow more slowly than most of the other economies in the world which had less capital per head, for example, an economy at E. Clearly the West German economy in the immediate postwar period was still considerably richer than most underdeveloped countries and at the same time growing much faster.

Moreover, this simple model becomes ambiguous when demographic forces are introduced. If we differentiate the production function $Y = F(N, L, K)$ with respect to time where Y, N, L, and K are output, population (labor force), land, and capital, respectively, we get, after some rearrangement of terms,

$$\frac{\mathring{Y}}{Y} - \frac{\mathring{N}}{N} = F_K s + \frac{\mathring{N}}{N}\left(\frac{F_N N}{Y} - 1\right)$$

where subscripts indicate marginal products, s is the savings fraction, and the dots indicate time derivatives. Both components of $F_K s$ are larger when K is smaller: thus the growth advantage of the destroyed economy. Yet it is possible that a shift in the second term could offset or exceed this, since the wage fraction of national output, $F_N N/Y$, could fall with a reduced K if the elasticity of substitution were less than unity.[10] Consequently, the traditional production function provides hardly more than minimal insight into the problem of regenerative growth.

Alternative Models

Modifying the traditional analysis just considered, each of the following models introduces another general concept: that post-destruction

8. If we dropped the assumption of aggregation, this higher return of new investment might be somewhat reduced by the fact that the production of capital goods might in itself use relatively large amounts of capital goods services which are now high priced factors. This could not eliminate the higher rate of return, however, since the higher price of capital goods services represents the whole of their return but only part of their cost. On the other hand, if capital goods production used relatively small amounts of capital goods services, the new return would be even higher than in the model used here.

9. We are presuming a positive elasticity of saving with respect to interest. For evidence see M. Boskin, "Taxation, Saving and the Rate of Interest," *Journal of Political Economy* 86 (1978), pp. 53–527.

10. The elasticity of substitution seems in fact to be substantially less than unity (see ibid.).

capital is not only relatively reduced in quantity, but is dislocated, or available only in forms inappropriate to the relative quantities of other factors available and/or to the relative demand for commodities then prevailing. This has two effects. First, it reduces the quantity of output by more than would be expected to result merely from the reduced quantity of capital and the normal production function. Second, it creates an opportunity for much more than normal growth from the new abnormally low level of output.

Model 1: Unadaptable Homogeneous Capital. First consider a modification of the traditional case to incorporate an idea recurrent in economic theory: that the ratios of capital to other factors are variable at the time of investment but thereafter are less variable or are fixed at the limit. Stigler has noted a property which he terms "adaptability," which to some degree would make these ratios as variable after investment as before.[11]

The effects of unadaptability can be intuitively seen if we modify the well-known example cited by the late Sir Dennis Robertson. If 10 men using 10 shovels are digging a ditch, what happens to output if someone steals 5 shovels? Perhaps it falls by close to 50%. To find any smaller long-run loss we must imagine the 5 remaining shovels transformed through depreciation into 10 inferior shovels with the same cost of production. Conversely, replacing the 5 good shovels would raise output by much more than would be accomplished by replacing the 10 hypothetical inferior shovels with 10 of the original quality.

The effects of unadaptability can be seen by reference to Figure 8.2. Consider an extreme case of complete short-run unadaptability, or fixed postinvestment proportions (the elasticity of substitution is zero in the short run). A loss of *AB* in capital would nullify a proportionate amount of other factors (*BD*). Output would fall by this proportion—to the isoquant I_1. In other words, the loss of *AB* because of unadaptability would cause output to fall as if the capital loss had been *AE* (for capital completely adaptable). Here, although postdestruction output is lower because of unadaptability, any increase in output caused by increased capital would for that reason be much higher. To reach I_3 from I_1, an economy in long-run equilibrium with a correctly adapted capital stock would have to accumulate *AE*, whereas the economy with unadapted capital would need only *AB*. *Therefore, the economy with unadapted capital FB can be expected to grow substantially faster than an economy with adapted capital FE (both having per capita output I_1).* In addition, given

11. George Stigler, "Production and Distribution in the Short Run," *Journal of Political Economy* 47 (1939), pp. 305–327. E. S. Phelps has given the term "putty-clay" to a related but broader concept in which unadaptability is total and, further, postinvestment

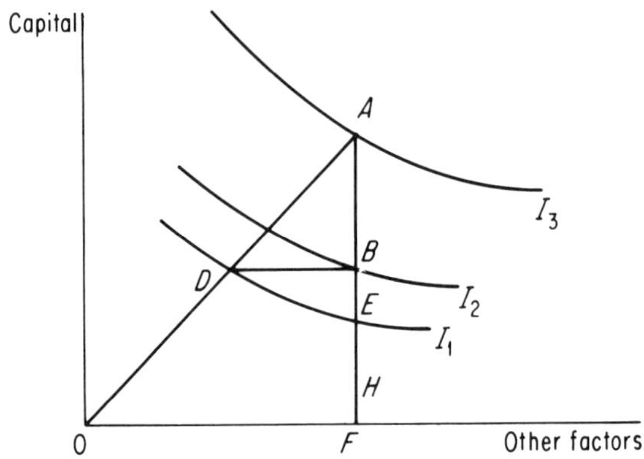

FIGURE 8.2. Unadaptable homogeneous capital.

some continuity in the production function, we may also expect that nation's economy to grow somewhat faster than that of some poorer economy, say at *H*. According to this unadaptability model, then, it is not really surprising that West Germany was able to recover so fast. Indeed it was precisely because of the vast original devastation that the rapid growth occurred.

Given unadaptability, rapid growth is effected through relative price movements. Because of the loss of capital, entrepreneurs are induced to apportion lesser amounts of capital to more of the other factors, resulting in higher marginal returns to capital. With perfectly unadaptable capital, wages and land rent would be placed under great pressure, the returns to all redundant factors would in principle fall to zero, and all national income would be absorbed by higher quasi-rents to capital. Even without such extremes, any degree of unadaptability would tend, by raising the returns to capital, to provide incentives to save and invest.[12]

Model 2: Factor Price Rigidity. Some degree of unadaptability may also result from imperfect flexibility in the prices of other factors. If we assume complete factor price rigidity, but no unadaptability for technological reasons, the loss of capital will have precisely the same effect on output as if there were complete technological unadaptability. Output is

---

technological change has no effect on output (Phelps, "Substitution, Fixed Proportions, Growth and Distribution," *International Economic Review* 4 [1963], pp. 265–288).

12. There is a potentially interesting dynamic programming problem here, since the designers of new durable capital would presumably foresee a change in relative factor costs as the future economy returns to normal.

higher with adapted capital (at B) than with unadapted capital (at D) because, given adaptability, the existing short supply of capital can be combined with the whole quantity of other factors. If the prices of these other factors remain constant, however, there will be no incentive to reach such combinations. The factor proportions used will produce the same marginal products as at A (or D), and the same quantities of other factors will lie idle as would happen in the case of technological unadaptability.

Given rigid factor prices, a devastated economy again has a growth advantage: The same increment of capital, AB, will raise it from I_1 to I_3. Although the factors will be combined in proportions such that the marginal product of capital will remain the same as at A, that increment of capital will result in the addition of other marginal products because it induces corresponding increments of other factors which had previously been idle.[13] Assuming rigid factor prices, these marginal products will not vary until equilibrium is restored. The per worker output of the utilized factors will remain constant, and increased employment will lead to rapid growth in output for the population as a whole. It is true, however, that no extra stimulus now exists to save and invest, because the return to the investor would be the same as at A.

Model 3: Unadaptable Heterogeneous Capital. Even further insight is gained if we allow for a heterogeneous capital stock while retaining the assumption that we can aggregate total output. If different types of capital are destroyed in different proportions, even greater and more rapid regenerative growth may be expected.

Consider the case of complete unadaptability where the production function is $Y = G(L, N, K_i, K_j)$ and K_i and K_j are two types of capital. For illustration, further suppose that they were about equal in capital value before destruction, that they are measured in units such that their costs of production are equal, and that 60% of K_i and only 40% of K_j were lost. With complete unadaptability, output will fall 60%. New investment will now concentrate only on K_i, however, and a new unit of K_i will reemploy not only some quantity of noncapital factors but a unit of K_j. Thus, according to our assumptions, the increased output will require half the cost as in the first model. Alternatively stated, the

13. The increment to total output from an increment of capital will thereafter be

$$dY/dK = F_K^A + F_N^A\, dN/dK + F_L^A\, dL/dK$$

where the subscripts indicate marginal products, the superscripts indicate where they are taken, and dN/dK and dL/dK are the ratios in which the factors are combined at Point A (or D). F_K^B and F_K^E (both greater than F_K^A) are the complete increments to output at B and E, respectively.

rate of return will be twice as great (subject to the qualification in Note 8), and again this extra high rate of return can be expected to stimulate greater saving and investment.

This is illustrated in Figure 8.3, which is similar to Figure 8.2 except that the two types of capital now appear along the axes. Thus the isoquants do not represent the whole production function but only a "slice" holding noncapital factors constant; therefore movements along the ray *OM* do not represent constant returns to scale. An economy originally at *M* that suffers a loss of *MP* in K_i moves to an output per head equal to that of an undamaged economy at *R*. The devastated economy has a growth advantage in that the accumulation of *MP* of K_i will move it to *M*, while some other intact economy at *R* must accumulate both *MP* of K_i and *RP* of K_j to accomplish precisely the same rise in per capita output.

Model 4: Adaptable Heterogeneous Capital. Even if capital is adaptable, disproportionate destruction followed by capital replacement will generate an unusually high growth rate. Referring to Figure 8.3, compare a destroyed economy with adaptable capital at *P* with a "normal" economy at *R*. The damaged economy has a higher output per head, but if the factors are normally complementary a marginal increment of K_i at *P* will be more productive than an increment of either form of capital at *R*. This is because the K_i increment will have a much larger supply of complementary K_j available at *P* than at *R*. For the economy in equilibrium at *R*, the marginal return to investment in either capital will be the same. For the ravaged economy at *P*, all investment will be K_i; therefore investments will be more productive than in the other economy at *R*.

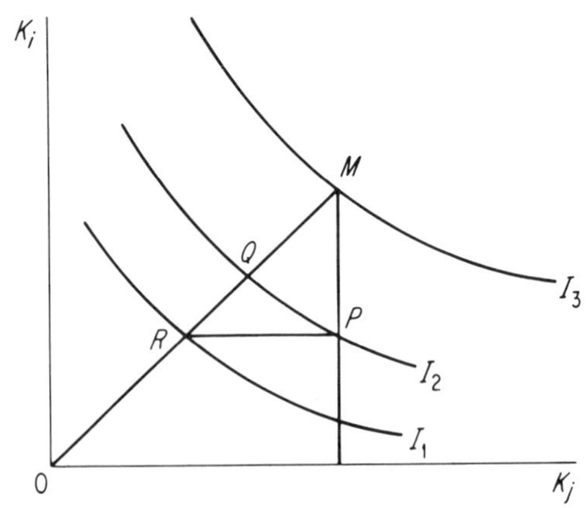

FIGURE 8.3. Heterogeneous unadaptable capital.

Moreover, and for the same reasons, growth at *P* will be more rapid than at Q with an equal per capita income or at *M* with a higher per capita income.

In this case of heterogeneous and adaptable capital, the basic growth advantage of a destroyed economy lies in its divergence from the equality of marginal-production cost ratios and marginal-product ratios. The underutilized (even if fully employed) stock of one form of capital raises the marginal product of investment in the other. A return to optimum equilibrium proportions generates higher returns than would simple capital accumulation on all fronts.[14]

Model 5: Disaggregated Output. A final and fairly obvious way in which postdestruction capital may take inappropriate forms becomes apparent when we drop the assumption of aggregation. Different commodities will, at least in part, use different forms of capital which either will not be transferable or will be transferable only at a cost. From this premise two conclusions follow. First, even if none of the earlier difficulties occur in the production of each final good, a greater proportion of production capital may be destroyed for one commodity than for the other. Second, even if all capital were destroyed proportionately, the new relative quantities will not conform to the new relative demands, which will have changed with the decreased level of income.[15]

Except in the unlikely event that these two forces precisely offset each other over the whole range of final goods, an output index with predestruction weights will underestimate the drop in real income: The quantity of capital has not only been reduced, but it has also been misallocated among commodities. A "true" output index would show these effects, but it would have to include consumer surpluses. Conversely, new capital formation will be concentrated upon those goods which have risen in relative price, and an output index with correct postdestruction weights will show accelerated growth for these reasons. Again, a true index would show a decline in this effect as the disequilibrium relative quantities were corrected.

Changing Technology

In all of these models we have maintained the assumption of a constant technology. If we relax this assumption, abnormal growth can be

14. The qualification in Note 8 would modify but not eliminate this growth advantage.

15. Of course with good luck some of the first effect will offset the second; that is, the disproportionately high capital destruction will happen to occur in those final goods for which there will be a disproportionate reduction in demand at the lower income level. With bad luck, they will reinforce each other.

expected to continue past the previous highest absolute level of income. With nonembodied technical change this will hold so long as the various distortions exist in the capital structure. With embodied technical change the previously noted disequilibrium incentives for saving and investment will be further enhanced. Only when these various "shortages" and distortions are resolved will the period of recovery end and a "normal" long-run trend rate of growth be resumed.[16]

TESTABLE IMPLICATIONS AND EMPIRICAL EVIDENCE

It is reasonable to assume that some elements of all of these models were present in the postwar West German economy. The primary prediction of this theory of regenerative growth (or, if one prefers, this set of subtheories) is that when we observe a degree of physical destruction and a consequent fall in per capita income, we will subsequently observe (*a*) an extraordinary rate of growth followed by (*b*) a declining rate of growth.

The theory also yields several other predictions. All the models predict further that (*c*) the fall in output will be "large" compared to the destruction of physical capital, given what we know of long-run aggregate production functions. Models 1, 3, 4, and 5 predict that (*d*) wages will fall, (*e*) real interest rates will rise, (*f*) the share of income going to capital will rise, and (*g*) the saving rate will be high. Of course, it is the combination of (*e*) and (*g*) which, with flexible factor prices, produces the primary prediction (*a*). If factor prices are rigid, as in Model 2, growth occurs by way of greater employment. This model further suggests (*h*) that unemployment will initially be high, while Model 3 suggests (*i*) some unemployment of capital. The theory predicts that all these forces will diminish over time.

Many of these results are to be expected from neoclassical production theory, particularly if we add the stipulations that the elasticity of substitution is less than unity and that the elasticity of saving with respect to real returns is positive. What the regenerative growth theory emphasizes is, first, the applicability of neoclassical theory and, second, the extremely low elasticity of substitution to be expected in the short-run

16. Although stated somewhat mysteriously, the dissipating effect was anticipated by Bazarov: "Since the greater the deviation from equilibrium, the more strained are the inner powers of cohesion seeking to restore the deformed system to a state of equilibrium, it is obvious that the rate of speed of the recovery process must slacken in proportion as the difference diminishes between the given state of the system and the state of its stable equilibrium." Quoted in Spulber, *Soviet Strategy*, pp. 283–284.

postdestruction situation because of the inappropriate nature of the capital stock.

These testable implications directly determine what empirical evidence is relevant for the prewar and postwar periods. Unfortunately, that evidence is incomplete, but of all the nations that experienced extensive war destruction, West Germany provides one of the best opportunities for empirical testing. Some information is available on (*a*) real national product per capita, (*b*) rates of growth of real product per capita, (*c*) capital stock per capita, (*d*) capital utilization, (*e*) rates of unemployment, (*f*) real wages, (*g*) the proportion of income saved and invested, and (*h*) factor shares of income.[17] Many of these series are, however, somewhat fragmentary and subject to error; particular caution is required in interpreting data for the years before 1950.

No one questions that per capita real income declined drastically between the prewar and postwar periods.[18] Table 8.1 suggests a fall in per capita income between 1938 and 1947 of more than 50%. Between the years 1938 (or 1939) and 1946 the fall was certainly sharper.

Supporting evidence for a decline of this general magnitude is given in a study by Mendershausen.[19] Although he provides no comparable national income estimates for 1938 and 1946, he does give interwar comparisons of industrial production and of agricultural production. By his estimates, industrial production in 1946 in the bizonal area was 29% of that in 1938, and in the Federal Republic food production was only 67% of an average for the years between 1935 and 1939. Taking into consideration the growth of population, which was about 12% between 1938 and 1946, the postwar per capita levels are further reduced to little more than 25% of the 1938 level for industrial production and to slightly less than 60% for foodstuff production. Certainly a 75% decline in the former and a 40% decline in the latter are consistent with aggregate income per capita reductions approaching 60% for 1938–1946. Weighted by the approximate shares of national product stemming from industry and from agriculture in 1949, the results suggest a decline in income per capita exceeding 60% between 1938 and 1946.[20] Similarly, Balogh suggests a

17. This list, of course, does not include all relevant data, and even some of these series are fragmentary.

18. All comparisons are based on the area which corresponds to postwar Germany, the Federal Republic of Germany.

19. *Two Postwar Recoveries*, pp. 5–8. On the basis of evidence from *Industrial Statistics, 1900–1957*, OOEC, Paris (1958), Table 2, Janossy shows a decline in *aggregate* industrial production between 1938 and 1948 of approximately two-thirds (see his *End of the Economic Miracle*, p. 43).

20. Wallich, *Mainspring*, p. 40. In 1949, the contribution of agriculture (including forestry) to national income was about one-fourth that of industry (excluding construction). A

decline in general production per capita of over 70% between 1938 and 1946.[21]

Such exceptionally low levels of real per capita income did not persist, however, and the early postwar years produced extraordinarily high rates of growth. Though the early data are crude, those from Table 8.1 suggest an average rate of growth of real per capita income of almost 16% from mid-1947 through mid-1951. In contrast the table shows that the average growth rate fell to about 7% between 1951 and 1955.[22] More reliable evidence on the growth rate for the post-1950 period is given in Table 8.2. This evidence supports the view of a declining trend in the growth rate, and Denison gives estimates of average growth rates for West Germany of 8.9% from 1950 to 1955 and of 4.1% from 1955 to 1962.[23] Overall, there can be little doubt that a distinct downward trend followed the high rate of growth which marked the immediate postwar years.

The primary predictions of the model appear to have been fulfilled also in Japan, Greece, Russia, and other countries after World War II, in France after World War I, and "often," if Mill is correct, before 1848. This is perhaps the most pervasive element of the theory, its effect being observable across the whole spectrum of social, cultural, technological, and political differences between nations and over time.

Because the interwar years were marred with chaotic economic conditions and because of differing circumstances between the Weimar Republic and the Federal Republic, it is hazardous and perhaps not too meaningful to attempt to pinpoint the resumption of "the" long-run growth trend. However, the evidence indicates an average growth rate of between 3 and 4% from 1925 to 1939,[24] which would suggest that the regenerative forces had run their course by the early 1960s.

---

substitution of 1936 weights makes no significant change in the results. It is highly unlikely that the fall in real GNP per capita from 1938 (or 1939) to 1946 was less than 60%, according to official government sources. With an index of 1950 (=100), real GNP per capita in 1938 was 152 and in 1939, 163. If the growth rate from 1946 to 1950 was similar to those suggested in Table 8.2, and at least not less than those for the years 1950–1955, this implies a fall in real GNP per capita well over 60%.

21. T. Balogh, *Germany: An Experiment in "Planning" by the "Free" Price Mechanism* (Oxford: Basic Blackwell, 1950).

22. Although such data do not inspire great confidence, especially for year-by-year comparisons, they serve reasonably well for such 4-year benchmark comparisons. Moreover, even when much room for error is allowed in the data, the order of magnitude in the differences in the growth rates between the late 1940s and the early 1950s leaves little doubt that a significant drop occurred in the growth rate between 1947 and 1955.

23. Edward F. Denison, *Why Growth Rates Differ* (Washington, D.C.: The Brookings Institution, 1967), p. 18.

24. From statistics generously supplied to us by the Statistics Office, Weisbaden, Germany.

TABLE 8.2
Rates of Growth of Real National Product Per Capita

Year	(1) Percentage	(2) Percentage
1947–1948	16.0	
1948–1949	13.8	
1949–1950	16.7	
1950–1951	15.6	9.0
1951–1952	5.6	8.3
1952–1953	6.4	7.6
1953–1954	7.0	6.3
1954–1955	9.3	10.4
1955–1956		6.0
1956–1957		4.4
1957–1958		2.4
1958–1959		6.5
1959–1960		7.8
1960–1961		3.6
1961–1962		3.0
1962–1963		1.9
1963–1964		5.7
1964–1965		4.0

Source: Column (1) is derived from Table 8.1; Column (2) is derived from official government statistics generously supplied by the Statistics Office, Weisbaden, Germany (the years 1950–1960 are for Bundesgebiet ohne Saarland and Berlin).

Consider now our Prediction (*c*): an "abnormal" initial fall in output relative to that expected from the loss of capital. According to Mendershausen, national wealth was reduced by about two-thirds though World War II, of which 40% was due to loss of territory.[25] Adjusting for population increase, the loss in per capita terms was about 50%.

An alternative but less comprehensive view is given by Krengel, who has made estimates of gross fixed assets in industry.[26] Adjusting for population change, he derived a reduction in per capita fixed assets in manufacturing of only about 7% for 1938–1946. Negative net investment

25. Mendershausen, *Two Postwar Recoveries,* p. 27.

26. "Some Reasons," p. 5. Krengel's definition of industry is fairly comprehensive, including mining, processing industries, raw materials production, engineering industries, consumer goods industries, and some foodstuffs and luxuries. Unfortunately, he excludes housing. See his Table 6, p. 19. It should be noted that our comparisons of physical capital per capita reflect approximately the same sectors in terms of "per worker"

and dismantling from 1946 through 1948, however, increased the per capita reduction to approximately 15% for the period to 1948.

Total destruction undoubtedly exceeded that of industrial capacity, especially in view of the extent of damage to the transportation sector and to residential districts. For our purposes, an acceptable general order of magnitude suggested by the evidence would be that physical capital per capita declined perhaps as much as 50% and almost certainly more than 15% between 1938 and 1946.[27]

In light of what economists have estimated to be the contribution of capital to the growth of output per labor-hour, these capital losses were *not,* in fact, large relative to the decline in per capita income. Denison, for example, found that in the United States an increase of 1.2% per year in (physical) capital per employee over the period 1909–1957 produced a rise in annual output of about .23% per capita,[28] or a marginal product of investment of roughly 20%. On the other hand, a 50% fall in capital (to take the larger of the above figures), accompanied by a larger fall in income per head, implies a marginal product of over 100%. The finding of this anomoly concurs precisely with our Prediction (*c*).

Model 3 suggests that when capital is both heterogeneous and unadaptable some part of it will remain unemployed despite the drastic fall in the overall quantity. Krengel's data appear to confirm this fully. His estimates of capital utilization (in "industry") indicate rates of 95% of capacity in 1939 but only 49% in 1948.[29] As predicted, this situation improved rapidly until by 1951 utilization was unusually high.[30]

Model 2 predicts that unemployment may rise in a postdestruction era, because of rigid factor prices, but that it will decline over the period of rapid growth. There is some evidence that this was occurring in West Germany. Table 8.3 shows unemployment figures starting with 1950.

---

except for 1948–1955, a period of unusually high measured unemployment. For a comparison with those years, a measured decline in per capita terms would exceed that per worker.

27. Evidence in support of the higher figure is goven by Wallich, *Mainspring,* p. 200.

28. Edward F. Denison, *The Sources of Economic Growth in the United States and the Alternatives before Us* (New York: Committee for Economic Development, 1963). Calculated from data on pp. 85, 141, and 270.

29. Krengel, "Some Reasons," p. 13. Such estimates of utilization admittedly are very crude. They attempt to measure actual output in a given year as a percentage of "full capacity potential" output in the same year. Of course, any determination of "full capacity potential" must be quite arbitrary if capital is adaptable (at least partly) and labor and capital substitution is possible. Nevertheless, for very large changes, the estimates serve a useful purpose.

30. Ibid.

TABLE 8.3
Rates of Unemployment, 1950–1966

Year[a]	Percentage unemployed[b]
1950	11.0
1951	10.4
1952	9.5
1953	8.4
1954	7.6
1955	5.6
1956	4.4
1957	3.7
1958	3.7
1959	2.6
1960	1.3
1961	.8
1962	.7
1963	.8
1964	.8
1965	.7
1966	.7

Source: See Table 8.2.

[a] From 1950 through 1958, Bundes gebeit ohne Saarland.

[b] In percentages, der beschäftigten Arbeitnehmer.

It is true that official unemployment was very low until the monetary reform in mid-1948 and rose sharply thereafter; however this was probably due in large part to the extreme distortions produced by (economic) controls and rationing in this period. Wages and prices were being held at 1938 levels despite the massive increases taking place in the money supply, but with the low wage went a ration book permitting the holder to buy rationed goods at the artificially low prices. In real terms, this constituted a large subsidy to the employee at no cost to the employer.[31]

The shortage of employment and its subsequent reversal is also reflected in the evidence on average weekly hours worked. Contrary to what might be expected with a huge effort "needed" to rebuild the economy, the average weekly hours worked declined in the postwar years. A comparison of the average number of hours worked per week

31. Norman Macrae, "The German Lesson," a special survey in *The Economist* (London), October 15, 1966, pp. i–xxxii. See also Wallich, *Mainspring,* pp. 288–297.

shows a decline from approximately 50 hours for males and 48 hours for females in 1938 to 40 hours for males and 35 hours for females in 1946.[32] This trend reversed itself and in 1948 work hours for males were nearly 43 per week; the rise continued to 47 hours per week in 1949, and remained at an average of between 48 and 49 hours per week in the early fifties. A similar trend, but at a lower level, was true for females.

Although the trend of real wages was steadily upward during the postwar years, in the immediate postwar years real wages were far below those earned in 1938. Based on an index of 100 for real weekly earnings for all workers in 1938, such earnings were only 66 in June, 1948, but then rose to 101 in March, 1951, and to 127 in November, 1954.[33] This upward trend continued, but the rate of advance was already slowing by 1950, as the theory predicts. The yearly percentage increases in real wages between 1948 and 1954 were respectively 22, 18, 5, 7, 7, and 4%.[34]

It is less easy, with the evidence available, to test the theory's predictions as to the capital share in national income and the rate of saving and investment. This is partly because all national income data fail to separate out factor shares for a significant portion of the economy, and particularly in postwar West Germany this was a rapidly changing fraction. The evidence is also severely clouded by massive government intervention in, and distortion of, the capital market.[35]

Nevertheless there is evidence that labor's share fell. Balogh reports that "the share of wages in net *industrial* [italic added] production decreased from 50 percent in 1936 (the heyday of Nazi rearmament) to 42 percent at the end of 1948."[36] Unless this was offset by increases in other sectors, the labor share of national income must have fallen. More complete evidence on the early postwar years is not available, but for later

32. Data on weekly hours worked are from *Wirtschaft und Statistik*, 1938, Bundesministerium fur Arbeit, *Hauptergebnisse der Arbeitsund Sozialstatistik* (1953), p. 104, as reported in Wallich, *Mainspring*, pp. 289, 301. For corroborating evidence see Balogh, *Germany*, p. 30. He reports a "lengthening of the working week from 82.5 per cent of 1938 in June 1948 to 89.7 per cent in December 1948 and 94.9 per cent in September 1949."

33. From the *Statistisches Jahrbuch, Wirtschaft und Statistik* as reported in Wallich, *Mainspring*, pp. 297–298. Also see Balogh, *Germany*, p. 35, which reports that "the real purchasing power of wages, considering the increased regressiveness of direct taxation and social security dues, fell to 60–65 percent of pre war."

34. Wallich, *Mainspring*, pp. 297–298.

35. A brief account of these distortions may be found in K. F. Maier, "Has Western Germany a Liberal Market Economy?" in *Banca Nazionale del Lavoro Quarterly Review* 5 (1952), pp. 37–43.

36. Balogh, *An Experiment*, p. 35

years Wallich reports that the fractions of national income going to wages and salaries were approximately 64% in 1949, 63% in 1950, 61% in 1951, 63% in 1952, and 65% in 1953 and the first half of 1954.[37] The comparable fraction in 1936 was 61%.[38] It can be concluded tentatively that labor's share of national income probably fell between 1936 and the immediate postwar years and then rose in the 1950s above the prewar level. This upward trend continued haltingly through the 1950s and into the early 1960s.[39]

Similarly, the evidence on saving and investment as a portion of national income is fragmentary for the immediate postwar years. Gross investment in fixed assets did rise significantly between the late 1920s and the period of 1949–1953—from 18–19% to 25–29%—but similar comparisons cannot be made between 1938 and 1946 (or 1947) because of inadequate data.[40] Though limited, the evidence is consistent with Models 1, 3, 4, and 5. By the late 1950s, however, other stimuli may have counteracted the dampening effects of regenerative activity, because gross investment as a percentage of gross national product continued to increase between 1950–1954 and 1955–1962.[41] It seems just as likely, however, that the increased flow of saving resulted from the removal of many of the government's disincentives to the free flow of capital.

A NOTE ON HUMAN CAPITAL

Further insight into this capital-dislocation theory of regenerative growth can be gained by contrasting it with an alternative single line explanation that has been put forth. In attempting to account for the "rapid recovery of countries that had suffered severe destruction of plant and equipment during the war," T. W. Schultz has argued that

> economists . . . overestimated the prospective retarding effects of these losses. . . . The explanation that now is clear is that we gave altogether too much weight to non-human capital in making these assessments. We fell into this error, I am convinced, because we did not have a concept of *all* capital and, therefore, failed to take

37. Wallich, *Mainspring,* p. 53.

38. Ibid.

39. Denison, *Why Growth Rates Differ,* p. 38, reports labor's share of national income at 73.7% for 1950–1954, at 73.3% for 1955–1959, and at 74.2% for 1960–1962.

40. From *Statisches Jahrbuch,* 1937 and 1953, *Wirtschaft und Statistik,* April 1954, and Bank deutscher Lander *Monthly Report,* March 1953, as reported by Mendershausen in *Two Postwar Recoveries,* p. 49.

41. See Denison, *Why Growth Rates Differ,* p. 118.

account of human capital and the important part that it plays in production in a modern economy.[42]

There are several senses in which human capital can be "important." We would fully agree to its importance in a modern technologically advanced economy, in that it accounts for a large fraction of national income, creates a high per capita income, and permits the absorption of domestic and foreign technical progress. But this does not necessarily affirm its unique place in the destruction–regeneration process.

If an abundance of human capital could prevent a "large" fall in output despite considerable destruction of physical capital, then recovery might be achieved fairly quickly even with modest growth rates. In this case, human capital would be a reasonably good short-run *substitute* for physical capital. But, as we have shown, this is just the opposite of what happened. Indeed, if economists had used data on the role of capital in the long-run production function and on the extent of capital loss in West Germany, they would have underestimated, rather than overestimated, the "retarding effects" of the losses.

As another possibility, an abundance of human capital might prove highly *complementary* to physical capital in the short run if output has fallen sharply because of physical destruction. In this case, the loss of physical capital has resulted in an abnormal fall in income and subsequently in a high marginal product of physical capital and a low marginal product of human capital. This of course is precisely what we believe was the case, but not because human capital was in any sense a more vital cooperating factor than, say, very productive land. Human capital *may* account for a before-and-after high level of per capita income, as we believe to have been the case in West Germany, but in another economy oil wells might play a similar role. In either case, the clue to the observed phenomenon is that in a situation of recovery following devastation, an inappropriate substitution for physical capital is being made on a short-term basis.

SUMMARY AND CONCLUSION

We have argued that for a variety of reasons a postdestruction stock of capital is dispersed in inappropriate forms and quantities with respect to complementary capital and other inputs, and with respect to the demands of consumers. In other words, the short-run elasticity of substitution is very low and the drop in income disproportionately large. Conversely, correction of the most critical dislocations will produce an ex-

42. "Investment in Human Capital," *American Economic Review* (1961).

traordinarily high payoff and will provide incentive for high saving and investment, both components making for rapid regenerative growth. The evidence in West Germany is highly consistent with this conclusion, which would appear to apply equally in other countries.

It could be argued that all of this is fairly obvious; it is merely neoclassical production theory with the addition of short-run bottlenecks (the popular phrase for low elasticities of substitution). We are inclined to agree. Yet one should remember that a spate of literature attributes the "surprising" examples of postwar recovery to a host of special factors, many derived from man-in-the-street sociology and popular stereotypes and still others from misapplied Keynesianism. Little or no attempt has been made to apply to the issue the production theory long developed by economists. In fact, as Norman Macrae has pointed out:

> One of the few long-term German economic surveys at the end of 1947, much praised by some British and American economists at the time, was solemnly prophesying that so long as Germany remained partitioned "only death or the emigration of 20 million Germans can effectively ease the food situation.[43]

If we should ever be so unfortunate as to have to analyze comparable situations in the future, let us hope that the economics profession will have achieved more historical perspective and more faith in its own theory.

Gary Walton's "Quantitative Study of American Colonial Shipping" not only served as his Ph.D. dissertation at the University of Washington in 1966, but proved a springboard for a series of studies and articles on the colonial economy which have profoundly altered the picture of the role of shipping and trade in the formative years of our country. In 1972 Walton collaborated with another of North's students, James Shepherd, on **Shipping, Maritime Trade, and Economic Development of Colonial North America.** More recently Walton and Shepherd authored **The Economic Rise of Early America** (1979) Walton also authored (with Erik Haites and James Mak) **Western River Transportation: The Era of Early Internal Development, 1810–1860** (1975) and (with Roger L. Miller) **Economic Issues in American History** (1978). After the death of Ross Robertson, Walton undertook to revise his classic text, **History of the American Economy,** the fourth edition of which appeared in 1979.

Walton has served as editor of **Explorations in Economic History** since 1973, with James Shepherd as coeditor in 1979 and 1980, and has edited or coedited three other books as well. After teaching at Ohio State University, Indiana University, and the University of California, Berkeley, Walton was appointed Dean of the College of Business and Economics at Washington State University in 1977. He was later Dean of the School of Business at the University of Miami. He is currently Dean of the Graduate School of Administration at the University of California, Davis.

43. "The German Lesson," p. viii.

Walton is joined by coauthor **Donald Gordon,** who was himself a colleague of Douglass North at the University of Washington from 1950 to 1966. He was thus close to the birth of part of the new economic history and taught several of the authors of the present volume, including Ransom, Sutch, and Walton. Gordon has since taught at several other universities, has served in a temporary capacity in Washington, D.C. and Ottawa, Canada, and is now Director of the Center for the Study of Business and Government and in the Department of Economics and Finance at the Bernard M. Baruch College of the City University of New York. He has published in the history of economic thought, on growth theory, on unemployment theory, on methodology and on various aspects of public policy. He was recently honored as President of the Western Economic Association.

Part III

Property Rights and Institutional Change

What we need is a body of theory which encompasses the traditional models of the economist and both widens its scope and allows us to include an explanation of the formation, mutation and decay of organizational forms within which man cooperates or competes. . . . It is one question to ask how the basic institutional environment is formed and modified. We need to know much more. It is still another question to ask what the consequences are of any set of basic decision rules.

Douglas C. North

The Journal of Economic History
March 1971

Chapter 9

Institutional Change Through the Supreme Court and the Rise of Transfer Activity

Terry L. Anderson and P. J. Hill

The complete independence of the courts of justice is peculiarly essential in a limited Constitution. By a limited Constitution, I understand one which contains certain specified exceptions to the legislative authority; such, for instance, as that it shall pass no bills of attainder, no **ex post facto** laws, and the like. Limitations of this kind can be preserved in practice no other way than through the medium of courts of justice, whose duty it must be to declare all acts contrary to the manifest tenor of the Constitution void. Without this, all the reservations of particular rights or privileges would amount to nothing.

—Alexander Hamilton

The court system described by Hamilton in this quotation from the 78th *Federalist* paper is certainly consistent with the kinds of institutions that Douglass North has argued are a necessary part of the growth process. Moreover, in his work with Lance Davis, Professor North has emphasized the contributions of the court system in the institutional change process. "Since most of the rules governing business behavior lie rooted in either the Constitution or the common law, the courts have played a particularly important role in determining this part of the institutional environment."[1]

1. Lance E. Davis and Douglass C. North, *Institutional Change and American Economic Growth* (Cambridge: Cambridge University Press, 1971), p. 70.

EXPLORATIONS IN THE NEW ECONOMIC HISTORY

ISBN 0-12-580080-0

What Douglass North has made us realize is that the court system will influence, and be influenced by, institutional change. The *Federalist's* faith in the court system as a means of preserving liberty and property rights seems naive in light of the models that Professor North has developed. Institutions are at least in part determined by the constitutional interpretations laid down by courts. Therefore, we should expect wealth-maximizing individuals to invest resources in trying to influence these decisions. Furthermore, to the extent that Supreme Court interpretations condition the security of private rights, we should expect those interpretations to lead to efforts to effect institutional change. North has postulated that when gains in efficiency appear realizable from institutional change, entrepreneurs will initiate such efforts. We believe his work documents the validity of this position.

It is an extension of this model that we examine in this paper. We argue that wealth maximizers will rise to any occasion (not just efficiency-producing occasions) to capture potential gains for themselves. As their goal is wealth maximization and not efficiency, we can just as well expect their attempt to be to obtain transfers of wealth as to increase aggregate wealth. To the individual, the relevant question would be which attempt would yield the higher return at the margin. From a social perspective, however, the results from these two alternatives are very different. What follows is an approach to the Constitution and its interpretation which illustrates this difference between productive activity and transfer activity and which links Supreme Court decisions to the predictable choices individuals will make between the two. We begin with a framework that implies that transfers lead to socially wasteful activity. Historical evidence from nineteenth-century Supreme Court interpretations is then presented to illustrate the transformation of the United States from a productive society to a rent-seeking transfer society.

PRODUCTIVE VERSUS TRANSFER ACTIVITY

Our approach is the mode of analysis derived from the public choice paradigm. Taking the individual as the unit of analysis, this approach emphasizes the exchange nature of the relationship between the state and members of the state. Given some starting point of endowments or rights, the members of the society agree to form a society which recognizes these rights as legitimate and is empowered to enforce them. Individuals accept some limits upon their actions in exchange for the protection of these sanctified rights and for the production of public goods by the state. James Buchanan offers a conceptual summary of the public-choice–contractarian paradigm.

From a
(1) natural distribution, a
(2) constitutional contract is negotiated, from which, in turn,
(3) post constitutional contract become possible, through
(a) private-goods trade (good rival in consumption) and/or
(b) public-goods trade (goods nonrival in consumption).[2]

In this paradigm, the function of the constitutional contract surpasses the interest group view that constitutions are "designed to protect groups sufficiently powerful to obtain constitutional protection for their interests."[3] The concept assumes that members of a society agree that certain fundamental rights are to be protected from the short-run pressures of interest groups and, therefore, they restrict the power of government (the legislature) to hand out favors which transfer these rights. Under such a system, the function of the legislature is simply to provide the public goods that the society desires. The role of the independent judiciary is clear in this framework; it is to negate any "deals" that violate the terms of the original agreement. Failure to perform that function results in social waste as the following analysis illustrates.

In any society, an individual's wealth position depends on the extent to which he has access to the use of resources. His efforts to alter this access and, hence, his wealth position can be categorized as producing positive-, zero-, or negative-sum results for the society. Consider the following three possibilities.

1. Individual wealth accumulation in our society perhaps most frequently results from production and exchange. A well-defined and well-enforced bundle of rights allows the decision maker to use resources in such a way as to maximize the production of goods he desires or of goods that can be traded for such desired goods. Given a set of rational decision makers, such production can yield only positive results. Furthermore, when trade results in an exchange of goods of a relatively low value for goods of a relatively high value (as perceived by the individual traders) no party to the exchange can be left worse off. The results are positive-sum and Pareto optimal. This quest for gains from trade moves resources to their highest-valued alternatives.

2. A second type of wealth-maximizing activity takes the form of definition and enforcement of exclusive rights where such rights were previously lacking. Consider the expansion of the American frontier during the nineteenth century. As population expanded into previously

2. James Buchanan, *The Limits of Liberty* (Chicago: Chicago University Press, 1975), p. 31.

3. William M. Landes and Richard A. Posner, "The Independent Judiciary in an Interest-Group Perspective," *The Journal of Law and Economics* 18 (1975), p. 893.

unoccupied regions, the owners of the new resource endowments found themselves with increased wealth and society found itself with increased production possibilities. These property rights, however, did not simply appear; as we have shown elsewhere, they were the product of definition and enforcement.[4] Professor Cheung has pointed out that the absence of exclusive rights to resources can lead to rent dissipation if entry is free. In his words, "There exist incentives to fishermen to restrict the *number* of decision units who have access to the fishing right. That is, even if each decision unit is free to commit the amount of fishing effort, the "rent" captured by each will be larger the smaller the number of decision units."[5] Of course, the fewer the resources needed to establish exclusive rights, the larger will be the gains. But in any case, definition and enforcement (like trade) serve to increase the return on resources utilized.

The establishment of exclusive rights yields a second social gain by forming, in turn, a basis for the trades just described. Individual rights embodied in the constitutional status quo offer "the basis upon which individuals may form expectations about the course of events, expectations which are necessary for rational planning."[6] As Ronald Coase noted in his seminal article on "The Problem of Social Cost,"[7] the assignment of property rights does affect the distribution of income and is in this sense a zero-sum game. But if such rights are not defined and enforced, what will ensure the equalization of private and social rates of return? The "static model would suggest *erroneously* that the assignment of rights remains always a zero-sum game."[8] However, it is these rules, within the constitutional status quo, which ensure that the ensuing game will be positive-sum.

3. A third type of wealth-increasing activity involves the transfer of existing access rights from one decision unit to another without a quid pro quo. Our interest here is not with transfers carried out voluntarily by the owners of rights, as in the case of charity whether organized privately or publicly. This type of transfer is similar to postconstitutional

4. See, for example, Terry L. Anderson and P. J. Hill, "The Evolution of Property Rights: A Study of the American West," *The Journal of Law and Economics* 18 (1975), pp. 113–179, and idem, "Toward A General Theory of Institutional Change," in Gordon Tullock, ed., *Frontiers of Economics* (Blacksburg, Va.: University Publications, 1976).

5. Steven N. S. Cheung, "The Structure of a Contract and the Theory of a Non-Exclusive Resource," *The Journal of Law and Economics* 13 (1970), p. 61.

6. Buchanan, *The Limits of Liberty*, p. 77.

7. Ronald H. Coase, "The Problem of Social Cost," *The Journal of Law and Economics* 3 (1960), pp. 1–44.

8. Buchanan, *The Limits of Liberty*, p. 78, emphasis added.

contracting in that it involves an implicit quid pro quo in the form of increased "personal satisfaction" for the giver. Rather, our concern is with *involuntary* transfers obtained under the threat of legal coercion. Although one might speculate that certain types of income redistribution from the "rich" to the "poor" are a form of charity, it is unlikely that import quotas, tariffs, and subsidies to farmers are designed for that purpose. Traditionally, such "transfers" have been viewed in terms of their redistributive and efficiency effects, both of which are important. This assessment, however, ignores the fact that "the prospect of the transfer leads individuals and groups to invest resources in either attempting to obtain a transfer or to resist a transfer away from themselves. These resources represent net social waste."[9] Anne O. Krueger has described this process as "rent-seeking." In her words, "In many market-oriented economies, government restrictions upon economic activity are pervasive facts of life. These restrictions give rise to rents of a variety of forms, and people often compete for the rents."[10] Individuals who suceed in the process will capture the value of the resources or the access rights transferred. Original owners will lose by the same amount, but both will employ resources to obtain or to safeguard these "rents," resulting in a negative-sum game.

Because of such potential resource consumption, rules against transfers may be requisite in establishing positive-sum games. As discussed earlier, the establishment and enforcement of previously nonexistent private property rights internalize the costs and benefits to the decision maker, giving him an incentive to pursue gains from trade. Such rights form the constitutional status quo. But what is to prevent a redefinition of these rights through the "legal" process in the form of special interest legislation? To the extent that such redefinition is possible, the expected value of transfer legislation will be positive. Unfortunately, total productive capacity will be reduced by the spending of resources in transfer or rent-seeking activity.[11]

The effect of judicial decisions that enforce legislative transfer deals can be shown graphically. Consider a situation in which the individual is faced with two employment alternatives for his resources, both of which will increase his wealth. If resources are combined to produce goods and services demanded by society and to engage in trade, wealth can be created. On the other hand, if those same resources are used to transfer

9. Gordon Tullock, "The Cost of Transfers," *Kyklos* 24 (1971), p. 642.

10. Krueger, "The Political Economy of the Rent-Seeking Society," *American Economic Review* 65 (1974), p. 291.

11. For a more definitive proof of this conclusion, see ibid., pp. 295–300.

wealth from one individual to another, a net loss in output will occur even though one individual is made better off. Wealth-maximizing individuals, therefore, face two values of marginal product schedules for their resources, shown in Figure 9.1, Panels *a* and *b*, as MB_T and MB_P, respectively. For a given upward sloping supply curve for resources (shown as *S* in Panel *c*) and a given MB_T, it is possible to derive a residual supply of resources available for productive activity at any price, shown as S_P in Panel *b*. Under these conditions, a total of $0B$ resources will be employed, with $0D$ devoted to transfer activity and $0F$ to productive activity. Now suppose that the independent judiciary enforces a price- or wage-control law even though it infringes upon freedom of contract. The result will be a shift to MB'_T since those gaining from such legislation will perceive a higher expected value and those losing will see a higher expected loss. The supply of resources for productive activity will decrease to S'_P; $0C$ resources will be employed in transfer activity and $0E$ resources in productive activity. Under conditions of less than full employment, more resources will be employed, but total output will be reduced to a point within the production frontier.

It is for this reason that "an independent judiciary is necessary to enforce the Constitution against the legislative and executive branches of government."[12] Fulfilling that role, it can greatly enhance the productive potential of an economy.[13] By enforcing the constitutional contract the judiciary can reduce the productivity of transfer activity and its attendant rent seeking. If, however, the independent judiciary functions simply as an enforcer of legislative deals, social waste can result. The Constitution provides a set of basic rules which neither the judicial, the legislative, nor the executive branch is at liberty to alter. When serving as a check on government and protecting individual rights guaranteed by the Constitution, the independent judiciary provides a necessary condition for the survivial of a constitutional democracy. On the other hand, by sanctifying legislative deals that modify the basic rules, the judiciary may as readily provide a sufficient condition for the decline of

12. Landes and Posner, "The Independent Judiciary," p. 887.

13. As Buchanan notes, the Constitution does embody "rights of membership in the polity, the collective organ of community, and this entity in its turn carries specified powers or rights to undertake the provision and financing of public goods and services." *Limits of Liberty*, p. 77. In other words, the state has a "productive" as well as a "protective" role. Transfers for the provision of public goods may consume resources in the rent-seeking sense, but the nature of public goods suggests that they constitute output which otherwise would not exist. The potential is present for positive-sum games.

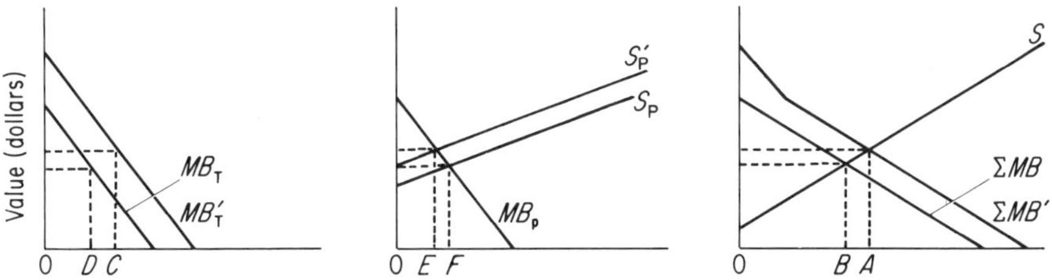

FIGURE 9.1. The impact of transfer activity and productive activity or resource allocation.

constitutional democracy.[14] Experience suggests that this latter tendency has given birth to the transfer society prevalent in the United States.

THE INITIAL CONDITIONS

The Constitution as framed in 1787 made transfers costly and hence reduced the potential marginal benefit from rent-seeking activity. In examining the United States Constitution and its impact on transfer activity, it is important to understand the tenor of the times in which it was written. The industrial revolution was in full swing in Europe, and particularly in England, accompanied by significant economic growth. While new forms of production, shifting demands, and growing populations promoted the idea of free mobility for factors of production, most of the governments of western Europe were still clinging to the vestiges of mercantilism—a doctrine that reduced mobility by interfering with markets through devices such as subsidies, quotas, and government-sanctioned methods of production.[15] Thus the framers of the Constitution, in setting specific limits on governmental power, were diverging sharply from Continental tradition.

On the other hand, the American Revolution and the Constitution it sired were consistent with the growing eighteenth-century libertarian philosophies from which two themes ring clear. The first is "the belief

14. Gordon Tullock suggests that a check upon the independent judiciary is within the authority of the other branches of government obligated to uphold the Constitution. He argues that a mere "myth of judicial supremacy" has led us to accept the Supreme Court as the ultimate power. "Constitutional Methodology," *New Individualist Review* 3 (1965), pp. 13–17.

15. For an example of institutional conditions in Europe, see Douglass C. North and Robert Paul Thomas, *The Rise of the Western World* (Cambridge: Cambridge University Press, 1973).

that power is evil, a necessity perhaps but an evil necessity; that it is infinitely corrupting; and that it must be controlled, limited, restricted in every way compatible with a minimum of civil order;" the second, is "the belief that through the ages it had been privilege—artificial, man-made and man-secured privilege, ascribed to some and denied to others mainly at birth—that, more than anything else except the misuse of power, had crushed men's hopes of fulfillment."[16] Even during the early years of conflict with the mother country, the colonists had believed they were acting within the principles of the English constitution to eliminate the evils of power. When it became clear that rights could not be secured under the English constitution, they demanded independence in accordance with John Locke's contract theory "which taught the right of the people, in seeking to secure their liberties, to establish *any* form of government."[17] Under the doctrine of natural law, the function of the state was to declare and make explicit the rights held by all men. The state did not create these rights; it simply secured them. As the English constitution had been allowing governmental power to abuse—rather than secure—rights, the Founding Fathers had reason to shape a constitution that imposed significant restrictions on the ability of the government body to promote rent seeking through transfers. Locke's theory convinced the colonists that they had the right to reverse the accumulation of power. Once independence was achieved, the question was what form of government would best assure that the same abuses would not reappear.

In the Constitution of the United States, the framers attempted to solve the problem by making explicit the limits upon our democracy. Supporters of the document were aware of both the "productive" and the "protective" roles of the state and equally aware of the possibilities for transfers inherent in these roles. Madison, writing in *Federalist #10,* expressed this recognition: "To secure the public good and private rights against the danger of such a majority function, and at the same time to preserve the spirit and the form of popular government, is then the great objective to which our inquiries are directed."[18] Madison's "tyranny of the majority" is another way of expressing the transfer form of wealth

16. Bernard Bailyn, "The Central Themes of the American Revolution: An Interpretation," in Stephen G. Kurtz and James H. Hudson, eds., *Essays on the American Revolution* (New York: Norton, 1973), pp. 26–27.

17. Martin Diamond, "The Revolution of Sober Expectation," *The American Revolution: Three Views* (New York: American Brands, 1975), p. 67.

18. See Clinton Rossiter, ed., *The Federalist Papers* (New York: New American Library, 1961), p. 80.

accumulation discussed earlier. The eighteenth-century attitude toward wealth redistribution is summarized by Professor Horwitz:

> The entire structure of legal and political ideas and institutions that emerged from the American revolution was devoted to erecting barriers that would prevent the redistribution of wealth and would assure that accumulations of wealth by the shrewd, the calculating, the ambitious, and the able would be protected.[19]

The intent to protect the rights of individuals from the whims of popular government is expressed in the decision rules embodied in the document. The process of amending the document, for example, was made costly by requiring approval of three-fourths of the states. Furthermore, for one issue (equal representation of each state in the Senate), only the explicit consent of the state itself could allow that state to be deprived of its suffrage. This provision, nearly equivalent to requiring unanimous approval, again indicates a belief in fundamental rights not subject to change or transfer by legislation.

Other evidence that the Constitution and its interpretation lowered the marginal benefits from transfer activity is found in several clauses which have been interpreted by the Supreme Court as providing a high degree of protection to vested or natural rights. However, before these clauses proved very effective in limiting the power of other units of government to alter rights or to carry out transfers, the appellate power of the federal judiciary had to be firmly established. Under the Constitution, the authority of the Supreme Court over state laws and over decisions rendered in state courts was not entirely clear. Following common law precedent, in the 1816 case of *Martin* v. *Hunter's Lessee,*[20] The Court decided it did have the right to review the decisions of state courts. This was crucial to the supremacy of the Constitution; without such appellate jurisdiction, constitutional restrictions would have applied only to federal laws.

One clause of particular importance for reducing the marginal benefits of transfer activity was that covering contracts (Article 1, Section 10). Under this clause, "No state shall . . . pass any Bill of attainder, ex post facto law, or law impairing the Obligation of Contract. . . . " An early and famous case in 1810 involving the contract clause was *Fletcher* v. *Peck*[21] (sometimes called the Yazoo Land case). This concerned an at-

19. Morton J. Horwitz, "The Legacy of 1776 in Legal and Economic Thought," *The Journal of Law and Economics* 19 (1976), p. 622.

20. I Wheaton 304 (1816).

21. 6 Cranch 87 (1810)

tempt by the Georgia legislature to rescind a land grant made in a previous legislative session because of fraud in the original action. Writing for the majority, Chief Justice Marshall concluded that since third parties had now entered into contracts involving the land, those contracts could not be abrogated. Moreover, "It may well be doubted whether the nature of society and of the government does not prescribe some limits to the legislative power; and if any be prescribed, where are they to be found, if the property of an individual, fairly and honestly acquired, may be seized without compensation?"[22] In this case, Marshall's decision relied partly upon the general principle of vested rights and partly upon the specific prohibitions against impairing the obligation of contracts. The effect was to prevent a legislative transfer.

The power of the contract clause was restipulated and expanded in *Dartmouth College* v. *Woodward* (1819).[23] In this case, the Court ruled that a governmental grant of an article of incorporation was thereafter to be viewed as a contract immune to government interference. As this meant that contracts between the State and private parties were as inviolable as those between two individuals, the decision might appear to have opened the way for a general granting of monopoly privilege, thereby increasing the marginal benefits of rent seeking. Other forces, however, were at work to prevent the marginal benefit curve from shifting significantly. First, the commerce clause (Article 1, Section 8) was used to invalidate several state-sanctioned monopolies on the grounds that these interfered with the power of the federal government to regulate commerce. Second, another Supreme Court action in *Charles River Bridge* v. *Warren Bridge* (1837)[24] interpreted the grant of privilege by the state very narrowly, holding that such grants did not restrict the power of the state to grant like privileges to potential competitors. Because this essentially allowed monopoly profits to be eroded by subsequent state action, the marginal benefit of attempting to achieve such transfers was constrained.

Although the contract clause was invoked numerous times early in the nineteenth century to prevent legislative action that significantly altered rights, its effectiveness as a limit on such action gradually diminished because of Supreme Court decisions relating to the "bankruptcy cases." *Sturges* v. *Crowninshield* (1819)[25] negated a New York law giving relief to

22. James J. Smith and Paul L. Murphy, eds., *Liberty and Justice* (New York: Alfred A. Knopf, 1965) 1: 126.

23. 4 Wheaton 518 (1819).

24. II Peters 420 (1837).

25. 4 Wheaton 122 (1819).

debtors, on the grounds that such relief impaired the obligation of contracts and was unconstitutional under Article 1, Section 10. The New York law in question had attempted to relieve insolvent debtors from obligations entered into prior to the passage of the law. A later law which stipulated that all subsequent contracts would be subject to bankruptcy proceedings was upheld in *Ogden* v. *Saunders* (1827).[26] The Court argued that because such a law became part of the contract, it did not violate the constitutional provision. Although this decision was crucial to bankruptcy legislation, it also weakened significantly the power of the Constitution to restrict legislative action. In effect, government was now permitted to alter any property rights involved in contractual exchange as long as that alteration preceded the contract. Thus, the freedom of property owners to use their property as they saw fit was appreciably reduced and, perhaps more important, the benefits of rent-seeking activity were appreciably increased.

Although the contract clause was thus losing effectiveness in limiting transfer activity very early in the nineteenth century, the commerce clause was increasingly potent in restraining the government from handing out special favors and privileges. For example, in an 1824 case, *Gibbons* v. *Ogden*,[27] the Court held that the power of Congress to "regulate Commerce . . . among the several States" meant that monopoly rights granted to steamship companies were invalid. Throughout most of the nineteenth century, the commerce clause frequently prevented actions by state legislatures that reflected immediate interests. It is interesting to note that although nothing in the Supreme Court decisions prevented the federal government from regulating commerce, for the first century of the nation's existence, the Congress did not act in this arena. In fact, prior to the Civil War, the only use of the commerce clause by the Supreme Court was to negate state statutes.

Although the preceding argues that transfers of income and wealth were difficult to obtain in the nineteenth century via the federal government, the fact is that some such transfers were carried out. Congress and the Supreme Court did allow rent seeking in at least two major areas: tariffs, and subsidies for transportation improvements including the rights of eminent domain.[28]

Trade policy was a major issue in American politics both prior to and

26. 12 Wheaton 213 (1827).

27. 9 Wheaton 1 (1824).

28. For an excellent discussion of eminent domain laws, see Harry N. Scheiber, "Property Law, Expropriation, and Resource Allocation by Government: The United States, 1789–1910," *The Journal of Economic History* 33 (1973), pp. 232–251.

immediately after the American Revolution. Although the Constitution did away with internal trade barriers, no such prohibition existed against federal enactment of external barriers. During early sessions a few in Congress advocated absolutely no government intervention, but "general agreement had apparently been reached that one function of government should be to stimulate all nationally beneficial occupations and enterprises."[29] Congress responded to this opportunity throughout the nineteenth century with numerous laws either lowering or raising the tariff, and such laws did represent an opportunity for rent seeking.[30]

Public assistance of transportation was another potential area for major transfers. As there was no constitutional clause prohibiting such action, about three-fourths of the total investment in canal construction prior to the Civil War came from government sources.[31] Government aid to railroads, although not such a large portion of the total, was still significant. Of course, subsidies to social overhead capital do not *necessarily* represent transfers; some might be required to equate private and social returns, as Professor Scheiber argues was the case with certain nineteenth-century expropriations.[32] Nonetheless, while this argument was the rationale for many grants, it is probably true that at least some did represent coercive transfers of wealth between members of the population.

In addition to transfer activity at the federal level, state and local governments were involved in altering the property rights structure. Between 1800 and 1830, "most of it [regulation] was undertaken by the states, not the federal government."[33] Here, again, transportation was one of the dominant areas of intervention, with states owning roads, canals, and railroads. States also passed legislation regulating the quality of commodities produced within the state, fixing interest charges on debt, and in certain cases setting wages, fees, and even prices on some

29. E. A. J. Johnson, *The Foundations of American Economic Freedom* (Minneapolis: University of Minnesota Press, 1973), p. 200.

30. For a discussion of arguments surrounding the tariff laws, see Richard Edwards, "Economic Sophistication in 19th-Century Congressional Tariff Debates," *The Journal of Economic History* 30 (1970), pp. 802–838.

31. Lance E. Davis, Richard A. Easterlin, William N. Parker *et al.*, *American Economic Growth: An Economist's History of the United States* (New York: Harper and Row, 1972), p. 497.

32. Harry N. Scheiber, "The Road to *Munn:* Eminent Domain and the Concept of Public Purpose in the State Courts," in *Perspectives in American History* 5 (1971), pp. 329–402.

33. Lawrence N. Friedman, *A History of American Law* (New York: Simon and Schuster, 1973), p. 157.

products.[34] Much emphasis has been placed on the precedent of state regulation,[35] and its importance should not be ignored.

On the other hand, the magnitude of transfer activity at all levels of government during the first three quarters of the century should not be exaggerated. Professor Lawrence Friedman says that despite this regulation,

> 19-century government was no leviathan. Even in the large Eastern states, its hold over the economy was weak. Many programs must have existed only on paper. Many of the inspection laws, licensing laws, and laws about weights and measures were feeble and vapidly enforced.[36]

Cases like *McCulloch* v. *Maryland*[37] limited the state's power to tax on the grounds that with such power came the capability to destroy what was taxed. Even Professor Scheiber agrees that "the heyday of expropriation as an instrument of public policy designed to subsidize private enterprise can probably be dated as beginning in the 1870's. . . . "[38] In the words of James Willard Hurst, the first three quarters of the nineteenth century were characterized by a "release of energy."[39] Freedom of contract and a laissez-faire philosophy were the rules of the day. However, the last quarter of the century and the first decade of the next witnessed a dramatic shift in constitutional interpretation which significantly raised the effectiveness of transfer activity in the government arena.

THE RISE OF TRANSFER ACTIVITY

The changes in the last part of the nineteenth century were the culmination of pressures by numerous political and social forces. Foremost among these were a growing concern for the perceived maldistribution

34. See Oscar Handlin and Mary Handlin, *Commonwealth: A Study of the Role of Government in the American Economy, Massachusetts, 1774–1861* (Cambridge, Mass.: Harvard University Press, 1969); Louis Hartz, *Economic Policy and Democratic Thought: Pennsylvania 1776–1869* (Cambridge, Mass.: Harvard University Press, 1948); Morton J. Horwitz, *The Transformation of American Law, 1780–1860* (Cambridge, Mass.: Harvard University Press, 1977); and Friedman, *History of American Law.*

35. For example, see Scheiber, "The Road to *Munn.*"

36. Friedman, *History of American Law,* p. 163. See also Jonathan R. T. Hughes, "Transference and Development of Institutional Constraints upon Economic Activity," in Paul Uselding, ed., *Research in Economic History* (Greenwich, Conn.: JAI Press, 1976), p. 60.

37. 4 Wheaton 316 (1819).

38. Harry N. Scheiber, "Property Law," p. 243.

39. Hurst, *Laws and the Conditions of Freedom in the Nineteenth Century United States* (Madison: University of Wisconsin Press, 1964), Chapter 1.

of income, the problems of urbanization and deterioration of the environment, and the depletion of the nation's limited supply of resources.[40] Since most citizens blamed these problems on the market, it is not surprising that the government was called upon to use its coercive power to improve the allocation of resources. As we have seen, the initial interpretations of the Constitution left little room for the transfer of rights except through market transactions. But changes in the rules of the game in the late 1800s increased the possibility of nonmarket (noncompensated) transfers.

Although it is difficult to identify watersheds in the evolution of constitutional interpretation in the United States, one Supreme Court case does stand out as the beginning of a new era—*Munn* v. *Illinois* (1877).[41] As noted earlier, the government framework had on occasion been used to effect transfers prior to 1877. J. R. T. Hughes's recent work suggests that the history of the transfer process had its roots in colonial times.[42] Moreover, Harry Scheiber has pointed out that "the road to *Munn*" was a long one, following traditional mileposts of common law.[43] Colonial and even federal precedent for price control cannot be denied, but we should not lose sight of the effectiveness of constitutional limitations in restricting transfers. Even Hughes, whose main thesis is that nonmarket control has been with us since colonial times and that our history is not the "mother lode of the laissez-faire tradition,"[44] concludes that

> we went from mercantilism to neomercantilism with an intervening period, the period from independence to the 1870's when the dominance of the free market as the main method of social control waxed and waned, the period when the private economy continuously moved, by both spread and size effects, ahead of government regulatory power.[45]

With the *Munn* decision, transfer activity at the federal level increased. Government was now authorized to regulate private property, and the door to rent-seeking had been thrown open. Over time, this process has been used increasingly to alter the structure of wealth and power in our society. The *Munn* decision itself may have been a response to the

40. For a more detailed discussion of factors influencing institutional change, see Anderson and Hill, "Toward a General Theory of Institutional Change."

41. 94 U.S. 113 (1877).

42. Hughes, *Social Control in the Colonial Economy* (Charlottesville: University Press of Virginia, 1976).

43. Scheiber, "The Road to *Munn*."

44. Hughes, "Transference and Development of Constraints" p. 62.

45. Ibid., p. 52.

changing economic and social conditions of the time, but the forward-looking consequence of the *Munn* doctrine was the encouragement of transfer activity.

Agrarian unrest during the post-Civil War period had led to the Granger movement with its denouncement of monopoly power, of rate fixing, and of big business in general. In 1873 the Granger-controlled legislature of Illinois responded with a law fixing storage rates for grain warehouses. Wisconsin, Iowa, and Minnesota promptly followed by fixing rail rates within their boundaries. By 1877 it was essential to test the constitutionality of all of these laws in the case of *Munn* v. *Illinois.* In the majority opinion, Chief Justice Waite concluded that when "one devotes his property to a use in which the public has an interest, he, in effect, grants to the public an interest in that use, and must submit to be controlled by the public for the common good, to the extent of the interest he has thus created."[46]

Under the doctrine of police power, the Supreme Court had previously upheld the power of states incidentally to regulate economic activity. But the idea that private property used in the public interest was subject to public regulation granted to government broad new authority to interfere with contracts and private property. Such authority raised the returns to transfer activity by giving to nonowners the capability to affect resource allocation. Justice Field recognized the path-breaking nature of this decision and in his dissent said,

> If this be sound law, if there be no protection, either in the principles upon which our republican government is founded, or in the prohibitions of the Constitution against such invasion of private rights, all property and all business in the State are held at the mercy of a majority of its legislature.[47]

In other words, through this decision the independent judiciary had taken on the role of enforcing "legislative deals." The full impact of the decision, however, was not realized for several decades.[48]

A major reason for this delay was the rise of what is termed "substantive due process," believed by some to be the bulwark of laissez-faireism in the late nineteenth century.[49] The Fourteenth Amendment to the

46. 94 U.S. 126 (1877).

47. 94 U.S. 140 (1877).

48. In two later cases, *Nebbia* v. *New York,* 291 U.S. 502 (1934), and *Tyson and Bros.* v. *Banton,* 273 U.S. 418 (1927), the idea of business related to the public interest was expanded as a reason for regulation. In *Nebbia* v. *New York,* Justice Roberts said, "It is clear that there is no closed class or category of business affected with a public interest."

49. Edward S. Corwin, *Constitutional Revolution, Ltd.* (Claremont, Ca.: Claremont Colleges, 1941), p. 29.

Constitution, passed in 1868 as an effort to clarify the rights of the newly freed slaves, reads in part that "no State shall . . . deprive any person of life, liberty, or property, without due process of law." This, of course, resembled the Fifth Amendment which put the same sort of limitations on federal laws, but the restatement served as a procedural safeguard guaranteeing just compensation. Before the Civil War, due process had required that certain procedures be fulfilled before a person could be deprived of life, liberty, or property, but supporters hoped the Fourteenth Amendment would give more substance to those requirements.

Interpretation of the amendment during the last quarter of the century did introduce the concept of substance into due process, but it is not clear just how much this guaranteed private property against arbitrary or confiscatory laws. The earliest interpretations diverged little from the procedural notion of due process as seen in the *Slaughter House Cases* of 1873.[50] However, in *Davidson* v. *New Orleans* (1878),[51] vested rights took on more substance as the majority of the Court argued that a law transferring private property from Individual A to Individual B could be, in fact, a violation of due process even if it followed established procedures. The words of Justice Miller in this opinion sounded much like those of Marshall during the early national period, but their impact on vested rights was short-lived. In *Stone* v. *Farmers Loan and Trust* (1886)[52] the Court reemphasized the *Munn* doctrine in another rail regulation case but added—with the implication that this addition would provide substance—that regulation was not without limits. Four years later, in *Chicago, Milwaukee and St. Paul Railroad Co.* v. *Minnesota,*[53] the doctrine of substantive due process was expanded when the Court held that state regulation must be "reasonable." The definition of that word, however, was left to the independent judiciary.

Although this interpretation did provide some constitutional protection, the very question of the "reasonableness" of transfers of property left greater scope to the judicial review process. Could vested rights ever be ensured in such a situation?

> The question of the reasonableness or arbitrariness of a law could not be settled by reference to any specific constitutional provision or any absolute principle of law. A reasonable law was one that seemed sensible, plausible, and intelligent to the judges who passed upon it. What constitutes sensible, plausible, and intelligent public policy, however, is largely a matter of the individual's economic and social

50. 16 Wallace 36 (1873).
51. 96 U.S. 97 (1878).
52. 116 U.S. 307 (1886).
53. 134 U.S. 418 (1890).

> philosophy—his standard of values. When the Court applied the test of reasonableness to legislation, therefore, it measured the law against its own economic and social attitudes. If in the light of these attitudes the law seemed intelligent, the justices upheld it; if not, they declared it unreasonable, arbitrary, and a violation of due process of law.[54]

Thus it is clear that the due process clause offered little or no firm protection against transfers and was wholly subject to the notions of members of the Court. It is not surprising, therefore, that what was considered "reasonable" changed over time in rhythm with the economic and social pressures of the moment. In 1898 a Supreme Court decision held that regulating the hours of miners was reasonable; in 1905, in a similar case, the Court ruled that regulating the hours in bake shops was unreasonable.[55]

The lack of firm constitutional arguments and the relevance of nonconstitutional information became even more clear in *Muller* v. *Oregon* (1908).[56] In this case, the constitutionality of a 1903 Oregon statute regulating the working hours of women was at issue. Louis Brandeis was retained by the State of Oregon to argue its side and, in support of the "reasonableness" of the statute, he filed a brief consisting of only two pages dealing with constitutional arguments as against more than a hundred pages dealing with social conditions. Since reasonableness was the issue, he argued that evidence was needed on that question rather than on constitutionality.

With Court acceptance of the Brandeis brief, the rule of "higher law" lost much power. In turn, this increased the potential benefits of invoking judicial and legislative processes to acquire command over resources. Cases involving regulation of working hours, working conditions, prices, etc., swelled the court dockets. Regulatory agencies began to evolve and gained power to influence resource allocation. As a result, expanded opportunities for the coercive power of government to influence the allocation of resources and the distribution of income provided ever greater incentive to seek marginal benefits from transfer activity.

Other parts of the government's traditional functions were also being altered during this period in ways that made transfer activity more profitable. First, the power to tax was expanded. As late as 1875, the Supreme Court had held that a state law that authorized the use of tax

54. Alfred H. Kelly and Winfred A. Harbison, *The American Constitution*, 4th ed. (New York: Norton, 1970), p. 527.

55. *Holden* v. *Hardy*, 169 U.S. 366 (1898), and *Lochner* v. *New York*, 198 U.S. 45 (1905), respectively.

56. 208 U.S. 412 (1908).

monies for the encouragement of private businesses was unconstitutional.[57] However, by the beginning of the next century, taxes were recognized as an accepted method of regulating market outcomes. In *McCray* v. *United States* (1904),[58] for example, the Court upheld a statute that regulated margarine production by placing a 10¢/lb. tax on artificially colored margarine but only a .25¢/lb. tax on the uncolored product. The allowance of such a tax opened up a new arena for potential transfer activity and effectively removed the limits on the power of Congress to impose taxes for nonrevenue purposes.

Second, during the last quarter of the nineteenth century, the police power of the state was used increasingly to justify interference with contracts and the power to regulate interstate commerce used to justify federal intervention in the market. In *Champion* v. *Ames* (1903)[59] the Court, under the guise of controlling interstate commerce, upheld a law forbidding the shipment of lottery tickets. Two years later, in *Swift and Co.* v. *United States*,[60] the Court formulated the "stream of commerce" doctrine, holding that economic activities that might eventually be a part of commerce between the states were subject to federal control. This doctrine has expanded to the point where almost all production and distribution is now subject to such control because of its potential involvement in interstate commerce.

Clearly, changes in the institutional environment during the last quarter of the nineteenth century were responsible for increased transfer activity. It has been said that the history of lobbying is the history of all legislation; but it was only after 1880 that the level of these efforts, especially by industry and railroads, rose to new heights. In addition to illegal resort to bribery, companies ran their attorneys for public office, contributed generously to campaign funds, and handed out favors to elected officials. There was, in effect, a market in state legislative seats, and the outcomes even of gubernatorial and congressional races depended upon which company was able to buy the most votes.[61] Then, with the advent of the substantive due process concept and the rule of reasonableness, attention turned toward efforts to influence court decisions. The sidetracking of the *Munn* doctrine during this period is evidence of the power of business. During the period of Republican reign from 1868 to 1912, the court system, all the way from the Supreme Court

57. *Loan Association* v. *Topeka,* 20 Wallace 655 (1875).

58. 195 U.S. 27 (1904).

59. 188 U.S. 321 (1903).

60. 196 U.S. 375 (1905).

61. For an excellent review of this type of behavior aimed at securing political positions, see Carl Burgess Glasscock, *The War of the Copper Kings* (New York: Bobbs Merrill, 1935).

to lower federal and state judiciaries, found its ranks being filled with corporate lawyers sympathetic to the interests of big business.[62] The quasi-legislative power obtained during this era enabled the independent judiciary to determine not only the constitutionality of acts but also whether the transfer of rights from one individual or group to another was "reasonable." With this concentration of power, it is little wonder that resources were invested both to obtain and to prevent such transfers.

CONCLUSION

The twentieth century has witnessed a changing public–private mix in many economies throughout the world, and the United States is no exception. The fact that government at all levels has continually increased in size and scope has been emphasized by scholars from many disciplines, with those from economics, history, law, and political science leading the charge. Professor North's work on institutional change, one of the most noteworthy reports of this investigation, stresses the role of the institutional environment as an incentive to individual action. We here suggest that this environment also determines the mix between productive and transfer activity. His work poses a further question: What factors determine changes in the institutional environment? This paper has highlighted the role of the Supreme Court in this respect.

We have argued that between the periods of colonial governmental intervention under the guise of mercantilism and the changes that occurred during the last quarter of the nineteenth century, America's experiment with constitutional government was at least a partial success. Liberty and property rights were protected by the Constitution and the interpretation of that Constitution. The effect was to encourage productivity and discourage rent seeking. By 1915, however, the major barriers that the Founding Fathers had erected against large-scale legislative transfers had been drastically lessened or removed altogether. The general reverence for natural (vested) rights had diminished, its final appearance in a Supreme Court case having been in 1875. The contract clause, formerly a bulwark against transfer activity, was greatly weakened by the bankruptcy case of 1827. The commerce clause had advanced from its status merely as a limit on state action to serve as justification for federal intervention. And the due process clause, which had originally been viewed as a revival of vested rights in the move from

62. For a more lengthy discussion of this rising transfer activity in conjunction with due process, see Kelly and Harbison, *American Constitution*, pp. 510–524.

procedural to substantive due process, had subsequently been shackled by ambiguity in the rule of reasonableness. All of this, coupled with changes in the constitutional interpretation of "the public interest" in *Munn* v. *Illinois,* meant that the groundwork had been laid for a major rent-seeking society. The expected value of transfer activity had risen.

Not all of the transfer activity took place immediately; in fact, a major increase awaited the coming of the Great Depression and the resultant New Deal policies. However, although important constitutional battles erupted during the New Deal, most of the alterations in the basic decision-making framework had settled into place several decades earlier. The Depression created a strong incentive for such transfers, but prior changes in interpretation of the Constitution made transfer activity much more likely to succeed. In short, the major reason why transfer activity has attained its present level rests with constitutional interpretations by the independent judiciary between 1875 and 1910. America's experiment with constitutional democracy was successful during the first half of the nineteenth century because of the independent judiciary. But that same judiciary has since eroded constitutional limits by supporting self-interest legislative deals. Herbert Stein's statement that "no one can imagine the court finding anything in the economic field unconstitutional"[63] suggests that we indeed have become a transfer society.

ACKNOWLEDGMENT

We thank the Hoover Institution for its support of this project while Terry Anderson was a National Fellow. This paper is a summary of our book, *The Birth of a Transfer Society* (Stanford, Ca.: Hoover Institution Press, 1980).

Terry Anderson studied with North from 1968 to 1972. His thesis concerned the economic growth of seventeenth century New England and was submitted in 1972. In that year he went to Montana State University as an Assistant Professor.

Anderson extended his work on the early New England economy with a parallel study of economic growth in the Chesapeake Colonies. He is also known for research carried on with P. J. Hill on the role of property rights on the frontier of the American west. They have completed a book entitled **The Birth of a Transfer Society** which adds to North's work on institutional change. Anderson and Hill are also working with North on a revision of North's **Growth and Welfare in the American Past.** This chapter is an outgrowth of a larger project initiated while Anderson was a National Fellow at the Hoover Institution on War, Revolution, and Peace. Terry Anderson is now Professor of Economics at Montana State University. **P. J. Hill**, one of Anderson's colleagues, joins him in this chapter.

63. Herbert Stein, "Grounds for Pessimism," *The Wall Street Journal,* December 12, 1974.

Chapter 10

The Market and Government-Sponsored Industry

Philip R. P. Coelho and David R. Knowles

Currently there are two major hypotheses over the nature and objective of government intervention in a market economy. The straightforward reformist hypothesis argues that government intervention results from "market failure,"[1] defined as either a breakdown of the competitive process or the incidence of externalities (positive or negative).

This first hypothesis has been used to justify government action in a multitude of instances. The establishment of the entire gamut of agencies that dot the American scene may be attributed to the hypothesis that the market has somehow failed to allocate resources in a "socially optimal" way. Well-known examples of such creations include the Environmental Protection Agency (EPA), the Securities and Exchange Commission (SEC), the Interstate Commerce Commission (ICC), the Occupational Safety and Health Agency (OSHA), and the Federal Communications Commission (FCC). As the "socially optimal" allocation of resources is not obvious, political authorities have delegated its determination to an assortment of bureaucracies. Besides spawning a host of bureaucrats and regulations, this has produced a sizable literature on the behavior of bureaucrats and agencies.[2] Without

1. The reformist hypothesis was clearly dominant among intellectuals and economists until very recently. Examples are abundant throughout the literature. For an elementary exposition of this hypothesis see Paul A. Samuelson, *Economics,* 10th ed. (New York: McGraw-Hill, 1976), Chapters 8, 26, 40.

2. Thomas E. Borcherding has edited an extremely valuable book on this topic: *Budgets and Bureaucrats: The Sources of Government Growth* (Durham, N.C.: Duke University Press, 1977).

EXPLORATIONS IN THE NEW ECONOMIC HISTORY

ISBN 0-12-580080-0

undertaking a review of this literature, we simply want to make the point that it affords no consensus upon what motivates agencies or bureaucrats. One theory is that the motivating force behind agencies is budget maximization,[3] another says managerial utility maximization,[4] still another states that the motivating force depends upon whether the commissioners of the agency have fixed-term appointments or indefinite tenure,[5] and finally, it has been suggested that mere survival is the dominant motivating force behind agency actions.[6] Regardless of how one views this plethora of ideas, one point of agreement has emerged: Economists, by and large, have rejected the hypothesis that there is some ideal "public interest" to which these agencies and bureaucrats devote their energies.[7] Consequently, even if we accept the reformist argument in explaining beginnings of these agencies, we still have not a widely agreed upon description of why they behave as they do.

The second main hypothesis advanced to explain government intervention treats it as a response to the desire of an industry group to be protected from market forces.[8] This hypothesis encounters fewer intellectual difficulties than the reformist hypothesis, but it does raise some questions. Instead of postulating that market imperfections result

3. William A. Niskanen, *Bureaucracy and Representative Government* (Chicago: Aldine Atherton, 1971).

4. See Oliver E. Williamson, *The Economics of Discretionary Behavior: Managerial Objectives in a Theory of the Firm* (Engelwood Cliffs, N.J.: Prentice-Hall, 1964).

5. Ross D. Eckert, "On the Incentives of Regulators: The Case of Taxicabs," *Public Choice* 14 (1973), pp. 83–99.

6. Philip R. P. Coelho, "Rules, Authorities and the Design of Not-for-Profit-Firms," *Journal of Economic Issues* 10 (1976), pp. 416–428.

7. Douglass C. North has coauthored an entire book on the theme that there is no ideal "public interest" (Douglass C. North and R. L. Miller, *The Economics of Public Issues,* 4th ed. [New York: Harper and Row, 1978]). A sampling of chapter titles may give a flavor of this book: "The Economics of Usury Laws" (Chapter 11), "The Economics of Prostitution" (Chapter 9), "The Economics of Juries" (Chapter 15), and "The Economics of Welfare and the Elimination of Poverty" (Chapter 33). The entire text is devoted to explaining the economic consequences of attempts (usually by public bodies) to change free market behavior.

8. George Stigler and Milton Friedman are prominent proponents of this view. See Milton Friedman, *Capitalism and Freedom* (Chicago: University of Chicago Press, 1962); George Stigler and Claire Friedland, "What Can Regulators Regulate?" *Journal of Law and Economics* 5 (1962) pp. 1–16; George Stigler, "The Theory of Regulation," *The Bell Journal of Economics and Management Science* 2 (1971), pp. 3–21. This hypothesis and the first one are not mutually exclusive. Some authorities argue that the agency is first established in a fit of reformist enthusiasm and then gradually captured by the industry group. Gabriel Kolko, however, argues that the Interstate Commerce Commission was explicitly promoted by the railroad interest that it was purported to regulate (Kolko, *Railroads and Regulation, 1877–1916* [New York: Norton, 1970]).

in the demand for agencies, it postulates that political imperfections allow these agencies to come into being.[9] Furthermore, it treats the regulated industry as a homogeneous group, or, alternatively, it does not specify how the dominant coalition was formed. One further notable difficulty with this "capture" hypothesis is that of explaining cases in which (as sometimes happens) the agency's behavior goes against the perceived best interest of the regulated firms.

In this paper we wish to suggest an alternative hypothesis that may be useful in interpreting governmental behavior which would be inexplicable if sole reliance were placed upon either the reformist or the capture hypothesis. We are rejecting neither theory, because both appear to have some empirical validity. Our more modest aim is to argue that governmental agencies and bureauracies, once established, act so as to ensure their own survival over time.[10]

Government agencies are similar to most nonprofit firms in that they have no easily discernible or measurable objective function. We contend that this is the main distinction between profit- and nonprofit-oriented firms. The absence of a measurable unit of output for evaluating the performance of government agencies has led some researchers to contend that government agencies are directed by individuals who run the agencies in order to maximize their own utility.[11] We cannot accept this hypothesis because, in the absence of other constraints, the utility-maximizing administrator would be constrained only by time and the assets available to his agency; in the long run we would observe agencies destroying themselves to satisfy the whims of their administrators. If the agency is to survive, utility-maximizing administrators must be con-

9. Protection from market forces implies that some are benefiting at the expense of others. Under complusion by government, the outcome as determined by the market would be changed by the political process. Under the capture hypothesis we have assumed perfect markets, thus government intervention must result in an inferior allocation of resources. The Coase Theorem, as stated in "The Problem of Social Cost," *Journal of Law and Economics* 3 (1960), pp. 1–44, asserts that in the absence of transactions costs, negotiations between contending parties lead to an optimal allocation of resources. Suboptimal allocation, therefore, implies some barrier to negotiations—that is, imperfect political markets.

10. This hypothesis is not original. A number of amusing and insightful books, in developing this line of reasoning have led to "laws" such as "Parkinson's Law" and the "Peter Principle." Robert N. Kharasch, in *The Institutional Imperative* (New York: Charterhouse Books, 1973), has elucidated the hypothesis with humor and incisiveness; his "institutional imperative" is that "every action or decision of an institution must be intended to keep the institutional machinery working." This is nearly identical to our survival hypothesis.

11. For a review of the literature on this point see Coelho, "Rules, Authorities."

strained from damaging the long-run viability of the agency. The concept of partially constrained utility maximization is a more accurate hypothesis than unconstrained utility maximization; however, the constraints that evolve are so detailed and pervasive that the theory of utility maximization becomes totally elusive.[12]

The ordinary manifestations of utility maximization will not be observed in an organization that survives because of these constraints: Those who support the agency would withdraw their aid if it became apparent that the sole reason for the agency's existence was to satisfy the sybaritic whims of the organization's administrators.[13] Because the agency cannot survive without this support (it is, by definition, *non*-profit), a viable agency will not pursue administrative utility maximization as a goal but will act in such a way as to be seen making some contributions to society. Thus, by an evolutionary process, the procedures designed into it will encourage "constructive" actions by the instruments of the agency.[14]

These actions of the agency need not be cost effective and most likely will not be. The reason is that the agency, to survive, must please a constituency. Given that the agency is financed by revenues raised by general taxation, its burden upon the general public will usually be negligible. Even if substantial externalities were being corrected, if such benefits and the budget of the agency were spread over the entire populace the impact of its spending would not be generally noted. However, if the agency directs its spending at a few groups, then it can build itself a constituency. Note that in this case the public at large does not feel noticeably worse off, because the benefits it could have enjoyed would have been negligible; but when the benefits are targeted, the groups that receive the agency's largess will be substantailly better off.

12. In a recent review article, Harvey Liebenstein has made similar comments upon the theory of the (profit-oriented) firm: " 'The Missing Line'—Micro-Micro Theory?" *Journal of Economic Literature* 17 (1979), pp. 477–502.

13. It is our contention that the support would be withdrawn regardless of whether the taxpayer, Congress, or some other body is postulated as the ultimate financial supporter of the agency. *The Wall Street Journal* recently carried an exposé of a government agency (Karen E. House, "Growing Deadwood: At Agriculture Agency, Bureaucracy is Huge, and the Living is Easy," *Wall Street Journal,* April 12, 1977). We argue that this is just the sort of notoriety that will lead to curtailment of support and, unless the agency succeeds in mending its ways and its political fences, it will find resources drying up.

14. In an early and stimulating article, Armen A. Alchian first explicitly applied the evolutionary approach to economic problems: "Uncertainty, Evolution, and Economic Theory," *Journal of Political Economy* 58 (1950), pp. 211–221. For an elaboration of how the evolutionary hypothesis would work in this particular instance, see Coelho, "Rules, Authorities."

Our hypothesis, then, is that governmental agencies and bureaucracies will devote their energies to benefiting select identifiable groups in order to ensure their survival. This differs from the capture hypothesis (that industry groups virtually take over these agencies) in that the agency, rather than being a captive of the industry, is now in a symbiotic relationship with the industry. We can also ask the question of causation: Which comes first, the agency or the special interest group? Typically, the response has been the special interest group (the industry). Our hypothesis makes this response less certain. Casual empiricism suggests that the trucking industry was an infant and politically minuscule when first regulated by the Interstate Commerce Commission; the same is true for nuclear power and the Atomic Energy Commission. We believe that there are manifold cases where intervention came before the industry was large enough to generate a substantial lobby.

This hypothesis can also explain how the agency resolves conflicting demands among different groups: The agency favors the group that is more politically effective. This differs from some of the literature on social decision making[15] in which the dollar strength of a lobby is regarded as crucial in determining political support. Political effectiveness is not simply a matter of dollars but, more importantly, of the intensity and the numbers of people who hold a particular viewpoint.[16] These "passionate minorities" have an impact upon government that does not seem to be readily offset by an additional expenditure of funds. For example, the Interstate Commerce Commission (ICC) originally regulated railroads and later acquired the task of regulating interstate trucking. Because the trucking industry is much more atomistic that the railroad industry, we contend that (after the trucking industry reached some minimum size) lobbying from the truckers was more effective than that of the railroads. In both the trucking and the railroad companies, each of the officials and the major stockholders has one vote in the electoral process. But because the truckers vastly outnumber the railroaders, we predict that the former would have a more effective lobby and, consequently, would be favored by the ICC. The argument can be extended to say that in any dispute between two groups, one of which consists of a few large firms and the second of many smaller firms, the

15. See Mancur Olson, *The Logic of Collective Action* (Cambridge, Mass.: Harvard University Press, 1965).

16. The literature on public decision making abounds in examples of "passionate minorities," whereby a small group, intensely committed to one issue, may decisively affect the outcome. Financial resources are not a sine qua non for success. See Anthony Downs, *An Economic Theory of Democracy* (New York: Harper Row, 1957); James M. Buchanan and Gordon Tullock, *The Calculus of Consent* (Ann Arbor: University of Michigan Press, 1962).

agency will presumably favor the group of smaller firms because its lobby will tend to be more politically effective. The preceding statement has to be hedged to the extent that if the smaller group is highly fragmented it may not be cost effective for this group to band together to lobby if only a relatively small fraction of its income is derived from the regulated activity. We believe this is why American agricultural policy has favored commercial farmers over the much more numerous part-time farmers.

The remainder of this paper examines the hypothesis that government agencies seek to perpetuate themselves by creating and favoring a special interest group. Using government involvement with the tung oil industry as a particular example, we examine a government agency actively establishing and nurturing an industry and the symbiotic relationship that developed between them until, for exogenous reasons (acts of God), much of the industry was wiped out and government intervention disappeared. We examine why the program was terminated, how it differed from others, and the special circumstances surrounding it. The case is unique because when tung oil price supports ended in 1973, this represented the first termination of agricultural price supports in 25 years.

HISTORICAL SUMMARY

The tung tree was introduced into the United States in 1904 by the Americal consul general returning from Hankow, China.[17] From its in-

17. The tung tree *(Aleurites fordii)* produces a nut from which oil is extracted and used as a drying agent in a variety of products that require water resistance and a relatively short time for drying. Tung oil is a component of varnish, paint, other protective coatings, and insulation. In the United States before 1936, it was used almost exclusively by the varnish and enamel industry; thereafter, developments in paint technology made that industry the major user as a base for high quality paints. The addition of tung oil improves paint to be used for outside work in hot climates because it mitigates cracking, checking, and peeling. Other industrial uses for tung oil have been found in the manufacture of printer's ink, of masonite and some plastic, of brake linings, and in the insulation of electrical wires. Nevertheless, the paint and varnish industries have used over 80% of the total consumption of tung oil in the United States since World War II.

The tung tree was cultivated in the United States in a narrow belt of land running parallel to the Gulf of Mexico from Florida to east Texas and styled "the tung belt." The tree requires a soil of moderate acidity, 55–70 in. of annual rainfall, a long hot summer, and a winter long enough and severe enough to ensure an unbroken dormant season although at no point should temperatures go lower than 5–8° F. Temperatures even in the range of 28–30° kill the buds in early fall or in the springtime bloom stage. Such stringent requirements obviously limited the potential for commercially successful cultivation of tung orchards.

troduction in California it spread to the Southeast where, in 1913, tung oil was first extracted in the United States. Sizable commercial plantings quickly followed, the cultivation spreading so rapidly that by 1938 an estimated 200,000 acres were devoted to tung.[18] However, domestic production constituted a very small percentage of total tung oil consumption in the United States prior to World War II; for the years 1935–1941, domestic consumption of tung oil averaged over 100 million lbs. per year while domestic production was averaging only about 2.2 million lbs. for the 3 years that significant amounts were produced in the United States.[19] Imports, almost entirely from China, were severely curtailed in 1939 because of the Japanese naval blockade of China.

The Second World War and the reduction in supply caused the government of the United States to classify tung oil as a critical and strategic commodity; all available supplies were requisitioned for the military, chiefly as a waterproofing agent in the coating of bombs, shells, tank guns, and other hardware. Because of these military uses, tung oil was placed at the top of the list of strategic materials by presidential proclamation.[20] Concurrently, the Department of Agriculture (USDA) offered cash incentives to growers to increase tung oil production.[21] The wartime price of tung oil, its high place on the strategic material list, and the incentives offered by the Department of Agriculture rapidly expanded the acreage devoted to tung oil; by 1945 domestic tung oil production was over 10 million lb.[22] At the end of World War II, American producers once again faced foreign competition from China and from new

---

Tung nuts mature in the fall and drop to the ground; harvesting is not recommended before the sap dries (prices are lower for nuts with high moisture content). The tung tree has been estimated to produce enough oil for commercial purposes for 30 years after its first bearing at 3 years of age. The tung tree is grown commercially in southern China (its point of origin) and also in Argentina and Paraguay.

For detailed accounts of tung agriculture and conditions in the United States, see *Review of Reviews* 94 (1936), p. 4; U.S. Department of Agriculture, *Report of Tung Feasibility Study Group* (Washington. D.C.: GPO, 1969); U.S. Tariff Commission, *Tung Oil and Tung Nuts* (Washington, D.C.: GPO, 1960); George F. Potter, "The Domestic Tung Industry Today," *Journal of the American Oil Chemist's Society* 45 (1968), p. 281; Wilson W. Kilby, *History and Literature of the Domestic Tung Industry,* Technical Bulletin No. 56, Mississippi State University Agricultural Experiment Station (State College, Miss., 1969): and Charles E. Powe *et al., Cultural Practices and Costs and Returns for a Tung Enterprise,* Bulletin No. 733, Mississippi State University Agricultural Experiment Station (State College, Miss., 1966), p. 7.

18. Potter, "Domestic Tung Industry," p. 281.

19. U.S. Tariff Commission, *Specified Manufactured Dairy Products, Flaxseed and Linseed Oil, Peanuts and Peanut Oil, Tung Nuts and Tung Oil* (Washington, D.C.: GPO, 1953), p. E2.

20. USDA, *Tung Feasibility,* p. 20.

21. Ibid.

22. U.S. Tariff Commission, *Specified Manufactured Products,* p. 34.

producers in South America.[23] "In addition, alkalies, resins and other chemically produced substitutes were developed. Likewise, a steadily increasing quantity of tall oil was produced as a byproduct of the pulp and paper industry and processed into products for drying oil use."[24] Faced with competition from both substitutes and foreign competitors, the domestic tung oil industry needed help.

In 1949 legislation was passed that insured tung oil a price support between 60 and 90% of parity. Together with the Communist takeover in China, this legislation would have seemed to insure the viability of the domestic tung oil industry. However, two other developments intervened: The first was a continual erosion of tung oil's traditional markets to lower priced substitutes; the second was a steady increase in South American production of tung oil.[25] As a result, and in conjunction with a system of quotas on imported tung oil established in 1957, there have been periods ranging from surpluses, when the price was at parity, to times when prices were far greater than parity. These fluctuations accelerated the tendency to substitute other drying oils for tung oil.

Recently, tung oil production "[has been] plagued by recurring freeze damage, hurricanes and rising costs. . . . Hurricane Camille destroyed about two thirds of the 1969 producing acreage."[26] In 1971, fewer than 100 domestic producers were maintaining an economic-size orchard of 50 or more producing trees.[27] In 1973 Congress voted the extraordinary termination of the mandatory price support program for tung nuts.

GOVERNMENT INVOLVEMENT

From its inception the tung oil industry has received substantial government support. Information is not available about the amount of aid in the early years of the industry; however, we do know that the government was involved from the early 1900s. In the 1930s, the optimal areas for planting the trees in the United States were finally determined.

23. Ibid, p. E3.

24. U.S. Tariff Commission, *Tung Oil and Tung Nuts,* p. 34.

25. To these two reasons for the decline of the domestic tung oil industry we may add a third or a subsidiary reason: the notorious variability in production caused by the stringent climatic conditions required, the uncertainty of these conditions in the tung belt (see note 17) and particularly the frequency of hurricanes in that area.

26. U.S. House of Representatives, Committee on Agriculture, "Tung Nut Price Support Program," *Hearings before the Subcommittee on Soybeans and Oilseeds,* 93d Congress, 1st sess., March 21, 1973, p. 7.

27. Ibid.

> Although progress in developing the industry was at first slow, technical information supplied by the United States Department of Agriculture, state departments of agriculture, and private sources was instrumental in increasing tung tree plantings and production of the oil. This information covered soil conditions, planting methods, cultivation, fertilization, and expressing process.[28]

The Department of Agriculture funded research to improve the yield and quality of the tung tree until the early 1970s. Table 10.1 lists the recorded expenditures of the department on tung oil research. We surmise that these data are a lower boundary on the actual amounts spent: Overhead and other expenses such as general management may be included but in all probability they are not. In any case, given governmental accounting, it is most unlikely that these data are overestimates. Over the period for which we have some data (none earlier than 1935) the USDA spent $7,341,700 on research related to tung oil. We cannot say this was useless because foreign producers may have utilized some of the research, and this, in turn, may have resulted in lower prices of imported tung oil to American consumers. Total domestic consumption in the 20-year period from 1951 to 1970 averaged 39.9 million lbs. per year.[29] Valued at the support price that prevailed for 1960–1961 (24¢ per lb.), domestic consumption averaged slightly less than $10 million per year, while American production was a little more than half the total American consumption.[30] Consequently, USDA research expenditures averaged 2.5% of domestic consumption and 5% of domestic production. Although we cannot say that these expenditures were entirely in vain, to defend them we have to resort to circuitous reasoning or rely upon future events to provide ex post benefits.[31]

Besides indirect aid in the form of research expenditures, the government extended substantial direct aid to the tung oil industry. Table 10.1 lists the funds expended by the Commodity Credit Corporation (CCC) in a price support program initiated after World War II ended. China had by now resumed its role as a major exporter of tung oil and in 1947

28. Edmund C. Wood, *Tung Oil, A New American Industry* (Washington, D.C.: GPO, 1949), p. 2.

29. USDA, *Fats and Oil Situation* (Washington, D.C.: GPO, 1975), p. 20.

30. Ibid. U.S. production averaged 21.3 million lbs. per year for the period 1951–1970.

31. This presents a problem in measuring the productivity of government-sponsored research. A correct accounting would include unsuccessful as well as successful projects in calculating the rate of return. Zvi Grilliches recognizes this difficulty in his classic article, "Research Costs and Social Returns—Hybrid Corn and Related Innovations," *Journal of Political Economy* 66 (1958), pp. 419–431. However, we do not fully accept his contention that all increases in agricultural productivity were due to USDA and private expenditures upon plant improvements. This assumption ignores the increased productivity of other inputs—human and physical capital, fertilizer, and so forth.

TABLE 10.1
Government Expenditures on Tung Oil (in Thousands of Dollars)

Year	(1) CCC Losses	(1) CCC Gains	(2) USDA research expenditures
1935			2.2
1936			2.2*
1937			2.2*
1938			2.3
1939			140.0*
1940			140.0*
1941			133.5
1942			134.4
1943			128.4
1944			133.3
1945			143.5
1946			165.9
1947			164.0
1948			169.4
1949			174.8
1950			167.5
1951		234	159.2
1952	1		164.3
1953			154.5

Sources: (1) U.S. House of Representatives, Committee on Agriculture, Subcommittee on Soybeans and Oilseeds, "Study of the Tung Oil Program," *Hearings,* 92d Cong., 1st sess., March 21, 1973, p. 4. These data are reported for the fiscal year. At the end of fiscal year 1972, the CCC still had in inventory 27.8 million pounds of tung oil.

(2) These data come from two different sources. Those carrying an asterisk are estimates derived from U.S. House of Representatives, Committee on Agriculture, *Research and Related Services in the United States Department of Agriculture,* vol. 1, 61st Cong., December 21, 1950. On page 924, this report states that the annual allotment for tung products, disease control, and improvements varied from a low of approximately $120,000 to $141,000. On page 957 it is estimated that annual expenditures on investigation of tung utilization and processing varied from $1,500 to $3,000 between 1934 and 1938; from 1938 to 1942, annual expenditures were approximately $20,000. The numbers with asterisks in

(cont'd.)

and 1948 exported to the United States 121 and 131 million lbs. of tung oil, respectively. Prices of tung oil dropped from nearly 29¢ per lb. in 1947 to just under 20¢ in 1949. In Congress, two major reasons were promptly advanced for price supports:

> [First,] tung oil is a strategic and critical war material, vitally necessary to many industrial and commercial products that are essential either in peacetime or in wartime . . . [and, second,] supplies from China have been imported in greatly increased quantities and the price of tung oil on the open market in the United States has dropped to a point where domestic producers are facing disaster.[32]

32. U.S. House of Representatives, Committee on Agriculture, "Price Support for Tung Nuts and Honey," *Report Number 1027,* 81st Congress, 1st sess., July 12, 1949, p. 4.

TABLE 10.1 (Continued)

Year	(1) CCC Losses	(1) CCC Gains	(2) USDA research expenditures
1954	3		235.6
1955	295		236.7
1956	480		242.4
1957	206		246.9
1958	1		271.2
1959	1596		289.7
1960	998		261.1
1961	1325		290.8
1962		250	283.5
1963			290.0
1964			325.4
1965	98		290.8
1966	68		275.4
1967	371		238.0
1968	1916		364.5
1969	2916		294.0
1970	1010		261.2
1971	552		262.9
1972	1721		76.0
1973			24.0

1936 and 1937 are a simple mean of the high-low estimates for utilization and processing for those years. For the years 1939 and 1940 we added the estimates on utilization and processing to the minimum estimate given for improvements and disease control ($120,000, p. 924) to get the total of $140,000 for each of these years. These are in fairly close agreement with the other data that we have.

The rest of the data were acquired from a telephone conversation with Mr. C. Ronald Niemeyer of the Agriculture Research service of the United States Department of Agriculture, who kindly researched the problem at our request. He stressed that the material was not complete and that these figures should be regarded as estimates, albeit fairly reliable ones. From 1954 the program was transferred to the Agricultural Research Service and there may have been a more complete accounting of costs, explaining the large increase, or it may, alternatively, represent an arbitrary assignment of fixed costs.

The Congress seemed to be convinced that the domestic tung oil industry was on the verge of collapse.[33]

The Cassandras in Congress were premature; 2 years after the price support program was enacted in 1949, imports from China were reduced to 13 million lbs. and the price had increased by 50%.[34] The Commodity Credit Corporation, which was in charge of the price support program, had acquired 1.5 million lbs. of domestic tung oil specifically for wartime stockpiling (the Korean War was being fought at the time). Still, domes-

33. Ibid., p. 5.
34. See U.S. Tariff Commission, *Tung Oil and Tung Nuts,* Tables 3 and 6.

tic consumption decreased by almost 50% while the consumption of substitutes increased substantially. The events of the early 1950s had disproved the rationale advanced for support of the industry in the 1949 legislation. Although a war was being fought, tung oil consumption had decreased notably and the civilian economy was rapidly adopting substitutes. Nevertheless, the program remained. Through 1954 no substantial losses were incurred by the CCC in support of tung oil (see Table 10.1), but in that year a severe frost in the tung belt reduced domestic production by 60%, and in 1955 domestic production was less than a tenth of that in 1953. The year 1954 was also a benchmark when Argentina exported a record amount of tung oil to the United States, causing market prices to plummet at the same time that domestic production was decreasing significantly. Under normal competitive conditions this would have discouraged further domestic production. However, the industry enjoyed the third highest production level in its history in 1956. Prior to 1954, the CCC had gained over $200,000 in its transactions with the tung oil program; in the next 3 years it lost almost $1 million (see Table 10.1). Continued importation of tung oil from South America was becoming costly.

At the direction of the President, the Tariff Commission on March 22, 1957, instigated an investigation on tung oil. The Commission reported:

> On the basis of its investigation, the Commission unanimously found that tung oil was being and was practically certain to continue to be imported under such conditions and in such quantities as to render or tend to render ineffective, or materially interfere with, the price support program for tung nuts and tung oil undertaken by the Department of Agriculture. . . .[35]

On November 1, 1957, President Eisenhower issued a proclamation restricting imports of tung oil from South America to a total of 26 million lbs. through the growing seasons of 1958–1960. In essence this program was initiated to salvage an earlier program, and its effect was to further stimulate domestic production. (In 1958 a record 44.8 million lbs. of tung oil was produced.) It is instructive to note that all indications pointed to a declining industry: Consumption of tung oil had declined; competition from foreign producers had risen sharply; and domestic supply was curtailed by a series of unfavorable growing seasons.

From its inception in the United States, the tung oil industry was a ward of the government. The data in Table 10.1 show that government expenditures on price supports and research dating from the late thirties totaled over $18 million. This is certainly a lower boundary; we know of

35. U.S. Tariff Commission, *Annual Report* (41st) (Washington, D.C.: GPO, 1957), p. 21.

earlier government expenditures that were not reported, and the costs of investigations into the industry were also excluded.

The expenditures listed in Table 10.1 are also not entirely *economic* costs, nor are they a complete listing. These points can be illustrated with the aid of Figure 10.1.

In Figure 10.1 the subscripts "us" and "w" identify the variables for the United States and for the rest of the world respectively. Thus, $P_w - S_w$ is the supply curve of tung oil from the rest of the world and $D_{us} - D^u_{us}$ is the private (excluding government purchases) demand for tung oil in the United States. In the absence of any government intervention, consumers in the United States would purchase $0F$ units of tung oil at the price P_w (where domestic demand and the supply of the lowest priced tung oil intersect at Point G in the diagram).[36] No domestic production would result, because the lowest priced American supply would be more costly than the price set by the rest of the world.[37]

The substantial government intervention during the period of quotas enforcement is also illustrated in Figure 10.1. The supply from the rest of the world to the United States was limited by quota to an amount equivalent to $0X$; after that point only the domestic supply of tung oil was available to the American consumer. The line segment CS_E, the American supply of tung oil shifted to the right by the amount $0X$ (the import quota), is parallel to the American supply curve of tung oil (MS_{us}). Thus, the effective supply of tung oil to the United States is the dashed line P_wBCS_E.

36. The world supply of tung oil shown in Figure 10.1 ($P_w - S_w$) is drawn as invariant to the domestic demand of the United States. This is a simplifying assumption. An upward sloping supply curve would not affect the analysis; it would only make a complex diagram more complex. The United States imported approximately 20% of the total tung exports in the world during the decade from 1960 through 1969. See United Nations, Food and Agricultural Organization, *Production Yearbook* (Rome, Italy, various years). However, the data from the United Nations are flawed; during most years their statistics show world exports of tung oil as substantially different from world imports. (In the absence of extraterrestial trade, this is impossible.)

The United States fraction of total imports fluctuated from 16 to 27%. Although the level of United States demand may have had some impact upon world prices, the supply of tung oil on the world market was relatively competitive; consequently an upward sloping supply curve, while adding realism and complexity, would not change the analysis.

37. This was certainly true in the long run; currently, the United States does not produce enough to make a crushing mill for tung nuts economically viable. In the short run, American producers would and did produce some tung at prices below M because they could cover marginal costs: Since the tung nut comes from a tree, the *annual* costs of cultivation and harvesting are relatively low.

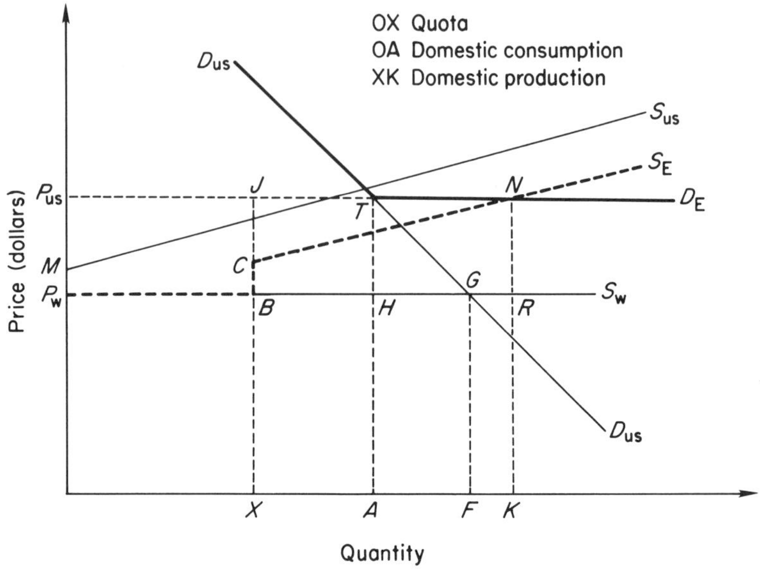

FIGURE 10.1. Supply–demand analysis of tung oil policies.

The government also influenced demand. Because the CCC supported the price of tung oil in the United States (P_{us} in Figure 10.1) above the world price,[38] domestic producers were encouraged to increase production beyond what consumers would buy, and the oversupply was purchased by the government at the support price. In Figure 10.1, government purchases are equal to the distance *AK*. Consequently, kinks appear in both the effective demand and the supply lines of tung oil in the United States. The effective demand curve, equal to private demand at prices above the support price, is completely elastic at the support price. In Figure 10.1, the effective demand curve is the heavy line $D_{us}TD_E$, the sum of domestic private demand plus CCC purchases.

For American consumers, the cost of these restrictions is represented by the area $P_{us}TGP_w$, or the differential over the world price paid by Americans plus the resultant loss in consumer surplus (*TGH*). If the demand curve were completely inelastic, thus eliminating the consideration of lost consumer surplus, the estimated excess cost to American

38. The United Nation's statistics on tung oil for the years 1958–1961 shows the price of tung oil in the United States averaging 11.9¢ per kg (equivalent to 5.4¢ per lb.) more than the world price.

consumers of tung oil would still be \$2.25 million per year.[39] Integrating to find the consumer surplus at an assumed elasticity of demand of −2, we find that an additional cost of approximately \$600,000 per year would be incurred.[40] On the basis of these rough calculations, we estimate that over the entire quota period the cost to tung oil consumers ($P_{us}TGP_w$) was between \$9 and \$11.5 million.[41] Not all this amount comprised overall economic costs, however, since a portion of it was transferred to domestic producers and to holders of the import quota. Such transfers sum to the area $P_{us}NCBP_w$, with *JCN* going to American producers of tung and $P_{us}JBP_w$ to holders of the quota. Consequently, the *economic* costs of the price supports and quotas, excluding transfers, are represented by the extra cost of producing tung oil in the United States (Area *CBRN*) and the lost consumer surplus (*THG*). Without quotas, the loss of consumer surplus would be eliminated and the economic costs reduced to *CBRN* alone. The costs to the taxpayer (the amounts listed in Table 10.1) are the government purchases of tung oil, multiplied by the purchase price less the price received by the government for the tung oil sold—equivalent to Area *BJNR* in Figure 10.1. This implies that in the absence of quotas the CCC would purchase the entire crop of tung oil produced in the United States, and starting in 1965 this is virtually what happened.[42]

It is not difficult to explain the time lag between the removal of the quotas (May, 1962) and the assumption of the whole purchase burden by the CCC. Real market forces are dynamic, not static as in our dia-

39. These estimates were derived by using the United Nation's data on prices (described earlier) and quantities as given by the USDA in *The Fats and Oils Situation* (Washington: GPO, 1975), p. 20.

40. These calculations are crude. From the evidence, it appears that the demand for tung was very price sensitive; but with an arbitrary choice of −2 for constant elasticity, it is estimated that domestic consumption would have been approximately 66 million lbs. if the American price had been equal to the world price during the quota period. This amounts to assuming a 5.4¢ per lb. price decline (see Note 35). The price in the United States averaged 26.4¢ and the world price 21¢ per lb. Domestic consumption was actually 41.7 million lbs. To find the loss in consumer surplus in the reducing hypothesized consumption of 66 million lbs. to 41.7, we integrated the area underneath demand curve, $q_x = c/p^2$; where q_x is quantity, c is a constant, and p the price. This is the general equation for a demand curve with a constant elasticity of demand of −2. Subtracting the relevant amounts yields the lost consumer surplus.

41. Even this is an underestimate. These calculations assume the quota was in force for only 4 calendar years (1956–1961) whereas it actually extended 6 months longer, from November 1, 1957, to May 1, 1962.

42. USDA, *Fats and Oils Situation*, p. 20.

gram, and the world supply of tung oil was and is volatile. The quotas were imposed when world supply–demand conditions were such that the world price was substantially below the CCC support price.[43] Between 1958 and 1962 those conditions changed. By 1961, the world price was equal to the price in the United States which, in turn, was above the CCC support price. Consequently, there was no real opposition to the removal of quotas in 1962, and market forces kept the market price above the support price until 1965.[44]

We have not included the estimated loss of consumer surplus in our calculations of the costs of government involvement, nor have we calculated the economic costs illustrated in Figure 10.1 and discussed earlier. In the absence of hard data, the assumptions that would have to be made for such analysis would admit a margin of error that we consider unacceptable. Furthermore, such calculations would confuse overall economic costs with the net out-of-pocket government expenditures that we wish to emphasize. Transfers between tung producers, consumers, and quota holders may or may not enter into the utility function of the public at large, but expenditures are debts that must be paid.

From Table 10.1 it can be seen that the imposition of the quota did not eliminate CCC losses. From 1958 to 1961, the agency lost another $4 million on its tung oil operations. The Tariff Commission recommended a further reduction in the tung oil quota to 14 million lbs. a year, but that case was lost with the turnabout in the world price. On May 1, 1962, the

43. We have used United Nation's prices rather than those from the USDA (appearing in USDA, *Fats and Oil Situations)*. The USDA and the UN statistics differ because each goes on a crop-year basis and much of the tung oil produced is from the southern hemisphere. The USDA statistics lead the UN statistics by one year. The following are prices of tung oil in the United States as estimated by the UN and by the USDA for the period 1956–1963.

Year	UN (in cents/lb.)	USDA (in cents/lb.)
1956	24.3	22.7
1957	23.2	21.4
1958	21.3	21.9
1959	22.8	21.9
1960	22.3	26.5
1961	27.7	35.2
1962	37.4	38.0
1963	37.4	26.7

44. USDA, *Fats and Oils Situation,* p. 20.

Kennedy administration eliminated the quotas and tung oil imports rose from 12.6 million lbs. in 1962 to 18.8 in 1963, and to 28.2 in 1964.[45]

The marketing of tung oil continued without substantial loss to the CCC from 1962 through 1964. The 1964 crop was close to a record, yet imports also continued at record high levels, and that combination caused market prices to plummet. By 1965, the CCC was once more purchasing tung and kept doing so in increasing amounts through 1972. Further, the administration indicated that another quota was out of the question: "This would go against our longstanding program of reducing trade barriers which has seen much progress since 1962. . . ."[46] However, for the first time the government allowed that the tung nut was no longer considered a strategic commodity, because of the developments of synthetics in the chemical industry.[47]

The drastic losses throughout the late 1960s and early 1970s, together with the elimination of all tariff quotas, forced the CCC to alter its operations. The agency started selling limited quantities of tung oil at periodic intervals for unrestricted delivery. This facilitated the acquisition by the CCC of all the domestic production.

> Prices have been such that CCC has for many years acquired virtually all of the domestic crop. On February 28, 1972, CCC had an uncommitted inventory of 32.8 million pounds of tung oil. With support on 1971 crops tung oil at 27.2 cents per pound and the current market under 11 cents, losses are running over 50% of the government's investment. With no revision in the legislation, future losses on the program can be expected to remain relatively high.[48]

To reduce the guaranteed parity was thought to be out of the question. Government economists placed the minimum cost of production (the break-even point) at 23¢ per lb. at a time when the market price hovered between 10 and 11¢ per lb.[49] Still, no new bills were initiated to check the 7 straight years of CCC tung oil losses, which obviously were not considered a relevant basis for program change.

It was largely due to recurrent freeze and hurricane damage to the tung groves that the output of tung oil in the United States had been so erratic. Because of these factors, together with the exclusion of "new" tung orchards from the price support program, few replacement plant-

45. USDA, *Present Plight of the Tung Industry*, (mid-1968 study, mimeograph, World Tung Oil Trade and Projections Table, Exhibit C).

46. U.S. House, Committee on Agriculture, "Tung Nut Price Support Program," p. 4.

47. Ibid., p. 5.

48. Ibid., p. 8.

49. Ibid.

ings have been made since 1960 and no new orchards have been established.[50] By 1972, most remaining trees were so old that without extensive investment the industry faced extinction.[51] Confronting this situation, Congress finally decided to phase out the price support program for tung oil.[52]

INDUSTRY CHARACTERISTICS

The domestic tung industry suffered through seven seasons since 1949 when frost damage alone curtailed potential production by more than half. Two hurricanes decimated orchards. Domestic consumption decreased 80% during the same period while all major substitutes, both natural and synthetic, were increasing or maintaining their market shares, yet the price of tung oil remained higher than those of substitute products.[53] (All major substitutes are produced in the United States, augmented by only minimal imports.)[54] Certainly the industry has never shown characteristics that would attract private investment. Indeed, it is apparent that tung oil production would not have survived beyond the early 1950s without firm governmental support in the forms of direct aid, research assistance, and quotas.

The question remains: Why was this industry so heavily subsidized? By any economic standard, much of the government's support since

50. The parity program was set up to include support for only the amount of trees then in existence (1949). Obviously, this would not be an inducement to increase acreage even if market conditions favored increased production.

51. Some farmers are still planting tung trees. The *Chemical Marketing Reporter* (December 8, 1975, p. 37) reports that some Mississippi farmers are planting a frost-resistant type. It would be ironic if the industry survives after government aid has been terminated.

52. Representative Paul Findley pointedly noted the abolition of the price support of tung oil:

> Mr. Speaker, yesterday . . . an important milestone was reached in farm legislation.
>
> It had been 25 years since the House approved the termination of any of the price support programs that were approved during the 1930's and 1940's. In short . . . we have treated these programs as if they were sacred and above careful reconsideration.
>
> Each year, we had appropriated funds for their continuance without subjecting them to a close scrutiny to determine if they were still needed or if they were doing the job they were designed to do. [U.S. Congress, *Congressional Record,* 93rd Cong., 1st sess. vol. 119, pt. 16, p. 20363.]

53. The total consumption of all these drying agents had been decreasing, but tung oil had been decreasing more rapidly than the others and its market share was falling. See U.S. Tariff Commission, *Tung Oil and Tung Nuts,* p. 33, Table 2.

54. See the appropriate table in United Nations Food and Agriculture Organization, *Trade Yearbook,* Vol. 28 (Rome, Italy, 1974).

1932 has been both capricious and useless. Although the potential for tung orchards may have been a legitimate subject for research in the 1930s, the handing out of a 700% return to tung oil producers during World War II was neither economic nor rational.[55] Incentives to increase production were ill-advised because of the 3-year time lag between planting and the first harvest. The rationale for concern over Chinese imports in the late forties was obviously not an economic one. Neither should there have been concern from a strategic standpoint, as both domestic substitutes and supplies from South America were then available.

Considerations of equity for the producer are the only rationale left. Congressional committee agendas from 1949 through 1973 are filled with equity considerations. In 1949 a House report stated, "thus this bill merely provides support for the acreage of tung nut trees which were largely brought into existence as a result of the war when we were cut off from supplies from China."[56] In 1956, another report emphasized that the American tung nut producers should be protected.[57] In the 1972 hearings, the producers felt it necessary to maintain price supports to keep the farmers on the farm or the laborers off the welfare rolls.[58] Finally, in 1973, the House hearings quoted John R. Rarick of Louisiana as saying: "I have tung producers in my district and it is embarrassing for them to go around and say that the Federal Government is phasing them out—that they are being replaced by Red Chinamen."[59] The most interesting aspect of these equity considerations is the total number of producers involved: From 1968 to 1972 approximately 100 producers had orchards of an economically viable size,[60] yet in that same period the CCC lost approximately $8 million in its support program. This would

55. *Business Week* ("Tung Oil's Boom," November 21, 1942, p. 4) reported that the Defense Supplies Corporation (a government buying agency) was paying tung oil producers "36¢ a pound for oil that costs 5¢ a pound from mature orchards." Unless World War II was expected to last well into the future, it was futile to encourage the planting of trees which would not yield nuts until their third year and would not reach half their normal maximum yield until the fifth year. (See Powe *et al.*, *Cultural Practices,* p. 7.)

56. U.S. House, "Price Support for Tung Nuts and Honey," p. 22.

57. U.S. House of Representatives, Committee on Agriculture, "Study of the Tung Oil Program," *Hearings before Subcommittee on Soybeans and Oilseeds,* 84th Cong., 2d sess., July 19, 1956, p. 19.

58. U.S. House of Representatives, Committee on Agriculture, "Tung Nut Price Support," *Hearings before the Subcommittee on Oilseeds and Rice,* 92d Cong., 2d sess., April 12, 1972, p. 22.

59. U.S. House, "Tung Nut Price Support Program" (1973), p. 22.

60. U.S. House, "Tung Nut Price Support" (1972), p. 7. An economically viable orchard was defined as an orchard with 50 or more producing trees.

average out to $16,000 per year per farmer; however, because production was not uniform, the support program benefited a few farmers a great deal and did very little for the rest. Congressional hearings in 1972 illustrated the true distribution of government aid:

> The largest single producer of tung nuts is located in Florida and has about 4,500 acres in tung, consisting mainly of older trees. According to our settlement records, the Commodity Credit Corporation acquired an average of 1,384,526 pounds of tung oil annually from this producer from the 1968, 1969, and 1970 crops. This would translate into an average annual loss to CCC of $229,831.32, based on the difference between the present support rate of 27.2 cents a pound for oil and current CCC sales prices of 10.6 cents a pound.[61]

During those years, the government of the United States was subsidizing one farmer almost a quarter of a million dollars annually to produce from 20 to 33% of the total domestic production.

SUMMARY AND CONCLUSIONS

If we ask why the federal government became so heavily involved in one rather peripheral industry, we cannot rely solely on either the reformist or the capture hypothesis as an explanation of government behavior. The domestic tung industry was too insignificant to "capture" the government bureaucracy that dealt with it. The reformist hypothesis may seem a little more plausible, particularly during World War II when tung oil was listed as a strategic commodity. Even here, examination reveals that the facts are not consistent with any argument concerning externalities. Tung oil was not necessary for the war effort: It was used as a drying agent on only a small fraction of the war material for which it was classified "essential," and adequate substitutes were at hand. Perhaps the government overreacted in the emergency atmosphere that prevailed in the early days of World War II, but this does not explain why tung oil was chosen. We postulate that a bureaucracy familiar with the fledgling tung oil industry had established a symbiotic relationship with it. We do not postulate a sinister or corrupt relationship; these agents were sincere in their belief that by aiding the industry they were serving the nation. Evolutionary processes will ensure that an agency acting from ulterior motives will not last long. In this case we may rephrase the adage and say, "Busy hands are the Devil's workers." Decision makers were not about to let impersonal market forces destroy an industry that they had labored long and hard to establish. The indus-

61. U.S. House, "Tung Nut Price Support Program" (1973), p. 15.

try was only too glad to acquiesce, and the result was a pyramid of policies, each designed to save a nonviable industry. Only acts of God, in the form of successive hurricanes and freezes that destroyed many of the tung orchards, finally caused the government to abandon life-support measures. We speculate that it was only after the numbers of farmers had been sharply reduced by natural disasters that the overwhelming concentration of price support payments into the hands of so few forced the political process to the point of terminating governmental support. A broader political base would have made such action much less feasible. As it was, hearings had to be held in two different Congresses (the Ninety-second and the Ninety-third) before the program met its end.

The lessons from the tung oil experiment are not encouraging to those who wish resources to be allocated more economically by the public sector. We speculate that the industry and bureaucracy would not have allowed the government intervention to cease without: (*a*) the rise in world tung prices in the early sixties that made the termination of the import quotas politically feasible; (*b*) the small and declining number of producers of tung oil; (*c*) the concentration of government support payments to the benefit of this handful of large producers; and (*d*) the successive natural disasters that literally and figuratively eroded the industry. Lacking such an improbable concatenation of events, it would seem unlikely that government programs, even those having no rational economic basis, could readily be dismembered.

Philip Coelho received both his M.A. and Ph.D. degrees from the University of Washington, where he was a student in Douglass North's classes. Since completing his doctorate in 1969, Coelho has taught in Canada and Hawaii. He was a member of the faculty at Washington State University until 1981; he recently accepted the position of Chair of the Department of Economics at George Mason University in Fairfax, Virginia.

Coelho's work with James Shepard on regional differences in prices and wages in nineteenth-century United States is an important contribution which explores some rich but previously neglected sources of information. Coelho is currently pursuing research on the federal government's direct involvement in business and nonprofit firms.

Coelho is joined by coauthor **David R. Knowles.** Knowles was Coelho's student at Washington State and is currently an Assistant Professor of Economics at Seattle University.

Chapter 11

Economic Behavior in the Ancient World

Gerald A. Gunderson

Moses I. Finley's *The Ancient Economy,*[1] published in 1973, has been generally acclaimed as a landmark in the study of classical history. The book is lucid, persuasive, and distills an enormous amount of evidence collected by its distinguished author. Of course, the work is much more than a review of existing knowledge: Finley uses his comprehensive recounting of the classical world to advance some specific characterizations about the structure and behavior of the ancient economy. It is at this point that the general praise for the book has often shifted to respectful skepticism, and for good reason, because generalizations of the sort Finley seeks to establish to a large extent, emanate from, one's view of economic history in any premodern period.

Finley's primary thesis is that ancient societies lacked both the sophisticated system of markets typical of modern Western economies and the maximizing or self-interested behavior which he associates with them. This view is representative of a significant amount of existing classical history[2] and the consequence of its general adoption—or nonadoption—

1. Moses I. Finley, *The Ancient Economy* (Berkeley: University of California Press, 1973).

2. See, for example, William I. Davisson and James F. Harper, *European Economic History,* Vol. 1, *The Ancient World* (New York: Appleton-Century-Crofts), Chapter 14; H. W. Pleket, "Technology in the Greco-Roman World: A General Report," in *Talanta: The Proceedings of the Dutch Archeological and Historical Society,* Vol. 5, 1973; N. J. G. Pounds, *An Economic History of Medieval Europe Systems in World History* (London: Longman Group, 1974), pp. 12–13; Stephen Vilgen, *Economic Systems in World History* (London: Longman Group, 1974), Chapters 8 and 9. A notable exception to this pattern is Douglass C. North's "Structure and

ISBN 0-12-580080-0

is so important for the practice of that craft that it should be scrutinized very thoroughly. Thus our interest in Finley's work is not to offer a specific review per se, but rather to examine it as the most explicit, articulate statement of that important premise.

One major implication of the view of behavior represented by Finley is that no generalizations or techniques that have been helpful in developing the history of more modern economic systems can be presumed to aid our understanding of the classical economy. In this sense Finley's work continues a long tradition by such well known scholars as Max Weber and Karl Polanyi who have argued that economic behavior—or at least that type described by neoclassical economic analysis—is a unique product of modern capitalistic environments. These scholars, Finley included, have not succeeded in providing an alternative view of economic behavior which is operational. Nor have they formulated or conducted any explicit tests for the existence of what they view as "capitalistic" as opposed to other types of economic behavior. This last issue, developed in the context of classical history, is the primary interest of this study.

Finley declares his view of economic behavior most specifically on page 22, where he states the belief that most economists would accept Eric Roll's definition of the economic system as "an enormous conglomeration of interdependent markets [where] the central problem of economic enquiry becomes the explanation of the exchanging process, or, more particularly, the explanation of the formation of price." Finley then goes on to conclude that "if a society was not organized for the satisfaction of its material wants by an enormous conglomeration of interdependent markets'. . . it would then not be possible to discover or formulate laws of economic behavior, without which a concept of 'the economy' is unlikely to develop, economic analysis [being] impossible." Thus Finley's effort to demonstrate that classical societies lacked any modern form of economic behavior comes down to a two-step argument. First, economic behavior is considered to be restricted to relatively sophisticated market economies. And second—to which he devotes most of the book—the classical world lacked anything like a developed system of markets. Ergo, modern-style economic behavior could not have existed in the ancient world.

M. W. Fredericksen, in a major review of *The Ancient Economy,*[3] has

---

Change in Economic History," *The Journal of Economic Literature* 3 (1978) pp. 963–978, which explicitly employs modern economic analysis to examine the ancient world.

3. M. W. Frederiksen, "Theory, Evidence and the Ancient Economy," *The Journal of Roman Studies* 65 (1975), pp. 164–171.

challenged Finley's empirical judgment that market activity and organization were relatively unimportant in classical times. Fredericksen acknowledges the existence of some of the caste, status, and agrarian structures in ancient societies which Finley saw as almost completely supplanting economic incentives. However, in a wide array of important sectors he demonstrates that market activity was much more prevalent than Finley sought to portray. Furthermore, he shows that in sectors composing a significant portion of the ancient economy, economic incentives were strong enough to cut across and dominate social divisions in the economy. Thus there appears to be strong evidence that one of the two central links in Finley's major thesis is doubtful.

Even if, upon further investigation of this important issue, Finley's view were to be upheld, the case for the absence of economic behavior in the ancient world would still be a long way from convincing. Both pivotal and dubious is the other major component of the argument, where Finley seemingly uncritically has accepted Roll's restriction of economic behavior to market system. In Note 16 of his first chapter he pointed out that scarce resources—usually assumed to be the basic expression of economic behavior—are not necessarily synonymous with markets, but he then dismissed any possible differences as unimportant for his purposes. However, this distinction is important; indeed it is critical for, and potentially destructive of, his main thesis. Most scholars specializing in economic affairs recognize that economic systems other than a market format can coordinate self-interested economic behavior. Markets are generally believed to promote the best possible use of available resources, given an existing set of consumer tastes. They are particularly advantageous when the volume of goods and services exchanged at some locality becomes large and a substantial reduction can be made in the resources required (per unit of output) to acquire information and arrange transactions.[4] On the other hand, a society may decide that a particular objective, such as growth or self-sufficiency or the expansion of a particular sector, is so important that central planning or some other form of centralized direction must be allowed to override

4. The development and subsequent decline of markets in the classical period, apparently through spontaneous private initiative and not by any substantial public intervention to those ends, seems consistent with this explanation. Organized markets appeared in both Greece and Rome in their earlier years as the volume of trade, especially that of distant waterborne commerce, increased. In the Roman case, markets declined in relative importance in the latter years of the Empire. Most scholars have attributed this to economic retrogression, including falling real incomes and an absence of economic innovation. Viewed from our perspective, however, an opposite inference becomes possible: People may have switched away from market organization because decentralization of economic activity reduced the relative gains from that format.

individual preferences. Or again, by way of example, groups acting in their own economic self-interest may in some circumstances choose to employ a traditional or tribal form of economic organization. When economic obligations and payments can be fulfilled within an existing social structure, the costs of erecting and operating a parallel economic structure are thereby saved. In addition, traditional structures are well adapted to minimize the conflict over food supplies in years when the harvest falls below normal and to reduce costs during changes in leadership of the hierarchy.

In other words, in a fair number of circumstances a society composed of self-interested individuals may choose an economic system not organized predominantly around markets. Judging by frequently encountered remarks about economic affairs in the classical period, Finley's misconception of this relation seems to be shared by many other scholars. Economic performance is often assumed to be constrained to a very rigid, narrow path, in which increases in urbanization, industrialization, and market organization are tantamount to improvements in economic affairs, and decreases are interpreted as regressions. Assumed declines in economic performance, in turn, are often attributed to a lack of economic motivation in the general populace. Thus the process becomes self-perpetuating, with the presumed lack of economic behavior being interpreted as economic decline and that, in turn, being taken as signifying a lack of rational economic behavior. What is obviously necessary is a precise statement of the nature of economic behavior followed by a careful test for that phenomenon in the ancient world. Such an investigation will almost certainly be restricted to qualitative indicators, for want of systematic quantitative evidence about the classical world. If such techniques can be devised, however, they could provide a test applicable in a wide range of premodern societies.

TESTING FOR THE NATURE OF ECONOMIC BEHAVIOR

To develop a definitive test for the nature of economic behavior we must go back to the source of the activity. All economic problems basically result from scarcity: a society's desire for more goods and services than it is currently capable of producing. In a world of plenty, each individual could obtain free all conceivable services provided by economic resources. There would be no concern about debts, finding the lowest price, obtaining a job, providing for retirement, eliminating poverty, or lobbying to enact most types of legislation—or to install the "right" legislators. Scarcity implies that not all wants can be satisfied at any given time; as a result, the production of a given good or service creates an opportunity cost in that the consumption of those resources forestalls the production of other goods or services. Thus the economy faces a range of choices or "trade offs" where each activity comes at the cost or sacrifice of some other desired good or service.

Even this limited exposition of the implications of scarcity suggests the fallacy in one example said to demonstrate the absence of economic motivation in the classical era. The failures of individuals to take advantage of attractive opportunities to invest capital or to reduce costs are frequently cited. Such illustrations are inconclusive, however, unless they recognize and control for the opportunity costs inherent in each situation. For example, in an earlier paper, "Technical Innovation and Economic Progress in the Ancient World," Finley surveyed various hypotheses seeking to explain why the Romans were so slow to adopt the water mill (generally acknowledged as an advance in technology).[5] After rejecting each of them, he concluded that the failure to adopt the innovation could be attributed only to a lack of entrepreneurial motivation. However, the range of alternatives he surveyed failed to include one other possibility, an omission that turns on the failure to distinguish between advances in the state of mechanical arts and advances in economic productivity. The water mill was an obvious advance in technology. Nevertheless, it was rather ill-suited for much of the ancient economy in that it substituted a capital resource for labor which was relatively cheap at that time. In other words, the limited adoption of the water mill can be explained by the fact that a manager or owner usually perceived that it was more cost effective to hire labor to grind grain by the old "backward" methods than to purchase the advanced machinery.[6]

Some of these considerations of the opportunity costs of labor and capital have been recognized in the discussion of labor scarcity, particularly as applied to the later Roman Empire.[7] However, the commentators almost universally have overlooked the role of land as an input, falling back on economic irrationality as an explanation when they en-

5. M. I. Finley, "Technical Innovation and Economic Progress in the Ancient World," *Economic History Review* 18 (August 1965), p. 38.

6. Pleket in "Technology in the Greco-Roman World" (p. 35) notes that a water mill cost 500, 750, or 1750 denarii more than a horse mill, a donkey, or a handmill respectively. He attributes the lack of water mills to the unwarranted reluctance of landowners to make an initial outlay which required a long wait before it was recouped. He could just as well have attributed their behavior to the high cost of capital, noting that it would have required relatively large savings in labor to recompense the depreciation and forgone interest which such an investment entailed.

7. Ibid., pp. 28–30.

counter techniques (usually in agriculture) that seem to be wasting some output. A characteristic example is K. D. White's observation that the Romans typically resorted to "second best" practices;[8] however, it appears that most of these reduced the amount of labor used per acre. Although this in turn reduced output per acre—hence the characterization of "second best" in terms of output—it also saved on labor per acre, allowing each worker to care for more acres per season. Thus Roman farming practices were not necessarily wasteful overall: They merely used land rather than capital as a substitute for labor. In view of many reports that land was abandoned in those periods, the apparent substitution of a cheaper factor for a more costly one seems to be a perfectly reasonable tactic.

A recognition of opportunity costs, such as those of capital in the case of the water mill or of land in the case of agriculture, thus invalidates many of the indicators previously used to judge economic behavior in the ancient world. What we need, however, is a measure that provides an unequivocal test of economic motivation whatever the specific circumstances; therefore we return to the basic axiom of scarcity. In such an environment each good or service is, in effect, in competition with all other goods. Thus if the price[9] of one good were to decrease while that of all others remained the same, economic behavior would imply a certain pattern of accommodation. The most likely response would be an increase in the consumption of the newly cheapened good because it would now be more attractive in lieu of other purchases. If the purchases of the cheapened good did not increase, some increase in the consumption of other goods should occur.[10] The logic of the latter implication is most obvious if we ask what it would mean for such responses not to occur. If, upon the decrease in price of one item, no increase occurs in the consumption either of it or of any other good, the implication is that surplus or redundant purchasing power exists. However, unexercised claims for goods nullify the presence of scarcity or of un-

8. K. D. White, *Roman Farming* (Ithaca, New York: Cornell University Press, 1970), pp. 450–454.

9. The use of money prices—or at least of terms that suggest them—does not affect the generality of the argument. Prices in the subsequent examples are best thought of as opportunity costs: Two units of Good A are equivalent to, or exchanged for, one unit of Good B, for example. Thus, a decrease in the relative price of A could be said to shift the ratio to three of A for one of B.

10. Among the goods upon which one might spend some of the "released" income from the lowered price would be the potentially confusing activity of saving. This is actually the process of purchasing a good called "future income." Thus, forms of nonspending that have the effect of increasing future income must be distinguished from behavior that fails to utilize present purchasing power while also creating no subsequent return.

satisfied wants. Thus we have one general test for the impact of economic behavior: In the face of changes in the relative prices of goods or services there should be corresponding adjustments in the relative consumption of goods.

An analogous process in the production of goods provides a second general test for economic behavior. A production unit combines the services of inputs from one or more of the three major categories: labor, capital, and natural resources. To achieve the highest possible return at any given time, the unit should employ that combination of inputs which (given their respective prices) minimized the cost of producing the prevailing level of output. Again, by way of contradiction, if its owners were not motivated to do so they would be, in effect, passing up some goods or services which they could otherwise claim. If the price of one of the inputs were to rise relative to all others, then production methods should be adjusted to economize on that (now) more expensive input.

A third basic indicator of economic motivation appears in the form of the response to an innovation that is an unequivocal improvement over existing techniques. In practice, most innovations do not embody such clear-cut advances over existing methods; while saving some types of inputs they may require increased use of another input, thus clouding their superiority until the respective prices of the inputs are weighed. This was the case in the example of the water mill, and similar complications appear in other innovations of the classical period such as the screw press, the wooden barrel, hypocausts, and soap.[11]

One important qualification should be noted here. Modern economic analysis builds on the premise that individuals in general act to maximize their own economic welfare, but it does not attempt to predict the behavior of specific individuals or business enterprises. That responsibility is willingly delegated to psychologists and entrepreneurical historians. Rather, economics seeks to predict the behavior of groups of individuals or businesses in response to changes in economic conditions. Consequently, all of the tests that have been here, and that will be applied in what follows, must relate to aggregate behavior.

This distinction between individual and group behavior also should be invoked for previous attempts to test for economic behavior in the ancient world. Most such attempts, as illustrated by Finley's examples in

11. A related process, which we shall encounter in more detail in what follows, involves subtle modifications of the new invention to adopt it to local conditions. This process takes both time and further investments; thus it could readily be interpreted as reluctant behavior, when, in fact, it represents a learning process.

The Ancient Economy, are interpolations from the responses of individuals; thus the common conclusion that self-seeking behavior was absent is unwarranted. In fact, the finding that individuals failed to adjust to some economic change is very much in line with the usual results of modern economic analysis. In any period, a single individual may fail notably to respond to some economic change within a given range; however the likelihood is great that enough individuals in a group will so react as to exemplify economic behavior. Most previous attempts to deny economic behavior in the ancient world are inappropriate and inconclusive precisely because they focus on individual examples. Only evidence of group adaptations, such as will be attempted in what follows, is a valid test for such behavior.

THE PROCESS OF TECHNOLOGICAL DIFFUSION

The distinction between technological improvements in general and those technological improvements which are unequivocally profitable in specific circumstances allows us to make an initial test for the restore of economic behavior. What is required—unlike the case of the water mill—is an invention that reduces the consumption of certain types of inputs but does not complicate comparisons by increasing the use of other inputs. That set of circumstances appears to be met in the improvements to millstones and to cores in oil presses. They allowed a saving of labor and probably of olives—relative to a given output of oil—but probably caused no significant increase in the cost of the capital item, the press itself. Available evidence, suggesting that this improvement was generally adopted relatively quickly, in contrast to the screw press,[12] indicates that the ancients were indeed influenced by a basic form of economic motivation. They adopted a given innovation only when on balance it was to their advantage to do so.

A set of three indicators therefore constitutes a test for economically motivated behavior in any society, however disparate in organization or time.[13] In principle, it is simply a matter of applying such measures to any given economy. In actual implementation, however, it is a compli-

12. Finley, "Technical Innovation," p. 29. The basic, comprehensive study of the issue is A. G. Drachmann, *Ancient Oil Mills and Presses* (Copenhagen, 1932).

13. Most of the examples offered by Finley to show that self-interested economic behavior was absent from the ancient world fail this acid test. For the most part they are extensive accounts of individual statements or actions which purport to show that economic considerations were unimportant. Seldom, however, does Finley consider whether the cited economic adjustments can be interpreted as responses to changes in relative prices (see, for example, our Note 25, following).

cated and time-consuming effort to specify and isolate instances that allow clear-cut tests of each, as the examples given here have probably suggested. Fortunately it is possible to investigate all three indicators within one comprehensive process which is much more conveniently observable and applicable with respect to the classical economy. Commonly termed the "diffusion of technology," the process incorporates the invention, refinement, and migration of new techniques and embodies a wide range of economic choices including the three developed here. Furthermore, it involves a pattern of economic adaptation which, even in the case of the classical world, would have left distinctive traces.

For convenience, the process of technological diffusion can be viewed as a series of sequential steps. Each of these involves one or more of the three economic choices that have been delineated and thus should have taken on certain well-defined characteristics if economic behavior prevailed. For example, a first step in the diffusion of technology is obviously that of its emergence. By this we do not mean the simple, dramatic, path-breaking "invention" commonly associated with the appearance of a new product. Rather, recent investigation indicates that the development of new lines of technology is a more gradual, extended process requiring the identification and solution of numerous small problems. Popularly conceived of as "Eureka!" or the flash of genius solving a major problem, invention is probably more realistically seen to be the patient working out of a jigsaw puzzle.

One implication of this gradual, extended view is that a new line of knowledge need not be worked out to completion by the inventors or at the location where the initiating discovery or conceptualization occurred. Indeed, where self-interested economic behavior is operating, one would expect this frequently not to be the case. In essence the development of new knowledge requires the solution to a series of "bottlenecks." Compared to the production of goods for which the technology is well established, these newer categories of production are best developed by employing resources of a relatively high level of creative ability, and training, and oftentimes by locating an enterprise so as to have access to specialized skills to solve problems as they arise. Newer technology is, in other words, relatively expensive but justifiable, in that extra expenses during the early phase of development are recouped by lower costs later on.[14] This tendency of developing technol-

14. The higher costs of production in the early years of development are also explained by an understandable orientation toward limited, high quality, or "luxury," markets, in that the product is still novel and relatively valuable.

ogy to move to (or to be joined by) relatively productive (and expensive) resources is commonly observed in modern economics and is a predictable procedure if higher quality inputs are complements, rather than substitutes, among themselves. The total output of an economy is generally maximized when a higher cost input (including that of any technology that is in the early stages of development for production) is used in conjunction with other higher priced (relatively productive) inputs. Lower priced (less productive) inputs should be similarly paired in their contribution to the overall maximization pattern.

The particular implication of this axiom most directly related to the interest of this study is that at any given time the development of newer technology should tend to coalesce in certain areas or sectors within the total economy. For the classical period, this would imply that although inventions might initially occur anywhere around the Mediterranean basin, a good portion of subsequent development of the new products or techniques should soon have been shifted to a fairly well-defined locality. Anyone reasonably familiar with classical history would quickly recognize two such centers of technological development: Athens in the three centuries or so prior to 150 B.C. and Rome—the city proper and adjacent provinces such as Latium, Compania, and Etruria—for approximately the next three centuries (until A.D. 150).

This impressionistic judgment about "innovative centers" is confirmed when we take a more systematic look at those lines of developing technology for which we have a passable record during the period. The four to which we shall devote special attention are wine, olive oil, pottery, and glass. None of these was a completely new product as of 450 B.C., but after that date all developed techniques or forms sufficiently new to create the special problems inherent in an emergent type of technology.

From approximately 450 B.C. to 150 B.C., Athens was one of the largest exporters of wine, olive oil, and pottery in the Mediterranean area. This dominance was especially marked among higher quality items in each of these product lines. After 150 B.C. the commanding position in the export of these three products shifted to Rome, apparently because of its own merits in the economic sphere. Although the Romans did achieve political control over Greece at about this time, they did not impose any restrictions that would have been severe enough to cause such a radical shift in what was then basically a competitive market. Thus Roman dominance appears to be best explained by their assumption of technological leadership in these products.[15]

15. There is still much we do not understand as to why a particular area should achieve technological leadership at any given time. Some important factors are recognized, how-

If we accept this designation of centers of technological leadership in the classical period, then a first test for economic behavior is possible. New lines of technology should be drawn to wherever the existing center(s) is (are) located at any given time. The first obvious implication is that (subject to the limits of available evidence) we should be able to observe such a migration. A second implication is that the initial discoveries or inventions are likely to be more widely scattered geographically than their subsequent phases of development.

The pattern of location of the four major products that we can trace appears to coincide with these expected guidelines. For example, various areas around the Aegean Sea had been producing and exporting wine for at least 6 centuries prior to 150 B.C. During that time, Greek colonies in Sicily, in southern Italy and France, and in southern Russia had begun to produce their own wine and to compete with the homeland for the export markets. Yet despite all these potential supplanters, the Greek homeland, specifically Attica in the later part of the period, retained its leadership in the development and use of new technology in productions. It was only with developments in central Italy, especially in the province of Campania in the second century B.C., that this focus of leadership shifted. Although many aspects of this Greek dominance are vague,[16] the technology must have been sufficiently progressive to ensure a competitive edge over cheaper foreign wines for more than 4 centuries. Thus the shift, when it finally occurred, indicated a rather basic relocation of economic functions in the Mediterranean area.

The experience in wine was closely paralleled by that of olive oil and pottery. Greek producers had similarly been able to maintain longterm leadership in those products, despite the appearance of numerous competing enclaves during the period, until developments in the local economy of central Italy succeeded in capturing them also.

One further indication that such centers of technological development functioned in the classical period is the experience of the fourth product whose diffusion can be traced during the era. It seems fairly certain that the technique of glassblowing was initially devised in Syria just prior to

---

ever, one of which is the size of the local market for goods. The larger the pool of local spending power, the higher will be the presumed return on a given innovation. A second factor is the availability of relatively skilled labor—probably the single most important resource for devising and modifying new technology. It seems reasonable to conclude that Rome was able to surpass Greece as the center of new technology in the second century B.C. because her stock in human skills approached parity with, while the size of her local market surpassed, that of Greece. Because such considerations may well have contributed to the rise of the Roman Empire, a better understanding of that process would be highly desirable.

16. See R. J. Forbes, *Studies in Ancient Technology* (Leiden: E. J. Brill, 1955), 3: 106–115.

the first century A.D. On the basis of this information and the above conceptual arguments, we could anticipate two results. The first would be that a good portion of subsequent production of blown glass would be shifted out of Syria to a locality whose endowment of resources was better suited for the development of new forms of products. The second prediction is that this type of production would be shifted directly to central Italy, the locus of development as of that date, not passing through now-supplanted Athens or any other area on the way. Both of these expected outcomes of economic behavior appear to have occurred. Coupled with the other pieces of evidence cited earlier, these developments indicate that economic organization in the classical era conformed spatially to the basic patterns we would expect as a result of self-interested behavior.

The second step in the diffusion process is more obvious and has been noted by students of the era. Once the initial—and usually most difficult—problems have been worked out, a technology should move outward from its development center. One reason is that as the technology becomes more standardized and simplified it can be put to work in a wider range of locations using less costly local resources. A second reason is that relocation often allows savings in transportation costs, either in moving the finished product to the consumer or in acquiring raw materials..

This process of diffusion was so apparent in the classical period that its incidence is scarcely questioned.[17] Yet a central implication of this activity for economic behavior has seldom been appreciated. Technology is transferred to new localities because someone gains from production at the new location. As suggested in our earlier discussions, the gain may take the form of lower production or transportation costs resulting initially in either a larger profit at given prices or larger sales at the same profit margin per unit. Thus the transfer of technology is an indication of economic behavior. In the absence of such motivation, there would be no reason to expend effort in relocating existing techniques. In that case, knowledge would tend to remain where it was first created, and in the unlikely case that it did move it would disperse in a random fashion. However, because the migration of new techniques in the ancient world was immediate and regular we dismiss that possibility.

A third test of economic behavior within the diffusion process con-

17. The decentralization of industrial techniques is perhaps most emphasized by F. W. Walbank in *The Awful Revolution* (Toronto: Toronto University Press, 1969); he makes it a central factor in the fall of the Roman Empire (see especially in Chapter 3). For the diffusion agricultural techniques see White, *Roman Farming*, especially pp. 187–189, 260–261.

cerns the sequence in which new techniques are likely to be transferred. We have noted that relatively new lines of technology tend to be worked out in localities offering more productive/expensive resources such as labor. Thus, in terms of output, the centers of new technology have a relative advantage in producing items of higher quality which are generally more complex or which require techniques with more skill. The implication is that the production of cheaper or more common grades of any given product is likely to be the first to move away from the developing center.

This pattern of diffusion seems amply confirmed by our knowledge of classical economic history. Not long after the Greek settlements of the Aegean area began to export wine, their markets were invaded by "cheap" exports from such colonial outposts as Sicily, the Bosporean Kingdom, and areas around the Black Sea. This spread of the production of lower quality wines continued from the fourth century B.C. with some apparent tendency for the outlying areas to upgrade some of their output and also to compete with the "medium" quality wines being produced in Attica. However, even in the face of emergent Roman domination of wine production in general, Athens was able to maintain its reputation as the source of the best wines until the first century B.C. The Romans, in turn, soon found their exports of wine being undercut by "cheap" exports from such developing areas as Spain and Gaul in the first two centuries A.D. One can recount similar patterns in pottery, olive oil, and glassware, but such detail is probably unwarranted here. The important point for our purpose is that not only the process, but also the observed order, of diffusion of technology supports the activity of normal economic behavior in the classical world.

CONSUMPTION PATTERNS AND TECHNICAL CHANGE

A fourth component of the diffusion of technology is the reaction of consumers to the process. In portrayals of ancient history, diffusion is frequently linked with a "cheapening" of the good in question. Sometimes, as is especially noticeable in discussions of molded pottery in the latter part of the Roman Empire, this is equated with a reduction in the quality of the good. This view assumes, in effect, that little in the way of net gain is achieved in the diffusion of technology because the increased quantity consumed is offset by a reduction in the quality per unit. Such an interpretation seems doubtful, however, in the absence of any major force to prompt such a trade off.[18]

18. In effect, the argument that "cheapening" will occur in the absence of any significant

Examined over the full range of goods for which we have information, rather than simply those few highly publicized examples such as pottery, the "broadening of consumption" seems to be best explained by a real reduction in the cost of those products. In the case of Greece, we know that whereas about 500 B.C. the enjoyment of wine was largely restricted to the richer classes, regular consumption had extended well down into the lower income strata by around 200 B.C.[19] Admittedly, the lower classes drank wines of the poorest quality, but the shift required something more than a mere watering down of expensive wines, since this pattern could have been produced 300 years perviously. A broadening consumption of olive oil during approximately the same period, as well as of glass vessels in the century or so after 50 B.C., suggests a similar substantial reduction in cost. If we are willing to go outside the four product lines upon which this study has focused so far, there are other examples of increasing consumption in response to lower prices during the classical period. One important case is found in agriculture, where a fairly extensive process of borrowing and experimentation in crop varieties and cropping techniques resulted in a sizable gain in agricultural productivity.[20]

As they typically have done in other times, consumers translated this increase in potential output per person into a more attractive diet; that is, they shifted toward varieties that required more resources per unit of output. About 500 or 600 B.C., the staples of both Greek and Roman diets had been porridges, broths, and groats. These had been supplemented by certain vegetables such as pulses and beans, by coarse bread, and by relatively small quantities of meat, with the Romans eating mostly mutton or pork, and the Greeks fresh or dried fish. Two or three centuries later, much of the earlier diet was considered fit only for the poor. Porridge had become far less prominent in Roman diets and, although

improvements in productivity must be based on a major change in consumer preferences. Large numbers of consumers would have been turning to these newer items in the absence of any increase in their incomes or relative changes among the prices of goods themselves. In other words, simply because they decided to do so—in the absence of any other initiating force—consumers are alleged to have substantially increased their consumption of such goods. This could have been accomplished, however, only if consumers had reduced their expenditures on other goods and that would mean, in the widely touted case of molded pottery, for example, that sizable numbers of individuals in the lower income categories must have been sacrificing some of such basic items as food, clothing, and housing. Thus, the case for "cheapening" based primarily on a degradation of quality seems unlikely.

19. Forbes, *Ancient Technology,* 3: 96–115.

20. Fritz M. Heichelheim, *An Ancient Economic History,* Vol. 3 (Leyden: A. W. Sigthoff, 1970), pp. 147–151.

still favored by the Greeks, it was now largely made from wheat flour rather than from barley. Both societies in general had increased their consumption of wheat bread, meat, fish sauce, spices, and, especially in the case of Rome, such fruits as apples, cherries, and peaches.[21] (The general increase in the use of finely ground flour is in itself noteworthy as a predictable result of the general improvements in milling techniques obliquely mentioned earlier.)

A second major change in consumption patterns was occurring as a result of a long-term, sizable reduction in the cost of producing iron. The production of iron, in a form cheap enough to be used for anything other than expensive jewelry or artwork, was probably initially developed in the Hittite Empire in Armenia not too long before 1000 B.C. Within a relatively short time the technology spread to much of the eastern hemisphere including India, northeastern Africa, and the Celtic areas of northwestern Europe as well as the more developed Mediterranean area. Technology did not stand still after the initial Hittite achievements however. In the next 1500 years a number of discernible improvements certainly reduced the cost of iron. (Probably other more subtle improvements are not evident in the archaeological record.) We do know that about 500 B.C. the Celts devised the shaft furnace, a crude forerunner of the blast furnace. It was an improvement over the existing "bloomeries"—where iron was smelted on an open hearth much like that of a blacksmith shop—in that it provided for a more complete separation of the pig iron and slag and possibly also increased the efficiency of the smelting process by raising its temperature. Techniques that would produce the strong steel cutting edges of such tools as swords, knives, axes, and chisels began their long evolution soon after this date. The first step, which was to combine thin, tempered strips of metal, was an outgrowth of the invention of welding, developed in Greece in the seventh century B.C. However, satisfactory results were not consistently acheived until the second or third century A.D. The delay is fully understandable in view of the ad hoc metalurgy then available to determine the proper combinations of welding, carbonizing, quenching, and fast tempering required. The productivity of iron production was further improved by the development of bellows in the latter days of the Roman Empire and may also have been aided by the use of casting. The latter invention appears in Chinese iron production in the second century B.C. and was used in other materials, such as pottery, in Europe during this time.

Thus we can make a reasonable case that iron production and fashion-

21. Forbes, *Ancient Technology,* 3: 96–101.

ing improved significantly during (a somewhat extended version of) the classical period. This should have resulted in a reduction in the cost of iron and then, if our expectations about economic behavior are valid, in a large increase in its use. Such an expansion will probably be generally acknowledged, but some elements are sufficiently far-reaching and intriguing to warrant attention here. One major result was the extensive adoption of metal tools in woodworking. Many of the basic tools, such as saws, drills, and planes, still used by carpenters today became commonplace in the Greco-Roman period. This was an obvious aid to building construction, but an even more noticeable effect was the first widespread appearance of household furniture. Perhaps even more important was that for the first time the construction of large wooden ships now became feasible. This, in turn, explains much of the increase in commerce and specialization in the Mediterranean area. Without that development it is difficult to picture such highlights of the classical period as the prominence of Athens or the rise of the Roman Empire.

The extensive adoption of metal implements in agriculture and the military[22] also seems noteworthy. Although historians have generally tended to play down the prevalence in agriculture of large pieces of capital equipment such as water mills or thrashing sledges, some have remarked on the wide use of metal hand tools by Roman farmers. These included the iron blades of sickles, scythes, and pruning knives and the iron heads of picks, mattocks, and shovels as well as the iron coulters and shares of a fair proportion of plows. One indication of the productivity gains of these implements over their (nonmetal) antecedents is that the Roman agriculturalist Columella recommended that farmers keep a reserve supply of such tools (or retain a blacksmith to repair them) rather than waste labor while they were unserviceable.[23] Thus there is every reason to conclude that as iron became less expensive in relation to other resources, more of it was used in the ancient economy, as befits a society motivated by the economic self-interest of its individuals.

It should be possible to test for other patterns attributable to economic behavior in the ancient world. There is, for example, the likely sequence that growth sectors of one era will in subsequent periods be superseded

22. Iron, of course, was almost universally used in swords, pikes, spears, armor, and shields by the major armies of the era. One might reasonably conjecture that its emergence as a relatively cheap material deterred the course of mounted warfare for almost a thousand years, which is to say that from the time of the Greek phalanx to about the third century A.D., heavily armored infantry was the dominant form of military organization.

23. As quoted by White, *Roman Farming*, p. 372.

and diminished by other sectors.[24] However, such demonstrations would probably not add significantly to the impact of the evidence that has been developed here. It does appear worthwhile to investigate one further pattern, in that its particular features also appear to provide some test of the behavior of "barbarian" populations outside the Mediterranean basin as well as insights into economic changes during that turbulent and perplexing period surrounding the end of the Roman Empire. The specific principle of economic behavior appropriate here is that new inventions or production techniques are most likely to be adopted in areas where the resource base is most favorable. Consider the wooden barrel introduced into the classical world at about the beginning of the first century AD from the northern Celtic areas. Obviously, one of the major inputs in its production was wood, a resource relatively cheaper in northern Europe than in the Mediterranean area. The site of its initial development is consistent with economic behavior, as is the rather skimpy evidence regarding its later diffusion. The barrel apparently was used extensively in such northern provinces as Gaul and appears in surviving illustrations of river commerce. Barrels were also used in Italy, but there is very little mention of their use in the more eastern provinces such as Greece. If we recognize that within some range barrels are portable—that is, they travel abroad from their production site—then the apparent spatial distribution of their use seems to coincide with the pattern expected from self-interested behavior. Cut-and-sewn clothing was also pioneered and adopted most extensively in the northern provinces of the Roman Empire. This included not only shirts and trousers, but also such related items as stocking, laced boots, and fibulae—a forerunner of the safety pin. Climate would seem to explain much of the greater incentive for these innovations to be developed in the North. The extra labor required to prepare the clothing could have been more than compensated for by the gain in warmth which, in turn, could be translated into savings in cloth (by reducing the

24. We can see some examples of that process of continual substitution within the same four major lines of technology we have examined. The market for olive oil was eroded by the introduction of soft soap, wax candles, and butter. Containers, either pottery or glass, received further competition from the introduction of the wooden barrel. This process of substitution is not deduced simply on the premise of economic behavior; it is a very likely result given one other plausible hypothesis—namely, that changes in an economy tend to make some fraction of existing economic activity particularly remunerative rather than affecting all sectors equally. From this, it would follow that economic behavior would create a corresponding pattern of growth sectors by concentrating much of the economy's innovative resources in those sectors.

need for more garments), in fuel, and by extending the work season outdoors. In other words, the advantage to the northern provincials in developing fitted clothing went well beyond the obvious provision of warmth. It also effected a tangible saving in the economy's stock of basic resources, particularly labor, which was becoming increasingly scarce in the latter period of the Empire. The labor saved by not chopping wood or not weaving cloth or not sitting idly by the fire on colder days could be converted into useful products.

Thus the northern provincials, in a portion of the Empire recognized as less Latin and more barbarian, also appear to have conformed to the basic laws of economic behavior. And this judgment, based on their reactions to differences in relative costs among resources, is reinforced when we consider their involvement with technology. A surprisingly large number of innovations came from this area in the latter part of the Empire. In addition to the barrel and tailored clothes, the region could claim credit for introducing soft soap, wicker furniture, hunting dogs, enameling, steel-edged tools, and an important collection of techniques in wagon and harness designs which increased the productivity of overland transportation. The precise time and location of each of these innovations will probably never be known. Our present knowledge is usually based on reports by Roman contemporaries who ascribed such items to northern origins. Nevertheless, it seems obvious that the provincials were ready to adopt those types of new technology which were profitable in their locality. Moreover, the available evidence seems to warrant an even more incisive judgment about their economic behavior: They not only adopted, but must also have been seeking to create, those new forms of technology which were especially productive in their particular localities. The land-abundant northern provinces with their large expanses of woodlands were well suited for such innovations as hunting dogs, improved wagons, and soap—this last made primarily from wood ashes and tallow.

BROADENING OUR EXPLANATIONS OF PREMODERN HISTORY

These observations on the economic "progressiveness" of the northern population emphasize one of the main themes that underlie the whole issue of ancient economic behavior. Much of the suspicion that the ancients did not behave by "modern" guidelines seems to result from the prevailing view that the classical economy—in particular the Roman Empire—was destroyed because it failed to respond to the challenge thrust upon it. It is believed that in order to sustain the ancient world it would have been necessary to increase output substantially. There was no such expansion; in fact, so the usual argument continues, there was a contraction. The model offered (usually implicitly) to explain this deterioration has several variants. One is that the ancients either were not interested in, or were socially constrained from, any sizable innovations in economic affairs. The idea is sometimes expressed that an industrial revolution would have been necessary for survival.[25]

This explanation reflects an unduly restricted view of what constitutes rational economic behavior. There is no compelling reason why such behavior must organize itself in the form of a particular social organization such as the Roman Empire. Admittedly, that form of political organization creates a large area within which goods, people, and ideas can move without hinderance. However, there are corresponding (opportunity) costs, the most obvious being the expense of maintaining a large standing army to protect the widely expanded boundaries.

In fact, when we recall that one of the main manifestations of eco-

25. A second major variant used to explain the (economic) destruction of the Roman Empire is that parasitic groups were on the increase. Such sectors as the cities, or the landlords, or the government are alleged to have been living off the productive sectors (usually agriculture). In view of the foregoing discussion, however, such explanations should evoke some skepticism. All sectors, regardless of the type of their output, can yield a positive product in that consumers place a higher value on their services in this function than in the alternative possibilities thereby denied. Moreover, unless almost all parties lack self-motivation, there are several possible ways for individuals to improve their economic position by bypassing the parasites among them.

Finley's extended discussion of the role of government in the ancient world (his sixth chapter) attempts to demonstrate that although ancient governments had inevitable effects on the economy, their decisions were almost entirely motivated by noneconomic considerations. Most of his evidence consists of specific examples of governmental policies or decisions where economic considerations were not explicitly recorded or, at least, appear to have been ignored. However, a proper investigation of economic behavior within the government sector requires awareness of the economic conditions prevailing at the time. That is, would the government have formulated the given policy if the costs of doing so had been higher (or lower) than in the reported circumstances? Several well-recognized general trends during the course of the Empire suggest that the govenrment did indeed respond to changes in economic rewards. For example, we know that by ancient standards both cities and interprovincial commerce were large relative to total economic activity, in the early years of the Empire, but that both decreased somewhat in the later period. It is not surprising, then, that the Roman tax collection system, which in the early Empire was based on urban collection units, later was shifted to a rural base of land values. A similar shift is evident in Roman military tactics. The early Roman armies were usually superior to their barbarian enemies and, understandably, disputes with alien hordes were customarily settled by force of arms. But as the military proficiency of the outlanders improved, the Romans increasingly resorted to defensive tactics, "buying off" potential invaders and even settling some of them on vacant lands within the Empire.

nomic behavior is a shift in patterns of consumption or production in response to changes in relative prices, then it would seem that such a shift in the dominant governmental structure can more plausibly be interpreted as an affirmation of economic behavior. It is generally believed that the cost of maintaining the Empire tended to increase (as a percentage of the total economic output) during the latter part of its existence. Scholars have often bypassed the rather obvious implication that, other things equal, this would make the Empire less attractive as a form of government over time. The usual approach has been to argue that the Empire was such a superior form of social organization that it would be retained "at all costs." At best this amounts to an arugment that in the ancient world the choices for alternative forms of government were few and the possibility of mixing parts of them quite limited. At worst, it amounts to a simple assertion that economic behavior was not present.

Thus, insofar as a cursory examination can show, the demise of the Roman Empire seems to coincide best with the expected response of a society motivated by economic behavior.[26] The decentralization of the western part of the Empire appears not as failure to respond to changing conditions but, rather, as a perfectly logical response to such a shift.

A myopic view of economic behavior also mars the general category of explanations typified by the argument that only an industrial revolution could have preserved the classical world from destruction. Although an industrial revolution indubitably can increase the output of an economy, it is not the only path to that end.[27] Indeed, given the economic conditions prevailing during those times, it would have been one of the least auspicious formats for the purpose. Neglecting some obvious problems about technological prerequisites, one can characterize industrialization as the centralizing of production in relatively large units to take advantage of the savings that such volume of production allows. These gains in the production process could be dissipated (and even exceeded), however, if the market for such products were dispersed and large amounts of resources consumed in transporting and distributing the goods to the consumers. Thus methods that would seem primitive from

26. A more specific analytic argument that the demise of the Roman Empire can be explained as a predictable response of an economically motivated populace to changes in opportunities is contained in Gerald Gunderson, "Economic Change and the Demise of the Roman Empire," *Explorations in Economic History*, 13 (January 1976), pp. 43–68.

27. This view has been propounded much more fully in the context of a discussion of the comparative experiences of the United States and England in the eighteenth and nineteenth centureis. See Gerald Gunderson, *A New Economic History of America* (New York: McGraw-Hill, 1976), Chapter 6.

our modern perspective, such as handicrafts or village workshops, might actually be cheaper than more "modern" forms.

Moreover, changes in the structure of the economy in the latter part of the Roman Empire actually encouraged a shift toward such embryonic forms of production. It is generally believed that economic activity underwent a major decentralization during this period, both from the larger cities to the countryside and from the older central provinces out to the less developed, peripheral areas. (The diffusion of technology discussed earlier certainly would prompt smaller and more dispersed economic units, on average.) This shift has been frequently noted but usually interpreted as a reduction in economic performance, because it appears as a "deurbanization," a "deindustrialization," and a "decommercialization." Other things equal, those reorganizations did incur the cost of giving up economies of scale. However, other things were *not* entirely the same. The decentralization allowed compensatory savings in distribution costs as well as gains from applying new technologies in outlying areas for the first time.

The (erroneous) belief that an industrial revolution was the only way out of the problems of the latter classical economy has frequently been accompanied by an assumption that growth could not have occurred in any other environment. Again this reflects a restricted view of the potential range of economic activity. It is generally recognized that output per capita can be achieved by increasing the amount of resources (land and/or capital) at the command of each worker. Ironically the "increasing labor scarcity" so frequently interpreted as evidence of economic distress in the ancient world was actually a manifestation of such a trend. The other potential source of growth, widely recognized only in recent years, consists of improvements in productivity or efficiency resulting in expanded output from the services of a given stock of resources. In the classical period, one cause of such growth would have been the diffusion of technology, as discussed earlier. Neither of these potential avenues of growth is precluded by the absence of industrialization. In fact, almost all of the evidence and arguments offered to demonstrate economic decay in the late classical period build on indicators which, like industrialization, capture only a fraction of this total economic process. The only comprehensive measure that is now available for the late classical world actually indicates an increase in output per capita.[28] This suggests that the ancients did take advantage of—and may well have worked to create—opportunities for economic advancement. And the magnitude of their effort was enough to more than offset the

28. Gunderson, "Economic Change and Demise of the Empire," pp. 43–68.

usual effect of resource depletion from production which, by itself, would have reduced output per capita.

Therefore, once appropriate methods are employed to detect it, evidence can be found of a considerable amount of rational economic behavior in the ancient world. This will be disconcerting news to many classical scholars, a good share of whose work in the field has rested on premises that imply just the opposite. From a somewhat more objective and altruistic standpoint, however, this conclusion should be considered good news for scholarship of premodern societies. It implies that examinations of such periods are no longer limted by the evidence directly available from each respective era but can be extended by drawing upon generalizations from other periods as well. In fact, should the commonality of human behavior that this study appears to have verified be upheld by subsequent examination, then the explanatory power of premodern history may be broadened considerably.

Gerald Gunderson presented "The Social Savings of Steamships" in 1967 as his dissertation at the University of Washington. He is widely known for his innovative textbook, **A New Economic History of America**, first published in 1976, and now forthcoming in its second edition. Gunderson's article in the **Journal of Economic History** on the origins of the Civil War (1974) was both provocative and controversial. Recently Gunderson has developed a research interest in the economy of the Roman Empire. His work in this area represents one of the few attempts—other than Douglass North's own work—to apply the New Economic History to the ancient economy.

Gunderson currently is Professor of Economics and designee of the Davis Chair in Economic and Business History at Trinity College in Hartford, Connecticut.

Chapter 12

Testing the Impact of Exclusive Property Rights: The Case of Enclosing Common Fields

Bennett Baack

Following the publication of Professor Coase's paper, "The Problem of Social Costs,"[1] economists have increasingly turned their attention to the study of property rights over scarce resources. The thrust of this effort has been to further our understanding of how legal systems respond to and influence the process of social and economic change. The incorporation into the standard theory of production and exchange of the terms on which property rights are assigned, enforced, and transferred has enabled the systematic analysis of a broad range of unresolved issues.[2]

One of the areas currently receiving attention is the nature of resource allocation under various forms of land tenure in agriculture. In an effort to establish the impact of alternative tenure arrangements such as fixed rent contracts, wage contracts, and sharecropping, writers have traditionally relied upon the neoclassical model of wealth maximization constrained by private property rights and a market system. In a reassessment of this approach, Steven N. S. Cheung has shifted the focus of study to the peculiar characteristics of private property as a constraint. He takes explicit account of private property as the exclusive right to the use of and income from land as well as the right to transfer its ownership. Professor Cheung's work has led to the conclusion that as long as

1. *Journal of Law and Economics* 3 (1960), pp. 1–44.

2. For an excellent review of the property right literature, see Eirik G. Furubotn and Svetozar Pejovich, "Property Rights and Economic Theory: A Survey of Recent Literature," *Journal of Economic Literature* 10 (1972), pp. 1138–1162.

EXPLORATIONS IN THE NEW ECONOMIC HISTORY

ISBN 0-12-580080-0

property rights are exclusive and transferable the various contracts in agriculture do not lead to different efficiencies of resource allocation as had been assumed in much of the traditional literature.[3]

A comparable reassessment of the consequences of land tenure systems not constrained by private property rights remains to be made. The difficulty of such an endeavor is that nonexclusive arrangements are extremely varied and have historically been subject to fundamental change. A frequently cited example is that provided by Harold Demsetz in his paper "Toward a Theory of Property Rights," where nonexclusive rights to the communal hunting territory of the Montagnais evolved over time into a system of private property.[4] In the property rights paradigm, nonexclusive rights form the basis of common property. By setting the theoretical framework for analyzing the impact on resource allocation of replacing common with private property, the article has encouraged others to enter the arena.[5] As Demsetz has recently observed, however, what is required to further our understanding of the problem is more empirical work and less "speculative theory."[6]

This paper investigates the allocation of labor during the transition from common to private property in land, combining economic theory with history to shed light on the question. The historical material is drawn from the enclosure of common fields in England during the eighteenth and nineteenth centuries. The paper is divided into two parts, of which the first discusses the general analytic framework and the second sets the theory against data compiled at a local level in the history of the enclosure movement.

3. Steven N. S. Cheung, "Private Property Rights and Sharecropping," *Journal of Political Economy* 76 (1968), pp. 1107–1122, and *The Theory of Share Tenancy* (Chicago: University of Chicago Press, 1969). By introducing transaction costs and risks, Cheung has also constructed a general analytic framework to explain why particular agricultural contracts are chosen under a system of private property rights. See his "Transaction Costs, Risk Aversion and the Choice of Contractual Arrangements," *Journal of Law and Economics* 12 (1969), pp. 23–42.

4. Harold Demsetz, "Toward a Theory of Property Rights," *American Economic Review* 57 (1967), pp. 347–359.

5. John McManus, "An Economic Analysis of Indian Behavior in the North American Fur Trade," *Journal of Economic History* 32 (1972), pp. 36–53; Omotunde E. G. Johnson, "Economic Analysis, the Legal Framework and Land Tenure Systems," *Journal of Law and Economics* 15 (1972), pp. 259–276; Terry Anderson, "The Evolution of Property Rights: A Study of the American West," *Journal of Law and Economics* 18 (1975), pp. 163–179; John Umbeck, "The California Gold Rush: A Study of Emerging Property Rights," *Explorations in Economic History* 14 (1977), pp. 197–226.

6. Armen Alchian and Harold Demsetz, "The Property Rights Paradigm," presented at the Thirty-Second Annual Meeting of the Economic History Association and published in *Journal of Economic History* 33 (1973), pp. 16–27.

THE ANALYTIC FRAMEWORK

The particular case of land tenure transformation to be examined is that which occurred in England during its emergence as the first industrial nation. As late as the end of the eighteenth century much of the land in England was still being farmed under the ancient system of communal property rights, which included the nonexclusive grazing rights held by certain individuals to the large cultivated fields, meadows, and wastes that surrounded the villages. As had been the custom for centuries, land use was determined by community-made decisions regarding what crops to plant and where to plant them as well as when to harvest. With the onset of the enclosure movement during the next two centuries the kaleidoscope of nonexclusive arrangements collapsed. Enclosure replaced existing common property rights with private property rights to land.[7]

For generations economists and historians have sought to ascertain the impact of enclosure upon the location of labor. One major consequence of the English industrial revolution had been a change in the tasks of workers. Whereas at the end of the seventeenth century, two out of every three workers were employed in agriculture, by the mid-nineteenth century only one in five workers made a living from the land.[8] To many, the observation that the enclosure movement and the industrial revolution occurred contemporaneously suggested that enclosure played a part in such a drastic reallocation of the labor force. The quest to identify such a role led to a historiography which has ranged from consistency to almost total contradiction between theory and evidence.

An early argument, which was to attain the status of nearly unassailable dogma, assigned a critical role to enclosure. According to this view, the enclosure movement resulted in the depopulation of the countryside and, consequently, provided a significant quantity of migratory labor which was subsequently employed by industry. Arnold Toynbee in his lectures on the industrial revolution singled out the enclosure movement as being responsible for decreasing rural population and increas-

7. There are several excellent primers on property rights to land in England. See, for example, Frederic Pollock, *The Land Laws* (London: Macmillan and Co., 1883) and A. W. B. Simpson, *An Introduction to the History of the Land Law* (Oxford: University Press, 1961).

8. Simon Kuznets, "Underdeveloped Countries and the Pre-industrial Phase in the Advanced Countries: An Attempt at Comparison," in A. N. Agarwala and S. P. Singh, eds., *The Economics of Underdevelopment* (New York: Oxford University Press, 1963), p. 143; Phyllis Deane and W. A. Cole, *British Economic Growth, 1688–1959* (Cambridge: University Press, 1962), p. 142.

ing pauperism.[9] Later, the Hammonds depicted enclosure and the subsequent changes in agriculture as a virtual social revolution which proved fatal to several classes of the agricultural population.[10] Paul Mantoux in his classic work on the industrial revolution asserted that enclosure so reduced the demand for labor that it "ultimately resulted in placing at the disposal of industry resources in labor and energy which made it possible for the factory system to develop."[11]

For all of the academic support of this view, however, there had also been studies revealing certain empirical deviations which, as it turned out, offered a portent of things to come. A case in point is the study by Reverend J. Howlett published in 1786. Using questionnaires and militia data in examining the influence of enclosure upon rural population, Howlett found strong evidence to suggest that enclosure did not decrease population but, on the contrary, increased it.[12]

More than a century later, E. C. K. Gonner conceded that in an intensive examination of census returns he had not found evidence that enclosure had led to depopulation in the countryside.[13] A reinvestigation of this question made subsequently by Arthur Redford in large measure substantiated Gonner's observations.[14] Despite such documented reservations by a few dissenting scholars, the traditional interpretation largely prevailed.

Not until the 1953 publication of a regional population study by J. D. Chambers was the accepted view of the impact of enclosure on the demand for labor severely undermined.[15] Chambers's methodology was a straightforward one. Taking a sample of villages, he categorized them as being primarily either agricultural or industrial at a point in time and then defined various classifications of agricultural villages according to whether or not at specified dates they had been enclosed and, if enclosed, how this was accomplished. Finally, he traced the rate of population growth for the different groups of villages over a period of time. His

9. *Lectures on the Industrial Revolution of the Eighteenth Century in England* (London: Longmans, Green and Co., 1937), Chapters 8, 9.

10. J. L. and Barbara Hammond, *The Village Labourer, 1760–1832* (London: Longmans, Green and Co., 1920), Chapter 4.

11. *The Industrial Revolution in the Eighteenth Century* (Oxford: The Alden Press, 1961), p. 183.

12. *Enquiry Into the Influence Which Enclosures Have Had Upon the Population of this Kingdom* (London, 1786).

13. *Common Land and Inclosure* (London: Macmilland Co., 1912), Book 3, Section 6.

14. *Labour Migration in England, 1800–1850* (Manchester: University Press, 1926).

15. "Enclosure and Labour Supply in the Industrial Revolution," *Economic History Review,* 2d ser. 5 (1953), pp. 319–343.

data, drawn from 119 villages in Nottinghamshire and covering the period 1801–1861, indicated that in those villages enclosed as of 1801 the mean value of population increased during the following 60 years.

The article by Chambers is considered by many economic historians to have been a watershed in the historiography on enclosure and the origins of the industrial labor force. An important reason for this is that, whereas previous empirical work had revealed contradictions between accepted theory and available evidence, Chambers suggested an alternative interpretation consistent with what had seemed to be disparate observations. In his view, although enclosure actually *increased* the demand for labor and thereby expanded employment in agriculture, the natural increase of the rural population was sufficient to create a surplus of labor from which the industrial labor force grew. As we have seen, the traditional argument was that enclosure decreased the demand for labor and thereby generated the industrial labor force. From the vantage point of hindsight, Chambers's turnabout in the interpretation of the labor impact of enclosure is remarkable.

The resolution of this issue would not only settle a long historical debate but would provide insight into the questions being raised in the current property right literature concerning the impact of evolving land tenure systems. Let us examine the effects of enclosure on the demand for labor when some land is privately owned and the rest is held entirely in common. Disregarding any effects that differing quality of land may have upon factor productivity, we merely consider the consequences of alternative property rights. Assume, then, that two homogeneous inputs, land and labor, are used to produce one output. Just how much labor would be employed upon enclosed land as opposed to common land can be determined in a simple two-factor model with fixed supplies of labor and land and a diminishing marginal product of labor.

In Figure 12.1, let AD represent the quantity of labor employed on land in the current period; AP_{NC} and MP_{NC}, respectively, are the average and marginal products of labor on common land while MP_{NP} is the marginal product of labor on privately owned land. If labor on private land is paid the value of its marginal product, the optimal volume of labor would be that quantity which would equate the marginal product with the marginal or opportunity costs of labor. The total wage bill would be determined by the wage rate times the quantity of labor employed, while the rent accruing to land would be that portion of the total product not paid out to labor. Where there is no private ownership of land, the total produce accrues to the owners of labor, which will then be employed on common land up to the point where its average product is equated to marginal opportunity costs. Accordingly, in equilibrium the

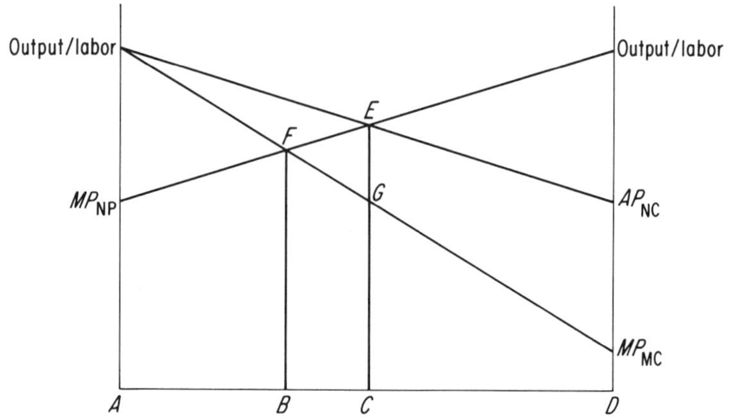

FIGURE 12.1. Labor employed on enclosed and uncommon land.

allocation of the given labor force *AD* will be *AC* employed upon common land and *CD* upon privately owned land. Although an equilibrium of the allocation of the labor force between common and private land has been attained, a misallocation of labor results from equating the average product of labor on common land with the marginal product of labor on private land.

Enclosure corrects the misallocation. On the formerly common land, labor is now employed up to the point where its marginal product is equated with opportunity costs. This occurs in the new equilibrium where *AB* of labor is employed on the newly enclosed land while *BD* is now employed on the initially private land. By comparing the areas under the marginal product curves (i.e., total product) we see that with the new equilibrium a total product equal to the area *EFG* has been gained by enclosure. This analysis also suggests that given the conditions described here enclosure will result in the migration of labor from the newly enclosed land to the initially enclosed land.

Although offering promising explanatory power, this analysis requires modification to make it applicable to the English enclosure movement, principally because ownership rights to land in the common fields of England during the industrial revolution varied widely in degrees of exclusivity. In the land tenure system, rights and privileges were established by custom and by oral as well as written contracts and agreements. Complex and multidimensional arrangements governed such factors as restriction of entry, duration of rights, and regulation of land use.[16]

Regarding the conditions of entry, rights of common to a given field

16. The following discussion of the English field system is drawn from the studies of D.

were held by a limited number of specified people and not by the general public. The majority of farmers were tenants rather than owner-occupiers, and the landowners received rental payments under several different types of tenancy.[17] In short, entry was restricted and rent accrued to landowners.

Property right arrangements also established the duration of common rights. For example, a fundamental concern of the tenure system was the grazing of livestock. Common rights to permanent pasture on a year-round basis were frequently held by those who had exclusive rights to the income generated from the production of grain on cultivated land. In the primarily arable areas of England the most prevalent form of husbandry was the three-field system. In annual rotation each field was subjected to a fall planting, a spring planting, and then was placed in fallow. As a general rule, common grazing rights were available on the fallow and, following the harvest, on the remaining two cultivated fields until spring plowing. Moreover, following the last crop of hay for the season, the rights to meadow land reverted to common for the winter grazing of livestock. Thus common rights ranged from year long to certain specified seasons of the year.

Finally, subject to a group decision-making process at the parish level, farmers adhered to a host of regulations concerning what crops would be grown, when and where to plant them, when to harvest, and how much livestock could be raised. This last matter was often determined by stinting agreements, a voluntary arrangement among those who held common rights to a given area to limit the number of livestock each raised, to prevent overgrazing.

In sum, because of all the restrictions and regulations making up the English land tenure system, the exclusivity of the rights to common land varied from those to enclosed land only in degree. Thus what have been traditionally termed "common rights" turn out to have been, in essence, partially exclusive rights.

In the context of this land tenure system, the analysis depicted in Figure 12.1 requires modification at the theoretical level which deals with land held under varying degrees of exclusivity.[18] On the basis of that analysis it was suggested that with unrestricted entry the quantity

R. Denman, *Origins of Ownership* (London: George Allen and Unwin Ltd., 1958), and Thomas E. Scrutton, *Commons and Common Fields* (Cambridge, 1887).

17. Lord Ernle, *English Farming Past and Present,* 6th ed. (Chicago: Quandrangle Books, 1961).

18. Such an exercise has been undertaken elsewhere. See Steven N. S. Cheung, "The Structure of a Contract and the Theory of a Non-Exclusive Resource," *Journal of Law and Economics* 13 (1970), pp. 49–70, and Ben Baack, "Potential Gains from the Enclosure of Common Land," *Journal of Agricultural Economics* 22 (1971), pp. 75–78.

of labor employed upon common land would be such that $AP_{NC} = MP_{NP}$. On the other hand, following enclosure the new equilibrium allocation of labor would equate labor's marginal product on both old enclosed land and newly enclosed land. What would be the allocation, however, if there were limits to entry on the "common" fields as was the case in England?

Consider Figure 12.2. Given exclusive ownership of land, an individual landlord (I) will maximize rent by equating the value of the marginal product of labor (MP_{NI}) with labor's opportunity costs (MP_{NP}). The maximum rent attainable is represented by the area *KGHJ* when *AB* of labor is hired for a total wage bill of *ABGK*. Assume a second individual (II) is now granted ownership rights to the same land. With I already employing *AB* of labor, the marginal product of II's first unit of labor is *HB*. Hence the marginal product curve is MP_{NII}. As II employs labor the marginal product of labor for I falls, and I employs less labor. The result is a higher marginal product of labor for II (MP^*_{NII}). Until in equilibrium, *AL* of labor is employed by I and *LM* by II. The total (reduced) rent to the ownership of land is now shared by I and II. If further entry is allowed the same process will ensue until in the extreme case of unlimited or free entry all rent will be dissipated and *AC* of labor will be employed upon what has become "common" land. This would be the situation depicted in Figure 12.1.

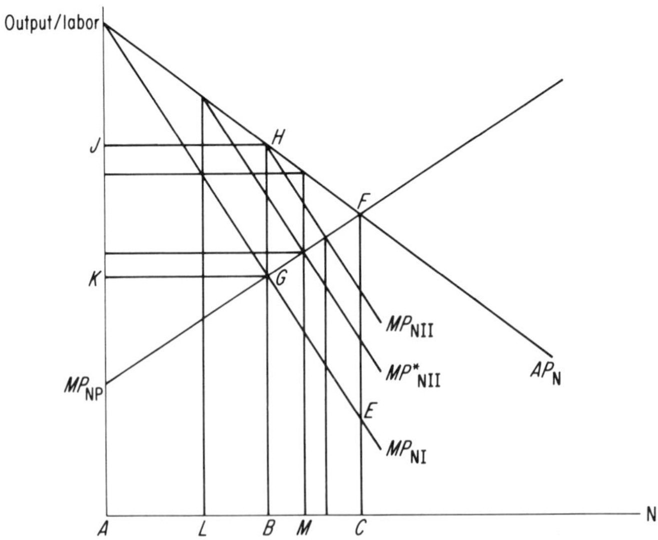

FIGURE 12.2. Labor employment during rent dissipation.

Among the many implications of the preceding analysis is the following: The less exclusive the property rights to common fields, the greater will be the labor force employed, and the greater will be the reduction of employment once enclosure occurs. Given the assumptions of these models, it follows that labor in any event will be reallocated from newly enclosed land to the initially enclosed land. This is just the reverse of the results obtained by Chambers in his study. In his sample of villages he found that population in general rose faster in the newly enclosed villages than in the remaining common and long-enclosed villages.

How could we account for this anomaly in light of the preceding analysis? One clue may lie in another economic variable undergoing change in agriculture during the industrial revolution. Throughout this period a whole series of innovations in husbandry was to a large extent transforming English agriculture. Among these were "new" crops including clover, sainfoin, ryegrass, mangels, swedes, and turnips.[19] Both the drainage of wet lowlands and the irrigation of pastures adjacent to streams by the floating of water meadows demonstrated increasing skills in water management. Field management also underwent change, with the introduction of four-course rotation, the substitution of convertible leys for permanent pasture, and the use of natural fertilizers such as lime, marl, and night soil. Innovations were being made also in animal husbandry. All together, the improvements spanned nearly the entire array of agricultural activity.

The impact of such new techniques on the demand for labor would ultimately have to be taken into account if their adoption were somehow related to enclosure. Unfortunately, what relationship, if any, existed remains unresolved in the historical literature. One school of thought asserts a positive and significant relationship.[20] The argument is that any individual farmer would be reluctant to implement new techniques in the unenclosed areas of the rural sector, since the returns generated would accrue to all of those holding common rights to the land: He would have to compare the cost of the contemplated activity, not with the total expected return, but with that lesser portion he would receive. On enclosed land, however, all benefits accrue to the individual. Another possibility suggested is that the owners of enclosed land would not bear any part of the positive transaction costs incurred by those who,

19. For an excellent discussion tracing the introduction of new crops into English agriculture, see E. L. Jones, "Agricultural Productivity and Economic Growth in England, 1700–1760," *Journal of Economic History* 25 (1965), pp. 1–18.

20. See the discussion in Peter Mathias, *The First Industrial Nation* (London: Methuen and Co., 1969), Chapter 3.

as holders of common rights, would have to reach agreement before implementing the new techniques. Through lower transaction costs alone the establishment of exclusive rights to income by enclosure might speed the diffusion of new husbandry. If we accept the general thrust of this argument for the moment, what are the empirical implications for our analysis?

Consider Figure 12.3. According to our previous analysis, following the enclosure of common land *BC* of labor would migrate from the newly enclosed land to the initially enclosed land. If as a result of enclosure the owners of the newly enclosed land incorporated new agricultural technology, the marginal and average products (MP^*_{NP}, AP^*_{NP}) would reflect this change. Owners of the initially enclosed land are assumed to be using the new husbandry. Only if, at the level of employment *C*, the new marginal product of labor MP^*_{NP} exceeded AP_{NC} would one expect to observe labor migrating from previously enclosed land to the newly enclosed land. In Figure 12.3, *C′* depicts such a possibility. Furthermore, the direction of the subsequent flow of labor following an enclosure would tell us something about the magniture of any difference in the level of technology between enclosed and unenclosed villages.

ENCLOSURE IN CHALKLAND PARISHES

In this section we turn to an empirical test of our theoretical framework, with data drawn from Chalkland parishes in the county of Hampshire. This area has several characteristics which make it particu-

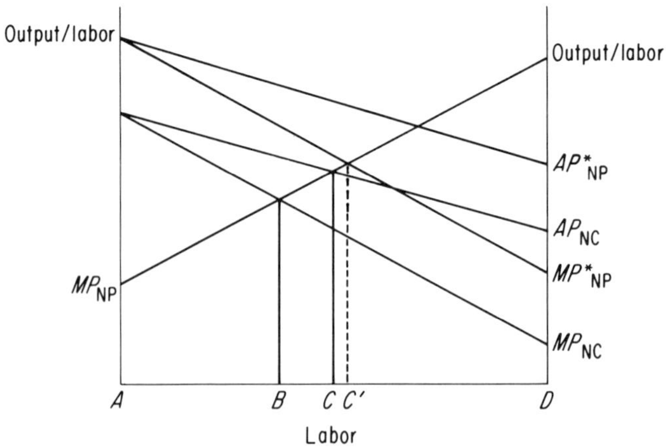

FIGURE 12.3. Effects of enclosure and new technology on labor migration.

larly useful for our analysis, among them that the 148 contiguous parishes comprise a relatively homogeneous land area and that the labor force was primarily agricultural during the eighteenth and nineteenth centuries. Throughout the period extensive enclosures occurred, as did conversions from old to new agricultural techniques.

Several qualifying points are in order. Although the analysis in the first section assumed the prices of output to be constant, this was not the case in England. The period of the Napoleonic wars, for example, brought rapid rises in the prices of agricultural goods. Following the wars, farm prices fell so sharply that historical literature classes the period as one of depression for agriculture. Such price fluctuations are not taken into account here, on the assumption that, given the homogeneity of the Chalklands, the changes would not significantly alter the labor demand as between parishes. As another qualifying notation: England was experiencing an increase of population during the period. In Hampshire the absolute level of population increased in both agricultural and industrial sectors. Without taking such change explicitly into account, the analysis in the first section has nevertheless suggested the direction of reallocation of the rural labor force when population, as well as property rights, is changing.

The Chalkland data reporting the allocation of labor are drawn from occupational census reports, the first of which was taken for Hampshire in 1801. These accounts divided occupations into three categories: families chiefly employed in agriculture; families chiefly employed in trade, manufactures, or handicraft; and all other families not included in the two preceding classes.[21] Between 1801 and 1831 the total number of families in the Chalkland parishes increased 40%, from 5162 to 7217. Table 12.1 summarizes the occupational returns and the share of the total families employed in each category. Although it grew rapidly overall, the Chalkland labor force remained primarily agricultural.

The analysis of Figure 12.1 in the first section suggests that the enclosure of land in the Chalklands should have led to a decreased demand for agricultural labor. To set the evidence against the model, two categories of parishes had to be established. Both had to be areas where no changes were underway in agricultural techniques, while at the same time one was experiencing enclosure and the other was not. The occupa-

21. *Abstract of Answers and Returns to the County of Hampshire* for the years 1801, 1811, 1821, and 1831. The occupational returns for 1801 listed persons employed, rather than families. An estimate was made of the number of families by dividing the total number of persons reported in agriculture for each appropriate parish by the average family size as of 1801 in those parishes.

TABLE 12.1
Occupational Distribution of Chalkland Labor Force

Census year	Percentage of total families in agriculture	Percentage of total families in manufactures	Percentage of total families in other
1801	.6164	.2429	.1407
1811	.6198	.2273	.1529
1821	.5931	.2711	.1358
1831	.5473	.2405	.2122

tional data from the two resultant groups of parishes are reported in Tables 12.2 and 12.3. Category A includes those parishes enclosed between 1770 and 1801 where the new agricultural techniques were in use; Category B includes those parishes newly enclosed during the period 1801–1831 and which, at the time of enclosure, were already being farmed under the new system of husbandry.[22] Category A therefore acts as a control group while Category B establishes the pure enclosure effect.

The analysis in the first section also demonstrated the possibility that changes in agricultural techniques could lead to the migration of labor from previously enclosed areas to newly enclosed areas. Just such an observation led Chambers to assert that, contrary to the then-accepted view, enclosure increased rather than decreased the demand for labor. Table 12.4 establishes a third category of parishes which allow a measure of the impact of technological change when it occurs contemporaneously with enclosure; it comprises all those Chalkland parishes enclosed during the period 1801–1831 in which enclosure was followed by initiation of the new husbandry.

The occupational data from the three groups of parishes can now be set against the analysis of the first section. The results are summarized in Table 12.5 which gives the percentage of growth in the number of families for each category of parishes. The first test is whether the relative ranking of the rates of growth of farm families is consistent with the model. The pure enclosure effect suggests that in an area where enclosure occurs, the rate of growth would be less than in an area already

22. The dates of individual enclosures in Hampshire were taken from L. Ellis Travener, *The Common Lands of Hampshire* (London: Hampshire Country Council, 1957), Appendix 1. The material regarding field systems was compiled from M. C. Naish, "The Agricultural Landscape of the Hampshire Chalklands, 1700–1840" (unpublished Master's dissertation, Lond University, 1960) and from the *Acreage Returns of 1801* preserved at the Public Record Office.

TABLE 12.2
Category A: Parishes Enclosed and Converted to the New Agricultural Technology by 1801

Census year	Percentage of Parish A families in agriculture	Percentage of Parish A families in manufactures	Percentage of Parish A families in other
1801	.5842	.2424	.1734
1811	.5984	.2325	.1691
1821	.5836	.2319	.1845
1831	.5298	.2828	.1874

enclosed, given that both employ the same technology. The evidence shown in Table 12.5 and depicted in Figure 12.4 is consistent with this proposition. Between 1801 and 1831 the Group B parishes where enclosure was underway had a 6.74% increase in the number of farm families. Over the same time period for the control Group A, the figure was 27.58%.

The analysis which considered the impact of technological change suggests further rankings. One would expect that in two areas undergoing enclosure, farm family growth in parishes converting to new techniques would exceed that in parishes already employing these techniques. The evidence is also consistent with that proposition. Over the 1801–1831 period the growth in the number of farm families in the third category exceeded that in the second. Furthermore, the observation of a higher growth rate in the third, where technology is changing, than in the first, where technology is given, is consistent with the analysis in the first section.

To this point the evidence has been in the form of the rate of growth in the number of farm families. Such an approach, however, does not account for the possibility that disparate initial populations may affect

TABLE 12.3
Category B: Parishes Enclosed during Period 1801–1831 and Which at Time of Enclosure Had Already Converted to the New Agricultural Technology

Census year	Percentage of Parish B families in agriculture	Percentage of Parish B families in manufactures	Percentage of Parish B families in other
1801	.5618	.2815	.1567
1811	.5515	.2509	.1976
1821	.4510	.4137	.1353
1831	.4466	.2402	.3132

TABLE 12.4
Category C: Parishes Enclosed during Period 1801–1831 and Where Enclosure Was Followed by Conversion to the New Agricultural Technology

Census year	Percentage of Parish C families in agrculture	Percentage of Parish C families in manufactures	Percentage of Parish C families in other
1801	.7394	.1899	.0707
1811	.7423	.1882	.0695
1821	.7705	.1603	.0692
1831	.7008	.1822	.1170

growth rates. A more complete test of the model would include an assessment of overall changes in whole shares, in addition to the percentage growth of individual group populations. Table 12.6, showing the shares of total Chalkland families in each occupation by parish type, indicates trends identical to those in the family growth tables. For example, the share of the total Chalkland farm families living in parishes of the third category rose over the period. The share living in the first also increased, but at a lower rate, while the effect of enclosure in the second group was to reduce its share of total Chalkland farm families. Accordingly, whether one looks at growth patterns or at share changes, the evidence is consistent with our framework of analysis.

In contrast to the traditional interpretation, the current view has been that enclosure increased the demand for labor. Although for the wrong reasons, as it now turns out, the traditional view was closer to reality than the current view. Ceteris paribus, the enclosure of land would reduce the quantity of labor employed. The extent of the reduction would depend upon the property right conditions of restriction, duration, and regulation which we have discussed. In principle, the closer the property rights are to being nonexclusive in nature, the greater the reduction of labor due to enclosure. The historical fact of an absolute increase of labor in English agriculture contemporaneously with the en-

TABLE 12.5
Percentage of Growth in Number of Families

Parish category	1801–1811	1801–1821	1801–1831
A	.0881	.2511	.2758
B	.0218	−.1271	.0674
C	.0846	.3696	.3867

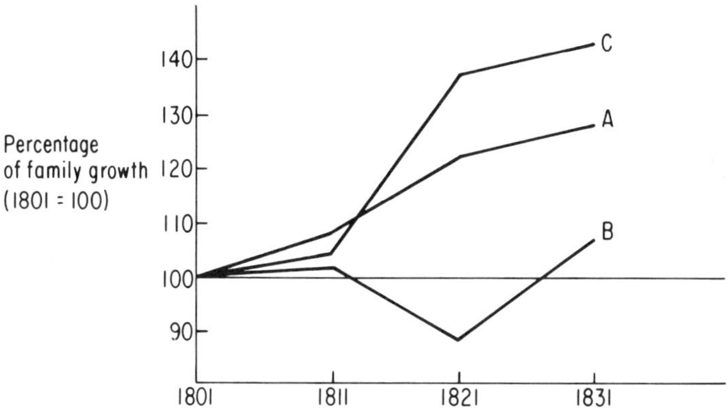

FIGURE 12.4. Growth in number of families by parish category during the period 1801–1831.

closure movement is not inconsistent with the analysis. Against the predictable reduction in the demand for labor due to enclosure must be set the impacts of population growth, of increasing demand for agricultural produce, and of the implementation of new agricultural techniques.

It has been our belief that some new insights into private property rights could be gained by further examination of tenure systems not under those constraints. In taking a step in that direction, this paper may also have shed some light on a long-standing historical issue relative to the demographic effects of the enclosure movement.

TABLE 12.6
Share of Total Chalkland Families in Agricultural and Nonagricultural Activities by Parish Type

Census year	Category A parishes	Category B parishes	Category C parishes
	1. Agriculture		
1801	.3567	.3312	.3121
1811	.3644	.3178	.3178
1821	.3838	.2486	.3676
1831	.3666	.2848	.3486
	2. Nonagriculture		
1801	.4081	.4152	.1767
1811	.3984	.4219	.1797
1821	.3991	.4413	.1596
1831	.3933	.4267	.1800

Ben Baack did his graduate work at the University of Washington where he received his Ph.D. in 1972. As a student in one of Douglass North's graduate seminars he became interested in the theory of property rights. Baack pursued this interest by writing his dissertation under North's direction on an economic analysis of the English enclosure movement. He was awarded an NSF Dissertation Fellowship which included a year-long study in England at Oxford University.

Since joining the faculty at Ohio State University, Baack has made several contributions to the literature on the enclosure maovement. His contribution to this volume reflects his continued interest in the theory of property rights. Baack is also interested in the role of government in the market place and has published works on American tariff policy during the nineteenth century. His current research is directed at an analysis of the interrelationship between economic events and the political process of defining public policy under the Articles of Confederation and the Constitution.

Baack is currently Associate Professor of Economics at Ohio State University. In 1979 Baack was awarded the Ohio State Distinguished Teaching Award.

Chapter 13

Customary Law, Markets, and Resource Transactions in Late Imperial China

Ramon H. Myers

In an essay examining Karl Polanyi's methodology, Douglass North again demonstrated his remarkable ability to identify new frontiers of research in economic history. Pointing out that economic historians had failed to take seriously either Polanyi's works or his basic challenge to the economics profession, North declared, "other allocation systems have characterized economic organizations and these other systems [were] not grounded in economic behavior."[1]

Stated in a different way, Polanyi had argued that only during the nineteenth century and in the Western world had the market become the predominant system for allocating resources. Throughout the rest of the world and before 1800 societies had primarily relied upon reciprocity and redistribution to serve that function. From his field research of transactions in Dahomey of West Africa and from his historical studies of transactions in the famous ports of trade, in early societies and empires, and in the economies of Athens, Mycenae, and Alalakh, Karl Polanyi had developed such concepts as reciprocity, redistribution, exchange, and household management of resources. He then used these concepts to theorize that in premodern times markets rarely emerged to allocate resources; instead, transactions filling that need were motivated by noneconomic factors, and allocative systems other than the market determined the exchange value of resources.[2]

1. Douglass C. North, "Markets and Other Allocation Systems in History: The Challenge of Karl Polanyi," *European Economic History Review* 6:3 (1977), p. 703.
2. George Dalton, ed., *Primitive, Archaic, and Modern Economies: Essays of Karl Polanyi*

ISBN 0-12-580080-0

Polanyi's followers and other scholars like M. I. Finley have further argued that the conventional tools of economic analysis have very limited application to the economies of early societies and that new concepts, developed in other branches of social sciences, are more useful in defining their actual operation.[3]

North replies, however, that economic contract theory as developed in recent years by such economists as Steven N. S. Cheung, Armen Alchian, and others offers the analytical tools to explain, without recourse to Polanyi's theoretical concepts, why different systems of resource allocation existed even in the absence of well-defined markets. Further, these different systems were rational responses by their organizers to certain kinds of transaction costs governing resource exchange, and it is on these costs that contract theory focuses in analyzing and explaining how these nonmarket systems functioned. In fact, North and a colleague already have effectively used this concept to explain why a system of resource allocation other than the market operated in late medieval Europe.[4] Because well-defined and enforced property rights were not widespread in Europe before the seventeenth century, transaction costs for resource exchange were extremely high, and for this reason the manorial system in feudal society emerged to determine allocation. North concludes his essay on Polanyi by asserting that the transaction costs approach to the study of premodern societies provides a "refutable explanation for these transactional modes" offered by Polanyi and other scholars.[5]

This essay tries to respond to North's proposal that economic historians ought now to identify the allocative systems of other premodern, nonwestern economies, using conventional economic analysis to elucidate how transactions were conducted. It also tries to do more. It advances the argument that the kind of resource exchange that took place

(New York: Anchor Books, Doubleday, 1968). See also S. C. Humphreys, "History, Economics and Anthropology: The Work of Karl Polanyi," *History and Theory* 8 (1969), pp. 165–212; and Paul Bohannan and George Dalton, eds., *Markets in Africa: Eight Subsistence Economies in Transition* (New York: Anchor Books, Doubleday, 1965) for examples of communities where the market was supposed to operate peripherally in determining resource prices.

3. Finley, *The Ancient Economy* (Berkeley and Los Angeles: University of California Press, 1973). Polanyi's students have generally applied the "master's" concepts of reciprocity and redistribution to the topics of research, but Finley develops other concepts such as a priviledged social order, status or prestige, centers of consumption, special role of the state, etc., to describe how the economies of the ancient Mediterranean world allegedly worked.

4. Douglass North and Robert Paul Thomas, *The Rise of the Western World: A New Economic History* (Cambridge: Cambridge University Press, 1973).

5. North, "Markets and Other Allocation Systems," p. 715.

between households, particularly the increased volume of such exchange in China after the seventeenth century, was primarily a function (*a*) of customary law which greatly reduced transaction costs and (*b*) of the activities of the state which both permitted customary law to operate and adjudicated disputes over transactions by respecting customary law.

The enduring empires of Asia have rarely been examined from the North perspective. Of course some scholars have tried to differentiate between certain Asian economies and the new enclave economies arising within them as initiated by Western regimes bent upon establishing their colonies. Examples of these are Marx's comments on India, where he introduced the concept of the Asian mode of production, and J. H. Boeke's study of Indonesia under Dutch rule, where he developed the concept of a dualistic society.[6] From both we note that Asian economies were supposed to have operated very differently from those of the West and that noneconomic behavior allegedly played a more important role in determining the allocation of resources.

This essay argues the opposite. I will first show that the economy of late imperial China expanded enormously to support a population of a size unprecedented in world history. Two economic factors made that achievement possible. First, the Chinese increasingly relied upon product and factor markets of a highly competitive nature to permit resource exchange, production, and distribution to flourish everywhere in the empire. Second, it appears that transaction costs for these marketing activities gradually declined over the period, permitting a greater volume of exchange of resources, goods, and services. The spread of customary-law practices, or private contractual exchange enforced by third parties and tacitly recognized as legal by the imperial state, seems to have accounted for this gradual decline in transaction costs. Let us examine late imperial China, beginning around 1400 but especially since the late seventeenth century and up to 1900, as we observe the character of economic growth, the market structure, and the role of customary law in reducing transaction costs.

LATE IMPERIAL CHINA

In very general terms we first should note China's principal achievements and difficulties during the past half millenium, keeping this balance sheet in full view when we next consider how the imperial state

6. For Marx's comments, see E. J. Hobsbawn, ed., *Karl Marx: Pre-Capitalist Economic Formations* (New York: International Publishers, 1964), pp. 61–97. Boeke, *Economics and Economic Policy in Dual Societies* (New York: Institute of Pacific Relations, 1953).

interacted with society, over time. Far more research must be done to measure these achievements and problems, but enough evidence is available to say the following.

First, during both the Ming and the Ch'ing imperial dynasties which spanned the half millenium between 1398 and 1911, China enjoyed several unusually prolonged periods of peace, social stability, and economic prosperity. During these intervals, the harvests were generally stable, without the severe fluctuations that plagued Europe during the same period. Meanwhile, China's population was growing, slowly but inexorably, unchecked by the Malthusian factors so prominent in premodern Europe. Simultaneously, the Chinese economy was expanding at a steady rate, until it reached a huge size in terms of both space and population.

Setting aside the issue of imperial administrative rule, let us consider only the increase in population and in cultivated land.

Around the year 1400, China's population probably ranged from 65 million to 80 million people farming between 25 and 30 million hectares of land of which a certain proportion, perhaps as much as 25%, was cropped more than once every year.[7] By 1600, population had increased to between 120 and 200 million people farming between 35 and 40 million hectares. Internal rebellions and an invasion from the North brought the Ming dynasty to an end, and in 1644 the Ch'ing empire began to take form, although 40 years passed before the country was unified and full control established over the empire. Reasonably reliable statistics for the mid-eighteenth century place population somewhere between 250 and 275 million people farming between 55 and 60 million hectares of land. By 1850, population stood at around 400–430 million, possibly farming between 60 to 65 million hectares (data for cultivated land are not available for that year). Internal rebellions then rocked the country, reducing both population and farm land, but by 1913 population had again increased to around 430 million persons farming some 90 million hectares of land. We observe in both dynastic periods that while population more than doubled, the cultivated farm land increased much more slowly. By the mid-nineteenth century, China supported a population much larger than that of western and eastern Europe and Russia combined. Further, China somehow managed to feed, clothe, and house close to a half billion people using only premodern technological sources of energy—wind, water, sun, and muscle power. Equally remarkable were China's other achievements; she maintained a large and efficient

7. The data cited in this paragraph are obtained from Dwight H. Perkins, *Agricultural Development in China, 1368–1968* (Chicago: Aldine, 1969), Chapter 2.

civil bureaucracy, a workable system of law and justice, a notably high level of functional literacy, and an ethos of civilized morality.

China was uniformly neither prosperous nor poor. Certain regions like the east-central provinces of Chekiang, Kiangsu, and southern Anhwei, as well as the southeast provinces of Fukien and Kwangtung, were quite wealthy as compared to the provinces of the southwest, northwest, and northeast. Between 1400 and 1580 and again between 1680 and 1850 China indeed suffered numerous poor harvests, but her granary system and resource reserves in the private sector prevented any prolonged regional declines that could affect the general trend of population growth or the expansion of foodgrain output.

As a further achievement, China supported this slow, sustained population growth in a unique setting of villages and small market town settlements. In spite of China's huge size, few lived in cities. G. W. Skinner has estimated that in 1893 the empire (excluding Manchuria and Taiwan) contained 877 urban central places having populations of 4000 or more, or a total urban population of 20.8 million.[8] Assuming a total population of around 394 million at that time, this would yield a rate of urbanization of only 5.3%. Certainly, the proportion living in cities did not increase during the Ch'ing period, and even after the rapid growth of the modern treaty-port cities along China's coast and large waterways after the 1880s, the urban population by the 1930s had reached only 9% of the total population. As many as 9 out of every 10 persons lived in small market towns and their surrounding villages.

The landscape was filled with thousands upon thousands of rural markets that were situated either in large villages or in very small rural towns in the 3500-odd counties [*hsien*] of the empire. Skinner has further estimated that in 1893 China may have had between 27,000 and 28,000 such marketing towns, each servicing an average of 15 villages, summing to more than 400,000 villages in all. Within the marketing area, designated by a market town and a cluster of 20–50 villages, even the least advantageously situated villager faced a round trip averaging only 5.4 miles to his own market center. Moreover, he could conveniently travel even to adjacent marketing areas[9] because the usual roughly hexagonal shape of the areas minimized the costs of local transportation.[10]

8. Skinner, ed., *The City in Late Imperial China*, "Regional Urbanization in Nineteenth-Century China" (Stanford: Stanford University Press, 1977), p. 224.

9. See John C. H. Fei, "The 'Standard Market' of Traditional China," in Dwight H. Perkins, ed., *China's Modern Economy in Historical Perspective* (Stanford: Stanford University Press, 1975), pp. 235–260.

10. Ibid., pp. 239–240.

As a result of these networks linking tens of thousands of villages, an enormous commodity exchange came to be transacted throughout the empire. As agriculture developed, specialization in trade and handicraft also flourished, and the low transportation costs within local marketing areas enabled the village and market town networks not only to supply their own agricultural and handicraft needs but also to exchange some of their products with other networks. The typical village family could participate in many activities: repairing structures and tools; spinning thread; weaving cloth; making decorative or useful objects from straw, bamboo, clay, or other materials; carting goods; hawking wares; clerking in stores; and, of course, farming the land.

How the landscape burgeoned with market towns and their satellite villages is well illustrated in the development of Ningpo city, and its hinterland in the northeastern portion of Chekiang province, as so brilliantly described by the Japanese scholar Shiba Yoshinobu.[11] Beginning in the late sixteenth century and continuing well into the late eighteenth, members of the literati sponsored and supervised considerable dredging and the reorganization of the water system on the Ningpo plain. The expansion of commerce and an influx of silver from overseas during this same period stimulated the demand for agricultural and handicraft goods until "a network of rural markets spread over the whole area."[12] Shiba's maps dramatically illustrate the increase of market towns across the Ningpo plain from the mid-eighteenth to late-nineteenth centuries. By the 1840s, about 70% of the farmers cultivated cotton, and the city of Ningpo flourished as a commercial center with numerous native banks financing trade of local products up and down the China coast as well as in the interior. Another recent study shows the growth of local marketing in Kwangtung province during the Ming and Ch'ing periods. The majority of these markets first evolved in villages, some operating on a periodic basis, others open year around.[13] Many specialized in the collection and sale of mulberries, silk cocoons, raw silk thread, fish, or poultry products, whereas others were open to all kinds of commodity exchange. More important, the largest increase of Kwangtung markets appears to have occurred in the seventeenth and eighteenth centuries.

Drawing from these thousands of small marketing areas were larger

11. Yoshinobu Shiba, "Ningpo and Its Hinterland" in Skinner, *The City in Late Imperial China,* pp. 391–439.

12. Ibid., p. 401.

13. Kazuo Hayashi, "Min-Shin jidai, Kantō no kyo to shi: dentōteki ichiba no keitai to kino ni kan suru ichi kosatsu" (A Survey of the Structure and Function of Traditional Markets: Fairs and Market Towns of Kwantung Province during the Ming and Ch'ing Periods), *Shirin* 63 (1980), pp. 69–105.

marketing centers in medium and larger cities and finally in the provincial and metropolitan urban centers. The reader should visualize a small urban continuum above the county township seat that linked prefectures to provincial capitals and these to their respective regional and national metropolitan centers. Staples like salt, cotton, cloth, rice, wheat, tea, and silk products flowed out of rural marketing areas into the urban markets; yet most commodity exchange still remained in the market places of large villages, market towns, and county seats.

The reader should realize that these achievements, like others mentioned earlier, were not without certain costs and difficulties which I will refer to as the dysfunctions of development. First, the distribution of wealth and income was highly unequal and remained that way over both the Ming and Ch'ing periods. Although in the early years of both dynasties large estates had dissolved and many households formerly lacking any property rights had gradually gained some, the slow rate of economic growth prevented a more equal distribution. While there is no firm quantitative measure of increasing divergence over time, China remained a society of income extremes. At the top was a wealthy class whose degree-holding numbers made up only 2% of the population yet received as much as 24% of income.[14] At the bottom of the ladder were those with little or no land, constituting probably between 20 and 25% of the households of most villages.[15]

A second dysfunction of development was the depletion of such resources as forests and fertile soils, especially on hills, and the pollution of large areas adjacent to the Grand Canal, to large lakes, and to various rivers. Throughout the eighteenth and nineteenth centuries the accommodation of ever more people upon the land led to ecological devastation almost ignored by communities and state.

A third dysfunction was that most inhabitants of cities, market towns, and villages endured low standards of living. The ordinary family lived very frugally in a modest dwelling and consumed a daily diet of coarse grains, vegetables, and tea. Little pork, beef, or fish was attainable. Although some reserves were kept on hand, two poor harvests in a row usually meant famine, disease, malnutrition, and death for many. Meanwhile the ordinary male adult and even women and children had to toil daily from sunup to sunset. In this society, labor triumphed over leisure, and hard work was the iron rule for survival.

14. Chung-Li Chang, *The Income of the Chinese Gentry* (Seattle: University of Washington Press, 1962) p. 327.

15. This estimate is based on a great number of Chinese and Japanese village studies of the 1920s and 1930s. See Ramon H. Myers, *The Chinese Peasant Economy* (Cambridge, Mass.: Harvard University Press, 1970), particularly Appendix A.

Yet the Ming and Ch'ing empires, in spite of dysfunctions, maintained themselves longer than most. Because the bureaucratic state played such an important role in promoting development, more for what it refrained from doing than for what it tried to do, we should examine the interaction of the state and society.

THE INTERACTION OF THE CH'ING STATE AND SOCIETY

In bureaucratically ruled empires, the state can interact with society in four possible ways and in various combinations of these. First, it may stand as a despot, extracting taxes and rents from its lands and mobilizing corvée labor for its projects. To continue long in this parasitic role, the state must have firm social and political control over passive subjects. Second, the state can carry out certain functions of its own, such as operating monopolies and managing its estates, without interfering in the lives of its subjects except to maintain law and order or for the empire's defense. Third, the state can strive to improve the allocative modes operating in society by advancing subsidies, instituting incentives, and pursuing a policy of "hands off" to liberate the forces of production. Finally, the state can itself undertake the allocation of resources by organizing monopolies, regulating trade, and managing specific marketing centers.

It is still too early in our studies of the Ch'ing economy to say which of the above combinations were used by the state, for how long, and in what intensity. Yet the general evidence strongly suggests that the state combined the role of noninterference or slight modulation of the private sector with very limited authoritarian allocation of resources so as to create a fairly beneficent economic environment for private enterprise.

Because the Ch'ing state ruled 18 huge provinces, some of which were strategic for defense and others for collecting revenue, the bureaucracy did not consider it necessary—and perhaps never even had the power—to reallocate tax revenues between provinces. Instead, provinces were permitted to retain a share of the taxes collected to fund the provincial sub-bureaucracies. Through taxes on land, salt, and imported foreign goods, the state managed its administrative system, maintained its army to preserve the peace, and provided for law and order.[16] The Ch'ing court, by virtue of the Manchu conquest, also had acquired certain territorial domains from which it collected rents and other revenues and in which local labor maintained its establishments and produced

16. Ramon H. Myers, *The Chinese Economy Past and Present* (Belmont: Wadsworth, 1980), Chapter 3.

special products for court consumption. The state bureaucracy also managed the salt and copper mining monopolies, supervised such public works as water control, the Grand Canal, and granaries, and tried to manage the copper component of the money supply. In sum, however, state control over resources and spending probably did not amount to any more than 6 or 7% of the empire's gross domestic product.

While the state bureaucracy was carrying out these limited functions, the household was serving as the basic producing and consuming unit.[17] Households were forever changing in size and form, enlarging when births exceeded deaths, contracting when deaths exceeded births. Every household experienced the general cycle of first forming, then enlarging, and finally dividing into segments which passed through similar cycles or disappeared entirely. In each cycle the Chinese household tried to build relationships with kin of the same patrilineal descent group. When their best interests dictated, they also transcended kinship to form ties with other units like guilds, religious cults, and secret societies. Depending upon its power or weakness, each descent group strove to form a lineage and these became important networks for economic gain and social advancement.

For economic gain, households singly or collectively performed productive and distributive functions within the agricultural, manufacturing, and services sectors of society. Some households pooled their savings to establish handicraft enterprises, small factories, stores, transport firms, vendors of services.

These partnerships probably never accounted for even a quarter of all the household activity in those same sectors, yet we should still consider households as involved in two discrete economic activities. First, they earned income by selling their factor services: Household members labored to earn wages, either in money or kind; they leased property or assets to earn rent; they loaned money to earn interest. Such activities required evaluation of potential buyers and decisions relative to the sale of factor services. Second, households organized their resources to produce goods or services to sell to other households through formal markets. They might hire labor and rent land to grow food or fibers for the market; they might operate a store or shop, manage a handicraft establishment, or engage in trade, near or far.

17. The household, in this essay, means a family plus any nonfamily members living under a single roof. The imperial state used the term household or *hu* as the basic socioeconomic unit for recording taxes, labor service, and population. Both as an accounting and a demographic unit, the household should be perceived as the basic organizer of production, distribution, and exchange.

We must remember that while earning income from these two economic functions—the sale of factor services and the sale of goods or services—the majority of Chinese households were still settled into the predominantly rural segment of the demographic landscape (as was equally true in western Europe during the same period). Within the rural–urban Chinese continuum of villages, market towns, and higher level urban centers, two major market systems were in operation for the allocation of resources: product markets and factor markets. Suppliers of rice, tea, cotton cloth, silk products, etc., competed with each other to produce for the market places. Some households specialized in farming to produce raw materials, others engaged in handicraft to process these materials, and still others served as brokers, carters, shippers, etc. to sell the finished products to standard markets and within the higher marketing centers. Commodity prices for products were competitively derived by haggling. Many examples of commodity markets could be cited, but the Hunan rice market serves as a case in point.[18]

Hunan province produced considerable rice for export, a large quantity being purchased by rise merchants in the nearby provinces of Kiangsu and Chekiang. Watching the movement of seasonal rice prices, the merchants, when the time was right, sent their brokers and boats to Hankow, Hsiang-yin, and Hsiang-t'an, the large market centers in Hunan province to which rice flowed from the smaller market towns. Meantime, the suppliers of rice congregated in small village and town markets had sold their rice after the harvest to brokers and merchants in exchange for cotton cloth, tea, metal, bamboo products, noodles, straw braid, fish, oil products, etc. (Many farming regions in Hunan of course specialized in these items, and suppliers marketed these for cash to purchase rice.) The large rice merchants outside Hunan, however, had already shipped their silver, copper cash, and even paper notes to the major Hunan markets because farmers supplying the rice needed that cash to purchase the many items they in turn required. As soon as brokers had purchased their rice, they shipped it to the large Hunan market towns like Hankow, where it was bought by other merchants and transshipped to the lower Yangtze markets in Kiangsu and Chekiang provinces. The rice market was highly competitive, with easy entry and exit for merchants, with prices uniformly prevailing or fluctuating according to the harvest and the strength of local and outside provincial demand, and with a fairly homogeneous product being transacted.

How could tens of thousands of markets operate so successfully with

18. Myers, *Chinese Economy, Past and Present,* pp. 93–94.

a multitude of products continually being produced, transported, and exchanged?

First, these activities were carried out under conditions of premodern technology with reliance on vast quantities of labor. Households progressively turned to labor-using, resource-saving methods, as did the state itself. For reasons too complex to treat here, the Chinese found the means to make certain resources more productive, while using labor in efficient ways to offset the growing scarcity of other resources such as timber, coal, and fertile land. It seems that by substituting labor to conserve scarce resources, the state and private economic organizations managed to produce a positive marginal physical product instead of continually diminishing returns or a zero marginal physical product.[19]

For example, when timber became scarce and more costly as fuel to produce salt in the east-central and southeastern provinces, private enterprise resorted to solar power methods which required larger quantities of labor. Again, in the state-managed copper mines in Yunnan province, when the rich surface veins were depleted the operators put more labor to work constructing shaft supports and draining water seepage, so deep mining was feasible. Finally, even in agriculture, family farms relied upon increased labor to apply larger quantities of organic fertilizer and to extend irrigation so as to crop the land more intensively. Other households expended considerable labor to transform hillsides into farm land.

As households came to use labor intensive methods exclusively, while conserving scarce resources, the character of the Chinese economy was increasingly assuming a new pattern of growth. Land productivity steadily rose, but labor and capital productivity increased scarcely at all except on an occasional once-and-for-all basis when innovations occurred in certain branches of handicraft industry, like cotton and silk. The capital stock—rudimentary in form and comprising only tools, small structures, and various systems of irrigation, water control, and roads—proved to absorb, rather than to displace, labor. The quality of capital stock changed very little, but its supply increased with steady population growth so that the capital–labor ration remained quite constant. Under these conditions of factor allocation and use, the output of goods and services probably expanded at the very slow growth rate of .2–.3% per annum, roughly equivalent to the growth rate of total inputs made up of capital, labor, and land. Total factor productivity, therefore, never provided any contribution to the expansion of output.[20]

19. Ibid., Chapter 4.
20. Ibid., Chapter 1.

All told then, tens of thousands of product markets were performing admirably, using labor-intensive methods of a premodern vintage to conserve resources and to support an empire whose population was steadily climbing from 200 million to more than 400 million by the mid-nineteenth century. But this was only part of the story. Informal *factor* markets were aiding the process with high efficiency by enabling households to correct for specific resource scarcities through exchanges with other households.[21]

Just as price signals in product markets informed merchants of how much to buy and conveyed to sellers clues of how much to supply to the market, so too did informal factor markets convey price signals for the exchange of scarce resources between households. Examples of resource allocative responses were the leasing and renting of land which took place within every village of the empire, the bidding for and supplying of credit between households, and the offering for hire and purchasing of labor services on either a short-term or a long-term basis. Although land, credit, and labor services were the key resources transacted in factor markets, one might also cite water supply and the maintenance of law, order, and peace, as well as security for commercial exchange, as other services transacted between households. Factor markets were extremely complex, and we are only now beginning to understand how these actually operated.

SYSTEMS OF ALLOCATION IN LATE IMPERIAL CHINA

Placing our discussion of resource allocation within the context of market structures and the prevailing production function of the Ch'ing period, let us now consider the various types of resource allocation that can theoretically exist and then examine how one of these became pervasive in the Ch'ing period.

Four principal types of resource allocation can operate separately or together in any economic system at any time. The first is reciprocity, where social units or individuals singly or collectively exchange resources at certain times according to prescribed social custom and cultural norms. The second is based upon a patron-client relationship, with the patron dispensing certain resources in exchange for those, usually labor, given by the client. The third type is resource allocation carried out by state command; social units in this case transfer resources to the state at zero price, at a price below current market value, or at terms more favorable to the social units. The final arrangement is contractual

21. Ibid., pp. 102–113.

agreement whereby two or more parties agree upon the terms of resource exchange which are then enforced either by themselves or through third parties.

In late imperial China all four types of resource allocation were found. At this stage of our research it is difficult to say which of these, either singly or jointly, characterized the economy during the Ming period. But by the Ch'ing period, the historical evidence strongly suggests, contractual exchange of resources became widespread.

To understand the probable reasons for this, it is necessary to consider the nature of officialdom in that period. First, the state had long depended upon detailed records based on a vast collection of information and its evaluation. This system, which had become highly sophisticated by the Ch'ing period,[22] was in the hands of extremely literate men who, to achieve their status, had passed difficult examinations leading to degrees which permitted them to enter officialdom. Along the way, they had also become aware of various punishments awaiting one who broke the law or governed improperly.[23] As a result, officials were understandably worried about their capability, within the entire institutional fabric of both state and society, to carry out the duties expected of them, but they also shared a human lethargy about carrying out those responsibilities with proper zeal. They naturally sought the most airtight ways of arranging transactions within the economy.

Meantime, as described earlier, the Ch'ing state had interacted with society in beneficial ways to encourage households and their economic organizations to take full advantage of markets and to conduct various transactions correcting for resource imbalances while still producing the highest value products for markets. This is not to argue that the Ch'ing state always initiated successful economic policies. But generally speaking, in the first century of Ch'ing rule and in many regions where the Ch'ing bureaucracy proved too weak to use its authority for extracting more resources, the private sector managed to take full advantage of expanding markets both for products and for factors.

Factor markets operate imperfectly if an absence of competition between owners and buyers of resources leads to an exchange of fewer resources at higher prices than would be the case if markets were more

22. For a brilliant discussion of this record-keeping system, especially the system and network of laws governing record keeping, see Thomas A. Metzger, *The Internal Organization of Ch'ing Bureaucracy: Legal, Normative and Communication Aspects* (Cambridge, Mass.: Harvard University Press, 1973), Sections 2, 3.

23. Ibid., Section 4. No other work in a Western language approaches the clarity and incisiveness of Metzger's treatment of the Chinese bureaucracy, particularly the societal values and norms which enabled it to operate as effectively as it did.

competitive. Further, factor markets perform imperfectly if the exchange of resources incurs high transaction costs which result in a lower volume of resources exchanged at higher prices than would otherwise be true.

Transaction costs result from three basic requirements of both buyers and sellers of resources: namely, information, accuracy, and enforcement. Information is needed about the availability of resources and the terms of exchange. Next, this information must be properly interpreted, assimilated, and used to reduce uncertainty, so that the respective parties to the transaction will produce the appropriate output and earn the proper income. Finally, there are additional costs for enforcing agreements. These three costs will vary depending on the ability of parties to obtain information, to evaluate it correctly, and to find means to enforce contractual agreements.

The higher these transaction costs, the lower the remuneration for owners and buyers of resources in the factor market. How can each type of these costs be lowered? First, the use of third parties to convey information and to bring owners and buyers of resources together reduces the cost of acquiring information. Second, the drawing up of contracts to counter all conceivable contingencies gives greater confidence and protection to both owners and buyers and helps to mitigate errors in judgment. Finally, the involvement of third parties makes these contracts more binding because an injured party can turn to the third party to enforce the original contract.

The practice of forming contracts between private parties had gradually emerged during the Ming period, but it appears to have greatly accelerated during the early Ch'ing period. In fact the Ch'ing state seems to have approved of these contractual agreements made through third parties in the private sector, and some historical evidence shows that Ch'ing officials even adjudicated contract litigation according to the customs that governed such agreements locally.[24] It appears that after the fourteenth century transaction costs in the private sector steadily declined from a previously high level because of this very reason—the spread of customary law, or private contractual agreements between households, often enforced through third parties. More and more resource transactions took place through transactional agreements made

24. For evidence that local magistrates adjudicated civil cases involving breach of tenure and credit contractual agreements, see David C. Buxbaum, "Some Aspects of Civil Procedure and Practice at the Trials in Tanshui and Hsinchu from 1789 to 1895," *The Journal of Asian Studies* 30 (1971), pp. 255–280; R. F. Johnston, *Lion and Dragon in Northern China* (New York, 1910; reprinted by Southern Materials Center, 1976, Taipei). The Buxbaum essay cites official adjudication in northern Taiwan in the late nineteenth century, whereas the Johnston work describes Ch'ing official adjudication in Weihaiwei port-city in Shantung in the early 1900s.

verbally or by written contracts. Many of the latter Ch'ing documents have survived to the present, and to these I now turn.

CUSTOMARY LAW AND FACTOR MARKETS

Although the imperial state always permitted private parties to negotiate agreements to exchange resources and to enforce these contracts, often through third parties, it expected the parties or households to shoulder these costs. The world of customary law certainly flourished throughout the Ch'ing empire and embraced what modern states today refer to as civil law.[25] I first point out some general characteristics of Chinese customary law and then cite some examples of contracts showing how these facilitated resource transactions between households for the purpose of correcting for resource scarcities within households.

Contractual agreements between private parties had common attributes of which I cite the following. First, in many surviving written contracts we find statements that the third party drawing up the contract can refer any future dispute between the parties to a state official for adjudication. For example, in a contract for adoption drawn up in Hou-chia-ying village of Ch'ang-li county in Hopei in 1792, an elderly man adopted his nephew and his wife as heirs to his corporate estate on the condition that the couple should perform ancestor rites after his death. A condition was inserted into the contract that the state should intercede if the terms of the contract were violated.

> After the adoption the heir will not try to leave the father, and the father cannot expel the heir. If either action takes place, the middlemen [12 men cosigned this contract] will appeal to the authorities to punish the offender. We fear that in the future any verbal agreement lacks concrete proof so we have drawn up this contract.[26]

Second, we also observe that written contracts followed a standardized format depending upon the type of resource transaction. Take the example of dividing the household corporate wealth between the male heirs, a custom in China since antiquity. Contracts for such a

25. Chinese customary law has been little analyzed by Western scholars, but it has been studied seriously by Chinese and Japanese scholars. In fact, thanks to Japanese government-sponsored surveys of Chinese legal customs, there has survived a vast treasure store of customary law documents which is only now being subjected to serious analysis. Much of what follows is based upon a current project in which the relationship of customary law to society and economy is being studied by me and by Dr. Fu-mei Chang Chen, research associate of the Hoover Institution, Stanford University.

26. Mindaishi Kenkyūshi, *Chūgoku tochi keiyaku bunshoshū* (Studies in Chinese Legal History: Land Laws and Laws Governing Transactions), (Tokyo: Tōkyō Daigaku Shuppankai, 1960), p. 335.

division always first mentioned why the household had been forced to partition the corporate estate, then identified all immovable assets in the estate and described in detail the terms of how each of these items was to be divided between the eligible male heirs. Then the contract went on to identify and describe the terms of how the movable assets of the estate were to be divided and, finally, how some corporate wealth might be set aside for the provision of the aged parents or used for a dowry or wedding trousseau by one or more daughters.

Rent contracts for leasing and renting land between owner and tenant also were standard in format irrespective of whether the contract had been drawn up by parties in Manchuria, North China, South China, or Taiwan except that contractual terms denoting the types of real estate varied according to the locale. Standard features for all land rent contracts were these: (*a*) names of the landlord and tenants; (*b*) precise land area and its four boundaries; (*c*) rental value; (*d*) period of lease; (*e*) time of rent payment, (*f*) cost-sharing when capital had been invested to improve the land; (*g*) terms of rent payment after a poor harvest and terms for determining rent in arrears; (*h*) procedures to expel one or more tenants in violation of contract; (*i*) terms for making rent deposit and its return. The first five items appeared in almost every rent contract. For example, a Nationalist Government survey of land tenure customs in nine provinces undertaken in 1931–1932 showed that the first five terms existed in every rent contract between owners and tenants, whether the owner was absent or not.[27] When Items (f)–(h) were omitted from a contract, rent disputes frequently erupted over the controversial topics. Finally, these contracts could be signed by either the tenant, the landlord, the middleman, the guarantor, or the scribe. Generally, the tenant and a middleman signed the rent contract.

A standardized contract format also governed the transaction of credit. The Chinese had developed an ingenious procedure for exchanging land for credit without the owner's giving up all property rights to that land. This custom or practice, referred to in Chinese as *tien,* dictated that a party in need of a large cash loan temporarily relinquish any private claim to his immovable asset, usually land.[28] When the borrower eventually repaid his loan his asset, or *tien,* was returned to him. We learn from historical records that *tien* contracts were in existence as early

27. Kuo-min cheng-fu shih-yeh-pu Chung-kuo ching-chi nien-chien pien-tsuan wei-yüan-hui, ed., *Chung-kuo ching-chi nien-chien hsü-pien* (Supplement to the Yearbook for the Chinese Economy), (Nanking, 1933), Vol. 2, Part 2, pp. (G) 70–100.

28. This discussion is based on Chung Nak-k'e, *Tien-tang chih-tu lun* (An Essay on the System of *Tien-tang*), (Shang-wu Publishing Co., n.d., n.p.).

as the eighth century. All *tien* contracts contained the following features: (*a*) name of the party drawing up the *tien* contract; (*b*) statement of how the borrower had acquired his asset; (*c*) reason for the *tien* contract; (*d*) location of the asset—if land, its four boundaries and the size or condition; if a structure, the number of rooms; (*e*) amount of tax the *tien* owner or creditor would pay while using the asset; (*f*) statement citing the right of the new owner of the asset to lease to a tenant (especially if former asset owner demanded to use it as a tenant); (*g*) time period for the *tien* contract; (*h*) statement indicating the right of original *tien* claimant to redeem the asset; (*i*) terms listing the new *tien* claimant's rights if original *tien* claimant failed to redeem the *tien*. These *tien* contracts were concluded by the formal statement of *k'ung-k'ou wu-p'ing* ("we fear that in the future any verbal agreement lacks concrete proof so we have drawn up this contract"), a date, and signatures by the original *tien* owner, a middleman, a witness, and a scribe. This format characterized *tien* contracts for every region in China.

Similar uniformities in other kinds of transactional contracts for resources can also be cited, and the examples that have been given held true in every region of the empire. For these written contracts to have been so widely used, numerous persons had to be skilled in negotiations and possessed of some functional literacy to draw up contracts between private parties. It seems that in every community, large or small, such persons could be found. They had been taught by their parents and/or by tutors to read and write a sufficient number of Chinese characters. Furthermore, they had obviously observed at firsthand, learned, and practiced the negotiating skills required to bring different parties together, to resolve and mediate differences, and to gain the trust of both parties that the contractual agreement was fair and would be enforced. Recent scholarship by Evelyn Sakakida Rawski certainly attests that functional literacy in rural China was adequate for these written contracts to be widely used.[29]

Turning to three examples of resource transactons, I cite actual contractual agreements between the parties involved. These examples pertain to the development of land and its long-term farming, to credit demand and supply for the financing of ceremonial expenditures to uphold the values of ancestor worship, and to the organization of large-scale irrigation works involving cooperation between many parties. Examples of

29. *Education and Popular Literacy in Ch'ing China* (Ann Arbor: University of Michigan Press, 1979). Rawski's path-breaking work describes the many forms of elementary education operating in the countryside, with numerous illustrations of the facility of rural people at writing and reading placards, contracts, etc.

other types of resource transaction could also be cited, but space does not permit.

Land Development

In the late seventeenth century when considerable land had become idle because of internal wars and foreign invasion by the Manchus, the Ch'ing state encouraged the reclaiming of old farm lands and the opening up of new by exempting several years' land tax and providing funds to buy seed and livestock. After receiving this property right by first obtaining land permits from local officials, many households still lacked physical resources to clear the land and plant crops; however, other families were willing to work their land if funds were advanced to make that land fertile. Both parties then drew up a contract defining their property rights and obligations. Numerous variants for these transactions existed, but the general contractual arrangement between the original owner and the new developer worked something like this.

In return for reclaiming the land and farming it, a tenant-developer would receive not only a certain share of the harvest, but also long-term property rights which enabled him, his heirs, and their successors to farm that same land as perpetual tenants. Also included were rights to use that land to obtain credit, to sublet it to another tenant, to sell that tenant right to another party, and to transfer that tenant right to a male heir. In turn, the tenant was required to pay to the original owner an annual rent, usually set as a fixed amount of product per unit of land. In most instances, these rents were fixed in perpetuity, although many owners by the second or third subsequent generation tried to raise them. The original owner was obligated to pay a land tax to the state. Many contracts contained clauses stating how the tenant was to pay the rent, at what times of the year, and the method of delivery. The following is an example of a long-term agreement between an original landowner and several of his tenant-developers.

Contract 1

Long-Term Rent Agreement between Landowner and Several Tenant-Developers

Lin Liao-liang, a land owner of Tung-lo encampment, has drawn up this deed for obtaining someone to farm my land. I own a plot of barren land located in Hsia-chü village, locally known as Chung-chou, on the east side [four boundaries are cited in detail]. These four boundaries are very clear. Because I do not have anyone farming that land, I have engaged Mr. Chuang Ch'i and Mr. Chuang Wei to farm it. They will supply their own labor-animals and seeds, and will endeavor to cultivate the land. We have met and agreed that the two of them will jointly give me 30 Mexican dollars. That silver has been paid in full. I will now make this land available to Mr. Chuang Ch'i and Mr. Chuang Wei to manage and farm [as they wish]. They now can manage that land as their permanent property [*yung-wei chi-yeh*], harvest its crops, and pay me rent. Each year they will pay me 5 *tou* of grain and 6 *tou* of hemp in full as ta-tsu rent. They must deliver that amount of rent to my granary, and any delay or non-payment of that annual rent will not be permitted. Should there by any delay or non-payment, this landowner has the right to cancel this contract and seek another party to farm that land. The present tenants dare not object to this agreement nor will they cause any trouble [about honoring this agreement]. This agreement was willingly concluded [by all parties]. We are afraid that a verbal agreement lacks concrete proof. Therefore we have drawn up this document for seeking a tenant as evidence. On this same day I have received in full 30 Mexican silver dollars as mentioned in this agreement.

Date: 1763_________ [signature left blank][30]

This type of agreement was common through east-central, southeast, and central China and even in Taiwan. The original property owner, in the eyes of the state, owned the land and paid the land tax. Rent contracts usually referred to his property rights as being the subsurface right, and there were many local terms expressing this property right: *t'ien-ku* (the bone of the land), *t'ien-ti* (the bottom of the land), *t'ien-ken* (the root of the land), *ta-tsu* (collector of rent). The long-term tenant possessed a property right referred to as the surface right, and contracts contained terms for this such as *t'ien-p'i* (the skin), *t'ien-mien* (the surface), or *hsiao-tsu* (long-term tenant). In other words, the Chinese had conceived of a dual property ownership arrangement for land which enabled households to reclaim and develop land when they could provide labor and in which they were guaranteed all gains from increased land productivity. Meantime, the original owners were guaranteed an annual fixed rent of around one-tenth of the yield irrespective of harvest fluctuations. Both parties could transfer their property rights to other households, and in fact did so, so that over the centuries this land peoperty system became extremely complex.

Many long-term tenant households sublet their original long-term leased land so that three parties came to claim the land's products. After a time, state officials became acutely aware that their land cadastre records did not correctly list the original landowning households who paid

30. Tai Yen-hui, "Ch'ing-tai T'ai-wan chih ta-hsiao tsu-yeh" (The Right to Collect Rents in Taiwan during the Ch'ing Period) in *T-ai-pei wen-hsien* (Journal of Local Historical Research of Taipei City) 4 (1963), p. 12.

taxes and actually farmed the land. By the twentieth century it had become impossible to consider land reform unless a new land survey were carried out, to identify which households actually owned the land and which farmed it. The goal then would be to recompense original landowners and confirm bonafide property rights to the long-term tenants. However, since—as has been mentioned—many long-term tenants had already developed new subtenants, further state action would have been needed to correct for inequities between those parties. The sheer complexity of this dual and sometimes triadic property-rights system made land reform prohibitively difficult and costly. Despite its faults, however, the shared-rights system had enabled agriculture to be rapidly developed in many parts of the country, especially in the South, and had given greater opportunity for the poor to acquire property rights and to obtain a foothold in villages.

Credit

As a patrilineal descent group, Chinese households engaged in ancestor worship and spent heavily for rituals such as the birth of a male child, the marriage of a son, and the death of an aged parent. Feasts and gift exchange were inherent in these rituals which every household performed at some phases of its life cycle. Often a heavy burden for members of the household, these rituals nonetheless served to reinforce the neo-Confucian ethic of ancestor worship. Grounded firmly in Confucian values and beliefs, each member of the household had a powerful commitment to work hard, to save, and to earn as much as possible to expand the household's corporate wealth or estate as an expression of filial piety to living parents and to the deceased. Moreover, it was an obligation to build that estate so that successive male heads of the household might have adequate resources to maintain the patrilineal descent line and to propagate ancestor worship.

Although ritual and compulsory gift-giving may not appear rational to modern eyes, these manifestations of Confucian cultural values undergirded powerful behavioral incentives which made the Chinese household a veritable economic engine of accumulation and population enhancement. Households developed routine procedures to obtain the necessary scarce resources, to manage their own resources more efficiently, and to earn the highest stream of annual income by which to build the corporate estate. One such transaction by households was to exchange a portion of the corporate estate, usually land, for the large sum of cash needed for a given ritual such as a marriage or a funeral. Households rarely had enough cash in hand for the requisite feasts and gift exchanges; therefore they transfered to another household, as surety for their borrowed cash, some portion of their corporate estate. This transaction, called the exchange of *tien*, functioned as follows.

A third party brought borrower and lender together, and then assisted both to draw up a contract involving these steps. First, the parties evaluated a portion of the corporate estate and agreed upon its location and characteristics. Next, they agreed on the amount of the cash loan. Third, they listed contractual terms for when the loan should be repaid, whether the borrower could still use the asset and pay a rent, whether the lender could sublet the asset to another household, etc. The contract was signed by the two parties, the middleman, and other witnesses. The lender was obligated to pay any taxes on the asset while he held it but, because he enjoyed all the income it produced, he collected no interest on his loaned cash. The borrower had the right to reclaim the asset at any time by repaying the loan, but if he failed to do so the lender acquired ownership. The following contract is an example of *tien* transaction in northeastern China.

Contract 2

A Contract for Mortgaging Land

I, Wang Lien-fu, a Captain in the Plain White Division of the Chinese Banner Troops, have drawn up the following mortgage contract (*tien*). Because I am too poor to make a living and cannot pay my taxes of money and grain, I have decided to mortgage the land attached to my house to Wang Yu-sung for him to develop and farm. I have agreed with all parties concerned that the mortgage price will be exactly 360 strings of cash. I will receive this amount in full without any deficit on the same day this contract is finalized. I fear there is not sufficient proof of our agreement, and I have drawn up this mortgage contract as evidence.

To wit, the registered land to be transferred to the holder of this mortgage totals 9 *tuan* 11 *jih* plus 4 *mou*. The period of mortgage will be 60 years. The eastern boundary of this land extends to the river; the west boundary extends to the base of the mountain; the north boundary extends to a ditch; and the southern boundary extends to a mountain top. If in the future the holder of this mortgage should build a house on land, I will repay him 3 silver taels plus building costs. If he reclaims any of the barren land, I will give him 1 silver tael for each *jih* of land which he farms.

Middleman: Tung Hsiang

Eyewitness: Ts'ui Wan-i

Scribe: Shao Yung-t'ai

Executed on Ch'ien-lung 36th year, 5th lunar month, last day (June 13, 1771)[31]

31. Source: *Chūgoku tochi keiyaku bunshoshū*, pp. 62–63 (152). Cited in Fu-mei Chang Chen and Ramon H. Myers, "Customary Law and the Economic Growth of China during the Ch'ing Period," *Ch'ing-shih wen-t'i* 3:5 (1976), p. 23.

Although I have not seen any cases where a borrower mortgaged part of the corporate estate for a loan to make capital investment expenditures, it is very possible that some households did borrow large loans for this purpose. Surveys of *tien* transactions in the early twentieth century generally show that borrowers used their loans for ritual purposes which enabled households to uphold Confucian values and beliefs. These norms, in turn, governed and conditioned the exemplary economic behavior of household members, orienting their activities to producing for the market and engaging in commodity exchange.

Irrigation

Water was an extremely important resource for making land more productive, and where farmers had developed irrigation projects to produce a stable water supply, they often obtained two crops every year (i.e., coarse grain followed by rice) or three crops every 2 years (i.e., winter wheat and summer coarse grains). The construction of irrigation projects often involved more than one village, but in any case a large number of households had to cooperate by supplying resources to build, maintain, and operate the project each year. Such large-scale enterprise required complex resource transactions among many households. To establish a rational basis for joint supply of resources and sharing of benefits, rules and procedures had to be drawn up in contractual form to ensure that all households complied. An example of such procedures follows, in the form of a customary law document that governed the operations of an irrigation system in Hsing-t'ai county of southern Hopei province on the northern China plain.

Contract 3

Revised Regulations for the Yung-chi Sluice in Hsing-t'ai county, Hopei

1. Each irrigation system worker (*lien*) is allowed to perform up to 7 *fen* labor. Each *fen* of labor will be rewarded 350 copper cash. The irrigation system manager (*lao-jen*) and subordinate-supervisors (*hsiao-chia*) who are paid for their labor services (*lien*) are subject to the same regulation.

2. The reward given to the *lao-jen* for his managerial services is minimal and not at all profitable. Those who are poor can hardly afford to take on such a responsibility. Therefore, we propose that each *li* (1/10 of one *fen*) of labor will be increased from 1 to 2 *ko* of wheat for payment to the *lao-jen*. The new rate takes effect next year, but the old rate will continue for the rest of this year.

3. Of those households exempted from performing labor services (*lien*) for the irrigation system, some are very poor and therefore unable to contribute to the man-

agement of the irrigation system. Therefore, their supervisors (*hsiao-chia*) must shoulder these costs. Those costs, however, will be apportioned to everyone registered in the *lien*, and those exempted households will not be required to bear those costs.

4. Where any land in the irrigation system has been pledged and given to the creditor to farm, the payment for water will be paid in full by the first day of the 12th month. Both debtor (*yao-ti*) and the creditor (*tang-chu*) will pay for the water used on that land. The creditor is not permitted to demand more water nor is the debtor allowed to reduce the amount of water. If the debtor is discovered secretly farming any irrigation land in excess of that stipulated amount pledged and transferred to the creditor, he will be fined an amount payable in kind of one unit of construction materials.

5. The *lao-jen* occasionally may ask those who have been exempted from performing labor services (*lien*) to take their turn patrolling the irrigation system. They will not complain about such an assignment, nor will they try to evade performing it by referring to some prior set of rules. For those who do not comply, they will be fined an amount according to their original *lien* assessment.

Signed the first month of Kuang-hsü 8th year (1882) by the *lao-jen*, Chiang Chao-hsiung, the *hsiao-chia* subordinate-supervisors, Ching Chi-ch'uan and five others, and the *lien* laborers. This document sets forth the revised regulations.[32]

This contract governed the way that many farmers in several villages along an irrigation canal contributed labor so that the supply of water could be smoothly distributed throughout a large land area. Similar detailed rules applied for the day-to-day upkeep and operation of irrigation systems in other parts of China. These arrangements conferred considerable enforcement authority on some given group of farmers who had obtained the support of the village council.[33] The contract indicates how Chinese households undertook complex cooperative arrangements to underwrite the costs for information and enforcement of large-scale projects to supply community services.

32. Source: *Chūgoku nōson kankō chōsa*, Vol. 6, p. 290. Translators' note: We do not possess the original version of the Yung-chi Sluice Regulations, and we do not know the exact date of its promulgation. However, we have a more recently revised regulation recorded in the 1919–1922 Yung-chi Sluice Account Book. This version is longer than the 1882 document. It contains, among other items, mention of a pay increase for the *lao-jen* from 2 to 3 *ko* of wheat for 1 *li* work unit. See Vol. 6, p. 300. Cited in ibid. 3:10 (1978), p. 15.

33. I have described how such an irrigation organization actually operated in villages of Hsing-t'ai county. See "Economic Organization and Cooperation in Modern China: Irrigation Management in Xing-tai county, Hobei Province," in *The Polity and Economy of China: The Late Professor Yūji Muramatsu Commemoration Volume* (Tokyo: Tōyō keizai shimpōsha, 1975) pp. 189–212.

CONCLUSION

This essay has pointed out China's unique growth characteristics in the late imperial period: a steady expansion of population with no perceptible long-term decline in per capita income; the application of more labor in substitute production processes to compensate for the decline in certain material resources with no evidence that marginal physical product return to labor was approaching zero; the spread of local markets throughout the empire; and the emergence of national markets for basic commodities such as rice and cotton cloth.

Two economic considerations appear to have made these achievements possible, and in some respects they resemble developments in western Europe—where economic development however, turned out very differently. First,highly competitive factor and product markets allowed for the exchange of resources and the production and distribution of goods and services by households within tens of thousands of small marketing areas, each no larger than 25–50 villages and a single market town. Second, households increasingly contracted with each other to exchange resources of all kinds by procedures based on what I have termed customary law. Because this implicit law reduced the costs of acquiring information, it better assured that contracts would be carried out and provided a means for their enforcement. The resultant decline in the transaction-cost/benefit ration for households encouraged them to undertake a greater volume of resource transactions than otherwise would have been the case.

Thus, as a consequence of law, the Ch'ing period was characterized by an increased exchange of resources, greater production for the market, and the growth of regional and national markets. Several other issues also related to customary law and the competitive market structure deserve brief mention.

In a patrilineal-descent family society like that of China, lineages or groups of households all bore the surname of the original lineage founder, and members convened to carry out the rituals. Within any lineage, the relationship between the powerful, wealthy households and the humbler ones often resembled that of patron and client. High status households were assumed to carry an obligation to protect and assist the weaker ones which in turn were expected to show deference and obedience to the authority of the strong. It remains to be seen whether such ties reflected the full extent of patron–client characteristics often observed in other societies. The subject deserves much more inquiry.

Although households of the same lineage sometimes interacted to share and exchange resources, this represented only a small part of the widespread and generalized contractual exchange of resources of which the examples cited in this essay are only a few. Moreover, when households rented and leased land on a contractual basis, such patron–client attitudes were rarely observed.[34]

As customary law came into acceptance throughout China and the imperial state looked upon this activity with approval—even consenting to adjudicate violations of contracts between private parties—these private contracts served as an effective device for greatly reducing transaction costs. Therefore, if transaction costs declined during the late seventeenth and eighteenth centuries, the exchange of resources between households must have increased enormously. That this very likely occurred is borne out by the great expansion of markets and market towns during these same two centuries.

The comparative efficiency of product and factor markets also made it feasible for households, by choosing alternative methods of production, to use a more abundant resource, like labor, to offset the growing scarcity of other resources like fertile land, timber, and minerals. If contractual agreements for exchanging resources helped the market mechanism to work effectively to eliminate scarcity,then improved markets perhaps inhibited the stimuli for households to tinker and to create new gadgets that might have produced labor-saving methods of production. As Mark Elvin perceptively noted some years ago in his classic study, *The Pattern of the Chinese Past,* "huge but nearly static markets created no bottlenecks in the production system that might have prompted creativity."[35]

It is quite possible that simply because markets were so highly competitive and worked so efficiently to offset resource scarcity, the economic potential was never perceived for a stream of innovations that could have led to labor-saving methods of production.[36] Let us assume that the success of highly competitive markets with reduced transaction costs actually did dampen technological innovation in China of the seventeenth and eighteenth centuries. Does this mean that Chinese society would not have responded to such innovations as the use of imported

34. For this argument see Ramon H. Myers, "North China Villages during the Late Qing and Republican Periods," in *Modern China* 6:3 (July 1980), pp. 243–266.

35. (Stanford: Stanford University Press, 1973), p. 314.

36. The innovations created by the Chinese during these centuries to offset certain resource scarcities were definitely output-increasing, as Oscar Lange has argued that innovations will be under perfect competitive market conditions. But with respect to the single firm, innovations may be either output-increasing or output-decreasing, as well as more factor-using. See Lange, "A Note on Innovations," in William Fellner and Bernard F. Haley, eds., *Readings in the Theory of Income Distribution* (Philadelphia: The Blakiston Company, 1951), p. 195.

Western technology even if the state had taken appropriate steps to make that technology available to households? That is a topic for future research.

ACKNOWLEDGMENT

I wish to thank Thomas Metzger and Fu-Meichen for commenting on an earlier draft of this essay: remaining errors are my own.

Ramon H. Myers received his doctoral degree in economics from the University of Washington in 1960. Douglass North served on his Ph.D. thesis committee.

His research has focused upon Japanese colonial economic development and Chinese economic and social history. In 1970 his book, **The Chinese Peasant Economy,** was published. He served as associate editor of **The Journal of Asian Studies** and was editor—manager of the journal **Ch'ing-shih wen-t'i** [Problems in Ch'ing History] between 1974–1979. His most recent book is **The Chinese Economy Past and Present** (1980).

Ramon Myers is currently Senior Fellow and curator—scholar of the East Asian collection of the Hoover Institution on War, Revolution, and Peace.

Index